79

Religious Secularity

RELIGION AND GLOBAL POLITICS

SERIES EDITOR
John L. Esposito
University Professor and Director
Prince Alwaleed Bin Talal Center for Muslim–Christian Understanding
Georgetown University

ISLAMIC LEVIATHAN
Islam and the Making of State Power
Seyyed Vali Reza Nasr

RACHID GHANNOUCHI
A Democrat within Islamism
Azzam S. Tamimi

BALKAN IDOLS
Religion and Nationalism in Yugoslav States
Vjekoslav Perica

ISLAMIC POLITICAL IDENTITY IN TURKEY
M. Hakan Yavuz

RELIGION AND POLITICS IN POST-COMMUNIST ROMANIA
Lavinia Stan and Lucian Turcescu

PIETY AND POLITICS
Islamism in Contemporary Malaysia
Joseph Chinyong Liow

TERROR IN THE LAND OF THE HOLY SPIRIT
Guatemala under General Efrain Rios Montt, 1982–1983
Virginia Garrard-Burnett

IN THE HOUSE OF WAR
Dutch Islam Observed
Sam Cherribi

BEING YOUNG AND MUSLIM
New Cultural Politics in the Global South and North
Asef Bayat and Linda Herrera

CHURCH, STATE, AND DEMOCRACY IN EXPANDING EUROPE
Lavinia Stan and Lucian Turcescu

THE HEADSCARF CONTROVERSY
Secularism and Freedom of Religion
Hilal Elver

THE HOUSE OF SERVICE
The Gülen Movement and Islam's Third Way
David Tittensor

MAPPING THE LEGAL BOUNDARIES OF BELONGING
Religion and Multiculturalism from Israel to Canada
Edited by René Provost

RELIGIOUS SECULARITY
A Theological Challenge to the Islamic State
Naser Ghobadzadeh

RELIGIOUS SECULARITY

A Theological Challenge to the Islamic State

—◦◦◦—

NASER GHOBADZADEH

OXFORD
UNIVERSITY PRESS

OXFORD
UNIVERSITY PRESS

Oxford University Press is a department of the University of Oxford.
It furthers the University's objective of excellence in research, scholarship,
and education by publishing worldwide.

Oxford   New York

Auckland   Cape Town   Dar es Salaam   Hong Kong   Karachi
Kuala Lumpur   Madrid   Melbourne   Mexico City   Nairobi
New Delhi   Shanghai   Taipei   Toronto

With offices in

Argentina   Austria   Brazil   Chile   Czech Republic   France   Greece
Guatemala   Hungary   Italy   Japan   Poland   Portugal   Singapore
South Korea   Switzerland   Thailand   Turkey   Ukraine   Vietnam

Oxford is a registered trademark of Oxford University Press
in the UK and certain other countries.

Published in the United States of America by
Oxford University Press
198 Madison Avenue, New York, NY 10016

Library of Congress Cataloging-in-Publication Data
Naser Ghobadzadeh.
Religious secularity : A Theological Challenge to the Islamic State / Naser Ghobadzadeh.
pages cm.
Includes bibliographical references.
ISBN 978-0-19-939117-2 (cloth : alk. paper)
1. Shi'ah—Political aspects.   2. Islam and state.   I. Title.
BP194.185.Q83 2014
320.55'7—dc23
2014011636

1 3 5 7 9 8 6 4 2
Printed in the United States of America
on acid-free paper

To my beloved late father, Ja'far Ghobadzadeh
An inspiring man of unconventional wisdom and wit

Contents

Acknowledgments

WATCHING THE AFTERMATH of Iran's 2009 election, I was struck with both great hope and a profound sense of helplessness regarding events at the other side of the world. In the months that followed, I had many conversations with fellow students and colleagues in Australia, who were surprised by the new image of Iran being presented by the media. During one such conversation over dinner in late 2009, my mind started racing when I was asked why my Ph.D. research did not focus on the political climate in Iran. Having worked on a completely different project for almost two years, it was not an easy decision to make—to suddenly switch topics. Looking back, I can say it was the best decision I could have made, as it profoundly impacted my academic life. I owe this decision, in some ways, to Lily Rahim, Judith Betts, Stephen Mills, Steve Curran, and to Mark Keevers, who contributed to that particular discussion that triggered the rethinking of my research topic.

This book is substantially my Ph.D. dissertation, which I completed at the University of Sydney in 2012. During the compressed process of writing my thesis, I was strongly supported and encouraged by my supervisor, Associate Professor Lily Zubaidah Rahim. I am most grateful to Lily for her significant contribution to this book through engagement with my ideas, critical feedback regarding my written work, and for the time she allocated to our frequent and lengthy meetings. I was also fortunate to have the support of my co-supervisor, Professor John Keane, who provided an invaluable contribution to the conceptual framework of this book. Despite his busy schedule, John was generous with both his time and his knowledge. It was through one of my discussions with John that the term "religious secularity," which I have developed in this book, was crafted.

I would like to express my gratitude to Dr. Estelle Dryland, Macquarie University, for her great assistance with this book. Estelle deserves special mention for providing assistance with my English writing and for helping me to develop skills that have proven invaluable throughout the project. I also owe a debt of gratitude to Professor Nikolas Kompridis, whose kind support offered me peace of mind to deal with the difficulties of the last stage of finalizing the manuscript.

Special thanks to my Ph.D. examiners, professors John L. Esposito, Abdullahi Ahmed An-Na'im, and Khaled M. Abou El Fadl, for their constructive comments. Professor Esposito, in particular, supported the publication of this book by Oxford University Press (OUP), and for that I am greatly indebted to him. I am also grateful to the anonymous reviewers of OUP for their constructive comments. The staff at OUP deserve special thanks for their patience and professionalism. In particular, Cynthia Read, the executive editor, and her assistant, Marcela Maxfield, afforded me all the support I needed, whenever I needed it. They both invested considerable time and energy in the production of the book.

This work owes much to the University of Sydney, without whose generosity and financial and intellectual stimulus it would have been nigh impossible to bring this work to fruition; in particular, the Endeavour International Postgraduate Research Scholarship (EIPRS), which allowed me to conduct my research. I have been fortunate to enjoy the kindness, insight, and support of many friends and scholars, with whom I have discussed ideas and who have read sections of my work and offered feedback. To name all of those to whom I owe thanks is not possible; but this does not mean that I am any the less grateful to them. Here, I will name only those who have contributed directly to this book: Arash Falasiri, Mary-Elizabeth Andrews, Nazanian Ghanavizi, Associate Professor Benjamin E. Goldsmith, Judith Betts, Professor Pippa Norris, Professor Shahram Akbarzadeh, Dr. Stephen Mills, Associate Professor Ariadne Vromen, Professor Louise Chappell, Dr. Rebecca Barlow, Sam Barnett, Melanie Brown, Colombina Schaeffer, Megan Parker, Dr. Stewart Jackson, Dr. Omid Tofighian, Dr. Ben Moffitt, Dr Timothy Laurie, Dr. Abolfazl Maasoumi, and Setayesh Nooraninejad.

Finally, the completion of this book would not have been possible without the support of my family and friends. Behnaz Ekhtiari, my brothers Siavash and Fazel, and Atefeh Fayyazi most generously provided me with much-needed materials from Iran: they went out of their way to source and send me works that were unavailable to me in Australia. Being away from home and family is not easy, but I was lucky to meet Khosrow Sadeghzadeh Milani and Fereshteh Kazazi, who have been generous with their love and care throughout these years. My frequent discussions with Khosrow, specifically on religious issues, proved very constructive.

I must also mention my brothers and sisters, in-laws, and, of course, my parents, who are a constant connection to my home in Iran. In particular,

I would like to express a personal debt of gratitude to my dearest friend Mohammad Fayyazi, who has always been a significant part of my personal and professional life. The conversations, ideas, and friendship we have shared throughout the course of this project have been invaluable. Without his unconditional support, study in Australia would not have been possible. Most importantly, I want to thank my wife, Bita Ekhtiari, whose unfailing support has played and continues to play a significant role in my personal and professional life. I would like to thank Bita for her patience, love, sacrifices, and enduring emotional support, without which I am convinced that I would never have completed this work.

Religious Secularity

Introduction

FROM THE SECOND half of the twentieth century, the quest for an Islamic state was an aspiration common to most Islamists across geographic borders and sectarian divides. Mainstream Islamic groups—including the Muslim Brotherhood and its affiliates across the Arab world; Jamaat-e Islami in the Indian subcontinent; and Shiite Islamists in Iran, Iraq, and Lebanon—all contemplated setting up Islamic states as a defining feature of their respective identities. Their aspirations climaxed with the establishment of the Islamic Republic of Iran in 1979; but, disillusioned by the failures of the Islamic state, this zeal was short lived. The notion of an Islamic state is no longer considered a desired political system. As well as being demonized in the West, it has also been depicted as an undesirable and forbidding choice in the Muslim world, evident in the lack of quest for Islamic states evinced by the world's mainstream Islamic groups. In Indonesia, the world's most populous and democratic Muslim-majority country, neither the leading Islamic organizations (including Nahdlatul Ulama and the Mohammadiyeh movement) nor the major Islamic parties are committed to an Islamic state. Turkey's Justice and Development Party (AKP) has no desire to convert the modernizing Turkish secular state into a Shari'a-based Islamic polity. And, following the "Arab uprisings" in the Middle East and North Africa, the more mainstream Islamists have not championed the establishment of an Islamic state, even though they continue to uphold Shari'a principles (Gerges, 2013).

Despite these trends, radical Islamists continue to aspire for the building of Islamic states, and, while marginal, these groups remain vociferous both in their demands and in their militant methods. Ansar al-Sharia in Tunisia, Yemen, and Libya; Boko Haram in Nigeria; Ansar Dine in Mali; and al-Shabaab in Somalia are a few cases in point. The Islamic groups that flourished under conditions of crisis and chaos in Syria—for example, the Jabhat al-Nusra, Ahrar ash-Sham, and the Islamic State of Iraq and ash-Sham (ISIS)—maintain their zeal for an Islamic state. The marginality of these groups is evidenced by the fact that no state in the Muslim world—nor any of the mainstream Islamic movements—offers them concrete support or official acknowledgement.

The lived reality of the Islamic state in Iran is of symbolic and practical importance mainly due to the fact that the Iranian-Shiite Islamists were the first in the modern age to seize political power and establish an Islamic state. Despite numerous existential challenges, the country's ruling clergy has managed to sustain the problematic political system; but their attempts to promote the Islamic state as a viable model in Sunni and Shiite countries have generally floundered (V. Nasr, 2003: 69). Despite the Islamic state's official policy of exporting Islamic revolutions, their particular politico-religious system of governance has remained confined to Iranian borders. More importantly, the very foundational legitimacy of the Islamic state remains contested, the reality being that the Islamic Republic is riddled with sociopolitical, economic, and theological contradictions (Adelkhah, 2000; V. Nasr, 2003; Roy, 1999). It is from this difficulty that a competing politico-religious discourse which refutes the religious foundations of the Islamic state has emerged. This book investigates this counter-discourse by developing the seemingly oxymoronic term "religious secularity" to highlight the paradoxes inherent in the Islamic state ideal. By this term, I mean the vision for the emancipation of religion from the state.

More than three decades after the establishment of the Islamic state in Iran, the very idea of an Islamic state remains contested. This contestation was starkly demonstrated by the political crisis that erupted in 2009. Widespread protests challenging the outcome of the presidential election were dramatically transformed into a protest movement challenging the legitimacy of the Islamic state. The cry "Where is my vote?" morphed into more far-reaching slogans such as "Death to the Dictator", "Down with the Islamic Republic", and "Independence, Freedom, Iranian Republic". Instructively, the word "Iranian" replaced "Islamic", which was at the centre of the 1979 revolutionary slogan calling for "Independence, Freedom, Islamic Republic". This discernible shift was followed by animated discussions within the country's political and scholarly communities interrogating the legitimacy and propriety of symbiotically fusing religion and the state.

The fragile legitimacy of the Islamic state is also evident in the societal context. The ruling clergy aspire to Islamize all aspects of Iranian life; but this is not born out of the aspirations and lifestyles of the younger generation

(Ladier-Fouladi, 2012). And, given that the younger generation were educated by an Islamized education system, this is somewhat surprising.[1] Earlier generations too, who revolted against the authoritarian secular state of the Shah, maintain a questionable commitment to political Islam (Khosrokhavar, 2007).[2]

In Iran, the notion of an Islamic state has also been systematically contested by reformist religious scholars. Abou El Fadl invites Muslims to reassess their understanding of religion in light of new challenges and changing conditions (2005: 283–284). Iranian religious scholars are engaged in just such an effort. Disillusioned by the authoritarian excesses of the Islamic state, these scholars, who initially contributed to the institutionalization of the Islamic state in the 1980s, have re-conceptualized the notion of political Islam. Arguing that an Islamic state is detrimental to religion, they propose an alternative conceptualization of state–religion relations from an Islamic perspective. This discourse, based upon religious sources, employs Islamic jurisprudential and theological methods. Rooted as it is in religious concerns, its primary goal is the emancipation of religion from state.

The ruling clergy's restrictive control of the political sphere has denied any political movement the opportunity to articulate a cohesive alternative to the Islamic state. However, the situation in Iran's scholarly circles has been somewhat different. Initially, the ruling clergy were not cognizant of the development of reformist discourse in scholarly circles and its growing influence on political practices. For this reason, the religious reformist scholars were treated with tolerance by the ruling clergy. Rather than launching overt attacks against the Islamic state, the former employed more subtle methods to undermine the clerical establishment. Not only were challenges channelled into diverse areas, but they were also embedded within theological discussion. Their more gentle, implicit, and sectarian manner of challenging the Islamic state, coupled with scholars' tactical retreats, robbed the ruling clergy not only of sufficient awareness of their criticism, but also of justification for taking measures against them.

Today in Iran, scholarly discourse occupies a place from which to offer cohesive and structured discussion that systematically challenges the Islamic

---

1. The education system was among the first areas to be targeted in the post-revolutionary era (i.e., to be Islamized). For a detailed discussion, see H. Godazgar, 2001, 2002; Golkar, 2012; Kamrava & Dorraj, 2008: 174–180; Shorish, 1988; Sobhe, 1982. However, the success of the Islamization of the education system is questioned seriously even by conservatives (e.g., see Kian-Thiebaut, 1999). For further discussion of the failure of the Islamic state to Islamize Iranian society, see Basmenji, 2005; M. A. Kadivar, 2014b; Khatam, 2009; Varzi, 2006.

2. For further discussion of the failure of the Islamic state to Islamise Iranian society, see Basmenji, 2005; M. A. Kadivar, 2014b; Khatam, 2009; Varzi, 2006.

state's unification of religion and state. The two most significant domestic political struggles against the authoritarian Islamic regime in Iran have been the reformist movement (1997–2005) and the Green movement (2009 onwards). Both were sparked by alternative religious discourse rather than by non-religious ideologies, which to date have remained largely ineffectual.

Religious reformist scholars include religious intellectuals and reformist clerics who believe in God and Shiism and evince incontestable respect for religious principles. Without exception, religion is at the core of their scholarly works. An ultimate goal for religious reformist scholars is to propose an understanding of religion that corresponds to contemporary conventions. In the political sphere, they argue that modern political ideas such as democracy, human rights, freedom, and secularity are compatible with Islam. This book interrogates the shift in their conceptualization of state–religion relations, an outcome of their lived experience in the Islamic state in Iran. They are opposed to the politicization of religion on the grounds that religion is God-given and the religious experience is by definition highly individualistic. Highlighting the esoteric layers of religious belief, religious reformist scholars argue that state intervention in religion disrupts and contaminates belief in God and the traditions of the Shi'a. Religion, as an absolute, metaphysical, God-given set of principles, should not be subjected to interrogation by mortals. State interference, then, is a travesty because it claims to possess the ultimate interpretation of religious principles and expects individuals to observe a unified and dictated understanding of religion.

The authoritarian secularism of the Pahlavi regime triggered a revolution in 1979 that resulted in the establishment of an Islamic state. Today, the Islamic state is challenged by a discourse that strives to liberate religious experience from state intervention. In order to characterize this discourse, I conceptualize the term "religious secularity", by which I mean the Islamic quest for the emancipation of religion from state. In this book, I will demonstrate the way by which this term encapsulates the complex and unorthodox characteristics of the political dimensions of the current religious reformation in Iran.

The Rise of Religious Secularity

Religious secularity, part of a broader enterprise of religious reformation in Iran, challenges the legitimacy of the Islamic state and draws attention to the detrimental impact upon both religion and state in their unification. Religious secularity discourse objects to both the politicization of Islam and authoritarian secularism, a political paradigm that has characterized the histories of Iran and the postcolonial Muslim world. While the main thrust of secularism is the emancipation of state and economy from religion, that of religious secularity is rooted in religious concerns—in particular, the liberation of religion from the state. Today in Iran, it is religious scholars, rather than politicians or political theorists, who are the leading proponents of religious secularity.

Religious secularity discourse is built upon two corresponding components: First, it calls attention to the disadvantages of the Islamic state to religion. While implementation of the Shari'a was proclaimed the primary aim of the Islamic state, Iran's experience has arguably demonstrated that the Islamic state transforms religion into a political instrument to justify state policy. This is clearly conceptualized in Khomeini's notion of *fiqh ul-maslaha* (expedient jurisprudence). According to this jurisprudential concept, the Islamic state is allowed to overlook Islamic principles, both worshipping and non-worshipping precepts, if it so decrees. This is one of many examples of how the jurisprudential character of the Islamic state of Iran subverts genuine religiosity by subjugating it to state policy. By insisting on the exoteric aspects of religiosity, the Islamic state not only disseminates hypocrisy, but also undermines the esoteric and spiritual dimensions of religiosity. Religious secularity invites the state to abandon its entrenched religious claims in order to cultivate genuine religiosity, whereby faith and religious practices are free of coercion by fellow citizens or state institutions.

The Islamic state was constructed upon the assumption that religion is capable of offering solutions to governance dilemmas in the modern age. Religious secularity disputes this all-encompassing understanding of Islam, which has given rise to unrealistic expectations of religion. By no means can governance be free of human error and failure; therefore, attributing state policies to religion simply shifts the responsibility for governance failures from government to religion. The advocates of religious secularity, who argue that Islam lacks specific guidelines for governance in the modern age, single out God and the hereafter as the two principle missions of religion. Religious secularity discharges religion from sociopolitical responsibility so that it may reclaim its credence. In fact, religious secularity defines the limits of religion in sociopolitical life and the limits of the reach of state in the religious domain. Not only is religion incapable of offering a blueprint for sociopolitical practices, but the state too is not sufficiently competent to be in charge of religion.

Demonstrating the inconsistency between the religious claims of the state and Islamic principles, religious secularity aims to safeguard the religious establishment from state intervention. In the case of Iran, not only have the traditional autonomy of the clergy and its pluralistic internal mechanisms been compromised, but the imposition of direct clerical political leadership has jeopardized the clergy's spiritual leadership. Religious secularity is an enterprise geared towards restoring the clergy's genuine spiritual aims and reputations.

Second, religious secularity discourse is based on the argument that Islam is compatible with the secular democratic state. Because providing religious justification for a secular political system is the primary objective of this discourse, it draws heavily upon Quranic verses and Islamic history, in which the case for secularity is implicit. Moreover, the principle of popular sovereignty deprives the state of any claim to having a sacred foundation and legitimacy through religious symbolism. By problematizing divine sovereignty, which is the linchpin of the Islamic state, religious secularity argues for the necessity of adopting popular sovereignty in the interests of capturing the true spirit of religion: justice. It provides an insight into the unpopularity of the Islamic clerical state—an unprecedented phenomenon in the Shiite world—within the traditional religious strata. The ultimate goal of religious secularity is to promote the democratic secular state as an alternative to the Islamic state. Religious secularity offers believers a more conducive environment in which to cultivate their faith. Under both autocratic secularism and the Islamic state, religion has been undermined in Iran. Due to these experiences with state power, religious secularity insists on the need to uncouple religion from the state in order to capture the spirit of religiosity.

The primary goals of religious secularity discourse are to invalidate the religious basis of the unification of religion and state and to offer religious justification for their separation. Religious secularity has emerged as a major competitor against the Islamic state because it reflects the religious sentiments of the people. As such, the raising of sensitive subjects such as the *hijab* and the consumption of alcohol has been side-stepped by reformist scholars at the current stage of Iran's political trajectory to avoid conflict.[3] Instead, reformist scholars have focused on questions of "why", rather than "how". The reformists' concern at this stage is to explain why the adoption of a secular democratic state is imperative in the Muslim world. How to go about implementing a secular democratic system is the project of another discourse.

---

3. While a few articles have been published on the role of religion in the public sphere, they do not address the policy dimension of implementing the concept of religious secularity. For example, see M. Kadivar, 2007b; Soroush, 2010c; Yusefi-Eshkevari, 2011.

Religious secularity blurs the boundaries between the "religious" and the "secular", conflating the terms into one. In the mainstream literature related to secularism, which is generally argued from Western Judeo-Christian perspectives, being secular is usually defined as antithetical to being religious (Taylor, 2008). In sharp contrast to this, as Islamic history shows, the border between the religious and the secular is neither pronounced nor properly understood in dualistic terms. This may provide an explanation for the difficulty in translating the term "secular" into native languages in the Muslim world. In keeping with this tradition, religious secularity discourse recognizes the distinction between religion and religious knowledge. "Religious" in this discourse refers to knowledge, not necessarily to religion itself. Religion, as the logic goes, is eternal and ultimate, tied to God and His will. Humans can never know the mind of God, as they are only presented with traces of Him in the Quran. Human knowledge of religion is, therefore, a worldly and temporary phenomenon, wholly dependent upon the discursive practice of human actors. Thus, to speak of religious secularity is to refer to the process by which human beings develop knowledge of religion in an earthly context. Religious secularity is not about living eternity in a pure form on earth: it is a process of interpretation, of coming to terms with a complex phenomenon.

This being said, the experiences of secular efforts in the Islamic context have differed from those in many Western countries.[4] Generally speaking, in the West the relationship between science and religion and the desire for worldliness was a major part of secularization. But, as these dimensions of secularism are already embedded in Islamic teachings, there is no need to contest them (Soroush, 2008c). In similar vein, religious secularity challenges the dichotomy between the religious and the secular; in the Islamic context, to be religious is to be secular and to be secular is to be religious. This is why the religious secularity discourse neither incorporates debate surrounding the science/religion conundrum nor engages in worldliness/next-worldliness speculation. Rather than being a philosophical-comprehensive project, religious secularity is a politico-religious discourse focused on depriving the so-called Islamic state of any transcendental claims.

Religious secularity discourse subscribes to the notion that it is neither possible nor prudent to privatize religion. Here it is important to distinguish

---

4. Given that the Western experiences of secularism and secularization are not homogenous experiences, this book does not intend to undertake a comparative study of Iran and the West. This, of course, does not mean precluding references to the West's experiences of secularization. Outlining the characteristics of the emerging secularity in Iran requires some reference to the Western experience.

politics from the state. Religious secularity advocates for public involvement of religion and acknowledges that through its contribution to civil society, religion preserves its role both in public life and the political process. However, religious secularity insists upon the importance of an institutional division of state (*doulat*) from religion. The category of state may well be questionable; but, given that it is not the aim of this book to examine the contested meanings of the concept of state, the issue of "what kind of state" is deferred. Under the prevailing circumstances in Iran, the principle aim of religious secularity discourse is to emancipate religion from state. In effect, religious secularity discourse offers a constructive vision for negotiating religion–state relations.

Religious secularity is imbued with normative, descriptive and strategic meaning. As a normative ideal, it offers an alternative to the unification of religion and state, an ideology that is the basis of the Islamic state. It is also descriptive inasmuch as it encapsulates the debates and initiatives of religious scholars who sanction revisionist political Islam but challenge the unification of religion and state from a religious standpoint. Furthermore, this conceptualization provides a pathway via which the Muslim world can accommodate modern democratic ideas. As a strategic concept, religious secularity simultaneously safeguards religion from politicization and emancipates religion and state. Synchronous with its rejection of Islamic fundamentalism and dogmatic secularism, religious secularity promotes negotiation, compromise, and conciliation to accommodate religious concerns within a secular state structure. In this way, religious secularity effectively negotiates not only the relations of politics and religion, but also those of religion and state.

This book uses the term "secularity" to distinguish the emerging discourse in Iran from the more general usage of related terms such as "secularization" and "secularism". According to José Casanova, the term "secular" is central to constructing, codifying, grasping, and experiencing "a realm or reality differentiated from the religious" (2009: 1049). The religious/secular dichotomy is rooted in this understanding of the secular. But, as suggested above, in the Islamic context there is no fundamental distinction between religion and the most important dimensions of the secular. The term "secularization" refers to a comprehensive historical process whereby religion loses its significance both in the individual and societal spheres. Individual belief in transcendental forces weakens, and, at the societal level, religion loses its influence in the public sphere through the prioritization of science, emphasis on worldliness, and the separation of church and state. By no means does my usage of the term "secularity" refer to this comprehensive process of weakening religion in individual and public life.

In this book, the term "secularism" refers to the political paradigm that is the outcome of the secularization process in a Muslim context.[5] Interestingly, secularism in Muslim countries was largely unique in that it drew from the experiences of secularism in Western countries. Whereas in the West, secularism was the result of long historical processes (secularization), secularism in the Muslim world was an ideology imposed for the sake of dominance, without any comprehensive societal process having taken place. For decades, secularism was adopted as a means of either suppressing religion or eliminating its role from public life in Muslim countries. Instead of being an historical process leading to the formulation and development of an ideology of secularism, political ideology has become the pretext for the proposed sociopolitical re-configuration of Muslim countries.

I intentionally use the term "secularity" in this book to clarify the distinction between the emerging discourse in Iran and the conventional understanding of secularism as a global paradigm. I concur with Scharffs, who distinguishes secularity from secularism. For him, secularity represents "an approach to religion–state relations that avoids identification of the state with any particular religion or ideology. . . and that endeavours to provide a neutral framework capable of accommodating a broad range of religions and beliefs" (2011: 110). In this book, "secularity" refers solely to a political project and does not introduce a new political paradigm. Secularity does not advocate the total elimination of religion from political practice; rather, it narrowly promotes the institutional separation of religion and state.

Unpopularity of the Islamic State

Secularism in the Muslim world is commonly perceived as an anti-religious project. Because there is no accurate translation of the term "secularism" in the Arabic, Persian, and Turkish lexicons, it remains an alien concept to Muslims. As a normative ideal, European models of secularism have typically been hostile to Muslims (Keane, 2000: 35). For much of the Muslim world, secularism is perceived as an imported, top-down ideology peculiar to authoritarian regimes. In recent years, however, stronger acknowledgement of the plural forms of secularism has emerged.

Egyptian scholar Nasr Abu Zayd, while approving the separation of religious institutions from the state, refuted the removal of religion from public

---

5. There are, of course, various definitions and understandings of secularism, see Ahdar, 2013; Casanova, 2009; Kenny & Smyth, 1997; Kosmin, Keysar, & Tabatabaei, 2007; Kurtz, 2010.

life (Abu Zayd, 2004; Abu Zayd & Eshkevari, 2005). Similarly, Algerian scholar Mohammad Arkoun distinguishes between "positive moderate secularism" and "negative extremist secularism" (2008). Acknowledging that "secularism" is a word imbued with unhelpful connotations in the Muslim world, eminent Islamic scholar Abou El Fadl stresses an important positive feature of secularism: "Secularism is necessary to avoid the hegemony and abuse of those who pretend to speak for God" (2003: 62). Rashid Al-Ghannouchi, a Tunisian scholar, speaks of French versus Anglo-Saxon secularism (Al-Ghannouchi, 2000, 2013; Esposito & Voll, 2001: 116–117), and, most recently, Abdullahi An-Na'im, who comprehensively questions the authenticity of the Islamic state has advocated that an inclusive secular democratic state is compatible with Islam as it safeguards the separation of religion from state but not religion from politics (2008). These scholars, who promote an inclusive understanding of secularism from their religious standpoints, table their arguments within an Islamic framework.

The Turkish AKP exemplifies the emergence of a new Islamism that challenges both the stereotypical image of political Islam and French-style secularism. The AKP's new Islamism is a response to Kamalist assertive secularism. While the AKP government operates within a secular political structure, it seeks to reconcile religiosity with secular politics.[6] Although their experiences have been different, Muslim-majority countries in South East Asia, such as Indonesia and Malaysia, have also opted in favour of the "quasi-secular state" paradigm (Elson, 2013; Hosen, 2013; Künkler & Stepan, 2013; Moustafa, 2014; Rahim, 2013; Seo, 2012).

In particular, religious secularity discourse has become a topic of growing importance following the Arab uprisings, as it questions not only state-dominated secularization, but also state-dominated Islamization. The volatile political situation in the Middle East and North Africa that has emerged following the Arab uprisings reinforces the proposition that religious secularity discourse is not confined to Shiite Iran. At the beginning of the Arab uprisings, the Egyptian Muslim Brotherhood reacted negatively to Ayatollah Khamanei's claim crediting Iran's 1979 Islamic revolution with the uprisings in the Middle East and North Africa region, stressing that the Egyptian revolution is not an Islamic revolution. A Gallup poll conducted following the fall from power of Egypt's president Hosni Mubarak showed

---

6. It is true that the Turkish AKP is in the midst of crisis due to Erdogan's authoritarian tendencies and corruption allegations, in particular after the Taksim Gezi Park protests and the 2013 corruption scandal. But it is preposterous to directly attribute this circumstance to AKP's religious characteristic. Like all other political parties, Islamic parties are prone to corruption.

that less than 1 percent of Egyptians favoured an Iranian-style Islamic clerical state (Michael, 2011).[7] Also, in his first interview after returning from exile to Tunisia, Rashid Al-Ghannouchi, the leader of Al-Nahdah, announced that an Islamic state was not an option for his country (Al-Ghannouchi & Bouazza, 2011). Despite increasing pressure from the Salafists, specifically from Ansar al-Sharia, Al-Nahdah remained loyal to its moderate discourse. To a large extent, Al-Nahdah is also to be credited with much of the new Constitution, which has been praised by both internal and international communities. Tunisia's new Constitution is described as a "progressive", a "model constitution" for other countries in the region, and an "historic landmark on [the] journey to democracy" (Aljazeera, 2014; Schemm & Bouazza, 2014; UNDP, 2014; United States Department of State, 2014).[8]

Nonetheless, by no means does Tunisia's promising transition represent a frequent pattern in the Middle East and North Africa region. The uprisings spawned cautious optimism regarding the constructive role of Islamic discourses in the region's political mosaics. However, this optimism has been variously impeded, among other reasons, by the flames of sectarian conflict (Syria, Bahrain, and Yemen); the failure of the Muslim Brotherhood in governance, which has led to the return of authoritarian rule (Egypt); and militia rivalries, tribal wars, and the risk of a failed state (Libya). Under these circumstances, transition to democracy is not only no longer on the horizon: it has become a long distant dream. Certainly, both Islamic groups and non-Islamic/religious forces are responsible for this lost opportunity for democracy. However, it would be far-fetched to impute this circumstance solely to the Islamic groups and their religious agendas. More specifically, there is little evidence that the demand for an Islamic state has contributed to the dimming of any democratization vision. Dispute over the form of state— that is, Islamic versus secular—never claimed a prominent place in the political rhetoric of the region in the post–Arab uprisings context, mainly because the idea of an Islamic state was never advanced by the mainstream Islamic parties as an option. For example, while there are many cleavages between the Muslim Brotherhood and Egypt's secular forces, these cleavages do not include political bargaining over the notion of an Islamic state.

In sum, there is little reason for optimism about the Arab uprisings in the present climate, irrespective of the fact that moderate Islamists enjoy

---

7. See also Akbarzadeh, 2014: 109–110; Roy, 2013b.

8. For further discussion of the constructive role of Al-Nahdah in Tunisia, see Cavatorta & Merone, 2013; Dalmasso & Cavatorta, 2013; Gerges, 2013; Hamid, 2014: 190–205; Hashmi, 2013; A. Stepan, 2012; Voll, Mandaville, Kull, & Arieff, 2012: 23–26.

immense political influence across the region. The quest for an Islamic state is missing from their political rhetoric: in effect, they pursue their policies within a secular political structure. This book is geared primarily towards religious secularity within an Iranian framework; but a comparative study undertaken to ascertain the potency of religious secularity discourse in the greater Muslim world would proven highly illuminating.

Iran's experience within the Muslim world remains significant for many reasons. Its first victory was against authoritarian secularization, which offered Iranian Islamists an opportunity to pursue their objectives from a powerful position. Esposito stresses that regardless of its Shiite character, the 1979 revolution "spurred" Islamic movements all over the Muslim world (1990). And, despite its failures and tarnished reputation, any shift in the Iranian politico-religious discourse will certainly migrate beyond Iran's borders. Iran, along with many secular-oriented Muslim countries, adopted a similar pattern of state–religion relations up until 1979 when the revolution set in motion a new paradigm. Iran has been an Islamic state for the last three decades; thus, contemporary debate among Iranian scholars pertaining to secularism has been strongly shaped by their lived experience of the Islamic state. And, while religious secularity discourse is a direct response to the Islamic state, it also bears the scars of authoritarian secularization, the approach adopted by the Pahlavi regime during its 60-year rule of the country.

Iran: A Chain of Backlashes

The first battleground between the religious and secular forces of Iran in the 20th century occurred during the Constitutional Revolution (1905–1911). The clergy's support for the Constitutional Revolution and their consent to parliament was conditional. They insisted on preserving the religious composition of both the judiciary and the educational system, restrictions on freedom of the press, and the supervisory veto power of the country's religious leaders. The secular forces that led the revolution spearheaded a system of parliamentary rule based on constitutionalism, a move that proved a major victory for secularism. The Constitutional Revolution failed to satisfy the clerics' demands, leaving the religious forces to regret their participation in the revolution (Afary, 2013; Arjomand, 1988: 52–54; Katouzian, 2010: 48; Momayesi, 2000: 45).

Tension between the secular and religious forces was further exacerbated during Reza Shah's reign (1925–1941). After his visit to Turkey in 1934, Reza Shah was determined to introduce Ataturk's authoritarian secularization project into Iran.[9] This modernization program proved a threat to clerical power as it was not only inspired by assertive secularization but would, according to Armstrong, "surpass Atatürk's ruthless secularization" (2000: 223). Reza Shah advocated major reforms of the judicial system, an intervention that culminated in the replacement of Iran's religious courts by secular courts in which the clergy had little to no privilege. He conscripted young clergymen into compulsory military service and imposed rigid restrictions on their lives. The wearing of clerical garb and the turban was forbidden. Similarly, a law was passed abolishing the veil, by extension forcing women to adopt the European dress style. Whereas before Reza Shah assumed power, the majority of children used to study in *maktabkhaneh,* or clerical institutions, under his uniform educational system, all boys and girls were obliged to attend schools in which the teaching of the Quran was prohibited (Cronin, 2003).[10] Reza Shah's secularization programs triggered major conflict with religious leaders—the Khoharshad riot of 1935, for example.[11]

Like his father, Mohammad Reza Shah (hereafter, "the Shah") pursued the same form of top-down authoritarian secularization during his rule from 1941 to 1979, although initially his authority was not overly strict. Between 1941 and 1953 he moderated the secularization project in an attempt to avoid conflict with religious leaders, who took advantage of these years to revive their influence and power (Esmaeili, 2007: 227–235; Esposito & Voll, 1996: 57). However, after the 1953 coup against the liberal prime minister Mohammad Mossadeq, the Shah's secularization programs intensified, marking the second stage of his reign (1953 to 1979) (Hashemi, 2009: 139). The enormous influence wielded by the clerics, which allowed them to resist the Shah's "anti-Islamic" inclinations, rendered conflict between a perceived despotic state and an increasingly influential clergy inevitable.

Almost 60 years of top-down authoritarian secularization neither sapped the influence of the clerics nor diminished the religiosity of the Iranian people. The Shah's secularization program failed to take root in the larger society (Benard & Khalilzad, 1979; Hashemi, 2010: 334; Mirsepassi, 2000: 65–95; V. Nasr, 2003). Keddie (2003) argues that while secularization was in tune with other social and cultural trends in the West, top-down authoritarian secularization in the Middle

---

9. For further reading about the similarities and differences of Reza Shah's and Ataturk's modernization programs, see Atabaki & Zürcher, 2004.

10. For a detailed discussion of Reza Shah's reforms, see Abrahamian, 1982: 102–148; 2008: 63–96; Arasteh, 1962; Arjomand, 1988: 59–86; Atabaki & Zürcher, 2004.

11. For further discussion of the conflict between the religious leaders and Reza Shah, see Amini, 2003; Basirat-Manesh, 2007; Goudarzi, Jawan, & Ahmad, 2009.

East provoked a backlash. Anti-secularism and anti-Westernization[12] were the chief slogans of this Ayatollah-led backlash, culminating in the 1979 revolution (Kamali, 2007: 381).

The toppling of the Shah saw state-dictated secularization replaced by state-dictated Islamization. The Islamic state did not hesitate to explicitly add "Islamization" as a prefix to legitimize its policies. "Islamization of law", "Islamization of the universities", "Islamization of the educational system", and the "Islamization of society" were just some examples of the phraseology utilized to legitimize top-down Islamization.

Today, this form of Islamization has provoked a backlash. Three decades after the introduction of the Islamization programs, the legitimacy of the unification of religion and state remains fragile. A group of religious scholars has effectively challenged the religious foundation of the Islamic state, but has not adopted a hostile attitude towards political Islam. Instead, they advocate a secular-democratic approach towards state–religion relations based on Islamic teachings, a discourse that affords them a middle-ground, or *wasatiyyah*, position between top-down secularization and top-down Islamization.

Drawing upon the Hegelian triad of thesis, antithesis, and synthesis, Iran's pre-revolutionary secularization program could be interpreted as a thesis that eventually created its antithesis. A synthesis of radical Islam and assertive secularism offers a middle course accommodating some features of secularism while rejecting others, particularly its anti-religious aspects. More importantly, it proposes a religious rationale for the secular democratic state, and through this it makes two corresponding contributions to the relevant literature. It not only introduces an evolving model of secularity, but also exposes the false dichotomy between secularity and religiosity. Although much of the relevant academic literature in the new millennium is critical of the secularization thesis, the secular/religious dichotomy continues to shape the debate surrounding secularism. Religious secularity proposes the possibility not only of the coexistence of religious and secularity, but also highlights the need to recognize the religious roots of an emerging model of secularity in the Muslim world.

Fall of a Theory

For a large part of the 20th century, secularization was assumed to be the inevitable destiny of the modern world. The widely held belief that the world

---

12.   Homa Katouzian argues that the anti-Western features of the revolution did not receive sufficient attention at the time; they later became the main character of the event, see Katouzian, 2010: 46.

would eventually abandon belief in religion was based on a somewhat simplistic assumption of a causal relationship between modernization and secularization (B. J. Berman, Bhargava, & Laliberté, 2013). Like urbanization, bureaucratization, industrialization, and rationalization, secularization was supposedly an integral part of modernization. Leading sociologists including Herbert Spencer, Karl Marx, Max Weber, and Emile Durkheim purported that religion would eventually disappear from public life. But, by the 1960s–1970s, this assumption was yet to be validated by empirical studies.[13] Acknowledging the complicated status of religion in the modern world, literature pertaining to the sociology of religion abandoned this formula. Peter Berger openly admitted that sociology was mistaken about secularization: "What I and most other sociologists of religion wrote in the 1960s about secularization was a mistake.. . . [The notion that] with more modernization comes more secularization was a mistake. [It was] a crazy theory. There was some evidence for it. But I think it is basically wrong. Most of the world today is certainly not secular. It is very religious" (1997: 974).

Provoked by the new findings, some scholars went so far as to press for the erasure of the term "secularization" from the sociological lexicon (D. A. Martin, 1969: 22; Shiner, 1967; Stark, 1999: 270; Stark & Iannaccone, 1994). However, scholarship did not positively respond to this suggestion, and even proponents of abandonment continued to use the term.[14] In contrast to the idea of abandonment, however, the concept of secularization, for some scholars, remained a useful analytical construct for explaining an important part of modern affairs. These scholars argue for complicated secularization theory as a response to a complicated religiosity of the contemporary world. One example of this effort was the 2004 work by Norris and Inglehart for whom rejection of the thesis in its entirety would have been a major mistake. Instead, arguing that the thesis should be updated, they proposed the concept of existential security as a way of revising the secularization theory. In their *Sacred and Secular,* the two authors argue that when, in the course of modernization, societies become wealthier and more secure, the need for religious values, systems, and practices decreases. This generalization, of course, ought to be understood as probabilistic, not deterministic, because specific factors in any given society make it impossible to predict exactly what will happen

---

13. A sizeable corpus of literature contains empirical evidence of both the qualitative and quantitative arguments put forward to invalidate anticipation of the secularization thesis in terms of the elimination of religion. Some of these works include Greeley, 1989; Hammond, 1985; Robbins & Anthony, 1981.

14. For example, ten years later, in *A General Theory of Secularization*, D. Martin (1978) clearly suggests that the term "secularization" was back in vogue.

(Norris & Inglehart, 2004). Similarly, for Steve Bruce, the secularization paradigm argues for "irreversibility" rather than "inevitability". Describing the revival of religion as a form of cultural transition, Bruce argues for the capability of the secularization thesis to describe the complicated situation of religion in the contemporary world (2002: 34–41).

The main body of scholarship has opted for a variety of perspectives, inviting careful examination of the diverse and complicated status of religion in the contemporary world. New scholarship softens the predictive feature of the secularization thesis and embraces a more analytical and descriptive account of the process of secularization. Backtracking on the universal claim of the traditional secularization thesis, new scholarship has evoked sectarian connotations to deal with the diverse modes and practices of religion in different parts of the world (Berger, 1999; Berger, Davie, & Fokas, 2008; Bhargava, 1998; 2009; Butler, Mendieta, & VanAntwerpen, 2011; Casanova, 1994; 2003; 2011; Chaves, 1994; Dobbelaere, 1984; 1999; 2002; Glasner, 1977; Hammond, 1985; Maclure & Taylor, 2011; Neuhaus, 2009; Stark & Iannaccone, 1994; Taylor, 2007; Yamane, 1997). This has sparked an enormous diversity of ideas, an outcome that provoked Hadden to suggest that critiques of the secularization thesis have produced "a hodgepodge of loosely employed ideas rather than a systematic theory" (1987: 598). It may be said that this situation is true, too, of the status of religion in Iran. Despite religion's powerful presence in the sociopolitical sphere, some studies claim a decline in religiosity and a decline in its role in the public life of Iranians (Abdi & Goudarzi, 2009; Ghobadzadeh, 2002; 2004; Hossein Godazgar, 2007; Rabiee, 2001; Rafipoor, 1997; Vahdat, 2011; Zooalam, 2000). The point I wish to make here is that even in the highly politicized presence of religion, secularization cannot be fully refuted.

Secularism[15] is commonly depicted as a gift from the civilized Western world to former colonies. This was particularly the case in the newly established nation-states in the Muslim world post–World War I, when postcolonial Muslim states adopted secularism as a political means of tackling the challenges associated with nation-building. This was evident in Mohammad Ali's reforms in Egypt in the late 19th century, Arab nationalism under Nasser, Ataturk's authoritarian secularization of Turkey, Reza Shah and his son Mohammad Reza Shah's emulation of Turkish secularization in Iran,

---

15. In addition to its sociological foundations, the notion of secularism in political science is also rooted in the works of political philosophers such as John Locke and Jean-Jacques Rousseau. For a detailed discussion of this background of secularism, see Kennedy, 2006: 91–180.

the Baathist secular movements in Iraq and Syria, the French secular model promoted in Tunisia under Bourguiba, and the programs put in place by the Algerian Front de Liberation.[16] By the 1970s, religious revivalism, particularly in the Muslim world, not only discredited the secularization thesis, but also posed a formidable challenge to its political project, secularism. In Muslim countries, the backlash against decades of state-imposed authoritarian secularization and the rise of political Islam resulted in the refutation of secularism in its totality (Arjomand, 1988; Esposito, 1997: 1–3; N. Keddie, 2003: 21–22; Lawrence, 1989; Mandaville, 2007: 48–57; S. V. R. Nasr, 1998; Roy, 2007: 62). However, the evolution of varying articulations of secularism has problematized this total refutation; in line with global scholarship, contemporary Muslim scholars have begun to acknowledge the varying models of secularism. While refuting some models, they promote others that are more suited to the religious nature of Muslim-majority countries.

From Secularism to Secularisms

The diverse experiences and "bewildering variety" of religion–state–society relations make it virtually impossible to present the Western experience in monolithic terms (Beaufort, 2008; Brown & Snape, 2010; Davie, 2000: 15; Hashemi, 2010; A. C. Stepan, 2011). It is widely accepted that divergent sociopolitical and religious contexts lead to varying experiences of secularism, recognition that not only provides descriptive and analytical illustrations of secular political systems, but is also sensitive to the different models of secularism from a normative standpoint. Explicit normative articulations of secularism have been proposed in response to the critiques of the applied models of secularism. The "liberal-pluralist", "principled distance", and "twin tolerations" models, to name but a few, are among the normative articulations of secularism.

Maclure and Taylor distinguish two ideal types of secularism—that is, "republican secularism" versus "liberal-pluralist secularism". In the case of the former, secularism favours moral equality, freedom of conscience, and the growth of a common civic identity. This, in effect, requires the marginalizing of religious affiliations and forcing them back into the private sphere. By contrast, secularism based upon the liberal-pluralist model is a method of "governance, [the function being] to find the optimal balance between respect for moral equality and respect for freedom of conscience" (Maclure

---

16. For further explanation of the secularization project in the Muslim world, see N. R. Keddie, 1997: 26–35.

& Taylor, 2011: 34). This model mandates that a secular state does not take exception to the presence of the religious in the public space. Similarly, state or public institutions are not allowed to grant greater value to members of a specific religion. Liberal-pluralist secularism intends to achieve optimal reconciliation between equality of respect and freedom of conscience (Maclure & Taylor, 2011: 27–36).

Rajeev Bhargava's "principled distance" model is based on the Indian experience, "where the instability or ambiguity of the secular/religious divide manifests itself and that therefore shows alternative modelling in comparison with European or North American variants" (Beyer, 2013: 665). This model contrasts with "mainstream Western secularism", according to which separation means mutual exclusion between religion and state.[17] In a secularism based upon "principled distance", religion may not assume special public significance antecedently defining the character of the state—but this does not mean that religion has no public significance at all. Bhargava advocates a flexible approach to the issue of inclusion or exclusion of religion and the engagement or disengagement of the state. In terms of law and policy, decisions depend upon the context, nature, and the state of relevant religions. In other words, "principled distance" opposes strict separation. Bhargava further states that religion either intervenes in or refrains from intervening in the affairs of state, depending upon which of the two options better promotes freedom, equality, or any other value integral to secularism. In similar fashion, the state may positively or negatively engage or disengage with religion, depending entirely upon which of the two better promotes religious liberty and equality (1998; 2009; 2013).

According to the "twin tolerations" model, there should be both distinction and a mutual respect between political authorities and religious establishments. Alfred Stepan argues that religious institutions should not have "constitutionally privileged prerogatives" to mandate public policy. At the same time, religious individuals and communities must have complete freedom to worship privately, to advance their values publicly, and to sponsor organizations and movements in the political sphere. However, their actions should not impinge negatively upon the liberties of other citizens or violate democracy and the law (2000; 2001: 27–35).

---

17. Modood has criticized Bhargava's generalization of Western secularism. Noting the different experiences of Western European secularism, he argues that neither the United States nor France are the best examples of the West, since they do not evince a mainstream practice of secularism. Similarly, Alfred Stepan argues that the separatist patterns of the United States and France are not norms in the Western context. Inspired by the notion of "multiple modernization", Stepan proposes "multiple secularism" to highlight the diversity of separatist patterns in the West, see Bhargava, 2009; Modood, 2010; A. C. Stepan, 2011.

Descriptive accounts of the varying models of secularism were initially introduced by distinguishing American secularism from the European experience. In particular, the difference between the French and Anglo-American models has invited different interpretations. Ahmet Kuru conceptualizes these two models, proposing the terms "passive" and "assertive" secularism. The first refers to the state's passive role in religious life—that is, how it avoids the establishment of religions, but allows for their public visibility. In the second (or assertive) model, the state actively excludes religion from the public sphere by confining it to the private domain. Kuru argues that assertive secularism emerged in France and Turkey as a result of antagonistic relations between republicans and the religious institutions during their secular state-building period. By contrast, in the American case, secular and religious elites reached an overlapping consensus on the separation of church and state, which resulted in a more passive form of secularism (2007; 2009).

An-Na'im, who distinguishes "authoritarian secularism" from "secularism as mediation",[18] claims that the former is typified by a top-down policy, which imposes secularism without promoting its principles among the population. By contrast, "secularism as mediation" offers an appropriate space in which social and political actors negotiate politico-religious issues through compromise rather than dichotomies of victory and defeat (2008). Tariq Modood proposes the dichotomous concepts of "moderate" and "radical" secularisms to explain a similar notion. While radical (or ideological) secularism promotes absolute separation of religion and state, the distinguishing feature of moderate (or inclusive) secularism is compromise. According to Modood, Western Europe, with the exception of France, conforms to the moderate secularism paradigm (2009; 2010). For the most part, the normative standpoint is embedded in the experiences of secularism. An-Na'im, for example, not only describes two leading models of secularism, but also advocates weak secularism. Similarly, Kuru and Modood promote passive secularism and moderate secularism as appropriate options for the Muslim world.

Multifarious descriptions of the applied models of secularism, along with diverse normative models, entail using the plural form "secularisms" to more accurately characterize religion–state relations (Berg-Sørensen, 2013; B. Berman, Bhargava, & Laliberté, 2013; Cady & Hurd, 2010; Calhoun, Juergensmeyer, & VanAntwerpen, 2011; Hashemi, 2009; Jakelic, 2010; Jakobsen & Pellegrini, 2008; Levey & Modood, 2009). Due to this diversity, it is no longer unusual to speak of a divergent model of secularity in the

---

18. An-Na'im also terms this model of secularism "weak secularism". For further information, see An-Na'im, 2009; 2010.

Muslim world. This book is built upon the space provided by new scholarship. In short, I argue that a new model of secularism is emerging within Iranian religious scholarly circles.

From Islamism to Islamisms

John Esposito, an eminent scholar of the Muslim world, maintains that the 9/11 attacks set back the efforts of progressive Islamic scholars for at least a decade (2011). It is true that 9/11 fuelled Islamophobia and re-energized Huntington's notion of a "clash of civilizations"; but one could also argue that it gave rise to the new millennium's focus on the Muslim world, shedding light on its internal diversity and complexity. But, in the process, misrepresentation of Islam and the Muslim world incensed the "silenced majority" or "less visible Muslim", to use Esposito's and El Fadl's terms, inciting them to raise the cry for a non-militant Islam (Abou El Fadl, 2005: 6; Esposito & Mogahed, 2007: ix).

Scholarship in the new millennium is attuned to these new voices of the Muslim world wherein moderate voices in particular have received special attention. Focusing on individual Islamic reformists, some scholarship expresses the progressive thought of Muslim scholars. Overall, these works provide progressive interpretations of Islamic teachings, that distinguish reformist discourse from radical Islam (Abu Zayd, 2006; Abu Zayd & Nelson, 2004; Mohammed Arkoun, 2006; Armajani, 2004; Baum, 2009; Eshkevari, Mir-Hosseini, & Tapper, 2006; Esposito & Voll, 2001; Ghamari-Tabrizi, 2008; S. Hunter, 2009; Johnston, 2010; Madaninejad, 2011; Safi, 2003; Soroush, Sadri, & Sadri, 2000; Taji-Farouki, 2004; Tamimi, 2001; Vahdat, 2000a; Vakili, 2001; Vogt, Larsen, & Moe, 2009). A thematic approach has also been adopted to introduce modern readings of Islamic scripts. Issues such as human rights, democracy, and secularism have received particular attention in this regard. Generally speaking, these works aim to challenge "Muslim exceptionalism", a view which depicts a contrasting relationship between Islam and modern ideas (e.g., democracy and human rights). These works can be read as efforts to demonstrate the compatibility of Islam with modern life (Abou El Fadl, 2002; 2005; Abou El Fadl, Cohen, & Chasman, 2004; An-Na'im & Baderin, 2010; Bayat, 2007; Esposito & Voll, 1996; Filali-Ansary, 2003; Gulen, 2006; Moussalli, 2003; A. Sachedina, 2001; A. A. Sachedina, 2009). Overall, these efforts not only acknowledge the public and political presence of Islam, but also outline a positive role for Islam in politics.

Efforts to conciliate Islam and modern political principles have sparked controversy over the notion of Islamism. It was not long ago that Islamism was considered identical with fanaticism, fundamentalism. and violence. New scholarship closely scrutinizes the internal diversity among those in the Muslim world who subscribe to political Islam. Recent articulations of the political dimensions of Islam have prompted some scholars to call for abandoning the term "Islamism" altogether (Alatas, 2010; Hanafi, 2010; Hussain, 2010; Rauf, 2010; Varisco, 2010). Other scholars, acknowledging the evolution of moderate notions of political Islam and the active participation of Islamists in the sociopolitical arenas, urge scholarship to move beyond the parameters of Islamism—that is, to widen the boundaries of what may be characterized as Muslim politics. "Post-Islamism", "post-fundamentalism", "new Islamists", and "beyond Islamism" are recently coined terms describing this new wave (Baker, 2003; Bayat, 2007; Browers & Kurzman, 2004; Burgat, 2003; Harub, 2010; Jahanbakhsh, 2003; Kian-Thiebaut, 1999; Mandaville, 2007; Roy, 2004: 58–99; Volpi, 2011).

To a large extent, Islamism was a response to secularism; it arose at a time when secular states in the Muslim world were in crisis (Mirsepassi, 2000: 189). A defining characteristic of Islamism was the rejection of the separation of religion and state, or secularism. Modern thought, however, recognizes that the diversity of Islamism invalidates the simple dual formula of separation versus unity. Esposito espoused this notion well at the beginning of the new millennium:

> Islamists will be challenged to demonstrate that an Islamic option can be sufficiently pluralistic and tolerant to incorporate diverse religious and political tendencies. At the same time, those who advocate a more secular orientation will be challenged to adopt and adapt modern forms of secularism that foster a true and open pluralism which responds to the diversity of society, one that protects the rights of believers and unbelievers alike (2000:12).

Today, the bulk of scholarly literature has moved away from simplifying Islamism–secularism relations within an antithetical framework. Muslim scholars have redefined secularism and invalidated the myth of the incompatibility of Islam and secularism from a religious perspective (Abu Zayd, 2004; Abu Zayd & Eshkevari, 2005; Akhtar, 2008; Al-Ghannouchi, 2000; An-Na'im, 2008, 2010; Muhammad Arkoun, 2008; Engineer, 2006; Fatah, 2008; Hanafi & Wahyudi, 2006; Soroush, 2010d; Wu, 2007; Zakariyya, 2005). This book's contribution to the literature is of a similar nature inasmuch as it

explains Shiite endeavours to re-conceptualize the secular state and its compatibility with Shiite Islam.

Scholarly and practical efforts in the Muslim world to reconcile the secular state with Islam have gained significant attention. Leading empirical
examples of the reconciliation of Islam and inclusive secular states such as
Turkey and Indonesia have been widely scrutinized (Assyaukanie, 2009;
Baran, 2010; Cinar, 2005; Cizre, 2008; Dressler, 2010; Heng & Ten, 2010;
Keyman, 2010; Künkler & Stepan, 2013; A. Kuru, 2013; A. T. Kuru & Stepan,
2012; Salim, 2008; Uysal, 2013; Yavuz, 2009; Yavuz & Esposito, 2003).[19] By
highlighting the diverse articulations of state–religion relations within the
Muslim world, the idea of the antithetical correlation between Islam and the
secular state is refuted. Esposito and Tamimi's *Islam and Secularism in the
Middle East* is an important contribution to the literature. In their endeavour to overcome polarization, they incorporate challenges to the conventional
notion of secularism and offers re-conceptualizations of secularism and political Islam, thereby promoting the reconciliation of Islam and the secular state
(Esposito & Tamimi, 2000).

In contrast to the Turkish state, Iran is widely cited as an extreme example of the incompatibility between Islam and secularism. However, subtle
shifts and possibilities of change cannot be discounted. Political developments in Iran, particularly during the reformist era (1997–2005), together
with the emergence of religious reformation discourse, have given birth to
a new scholarship about state–religion relations. A heterogeneous understanding of Islam–politics relations and the limits of religion in the political
sphere constitute emerging phenomena in Iran. Scholarship has offered a
clear understanding of the political shifts that occurred after the 1997 presidential election (Arjomand, 2009; Ashraf & Banuazizi, 2001; Basmenji,
2005; Bayat, 1997; Brumberg, 2001; Ehteshami, 2002; Gheissari & Nasr,
2006; Kamrava, 2011; Rajaee, 2007; Tazmini, 2009; Updegraff, 2006).
The epistemological developments generated in scholarly circles—the phenomenon Kamrava refers to as an "intellectual revolution"—constitute
another important dimension of the shift in the understanding of political
Islam (Boroujerdi, 1996; S. T. Hunter, 2009; Ramin Jahanbegloo, 2000; R
Jahanbegloo, 2007; Kamrava, 2003, 2008; Khosrokhavar, 2004; Kurzman,
2001; Madaninejad, 2011; Matin-asgari, 1997; Mirsepassi, 2010; Nabavi,
2003: 111–218; Sadri, 2001; Taghavi, 2007; Vahdat, 2004; Vakili, 2001). The

---

19. In light of the approval of a progressive Constitution in January 2014 and promising
political developments, Tunisia may offer another empirical example of the reconciliation
of Islam with an inclusive secular political system.

aforementioned developments have encouraged scholars to investigate the possibility of religion-oriented secularism in Iran's political sphere (Alizadeh, 2009; Javaherian, 2010; N. Keddie, 2003; Sadri, 2001; Schmid, 2003).

A work that is directly relevant to this book is Nader Hashemi's *Islam, Secularism, and Liberal Democracy*, which highlights the trend in Iran towards an "indigenous theory of Islamic secularism". Hashemi contends that failed secularization projects in the Muslim world stem from Islam's inner civilization ethos (2010: 329). He further asserts that religious discourse can contribute to the secularization process through the reformation of religion. In effect, Muslim reformists are developing their own brand of Iranian secularism.

However, Hashemi's pioneering work does not fully encapsulate the sophisticated debate among Iranian reformists, specifically religious scholars. He makes brief reference only to reformist use of religious theology to advance a new reading of Islam–state relations. Thus, questions surrounding what they are actually arguing for, how they structure their argument within the religious context, the particular model of secularism they are proposing, and whether or not they are articulating an indigenous secularism remain unanswered. As well, Hashemi's work does not recognize the possibility that liberal democracy may be unable to fully capture the indigenization process. Although Iran's religious reformist scholars promote democracy and a secular state, they are critical of liberalism and decouple liberalism from democracy (Mohammadi, 2000; Soroush, 1995b; 2000). Finally, Hashemi's work does not provide a clear understanding of what he refers to as an "indigenous theory of Islamic secularism". However, it must be acknowledged that his work offers an effectual point of departure for this book, and it is these unanswered questions that I intend to explore. Similar to the experience of the West, Hashemi recognizes that religious reformation in the Muslim world is a pathway towards developing a secular political structure. This book provides an insight into the current religious reformation in Iran within the context of the evolution of religious secularity discourse.

This work has been inspired by the conceptual framework offered by An-Na'im in his magnum opus *Islam and the Secular State: Negotiating the Future of Shari'a*. An-Na'im questions the legitimacy of an Islamic state by proposing three interrelated objections, the first of which refers to the lack of any record of "Islamic states" in the Muslim tradition. He regards the concept of an Islamic state as a postcolonial phenomenon rooted in the Western innovation of nation-state (2008: 7) and, on these grounds, challenges its efficacy. Acknowledging the diversity of interpretations among Muslim scholars, he asks: "How and by whom can such differences of opinion be properly and legitimately settled in practice in order to determine what is the positive law to be applied in specific cases?" (An-Na'im, 1998: 34). With regards to Iran, there has never been unanimous agreement on Islamic principles among the ruling clergy, let alone among dissenting religious leaders. Until his death in late 2009, Grand Ayatollah Montazeri, whose religious ranking was much higher than that of Khamanei, the current Supreme Leader, challenged the Islamic clerical state by providing alternative interpretations of Islamic principles. The lack of consensus on Islamic principles was highlighted by the appointment of female government ministers in August 2009, despite objections by several Grand Ayatollahs. But, supported by Ayatollah Khamanei, President Ahmadinejad confirmed the appointments.

An-Na'im purports that self-styled Islamic states such as Iran and Saudi Arabia are not capable of governing if they rigidly adhere to the regulations of the Shari'a (1998: 39). Hundreds of examples can be cited in which the ruling clergy in Iran have not only ignored Shari'a principles but even retreated from self-outlined religious regulations. One notable example was the creation of the Council for the Determination of the Interest of the Islamic State (Majma-e Tashkhis-e Maslahat-e Nezam). The Guardian Council, the country's religious watchdog, has the authority to nullify parliamentary endorsements if they are deemed incompatible with Islamic principles. In the early years of the Islamic state, many parliamentary endorsements were rejected on the basis of their incompatibility with Islam. In 1987, Khomeini ordered the setting up of a council to bypass this deadlock and overlook Islamic principles in the interests of the state. On another occasion, Khomeini reacted to then president Khamanei's statement that the authority of the Islamic government could be exercised only within the framework of the sacred law. In response, he insisted: "A government. . . [was] one of the primary commandments of Islam and has priority over all derivative commandments, even over prayer, fasting, and pilgrimage to Mecca" (quoted in Arjomand, 1988: 182).

Critical of the notion of an Islamic state on religious grounds, An-Na'im maintains that Islamic values are promoted when the state is neutral with regard to religion (2008: 3). He further asserts that an inclusive secular state is the only effective political system compatible with Islamic principles, traditions, and decrees. Highlighting the distinction between state and politics, An-Na'im favours a secular state based on the separation of religion from state, but not from politics. The statement "I need a secular state to be a Muslim" is repeated several times in his book, thereby highlighting the religious rationale for supporting a secular state. In sum, An-Na'im's argument provides a useful theoretical framework from which to analyse three decades of implementation of the notion of an Islamic state in Iran. My analysis of the Islamic Republic of Iran contributes to the academic literature by extending

An-Na'im's hypothesis regarding the theological and administrative tensions associated with the religious claims of an Islamic state.

A Scholarly and Latter-Day Discourse

This book focuses on the ideational power and influence of Iranian Shiite scholars. While there is occasional reference to arguments postulated by non-Iranian Islamic scholars, the study does not assert that religious secularity discourse is influential beyond Iranian scholarly circles. While there is specific and frequent reference to Shiite scholars in Iraq and Lebanon, due to their close relationship with Iran's religious strata,[20] this does not imply that religious secularity is an emerging discourse in these countries. Further comparative research is required in majority-Muslim countries before this claim can be made with confidence. It is also important to mention that there are many contradictions in Iran's lived experience of an Islamic state, due to the problematic incorporation of a "republican" dimension into the notion of Islamic state. The conflation of Islamism with republicanism begs further scrutiny that falls within the scope of the literature on the relationship between Islam and democracy, a subject outside of the province of this book's enquiry.

Religious secularity discourse first developed following a series of articles written by Abdulkarim Soroush in 1989,[21] which have since been widely acknowledged as precipitating a new phase of enquiry in Iran's politico-religious scholarly circles. Other scholars joining Soroush marked the polarization between the ruling clergy and their critics, who had become known as "religious reformists" and were soon supported by a number of journalists and politicians. This informal coalition developed into the reformist movement that has played a key role in Iran's politico-religious mosaic over the last two decades. This book examines the scholarly debate that has

---

20. In the contemporary world, there has never been a senior Ayatollah who has not been trained in Qom in Iran or Najaf in Iraq. Najaf used to be preeminent compared to Qom. This is why all Iranian Marja-e Taghlids undertook the main part of their training in Najaf. This is also true about the Grand Ayatollahs of Lebanon, such as Imam Mousa-Sadr, Muhammad Hussein Fadl-Allah, Mohammad Mehdi Shams al-Din, and Mohammed Jawad Moghniya. Moreover, many high-ranking Ayatollahs in Iraq, including Akhund Khurasani, Mahmoud Shahroudi, Khoei, and Sistani, were originally from Iran.

21. These articles not only underpinned contemporary religious reformation projects, but also generated other notions around their main thrust—that is, the separation of religion from religious knowledge. Soroush (1994) argues that whereas religion is a sacred, eternal, and fixed phenomenon, human knowledge of religion is a worldly, intermittent, and temporary phenomenon.

ensued between the ruling clergy and Iran's reformist scholars over the last two decades. However, there are many references to the Islamic state that are rooted in a much older historical discourse.

The notion of an Islamic state in modern Iran-Shiite history goes back to 1950, when a young, radical cleric named Navab-Safavi published a pamphlet promoted as the Constitution of the Islamic state. Compared to Khomeini's more academic articulation of the Islamic state, the pamphlet was not considered seriously by the scholarly community. Khomeini's lectures presented in February 1971, which were later compiled and published as a book titled *Islamic Government*, constitute the major theological case for the Islamic state. This study encompasses a wide time frame surrounding the religious secularity debate. Reference will be made to the early years of Islamic history, to historical debate, and to events in Iran.

Religious secularity has attracted a large group of scholars whose articulations have only strengthened through dialogue. Each and every one of the scholars discussed in this book plays an important role in the discussion. Some, like Soroush and Mojtahed-Shabestari, propose progressive interpretations of religious texts, while others, including Montazeri and Kadivar, communicate better with the masses and habitual believers. While Soroush and Mojtahed-Shabestari approach state–religion relations from theological-philosophical and civic perspectives, Eshkevari, Kadivar, and Montazeri's jurisprudential approach has launched an internal dispute regarding the jurisprudential state. This growing discourse has brought together an army of journalists, politicians, and academics embroiled in the religious reformation project. There is an internal dynamism that impels contributors to the discourse to complement each other's work. Despite their differences, the contributions of these scholars have formed the fount of a reformist discourse.

Religious secularity specifies the adoption of an inclusive democratic secular state in the Muslim-majority country of Iran. Decades of anti-religious, imported, top-down, and authoritarian secularism have tarnished the image of secularism. In this context, reformist scholars are faced not only with the challenge of articulating a new model of secularity, but also with managing the negative connotations associated with the term. To this end, they have exposed the disadvantages of the Islamic state to religion as well as the contradictions of the Islamic state vis-à-vis Islamic principles and traditions. Furthermore, by employing Islamic sources such as the Quran and hadiths within a jurisprudential and theological framework, they have articulated a robust religious rationale for the secular state.

The structure of this book is informed by two main arguments that form the foundational components of the concept of religious secularity: (1) the contradictions inherent in an Islamic clerical state and (2) the compatibility of Islam and a secular democratic state. The book unfolds additionally in thematic categories to support these goals. The religious claims of an Islamic state are crystallized into three forms: (a) claims of divine foundation for the state, (b) conflation of religion and state, and (c) the exclusive right of the clergy to political leadership. These themes, together with the two foundational pillars mentioned above, combine to form the six chapters of this book.

Chapter 1 scrutinizes the question of divine versus popular sovereignty, and introduces challenges to the notion that state authority in the contemporary world may be derived from divine sources. After providing a brief history of divine and popular sovereignty in Shiite Islam, this chapter targets the linchpin of Iran's Islamic state—that is, the doctrine of Velayat-e Faqih (rule of the Islamic jurist). The chapter intends to provide insight into the inconsistencies between divine sovereignty and Islamic precepts and traditions. Religious secularity discourse not only invalidates purported historical records of the sacred foundation of state in Islam, but also problematizes the notion of divine sovereignty from theological-philosophical and non-religious perspectives. As an alternative, Islamic history—along with jurisprudential-theological reasoning—is used to promote popular sovereignty as necessary to complement the spirit of religion. The main thrust of this chapter is to attest to the compatibility of Islam and popular sovereignty, which is an essential requirement of a secular democratic state.

Chapter 2 explicates the seeding of religious secularity by analysing the damage that the Islamic state has inflicted upon Islam. The formation of an Islamic state is claimed to have been inevitable in order to implement the sociopolitical dimensions of Islamic teachings. Politics, in this articulation, should be used to accomplish religious goals. However, the lived experience of the Islamic state in Iran has proven antithetical: religion has been employed as a tool to achieve political ambitions. This is not only evident in the policy-making processes of the Islamic Republic of Iran, but also conceptualized via the concept of *fiqh-ul maslaha* (expedient jurisprudence). Soon after the establishment of the Islamic state, the ruling clergy realized the multifarious realities of governance issues, which rendered the practice of many religious principles both impractical and impossible. In an attempt to deal with this dilemma, Ayatollah Khomeini claimed that governance was the core element of Islam; in brief, that religious precepts were subsidiary aspirations and instrumental to the implementation of governance. The second chapter shows how this shift led to the abuse of religion by the ruling clergy. The chapter also discusses how religious hypocrisy has grown in Iran, and

describes the shift towards the imposition of the exoteric dimension of religion by the Islamic state.

Chapter 3 critically analyses the unification of religion and state. The
exploitation of religion by the Islamic state provoked advocates of reformist
discourse to promote separation in order to emancipate religion from subjec-
tion to the state. A reinterpretation of the sociopolitical dimensions of Islam
is required to attest to the fact that Islamic teachings do not prescribe specific
guidelines for governance. This chapter contests the unrealistic expectations
of religion and re-prioritizes God and the hereafter as its primary mission.
It will be demonstrated that religion is questioned and weakened when held
responsible for governing politics wherein failures are bound to happen. The
third chapter also discusses why religion in general and *fiqh* (jurisprudence)
in particular, fail to execute the tasks of governance.

Direct political leadership by the clergy is another distinguishing character of Iran's political system. Chapter 4 examines the clerical establishment as a unique structure wherein politico-religious authority is indivisible.
After explaining the peculiarity of the clergy's claim to political leadership
in the Shiite tradition, the chapter will analyse the way by which Khomeini's
thought and political conduct led to widespread domination of the clergy in
the sociopolitical domain. The last part of the chapter explicates the process of
institutionalizing the clerical establishment in post-revolutionary Iran.

The primary goal of chapter 5 is to demonstrate the failure of the ruling
clergy to gain the support of the country's senior religious leaders. Khomeini
was the highest religious authority who subscribed to the politicization of
Islam in pre-revolutionary Iran; this pattern has somehow continued into the
post-revolutionary era. From the outset of the establishment of the Islamic
state, senior clerics resisted Khomeini's political discourse. The majority
of Marja-e Taghlids showed passive resistance by maintaining an apolitical approach. Furthermore, this chapter details the acts of resistance to the
clergy's direct political leadership, which on occasion led to political conflict.
The fifth chapter also investigates the alternative conceptualizations of the
clergy's role in the political sphere by traditional religious leaders. These
alternative formulations refute the clergy's exclusive right to political leadership, instead highlighting the role of the people in granting leadership. The
final part of chapter 5 discusses the failure of Iran's ruling clergy to promote
the clerical Islamic state model among other Shiite majority countries such
as Iraq and Lebanon.

The emergence of new religious scholars—namely, religious intellectuals—from the 1940s onwards fractured the clergy's monopoly of religious knowledge. In chapter 6, close examination of the contribution of

this group to the religious reformation process highlights how religious intellectuals continue to question the authenticity of the clergy as a genuine class in the Islamic context. Scrutiny of the educational and financial structure of the clergy reveals a conflict of interest in their politico-religious position, by extension challenging the clergy's legitimacy to claim political leadership. The sixth chapter also further problematizes the conflation of religious and political authority by discussing the ruling clergy's centralized authority in the form of politico-religious structure that contradicts Shiite jurisprudential-theological foundations as well as the Shiite decentralized structure. In practice, the experience of the Islamic state in Iran has exposed the comprehensive challenges associated with the unification of religion and state for both the clergy and Islam. The compromising of the clergy's autonomy, the dishonouring of dissident clerics, the interruption to the democratic process by preferment of Marjaiat, and the tarnishing of the clergy's reputation are analysed in this chapter. In conclusion, I argue that religious secularity compels clerics to retreat from political leadership in order to regain their spiritual credibility.

I

Shiite Discourses on Sovereignty*

The like power [God's power] have kings: they make and unmake their subjects, they have power of raising and casting down, of life and of death, judges over all their subjects and in all causes and yet accountable to none but God only.

KING JAMES I OF ENGLAND, 1609 (quoted in Hooker, 1996: 358)

All Muslims ought to obey the commands of the Valey-e Faqih [Supreme Leader] and submit themselves to his orders and prohibitions.. . . . Commitment to the Valey-e Faqih is not separated from commitment to Islam and the guardianship of the infallible Imams. . . . If there is a contradiction between the decisions/authorities of the Valey-e Faqih and subjects' volition and will, his decisions and authority take precedence.[1]

ALI KHAMANEI (2009), Supreme Leader of the Islamic Republic of Iran

THE MID-17TH CENTURY represented a landmark era for the principle of sovereignty in the West. The Treaty of Westphalia 1648 marked the end of the Thirty Years War and catapulted the international concept of sovereignty to the forefront. This was followed by the emergence of popular sovereignty in the face of the divine sovereignty of kings. With the execution of Charles I in 1649, so began the demise of the divine right of kingship in England. The Glorious Revolution of 1688 and the French and American revolutions in the

---

* A shorter version of this chapter appeared as Ghobadzadeh, N., & Rahim, L. Z. (2012). Islamic reformation discourses: Popular sovereignty and religious secularization in Iran. *Democratization, 19, 2, 334–351.*

1. All translations of Persian sources are the author's unless otherwise noted.

late 18th century advanced and institutionalized popular sovereignty in the West (Bukovansky, 2002; Morgan, 1978; Wootton, 1986). In addition to their profound influence on the English and French revolutions, philosophers of contractarianism, including Thomas Hobbes (1588–1679), John Locke (1632–1704), and Jean-Jacques Rousseau (1712–1778) consolidated their positions in the new epoch of political philosophy, in which popular sovereignty under-pinned the foundation of the state.

Although the study of divine and popular sovereignty has been relegated to political history in the West, it is a contemporary and pressing issue in Muslim countries, particularly in Iran. The quotation above by the current Iranian Supreme Leader, Ali Khamenei, is remarkable in its similarity to that of King James I of England. A quick search of the keywords "legitimacy" (*mashroiyat*) and "sovereignty" (*hakemiyat*) reveals the contested nature of these concepts not only in historical and scholarly works, but also in Iran's current political environment.

The ruling clergy's claim of divine sovereignty has had a significant impact on the country's political orientation. A recent example of this is the confrontation between Hashemi-Rafsanjani, head of the Assembly of Experts, and Ayatollah Mohammad Yazdi, a key member of the Guardian Council following the controversial election of June 2009. In his Friday prayer sermon delivered after the 2009 election, Hashemi-Rafsanjani maintained that without the republican basis of the political system and regular elections, the Islamic state lacks legitimacy. Challenging Rafsanjani's assertion, Ayatollah Yazdi stated: "The legitimacy of the government is given by God.. . . [A]cceptance by the people doesn't bring legitimacy to (an Islamic) government. Mr Hashemi-Rafsanjani ignored this important Islamic point and talked in both parts of his sermon yesterday as if governments are assigned only by the people" (AFP, 2009). Mir Hussein Mousavi and Mehdi Karroubi, the main opposition leaders, have reiterated the significance of popular sovereignty. According to Mousavi: "The people's will and vote are the source of legitimacy for political power" (2010). This sentiment is echoed by Karroubi in his critique of the authority of Valey-e Faqih[2]:

> The authority and domain of Velayat-e Faqih has been expanded so much, it is unlikely that God could have granted so much author-ity to the prophets and Imams. I don't even think God would have

---

2. *Valey-e Faqih* refers to the person who rules in the absence of the 12th Imam. *Velayat-e Faqih* refers to the principle of his rule.

considered such a right for himself in dealing with his people (quoted in AFP, 2010).

The controversy between divine and popular sovereignty has been widely discussed in many circles of Iranian society, from parliamentary debate and politicians' interviews to newspaper and journalistic articles. In response, strenuous efforts have been made to honour and legitimise the Supreme Leader, who represents the Hidden Imam and possesses the divine right to rule the country. There have been many cases in which political investigations or debates have been terminated following a speech or message by the Supreme Leader.[3] Officially, the last word on policy determination belongs to the Supreme Leader, who must be obeyed by each and every person and group. Many political activists and religious intellectuals have been imprisoned in his name. The debate surrounding divine versus popular sovereignty continues to animate contemporary Iranian politics and scholarship, and is central to the religious reformation discourse.

Sovereignty in the Shiite School

The discourse on divine versus popular sovereignty can be traced back to the Prophet Mohammad's demise in the seventh century CE. It is, in fact, the very basis of the Shi'a-Sunni division. When the Prophet died in 643 CE, Muslims were faced with two options to determine his successor. The majority of Muslims, the Sunnis, believed that governance was not a sacred matter and should be decided by Muslims, whose consent (baya'at) is the source of the ruler's authority. The minority group, the Shi'a, contended that the ruler possesses divine right and that God had appointed the Prophet's son-in-law, Ali, as the rightful successor. Thus, in Shiite austere theology, popular sovereignty cannot constitute a basis for legitimacy.[4]

The main branch of Shiism (Ithna Ashari, or Twelver Shi'a) purports that the right to govern was given by God solely to the 12 Imams, all of whom were ancestors of Imam Ali and believed to be infallible. Although some of the above 12 Imams claimed the right to rule, none—apart from Imam Ali— could form a government. Imam Ali ruled the Muslim world from 656 to

---

3. A recent example was the abandoning of a parliamentary investigation into the financial corruption of Vice President Mohammad Reza Rahimi. The Supreme Leader sent a concealed message to the parliament asking them not to proceed with the case.

4. This does not mean that contemporary Sunni states are more democratic than those of the Shi'a. Like other religious issues, the political thought of both the Shi'a and Sunni schools have evolved throughout Islamic history, according to a myriad factors.

661 as the fourth rightful caliph.[5] The ruling systems during the time of the infallible Imams were considered illegitimate by the Shi'a (Eshkevari, 2009b; Goudarzi, Jawan, & Ahmad, 2010). The 12th Imam, Mahdi, is expected to return to form a just government. Thus, by and large, messianic hope in the eternal existence of Imam Mahdi and his exclusive right to govern sanctioned a politically dissenting history for the Shi'a. It is unanimously accepted by Shiites that no specific person was appointed by God in the OCCULTATION ERA (the era extending from the second disappearance of the 12th Imam in 941 CE). For centuries the Shi'a expected the imminent reappearance of the Hidden Imam, a belief that mandated not only a passive approach to politics, but also complete rejection of non-divine kingships. For this reason, association with the temporal rulers was not an option in Shiite political theology.

This pattern continued to some degree until the Safavid era (1502–1736 CE), which represented a milestone as henceforth Persia became the centre of the Shiite world (Abisaab, 2004). Although the jurists were not in a politically dominant position during the Safavid dynasty (Rahimi, 2008: 2), Shiite political thought was employed to legitimise the king's authority over the nation. The Safavids appealed to the jurists, not only in pursuit of religious legitimacy for their governance, but also to enlist the jurists' support in converting the then-majority Sunni population of Iran to Shiism. Some jurists seized the opportunity to expand Shiism using the patronage offered by political power. But, the long-standing apolitical tradition necessitated conceptual revisions in Shiite political theology. In particular, jurists who were associated with the exercise of political power engaged in this re-articulation of Shiite theology. Mohaghegh Karaki (d. 1533), Muqaddas al-Ardabili (d. 1585), Mohammad Bagher Sabzeravi (d. 1679), Molla Muhsin al-Fayd Kashani (d. 1680), and Muhammad Baqir Majlisi (1627–1698) were among the more renowned jurists.[6] But, in no way does this imply that they subscribed to the notion of Velayat-e Faqih as it is articulated in by contemporary Shiite theology. Instead, they all tried, to various extents, to reduce the traditional hostility and gap between temporal political power and sacred canopy, with a view to justifying their cooperation with Safavids.

---

5. After the Prophet Mohammad, four caliphs led the Muslim peoples: Abu-Bakr, Omar, Othman, and Ali, who were known as the "rightful caliphs".

6. It is beyond the scope of this research to probe into the political theology of these scholars; but it is important to note that none of them claimed divine authority for jurists in the political arena. Neither did they grant kings divine sovereignty. For detailed explanations of their political thought, see Abisaab, 2004; Aienevan, Aghajari, Rahmati, & Moftakhari, 2010; Borji, 2006: 116–174; Calder, 1982a; Eftekhari, 2004; Jafaryan, 2008; Lakzaee, 1997; Matsunaga, 2000; Mazinani, 1996; Sultan-Mohammadi, 2001.

An enduring legacy of the jurists' association with the Safavids was the discord that emerged among them over religion–state relations. In the post-Safavid era, there were some jurists who believed that the king's authority could be religiously legitimized by the consent of jurists. While Mirzay-e Qumi, also known as Sahebe Ghavanin (1738–1815), and Kasheful Gheta (1743–1812) subscribed to this notion, others, including Sheikh Mohammad Hassan Sahebe Javaher postulated that the right to rule exclusively belonged to the Hidden Imam and, thus, could not be transferred to kings. From the 19th century onwards, Sheikh Morteza Ansari's discourse (1799–1864) dominated mainstream Shiite political theology. The first effective model of Marjaiyat (Mottahedeh, 2000: 2011) agreed with the general Shiite political thought that the 12 Imams were appointed by God and that they alone possessed the divine right to rule the Muslim world. Yet, in the OCCULTATION ERA, it is only the Hidden Imam who exclusively possesses divine politico-religious authority. Sheikh Ansari argued that the political authority of the Hidden Imam was not transferrable to jurists or kings. He further maintained that while the jurists possessed the same religious authority as the Prophet and the infallible Imams, they nonetheless had no political authority. For this reason, they were not in the position of legitimising the political authority of kings. From Ansari's standpoint, not only were all kings religiously illegitimate (Bashiriyeh, 2009: 241–246), the jurists' cooperation with kings was also sinful. He was opposed to any form of jurists' engagement in politics (Arjomand, 1988: 178).

Sheikh Ansari's apolitical discourse set the Shiite school's theological parameter for one-and-a-half centuries. The very idea of the indivisible and non-transferable right of the Hidden Imam to political sovereignty persisted unabated. This is why the political engagement of jurists remained marginal and political jurisprudence became an obsolete form of scholarship in the Shiite seminaries. Furthermore, few politically engaged clerics ever implied, either explicitly or implicitly, a claim to political leadership, let alone divine political authority. A epoch-defining event, which occurred in the early 20th century, was the Constitutional Revolution. Although members of the clergy became extensively involved in the revolution, in effect they did not alter their conceptual standing. As Feirahi contends, this experience was based on the continuation of Sheikh Ansari's theology (2005: 192).

The Constitutional Revolution not only compelled the clergy's political engagement, but it also provoked a theological discourse on the Shiite position vis-à-vis modern political thought. It is quite impossible here to justly explain the variety of positions adopted by the clergy at that time. But it is worth highlighting two salient points: First, the clergy were sharply polarized regarding constitutionalism.[7] Second, and more importantly, the theological heritage of this episode in the clergy's political history fortified the apolitical paradigm of the Shiite school. It offered contemporary reformists grounds upon which to discredit the doctrine of Velayat-e Faqih as a heretical innovation. In particular, the contributions of Akhund Khurasani (1839–1911), Sheik Mohammad Esmaeil Mahallati (1852–1924), and Alameh Mohammad Hossein Naeini (1859–1936) were of great importance, for they not only actively engaged in the Constitutional Revolution, but also bequeathed a conceptual and lexical framework in support of popular sovereignty. This explains the extensive citing of their works by contemporaneous scholars who promote religious secularity.

Mulla Muhammad Kazim Khurasani (also known as Akhund Khurasani), who was considered to be the best-known Marja-e Taghlid of the Shiite world, was also the highest-ranking clergy to actively support the Constitutional Revolution. Khurasani, who relied heavily upon reason *(aql)* to justify his support for constitutionalism, argued that absolute authority belonged solely to God. Employing a somewhat audacious initiative, he maintained that while the Prophet Mohammad and the infallible Imam's authority in the sociopolitical sphere was limited, they were nevertheless bestowed with absolute authority over religious matters on earth (Kadivar, 2006c: 10–13). Akhund Khurasani drew an elegant distinction between the Islamic state *(hokumat-e mashrou'eh)* and the legitimate state. For him, the Islamic state could be formed exclusively by the Hidden Imam. Therefore, in the OCCULTATION ERA, there are two forms of government: legitimate and illegitimate. Khurasani supported the Constitutional Revolution in order to form a legitimate government, but not as an Islamic state *(hokumat-e mashrou'eh)*.

Akhund Khurasani's writing constituted the Usuli Fiqh,[8] a Shiite school that underscores independent *ijtihad* and reasoning (Muhaqqiq-Damad, quoted in Farzaneh, 2010: 231). Khurasani was determined to engender the application of reasoning, particularly when it came to modern-day issues. This may explain why rather than citing the Quran or hadiths, he primarily employed

---

7. For a comprehensive analysis of the clergy's position during the Constitutional Revolution, see Algar, 1969; 1972; Bayat, 1991: 240–256; Haeri, 1977.

8. The Usuli differ from the Akhbari group in that they favour the use of *ijtihad* (i.e., independent reasoning to set new rules of *fiqh*) to assess hadiths and exclude traditions that are unreliable according to the convictions of the time and place. Since the crushing of the Akhbaris in the late 18th century, Usulis has been the dominant school of Twelver Shi'a and now forms an overwhelming majority within the Shiite denomination. For detailed discussions of the Usuli-Akhbari dispute, see Al-e Ghafur, 2007; Cole, 1985; Moussavi, 1985; Newman, 1992; Tabatabaee, 2005.

reason *(aql)* to support constitutionalism. There is no evidence in Akhund Khurasani's letters and statements that he drew upon religious sources, either the Quran or hadiths, to mandate constitutionalism as a religiously legitimate *(mashrou'eh)* form of governance. Rather, his point of departure was the interests and expedients of the nation and Islam. In a letter Akhund Khurasani stressed his pragmatic motivations:

> Our aim in taking such trouble is to bring a comfortable life for the people, to remove oppression, to support the oppressed, and to give aid to troubled persons. We would also like to carry out God's laws and to protect the Islamic land from the infidels' attacks. We intend to practice the Islamic concept of *amr-i bi ma'ruf va nahy-i az munkar* (to enjoin right conduct and forbid indecency) and other Islamic laws which are in the interests of the people (quoted in Haeri, 1976: 144).

Akhund Khurasani became involved in the Constitutional Revolution as part of his religious duty; but he assumed this responsibility based on certain over-arching precepts (e.g., "Commanding the Right and Forbidding the Wrong") or to fulfil his responsibility as a source of emulation (Farzaneh, 2010: 239–242; Kadivar, 2006c: 17). Because it was never his intention to realise a theological doctrine, he made the case based simply on the then-concurrent circumstances under which constitutionalism was a better option from a rational point of view.

The most renowned advocate of constitutionalism, Akhund Khurasani was supported by other clerics. The Shiite theological community strongly supported constitutionalism to pursue and protect the nation's interests, rather than materializing a Shiite political doctrine. Haeri asserted that "The three top *mujtahids* of Najaf, that is, Tihrani, Akhund Khurasani, and Mazandarani, together with their assistants and co-thinkers such as Na'ini and Mahallati, were very concerned with the welfare of the people and their being treated with justice" (Haeri, 1976: 152). In a joint fatwa, this three Marja-e Taghlids explicitly stated that, in the OCCULTATION ERA, people were the main source of political authority (Kadivar, 2006c: 21).

Neither his writings nor his activities suggest that Akhund Khurasani endorsed the clergy's political leadership. In fact, he completely rejected a pro-posal made by one of his disciples, Naeini, who urged him to call for an Islamic state and assume political leadership.[9] Naeini argued that by establishing an

---

9. This, of course, does not mean that Naeini promoted the clergy's political leadership during the Constitutional Revolution. Adopting a pragmatic approach, he subscribed to constitutionalism as a better option compared to absolute tyrannical monarchy. His book

Islamic state, disagreements among religious leaders would be resolved, the clergy would be able to institutionalize Shari'a, and a just Islamic state would be established. Akhund Khurasani refused Naeini's request not only from a theological point of view, but also based on the detrimental effect of the clergy's political leadership on Islam. He warned Naeini about the possibility of tarnishing the clergy's reputation in the event of direct political leadership. Akhund Khurasani numerated 21 reasons, all of which highlighted the negative consequences of the clergy's political leadership (Ghabel, 2011). In hindsight, Khurasani perceptively predicted what was to befall post-revolutionary Iran following the establishment of the Islamic state.

Sheikh Muhammad Ismail Gharavi Mahallati (1853–1924) also played an active part in the Constitutional Revolution. An important albeit lesser-known scholar, he not only repudiated the possibility of divine sovereignty during the OCCULTATION ERA, but was the first jurist in the religious circle to write a tract[10] promoting constitutionalism. Mahallati argued that there can be three types of government: (a) an Islamic state, (b) an absolute despotic monarchy, and (c) a limited and constitutional form of government. From Mahallati's viewpoint, the first type of government ought to be based on divine sovereignty, which solely belonged to the infallible Imam: But, given that the 12th Imam is absent, forming an Islamic state is presently impossible. Therefore, he argued, the choice would be between absolute tyrannical monarchy and a constitutional form of government. Every wise person would opt for a limited and constitutional form of political system. Mahallati further maintained that a constitutional political system would not only put an end to oppressive rule but would also protect Islam from infidels (Haeri, 1977: 100). Drawing a distinction between religious and temporal (*urfi*) issues, Mahallati asserted that parliament should not have any authority over religious matters. He promoted parliament as an institution to facilitate people's right to oversee their rulers (Varei, 2010: 111).

---

entitled *Tanbih al-Umma wa Tanzih al-Milla* (Admonishment of the Umma and the purification of the nation/religious community) is widely cited as the first quasi-democratic articulation of politics in Shiite history. Throughout his book, Naeini justified constitutionalism from a jurisprudential point of view. For a detailed explanation of his political thought and his contribution to the Constitutional Revolution, see Haeri, 1977: 101–234; Nouraie, 1975; Varei, 2003.

10. Mahallati's work *al-La'ali al-Marbuta fi Vojoob al-Mashroota* (The bound pearls on the necessity of the constitutionalism), was endorsed by two eminent Marja-e Taghlids, Akhund Khurasani and Ayatollah Abdullah Mazandarani. For detailed information about this book and Mahallati's political thought, see Husseinzadeh, 2003; Mahallati 2010; Mahallati & Rouhani, 2007.

The most iconic figure among clerics was Mirza Mohammad Hossein Naeini (1859–1936), whose book is widely cited as the main religious text-book promoting constitutionalism (Kadivar, 2014a: 358). Although known as the champion of constitutionalism, Naeini argued that legitimate governance was ultimately based upon divine sovereignty. Unlike Akhund Khurasani, he did not differentiate between the Islamic state (hokumat-e mashrou'eh) and the legitimate state. Fusing political legitimacy with religion, Naeini advo-cated constitutionalism based on the conviction that the right to govern was entrusted to the parliament by jurists (Varei, 2003: 59–61). Similar to the contemporary notion of the doctrine of Velayat-e Faqih, Naeini believed that, in the OCCULTATION ERA, jurists were assuming the role of the Hidden Imam in both his religious and political capacities. He asserted that the jurists, by virtue of their office of collective vicegerents of the Hidden Imam (niyabat-e um-e fughaha), should determine political issues (Naeini, 2003: 49). Naeini explicitly repudiated non-jurists' authority over political matters by arguing that it was the religious duty of jurists to dictate political issues (2003: 111–112). However, he was of the opinion that under the current circum-stance, direct political leadership by jurists was not viable. In other words, constitutionalism was perceived as a legitimate political system because the jurists endorsed it. Surprisingly, the notion of divine sovereignty remained marginal and unelaborated in his published work. Naeini alleged that his book included seven chapters; but he did not published two chapters due to a feeling that the Hidden Imam was not comfortable with the deleted chapters. The deleted chapters supposedly included a discussion of the status of jurists as collective vicegerents of the Hidden Imam in political matters. His reason for not publishing these chapters, he said, was that the scholastic quality of them did not properly correspond to the content of the book, which was meant to communicate with the laypeople (2003: 175). As suggested above, he may not have published it because there was no acceptance of his desired form of state (i.e., an Islamic state); a form of government, according to his politi-cal theology, led by jurists. No matter what explanation is given, Naeini did not promulgate divine sovereignty during the Constitutional Revolution. As a matter of fact, during this period, the notion of divine sovereignty remained totally marginal and negligible.

Overall, the Constitutional Revolution was an exceptional time in Shiite political history, as it witnessed the clergy proactively engaged in politics at the highest levels. However, by no means was their engagement aimed at implementing a specific Shiite political doctrine. Divine sovereignty was little more than a trivial claim, which had stagnated in conceptual and practical terms. Thus, from a theological perspective, the clerical engagement in the

Constitutional Revolution was not a breach of traditional Shiite political theology. However, this dominant theological approach had been ruptured by
the political thought of Ayatollah Ruhollah Mousavi Khomeini (1900–1989)
from the 1960s onwards. Although Khomeini did not explicitly challenge
dominant Shiite thought during the lifetime of the Grand Ayatollah Hussein
Broujerdi (1875–1961), in the absence of an eminent Marja-e Taghlid (source
of emulation), he and his revolutionary band of followers emerged as the leading Islamic vanguards of the 1960s (Rahimi, 2008: 3). Khomeini's innovative
doctrine of Velayat-e Faqih was the first in Shiite history to conceptualize the
direct political role of jurists. He pioneered the doctrine of the divine right
of jurists, which was implemented following the 1979 revolution (Kadivar,
1994: –4).

Velayat-e Faqih: A Doctrine of Divine Sovereignty

Paradoxically, the Constitution of the Islamic Republic of Iran acknowledges
both divine sovereignty and popular sovereignty (Martin, 2000: 163–164).
The Constitution acknowledges the direct role of the people in electing the
president and members of parliament and an indirect role for the people
in choosing the Supreme Leader (Valey-e Faqih) through the Assembly of
Experts. However, a meticulous reading of the Constitution reveals that the
source of state authority is inextricably bound to Islamic principles. And,
while the people are capable of exercising their rights within the religious
framework, they are not free to seek options beyond religion. Articles 2 and
4,[11] for example, expressly determine all legislation, policies, and programs
conditional to the observance of Islamic principles, which are presented and
safeguarded by the clergy. Article 72 clarifies this restriction in the following
way: "The Islamic Consultative Assembly cannot enact laws contrary to the
principles (*usual*) and decrees (*ahkam*) of the official religion of the country
or to the Constitution. It is the duty of the Council of Guardians to determine
whether a violation has occurred in accordance with Article 96". The Council

---

11. Article 1: "The Islamic Republic is a system based on belief in: (1) The One God (as
stated in the phrase 'There is no god except Allah'), His exclusive sovereignty and the right
to legislate, and the necessity of submission to His commands; (2) Divine revelation and its
fundamental role in setting forth the laws;. . ."
Article 4: "All civil, penal, financial, economic, administrative, cultural, military, political,
and other laws and regulations must be based on Islamic criteria. This principle applies
absolutely and generally to all articles of the Constitution as well as to all other laws and
regulations; and, the *fuqaha'* of the Guardian Council are judges in this matter". [trans-
lated by Hassan Khosravi]

of Guardians, which includes six jurists and six Islamic lawyers, ensures that all legislation conforms to Islamic principles.

The most pivotal articles of the Constitution relate to the notion of Velayat-e Faqih. Article 5 corresponds to the aforementioned constructed Shiite political thought, which dictates that the right to rule the Muslim world belongs to the 12th Imam. In the OCCULTATION ERA, the political authority of the infallible Imam is transferred to the clergy as part of their religious authority. Article 5 states:

> During the Occultation of the Wali al-Asr (may God hasten his reappearance), the *wilayah* and leadership of the nation [Ummah] devolve upon the just [*'adil*] and pious [*muttaqi*] *faqih*, who is fully aware of the circumstances of his age; courageous, resourceful, and possessed of administrative ability, he will assume the responsibilities of this office in accordance with Article 107.

In addition to the widespread jurisdiction granted to the Valey-e Faqih[12] in Article 110, Article 57 clearly states that all three main bodies—the judiciary, the executive, and legislative bodies—are under the supervision of the Valey-e Faqih.[13] The Constitution thus very clearly identifies divine sovereignty as a guiding principle for the Islamic Republic of Iran.

Ayatollah Khomeini was the chief architect of the religio-conceptual notion of divine sovereignty. Due to Khomeini's strong political aspirations, most of his writings are political in content. However, one book, entitled *Islamic Government: Governance of the Jurists*, is solely devoted to his thoughts on the jurisprudential foundation of the Shiite Islamic state. It is based upon 13 seminary sessions given by Khomeini in the early 1970s in Najaf, Iraq. As the title suggests, the doctrine of Velayat-e Faqih by no means refers to the representation of the people. *Valy*, in the Arabic language, means "guardian" or "custodian". Literally, it refers to a parent (specifically a father) or to one who is appointed to protect a ward.[14] Khomeini subscribed to the notion that

---

12. It is the same as Supreme Leader. Actually "Supreme Leader" is the political appellation for the Valey-e Faqih.

13. The powers of government in the Islamic Republic are vested in the legislature, the judiciary, and the executive powers, functioning under the supervision of the absolute Velayat-e al-Amr and the leadership of the Ummah, in accordance with the forthcoming Articles of this Constitution. These powers are independent of each other.

14. Mehdi Haeri-Yazdi challenges the political doctrine of Velayat-e Faqih by referring to the very meaning of the term. He argues that *velayat* refers to a relationship between a custodian and a ward—by no means can it be applied to governmental and political issues. He maintains that "[t]his relationship is not possible between a person and a group of people" (1994: 220).

the Prophet Mohammad and all 12 Shiite Imams possessed the divine right to be political leaders of the Muslim world. He maintained that

> When the Prophet appointed a successor, it was not only for the purpose of expounding articles of faith and law; it was for the implementation of law and the execution of God's ordinances. It was this function—the execution of law and the establishment of Islamic institutions—that made the appointment of a successor such an important matter that the Prophet would have failed to fulfill his mission if he had neglected it (Khomeini & Algar, 1981: 40).

Khomeini propounded religious reasons for the necessity of establishing an Islamic state in the OCCULTATION ERA.[15] He argued that just as the Prophet and the infallible Imams possessed political authority, the jurists possess the divine right to lead Muslim society. Embellishing some Shiite hadiths[16] with political features, he maintained that the political authority of the jurists did not differ from that of the Prophet Mohammad and the infallible Imams:

> The idea that the governmental power of the Most Noble Messenger was greater than those of the Commander of the Faithful ('a), or that those of the Commander of the Faithful ('a) were greater than those of the faqīh, is false and erroneous. Naturally, the virtues of the Most Noble Messenger (s) were greater than those of the rest of mankind, and after him, the Commander of the Faithful was the most virtuous person in the world. But superiority with respect to spiritual virtues does not confer increased governmental powers. God has conferred upon government in the present age the same powers and authority that were held by the Most Noble Messenger and the Imāms ('a), with respect to equipping and mobilizing armies, appointing governors and officials, and levying taxes and expending them for the welfare of the Muslims. Now, however, it is no longer a question of a particular person; government devolves instead upon one who possesses the qualities of knowledge and justice (Khomeini & Algar, 1981: 62).

---

15. For a detailed account of his argument about the notion of divine sovereignty, see Goudarzi et al., 2010; Khomeini & Algar, 1981: 40–54.

16. Specifically, he employs hadiths in which the Prophet or the infallible Imams ask Muslims to listen to the jurists after their departure. Offering an inclusive interpretation of these sayings, he argues that these hadiths are not just about religious authority but about political authority as well.

Khomeini explicitly challenged the view that Velayat-e Faqih should be indirectly chosen by people's vote through the mediation of the Assembly of Experts: "Velayat-e Faqih is not something created by the Assembly of Experts. Velayat-e Faqih is something created by Almighty God. It is the same guardianship of the Noblest Messenger" (2006: 95). Thus, the task of the "Assembly of Experts is to prove the Velayat-e Faqih. . .. [T]hey want to ratify something, which is told by Almighty God" (Khomeini, 2000: 27). On another occasion, Khomeini insisted on the primacy of the endorsement of the presidency by Velayat-e Faqih[17] over the people's vote: "Islam has made Velayat-e Faqih compulsory. If the president is not endorsed by Valey-e Faqih, [his presidency] is illegitimate and when it is illegitimate, it becomes *taghut* [oppressive government]. Thus obeying this sort of government is obeying *taghut*" (2006: 118).

It would appear that the Constitution and Khomeini's thought[18] on divine or popular sovereignty vindicates the doctrine of divine sovereignty. The people's role, specifically in terms of electing the ruler, is irrevocably bound to Islamic principles. The Islamic Republic is thus not based on the concept of popular sovereignty, in which people are seen as the ultimate source of state authority.[19]

Popular Sovereignty: A Recent Shiite Articulation

The primacy of divine versus popular sovereignty remains a key theme in the writings of almost all scholars who examine state–religion relations in Iran. As Iranian scholars interrogate the concept of divine sovereignty, it is worth noting that exactly the same point was debated during the process of secularization in 17th-century England. Nader Hashemi observes how sovereignty and property were debated by John Locke and Robert Filmer. Locke highlighted the issue of sovereignty at the beginning of the *Two Treatises of Government*. The determinant status of the issue in the secularization process in England is discussed by Hashemi in the following way:

17. After the election, the president should be endorsed by the Supreme Leader before offi-cially starting his presidency. Some argue that the winner's presidency will not be legiti-mate without this endorsement, in spite of his election by the people.

18. There is a counter-argument, according to which Khomeini's occasional confirmations of the centrality of subjects' role prove his subscription to a sort of dual-legitimacy. For a full demonstration of this, see Goudarzi et al., 2010.

19. For a detailed discussion of the current conservative clergy's argument about divine sovereignty in the Islamic Republic of Iran, see Kamrava, 2008: 94–112; Khosrokhavar, 2001.

Locke commences his attack on Robert Filmer (the leading intellectual champion of the "divine right of kings") by affirming that "Scripture or Reason I am sure does not anywhere say so notwithstanding the noise of divine right, as if Divine Authority hath subjected us to the unlimited Will of another" (2009: 71).

The correlation between the rise of popular sovereignty and secularism in the West is not confined to the British case. During the French Revolution, secularism and popular sovereignty were promoted in place of the divine right of kings (Sajo, 2008: 628). Jean-Jacques Rousseau played a crucial role in the formulation not only of French secularism, but also of modern political thought in which popular sovereignty is predicated (Bertram, 2004: 97–127). This chapter of Western political history is mirrored by the current situation in Iran. Popular sovereignty is a central theme among reformist religious intellectuals who seek to challenge an authoritarian interpretation of religion. The religious reformation discourse endeavours to offer a democratic reading of religious sources by arguing that Islam positions subjects as the source of state authority. Religious intellectuals in contemporary Iran employ jurisprudential argumentation, historical records, and theological/ philosophical and non-religious discourses when advocating the principle of popular sovereignty.

There are different approaches to the concept of sovereignty given the different levels of progressive conceptualization among reformist scholars. While scholars such as Soroush and Mojtahed-Shabestari advocate unconditional popular sovereignty, Ayatollah Montazeri proposed a progressive version of the religious, democratic state, in which people were encouraged to choose a just jurist as their political leader. Another distinctive element among the reformist scholars is their different epistemological approaches when disputing divine sovereignty. In actual fact, their epistemological perspective is based on a democratic notion of popular sovereignty. The doctrine of Velayat-e Faqih is a jurisprudential articulation of the notion of divine sovereignty, notwithstanding the fact that disputes against this notion extend beyond the jurisprudential framework. Reformist scholars question acclaimed historical records of the political authority of jurists, and pose theological/philosophical, even non-religious challenges to the notion of divine sovereignty in arguing for popular sovereignty. Focusing on religious intellectual approaches, I have divided the following argument for the compatibility of Islam and popular sovereignty into three sections: the jurisprudential approach, challenges from an historical perspective, and non-jurisprudential challenges.

Jurisprudential Approach

As with the ruling clergy, reformist scholars are of the opinion that Islam includes political precepts. It is, therefore, the religious leaders' responsibility to provide Muslims with a religious conceptualization of politics. Religious sources, that is, the Quran, the hadiths, and traditions, constitute the foundation of their conceptualization. In terms of political Islam, the same Quranic verses and hadiths are used by both conservatives and reformists within a jurisprudential framework. While conservatives present an authoritarian interpretation of these sources to justify the concept of divine sovereignty, reformists read these sources as justification for popular sovereignty.

Within the aforesaid jurisprudential framework, there is a significant difference between the OCCULTATION ERA and the lifetime of the infallible Imams. All political systems governing the Muslim world during the lifetime of the infallible Imams (from 632 to 941 CE)[20] were considered illegitimate because the infallible Imams were appointed by God and possessed the divine right of political and religious authority. As briefly explained above, there have been profound disagreements among Shiite scholars about the Shiite ideal of political governance in the OCCULTATION ERA.

Jurists' Divine Authority

Mohsen Kadivar, a visiting professor of religion at Duke University, has challenged the legitimacy of the notion of divine sovereignty by providing different readings of the same jurisprudential sources used by the ruling clergy. Following his comprehensive reading of the Quran, Kadivar reaches the conclusion that only six appointive positions are mentioned in the Quran, of which none are endowed with divine political authority for jurists. He depicts three forms of authority for a prophet: (a) prophetic authority (i.e., acting as a messenger), (b) spiritual authority, and (c) political authority. He contends that some prophets had only the first authority. Some, including the Prophet Mohammad, possessed all three appointive authorities. From Kadivar's viewpoint, the people are neither the source of Mohammad's prophetic nor sociopolitical authority. In contrast to scholars such as Mojtahed-Shabestari, Haeri Yazdi, and Eshkevari,

---

20.   Imam Ali's governance (656–661 CE) is considered by the Shi'a as the only legitimate rule in early Islamic history. From an historical point of view, it was the only Shiite state headed directly by a Shiite religious leader until the formation of the Islamic Republic of Iran, when religious leaders directly took political control. As El Fadl writes: "Until recently neither Sunnite nor Shiite jurists ever assumed direct rule in the political sphere" (Abou El Fadl, Cohen, & Chasman, 2004).

Kadivar maintains that the religious and sociopolitical authority of the Prophet is directly conceded by God. He extends this articulation to the infallible Shiite Imams. Referring to a Quranic verse,[21] he outlines the Quranic source of the sociopolitical role of the infallible Imams. He also lists various hadiths, in which the divine source of the sociopolitical authority of the infallible Imams is affirmed (Kadivar, 2000b).[22]

Kadivar contradicts the doctrine of Velayat-e Faqih by questioning the extension of this sociopolitical authority to jurists in the OCCULTATION ERA. He maintains that nowhere in the Quran is there reference to the proclaimed appointment of jurists to sociopolitical leadership. Based upon his review of the relevant hadiths, Kadivar argues that jurists possess only two appointive positions: judgment and *efta* (the authority to issue religious decrees). He identifies ten hadiths that Ayatollah Khomeini, the founder of the doctrine, and its other proponents refer to as the religious basis of the doctrine of Velayat-e Faqih. In reviewing these hadiths, Kadivar concludes that only two are rooted in the Shiite tradition.[23] He argues that these hadiths correspond to the trusteeship of jurists and their religious authority vis-à-vis educating and promoting Shari'a principles. They do not provide religious justification for

---

21. Verse 5:55: "Your guardian can be only Allah and his messenger and those who believe, who establish worship and pay the poordue, and bow down (in prayer)" [translated by Marmaduke Pickthall].

إِنَّمَا وَلِيُّكُمُ اللهُ وَرَسُولُهُ وَالَّذِينَ اَمَنُواْ الَّذِينَ يُقِيمُونَ الصَّلَاةَ وَيُؤْتُونَ الزَّكَاةَ وَهُمْ رَاكِعُونَ

22. In order to publish a book in Iran, one needs pre-permission from the Ministry of Culture and Islamic Guidance. When Ahmadinejad came to power, most reformist scholars could not get permission to publish their writings. Similar severe restrictions applied to journals. By force of circumstances, reformist scholars opted to use the Internet. Thus, their recent works are usually published on their websites. This is why many citations do not include page numbers in this book.

23. These two hadiths read as follows: (A) "The Most Noble Messenger (s) said, 'The *fuqahā* are the trustees of the prophets ('a), as long as they do not concern themselves with the illicit desires, pleasures, and wealth of the world.' The Prophet (s) was then asked: "O Messenger of God! How may we know if they do so concern themselves?" He replied: 'By seeing whether they follow the ruling power. If they do that, fear for your religion and shun them'" [translated by Hamid Algar].

علي عن ابيه، عن النَّوفلي، عن السكوني، عن ابى عبد اللهِ، عَلَيْهِ السّلام، قال قال رَسُولُ اللهِ (ص) الفُقَهاءُ أُمَناءُ الرّسُلِ ما لَمْ يَدْخُلُوا فى الدّنيا. قِيلَ يا رَسُول اللهِ وَ ما دُخولِهم فى الدّنيا؟ قال: اتِّباعُ السّلْطَانِ. فَاذا فَعَلُوا ذلِكَ، فَاحذَرُوهُم عَلى دِينِكُمْ

(B) "Imām Ja'far as-Sādiq ('a) said: 'The scholars are the heirs of the prophets, for although the prophets bequeathed not a single dīnār or dirham, they bequeathed their sayings and traditions. Whoever, then, acquires a portion of their traditions has indeed acquired a generous portion of their legacy. Therefore, see from whom you may acquire this knowledge, for among us, the Family of the Prophet, there are in each generation just and honest people who will repel those who distort and exaggerate, those who initiate false practices,

jurists' political authority in the OCCULTATION ERA (Kadivar, 2000d: 9). Thus, jurists today do not possess the political authority to lead Muslims, in contrast to Prophet Mohammad and the infallible Imams.[24] Kadivar concludes that the divine source of the jurists' political authority, as proclaimed by the doctrine of Velayat-e Faqih and the Constitution of the Islamic Republic of Iran, is rooted neither in the Quran nor in the hadiths. "Velayat-e Faqih, be it of religious or civil order, appointive or elective, absolute or conditional, lacks credible religious foundation for its operation in the political sphere" (Kadivar, 2002b).

Kadivar not only questions the religious validity of the doctrine of Velayat-e Faqih, he contributes to Shiite political thought by proposing a quasi-democratic reading of the religious sources. Adhering to the notion of political Islam, Kadivar asserts that Islam is not confined to the private sphere, but includes sociopolitical dimensions (Kadivar, 2002b; 2003a). He promotes a state based on popular sovereignty on the grounds that Islam does not recommend any specific form of state. To quote Kadivar, "Islam acknowledges that human faculties are capable of finding appropriate solutions in these fields [forms of political systems]. In other words, politics is a matter of intellect, and the ability to reason is a human trait" (2002b).

He further asserts that competing political models can be presented if they do not contradict the tenets of the Shari'a (Kamrava, 2008: 165); people of different times and different societies are allowed to articulate their preference. This approach places the people as the source of state authority in Muslim society. Kadivar argues that the Quran and the many hadiths support the notion of human competency in determining appropriate solutions. In addition, he maintains that Islam will play its role in politics through the political contributions of Muslims, rather than through the dominance of the jurists. He does not derive the notion of a democratic government from

---

and those who offer foolish interpretations [that is, they will purify and protect religion from the influence of such biased and ignorant people and others like them'" [translated by Hamid Algar].

عن محمد بن يحيى، عن أحمد بن محمد بن عيسى، عن محمد بْن خالد، عن ابى الْبختري، عن ابى عبد الله (ع)، قال: إنَّ الْعُلَماءَ وَرَثَةُ الْانْبِياءِ. وَ ذاكَ أنَّ الْانْبِياءَ لَمْ يُورِثُوا دِرْهَماً وَ لا دِيناراً؛ وَ انَّما أوْرَثُوا أحادِيثَ مِنْ احادِيثِهِمْ. فَمَنْ أخَذَ بِشَيْءٍ مِنْها، فَقَدْ أخَذَ حَظًّا وافِراً فَانْظُروا عَمَّنْ تَأْخُذُونَهُ. فَإنَّ فِينا، اهْلَ الْبَيْتِ، فى كُلِّ خَلَفٍ عُدُولًا، يَنْفُونَ عَنْهُ تَحْرِيفُ الْغالِينَ وَ انْتِحالَ الْمُبْطِلِينَ وَ تَأْوِيلَ الْجاهِلِينَ

24. Kadivar has another theory about the political authority of the infallible Imams, which has attracted heated debate in Iran. His notion of ulemay-e abrar (pious clerics) proposes that the notion of the infallibility of the Shiite Imams is not rooted in early Islamic history. From an historical point of view, he argues, it has evolved and dominated Shiite thought since the mid-11th century, see Kadivar, 2006a.

Islamic teachings, but claims that democracy is an appropriate political system for the Muslim world because it is the best product of human reasoning and experience:

> [D]emocracy is the least erroneous approach to the politics of the world (please note that least erroneous does not mean perfect, or even error free). Democracy is a product of reason, and the fact that it has first been put to use in the West does not preclude its utility in other cultures—reason extends beyond the geographical boundaries. One must adopt a correct approach, regardless of who came up with the idea (Kadivar, 2002b).

Radical political Islam in general, and the doctrine of Velayat-e Faqih in particular, evolved from Islamic jurisprudence rather than Islamic theology or philosophy. Jurisprudential reasoning is pivotal to the arguments advanced by opponents of the doctrine. In order to de-legitimize the doctrine of divine sovereignty, Kadivar disputes the readings from the relevant Quranic verses and hadiths, leading him to conclude that there was no jurisprudential justification for divine sovereignty in the OCCULTATION ERA. Kadivar's audiences are composed of a unique cluster of religious people and those located between the religious leadership and progressive intellectuals such as Soroush and Mojtahed-Shabestari. Kadivar finds his audience among the educated as his ideas reaffirm their strong religious commitment. As a cleric employing a jurisprudential approach, Kadivar's religio-political ideas pose a potent internal challenge to the notion of Velayat-e Faqih. They also explain his imprisonment for 18 months in 1999–2000 (Matsunaga, 2007: 328).

Theory of Elect versus Theory of Appointment

The late Ayatollah Montazeri (1922–2009), Iran's highest-ranking reformist jurist, while working within a jurisprudential framework, conceptualized a quasi-democratic notion of the doctrine of Velayat-e Faqih. Although differing in many aspects, Kadivar and Montazeri had at least something in common: their common jurisprudential approach challenged the supposed divine right of political authority by jurists. Like Kadivar, Montazeri was also of the opinion that the Prophet Mohammad and the infallible Imams possessed a sacred right to political leadership. However, in contrast to Kadivar, he reserved his preference for jurists' political leadership in the OCCULTATION ERA. Montazeri, one of the key rhetoricians of the doctrine of Velayat-e Faqih and head of the first Assembly of Experts, supported the inclusion of Velayat-e Faqih into the Constitution. It is worth noting that in the Khomeini-approved draft of the Constitution, Velayat-e Faqih was not included. Had Montazeri not contested Khomeini's decision, he would have been appointed the second Valey-e Faqih within 68 days.[25]

Committed to the notion of the Islamic state, Montazeri promoted a democratic version of Velayat-e Faqih, (Akhavi, 2008: 647). He maintained a rigid adherence to political Islam and to the doctrine of Velayat-e Faqih. He argued for the direct engagement of the clergy in politics:

> The jurists' ignorance of sociopolitical issues and their reluctance to engage in improving people's situations and to assume responsibility in an Islamic government is not acceptable before God. It is *vajeb* [religiously indispensable] for jurists to acquire the necessary sociopolitical knowledge and to bear some responsibility in an Islamic government (Montazeri, 2000d: 99–100).

Like the ruling clergy, he did not doubt that the divine source of political authority resided with the Prophet Mohammad and the infallible Imams (Abdo, 2001: 18; Montazeri, 2000d: 122–178). However, he distanced himself from the ruling clergy by questioning the notion of generic appointment *(nasb-e um)*,[26] according to which all just jurists were appointed by the infallible Imams to lead political positions in the OCCULTATION ERA. In other words, although no specific person was appointed as leader of a Muslim society in the OCCULTATION ERA, all just jurists simultaneously possessed the divine right of political authority. Montazeri questioned the practicability of a form of government based on generic appointment. Proposing five possible scenarios[27] from which to elect one of the jurists as ruler, he concluded that it was impossible to have a functional form of government based upon the notion of generic appointment (Montazeri, 2000d: 188–214).

Providing a new reading of the religious sources cited by the proponents of generic appointment, Montazeri concluded that the relevant Quranic verses

---

25. Montazeri, the designated successor of Khomeini, was appointed by the Assembly of Experts on November 24, 1985 and dismissed by Khomeini on March 26, 1989. He was the shadow Valey-e Faqih for more than four years.

26. *Nasb-e um*, as opposed to *nasb-e khas* (specific appointment) refers to the divine appointment of certain persons (e.g., the Prophet Mohammad and the 12 Imams).

27. For a detailed discussion of these five scenarios, see Akhavi, 2008: 664.

and hadiths only outlined the qualifications of the Islamic ruler (Montazeri, 2000d: 213–282). He argued to the effect that

> According to the Quranic verses and hadiths, only the qualifications of the sovereign can be extracted, but not more than these qualifications. This is not a basis for the appointment of jurists in the contemporary era; thus, appointment of a jurist to the position of sovereign by the infallible Imams is not proven (Montazeri, 2003: 35–36).

Montazeri's rejection of the notion of generic appointment due to its religious implausibility was a point of departure from which to introduce his "theory of elect" (*nazariy-e nakhb*). In contrast to the "theory of appointment" (*nazariy-e nasb*), he saw the theory of elect as providing religious justification for the source of state authority in the OCCULTATION ERA. He maintained that "In contrast to the theory of appointment, according to which the jurists' right to govern is directly legitimized by appointment by God, in this theory the source of state legitimacy. . . is the people's election not divine appointment" (Montazeri, 2008: 24).

Drawing upon 26 reasons,[28] Montazeri argued that from a jurisprudential point of view, the people's consent was the only legitimizing source of the Islamic state in the OCCULTATION ERA. He wrote: "It is certain that the external actualization of a just government, and its consolidation and continuity, are forever dependent on the consent of the people" (Motazeri cited in Abdo, 2001: 13). Montazeri provided a democratic interpretation of key Quranic verses and hadiths. According to his readings of the shura (consultation) verses of the Quran,[29] consultation includes the process of selecting which sovereign and Quranic commands to consult. It is not confined to the process of governance (Montazeri, 2000d: 288–290). Allegiance (*baya'at*), which has a strong tradition in Islamic history, and through which the Prophet and Imam Ali assumed political leadership, was frequently cited by Montazeri to justify the need for a voting system (Montazeri, 2000d: 305–326). After scrutinizing the method of governance in the Islamic state from a jurisprudential point of view, Montazeri contested the proclaimed absolute authority of the

---

28. For details of his argument pertaining to these reasons, see Montazeri, 2000d: 283–326.

29. "and those who answer the call of their lord and establish worship, and whose affairs are a matter of counsel, and who spend of what we have bestowed on them" [translated by Marmaduke Pickthall].

وَالَّذِينَ اسْتَجَابُوا لِرَبِّهِمْ وَأَقَامُوا الصَّلَاةَ وَأَمْرُهُمْ شُورَى بَيْنَهُمْ وَمِمَّا رَزَقْنَاهُمْ يُنفِقُونَ

Valey-e Faqih, arguing that even the Prophet Mohammad and the infallible Imams did not possess absolute authority:

> He [Valey-e Faqih] cannot interfere in all the affairs, particularly the affairs that fall outside his area of expertise, such as complex economic issues, or issues of foreign policy and international relations.. . . The most important point to be highlighted is that Islam is for the separation of powers and does not recognize the concentration of power in the hand of a fallible human being (cited in Abdo, 2001: 11).

According to Montazeri's understanding of Velayat-e Faqih, the latter possesses authority and expertise only in religious issues (Kadivar, 2002b). He did not consider Velayat-e Faqih a lifetime position, but saw it simply as a monitoring position rather than an executive body. In the words of Montazeri:

> [T]he selection of *Faqih* does not necessarily mean a jurist's governance and his intervention in executive arenas. The main goal is to have him monitor the laws of the country to [make sure that] they are Islamic. This should be the case when people want to develop an Islamic state, to pass and enforce Islamic law. An unelected jurist does not have any responsibility except to guide and expound his ideas to the people. A jurist cannot impose his ideas—even with the help of the minority—upon the majority of people (2008: 22–23).

Although beyond the scope of this study, some mention should be made here that in the "elective, conditional doctrine of Velayat-e Faqih" proposed by Montazeri, the Valey-e Faqih is accountable to people and not to God. He is chosen for a specific term like other political authorities (Kadivar, 2004: 64, 69). Finally, a key aspect of Montazeri's political thought was the acceptance of a social contract as the source of state authority. In line with contractarianism, Montazeri saw state authority as stemming from a contract between subjects and sovereign. Through 1,300 years of Shiite history, Montazeri was apparently the first jurist who dared to employ a religious rationale to frame state–society relations along the lines of a social contract, akin to the tradition of Locke and Rousseau (Soroush, 2004d; 2009b). A direct quotation from Montazeri is worthy of mention:

> From a rational and religious point of view, the electing of a sovereign by the people. . . is of necessity a social contract, which is indispensable when it is developed and contracted through allegation. When elected, the sovereign is responsible for carrying out delegated tasks due to the

contract's conditions and limitations. People ought to support him and obey his order unless he violates religious principles or the rules of the contract (2003: 36).

My inclusion of Ayatollah Montazeri in a study on secularity may seem a little odd, particularly in light of his high-ranking religious status and role in articulating and implementing the doctrine of Velayat-e Faqih. Until his demise in December 2009, Montazeri never abandoned his commitment to the doctrine of Velayat-e Faqih, although he repeatedly apologized for saddling the country with a despotic regime (Milani, 2010). His valuable contribution to the emergence of religious secularity should not be overlooked. The quasi-democratic elements in his political thought are of fundamental importance due to the prominent position he held within the Shiite clergy, thereby paving the way for progressive thought from within the heart of the traditional Shiite school.

Montazeri, who is considered to have been one of the highest-ranking Marja-e Taghlids in the contemporary Shiite world, exercised considerable influence over the religious. Along with huge numbers of religious emulators, his religiosity was greatly respected by the Iranian masses, even if they did not agree with his political standpoint. This is evident in the large numbers who gathered to mourn his death in Qum. There are four persuasive justifications for the inclusion of his reformist ideas, particularly those that pertain to popular sovereignty,[30] in research into the shift from radical political Islam in Iran.

First, in view of his scholarly and political background, Montazeri's reformed concept of Velayat-e Faqih represents an internal shift among the opponents of political Islam. This shift was a direct consequence of the empirical experience of the Islamic state. Second, Montazeri's propositions continue to hold sway among the masses, the non-educated, and the habitual believers for whom the Marja-e Taghlids play a key role. A particularly important point is that the ruling clergy attract strong support from elements of this cluster. I do not suggest that Montazeri's ideas deprived the Islamic state of the support from the country's deeply religious people, but rather that his ideas competed with the ruling clergy for the very same audience.

---

30. His humanitarian ideas, specifically in terms of human rights and women's rights, were very important as well. At his memorial ceremony, Shirin Ebadi, the 2003 Nobel Laureate for Peace, referred to him as "the father of human rights". See http://www.bbc.co.uk/persian/iran/2009/12/091220_wmt-montazeri-soroush-ebadi.shtml.

Third, Montazeri subscribed to the notion of popular sovereignty, albeit subject to certain conditions. Although these conditions distanced his ideas from a truly democratic conceptualization of politics, the underlying demo-cratic sentiment had an impact on significant numbers of the population. It is not realistic to expect habitual believers to concur with the more progres-sive and democratic readings of religion–state relations offered by religious intellectuals. However, Montazeri's ideas concerning religious reformation were well communicated to the country's deeply traditional religious com-munity. Finally, Montazeri's influence in the Qom seminary and among the new generation of clergy should not be overlooked (Abdo, 2001: 11). He taught many students in both the pre- and post-revolutionary eras, many of whom now comprise the ruling clergy—including the current Supreme Leader, Ali Khamanei—and the Iranian scholarly circle, which includes Ayatollah Sanei, Mohsen Kadivar, Hassan Yousefi Eshkevari, and Emad Ad-din Baqi. Their leading roles in the future of the Shiite school are demonstrated in their con-tribution to the current religio-political discourse (Rahimi, 2008: 6).

Questioning the Religious Basis for Divine Sovereignty

Like Montazeri and Kadivar, Hassan Yousefi Eshkevari objects to the notion of divine sovereignty, placing people instead as the source of state author-ity. Currently residing in Italy, Eshkevari is the director of the Ali Shariati Research Centre. As a cleric, he actively contributed to the 1979 revolution and served as a member of the first parliament of the Islamic state. Later, his revisionist ideas alienated him from the ruling clergy, resulting in his imprisonment from 2000 to 2005 and defrocking by the Special Clerical Court (SCC). From Eshkevari's perspective, "both legitimacy and acceptance of the government and its leaders should come from popular elections. And the responsibility for elections rests on the shoulders of the people, not with God, or His prophet, or religion" (quoted in Kamrava, 2008: 140). Eshkevari argues that the holy text does not include governance issues. For him, issues of governance are not directly related to Islamic principles nor do they consti-tute a part of the practical requirements of Islam such as praying, fasting, and pilgrimage (*hajj*). He maintains that

there is no definite and solid rationale and textual evidence to sup-port [the claim] that government is [one] of the religious rulings. For instance, there are Koranic verses about prayers, fasting, hajj, alms-giving, etc. Are there such verses or even Sayings available about

government? Religious rulings are legislated through textual authority, and no one has the right, through his own understanding or *ijti-*
had, to legislate a new matter in the name of religion and religious law
(Eshkevari, Mir-Hosseini, & Tapper, 2006: 88).

Eshkevari further argues that the form and method of governance constitute
a human phenomenon, defined entirely according to time and place. A blueprint for government cannot suit every society and epoch. Eshkevari contends
that even the Prophet Mohammad's government in Medina was a product of
his time and place. He writes:

> When the Prophet established a government, in ruling and dealing
> with the affairs, large and small, of Medina, he employed his own per-
> sonal acumen and tact, in the best possible way at the time. Even if we
> consider the Prophet's leadership to be an aspect of his prophethood,
> and therefore divine, there is still no doubt that the vast majority of the
> Prophet's social and political decisions came from his own discern-
> ment and discretion (Eshkevari et al., 2006: 87).

Eshkevari advances Montazeri's interpretation of the consultation verses of
the Quran by including another verse (*Al-Imran* 159) to supp\ort the argument for popular sovereignty. These Quranic verses, he argues, explicitly
prove that the Prophet consulted people about governance and administrative
matters. According to Eshkevari, "this consultation begins with the establishment of the state and the election of statesmen" (Eshkevari et al., 2006: 90).
Through his reading of the Quran and the Prophet Mohammad's traditions,
Eshkevari concludes that

> in any time or place, Muslims create their desired government and
> choose properly qualified people to rule them; the legitimacy and
> acceptability of the government and the rulers comes from their elec-
> tion by the people, from nowhere else. Thus the responsibility for this
> election is with the people themselves, not with God, the Prophet or
> religion (2006: 90).

However, his objection to the appointive sovereign has not dissuaded
Eshkevari from political Islam. He argues that religion is not just a personal
issue, bound solely to individual–God relations, but has large and important social dimensions. Highlighting justice as the main objective of Islam,
he purports that a democratic government is compatible with Islam in the

contemporary era and would facilitate this objective. Arguing that democracy has been the most effective, logical, and Islamic way of administering society, albeit not free of error, Eshkevari proposes that Muslims devise a new model of democracy, one that is free from the flaws of liberal and social democracy (Eshkevari et al., 2006: 73–100; Kamrava, 2008: 135–136).

Challenges from an Historical Perspective

The Islamic state of Iran has made a conscious effort to construct a narrative supporting the doctrine of divine sovereignty in Islamic historiography. In this regard, the Prophet Mohammad's governance in Medina, the five years of Imam Ali's caliphate, the third Shiite Imam Hussein's uprising at Karbala, and the direct political engagement of religious leaders in Shiite history have been narrated by the ruling clergy. By contrast, challenging the doctrine of divine sovereignty is integral to religious reformation discourse. Although some reformist scholars such as Montazeri and Kadivar accept that the Prophet Mohammad and the infallible Imams possessed divine legitimacy to rule the Muslim world, others, such as Haeri-Yazdi, Eshkevari, and Bazargan, offer alternate readings of Shiite history. The doctrine of divine sovereignty is depicted as a recent and peripheral concept within the Shiite school.

Prophecy and the Caliphate

Mehdi Haeri-Yazdi (1923–1999), in his pioneering work[31] *Hekmat va Hokumat* (Wisdom and government) published after the 1979 revolution, questioned the religious basis of divine sovereignty. The eldest son of Sheikh Abdul Karim Haeri-Yazdi, founder of the Qom seminary, he served as the seminary's representative in the United States and Canada, where he helped to establish many Islamic institutions. He taught Islamic courses at the universities of Harvard, McGill, Toronto, Michigan, and Oxford in the 1960s and 1970s. Haeri-Yazdi was the first Iranian ambassador to the United States after the 1979 revolution; but he was later confined to teaching alone as a result of his objections to the Islamic state. One of his historical objections to the doctrine highlighted the differences between prophecy and Imamat (the position of divinely appointed politico-reliogus leadership), on the one hand, and the caliphate on the other. Haeri-Yazdi maintained that both positions of

---

31. Haeri-Yazdi's book was never published in Iran due to the official censorship policy, which demands that all writers first seek permission from the Ministry of Culture and Islamic Guidance.

prophecy and Imamat were God-appointed positions, which were not dependent upon the allegiance of the people to be considered legitimate. He argued,
though, that the caliphate was a worldly position, which "does not have any
rational, theological or faithful liaison with the highly respected positions of
prophecy and pontificate. The caliphate is a sociopolitical position, which is
just a result of subjects' allegiance" (Haeri-Yazdi, 1994: 214).

Haeri-Yazdi further argued that sometimes people choose their prophet or
Imam as their political leader—as was the case with the Prophet Mohammad
and Imam Ali—and sometimes they do not. So, he concluded, the Prophet
Mohammad and the infallible Imams did not posses divine right in the political arena, any more than the jurists did in the OCCULTATION ERA.

Another objection raised by Haeri-Yazdi also targeted the historical record
of the doctrine of Velayat-e Faqih in Islamic history. Viewing the concept as an
innovation in the Islamic jurisprudential tradition, he argued that Velayat as
a political notion was developed less than two centuries ago by Molla Ahmed
Naraghi (1829–1771), who imbued the term with political meaning to justify
his cooperation with the king. Haeri-Yazdi maintained: "From an historical
point of view, the notion of Velayat in terms of governance finds no mention
in Islamic jurisprudence. No single jurist of either the Shiite or Sunni traditions has argued that in addition to their right to judge and issue fatwas,
jurists possess the right to rule and lead a country" (Haeri-Yazdi, 1994: 221).

Velayat-e Faqih: A Recent Innovation in the Shiite School

Like Haeri-Yazdi, Kadivar sees the concept of Velayat-e Faqih as a recent
innovation in the Shiite school. Having traced the concept's genealogy in
Shiite history, he concludes that Velayat-e Faqih lacked any political characteristic for a large part of Shiite history. Kadivar divides Shiite political
history into six phases, in which the ideal of divine right for the political
authority of jurists is peripheral. According to Kadivar, in the first seven
centuries after the OCCULTATION ERA, there was no sign of Velayat-e
Faqih in Shiite scholarly thought. He maintains that "[t]he idea that political affairs constitute a religious duty for jurists never sprang in the minds of
Shiite jurists in this phase" (Kadivar, 1999b). He further asserts that when
the Shiite jurists were faced with the challenges of governance during the
Safavid dynasty, a division between political affairs and religious affairs
emerged for the first time within the Shiite school. During the Safavid era,
an agreement was reached between the jurists and kings, allowing the former to occupy a leading position in the religious sphere. However, jurists

began to legitimize the political status of the kings; prior to this era, the infallible Imam (i.e., the 12th Imam) was the only legitimate sovereign in Shiite political thought. For the first time then, Shiite scholars accepted the sovereignty of the Safavid kings as legitimate in religious terms. However, Kadivar maintains that there was no sign of any direct jurist intervention in politics during this phase.

He suggests that the political notion of Velayat-e Faqih is rooted in Molla Ahmed Naraghi's thought: "Molla Ahmad Naraghi (died 1829), a jurist during the Fath-ali Shah Reign (1797–1834) was the first to propose the idea of jurists managing Muslims' worldly affairs, a proposal not previously advanced by any jurist. Thus, the notion of political guardianship of jurists has only been countenanced over the last 150 years" (Kadivar, 1999b).

Kadivar maintains that during the Constitutional Revolution in Iran (1906–1909), the citizens' right in the political sphere was acknowledged by leading Shiite jurists. During this phase, the dominant ideal, developed specifically by Allameh Naeini (1860–1936), recognized subjects as the source of state authority. As such, the clergy supported the establishment of a parliamentary system and actively took part in the Constitutional Revolution. In Kadivar's view, Ayatollah Khomeini's doctrine of Velayat-e Faqih signaled a landmark shift in Shiite political thought. Following the 1979 revolution, the direct engagement of jurists in the political sphere was introduced for the first time in Shiite history.

For Kadivar, Velayat-e Faqih dates back less than two centuries and is thus "a mere blinking of an eye compared to the age of Shiite jurisprudence" (Sadri, 2001: 256). He has systematically challenged the organized efforts of the Islamic state by documenting and conceptualizing the doctrine of Velayat-e Faqih. Kadivar delineates a new trend in the contemporary Shiite world—that is, an alternative to Velayat-e Faqih that incorporates democratic features of governance. Similarly, Ayatollah Montazeri, Mohammad Mehdi Shams al-Din (1933–2000), and Mehdi Haeri-Yazdi challenge the legitimacy of a divine Islamic state, advocating popular sovereignty within an Islamic framework (Kadivar, 1999b). Babak Rahimi's review of Ayatollah Montazeri and Ayatollah Sistani's ideas led him to conclude the following: "What the two religious figures share. . . is a vision of democracy backed by the Islamic ideals of justice and piety, by which they understand them to be compatible and even necessary in empowering a just political community" (2008: 14). Led by Ayatollah Salehi-Najafabadi and Ayatollah Montazeri, the increase in the number of proponents of elective rule after Khomeini's demise has been significant (Eshkevari, 2010d: 91).

The Prophet as a Messenger

Khomeini purported that the Prophet's governance was approved by God and that God elevated him to the status of the caliph of God on earth (Khomeini, cited in Goudarzi et al., 2010: 105). By contrast, both Mojtahed-Shabestari and Eshkevari characterize the Prophet Mohammad's governance in Medina (622–632 AS) as a factual phenomenon that did not constitute the Prophet's divine mission. Mojtahed-Shabestari further argues that no prophet in history possesses the right to rule a nation. "In principle, the prophets' role throughout history has been that of messenger, not of ruler. . . . [T]hus, the task of establishing social institutions and setting goals for social and political institutions and developing rules to regulate their political systems is delegated to human beings by all religions" (Mojtahed-Shabestari, 2005: 512). Distinguishing between "factual Islam"—which developed throughout history—and "Islam as God's message", Mojtahed-Shabestari argues that "in Islam according to God's message, which is conveyed by the Prophet, no universal framework is set for governance" (2005: 519). He regards the Prophet Mohammad's ten-year rule of Medina as an historical fact, not as integral to his religious mission. For Mojtahed-Shabestari, the Prophet's governance was no more than worldly power afforded by a people who invested confidence in him. As such, the shura (consultation) verses of the Quran were a means of addressing the issues of governance. Importantly, the Prophet did not claim Velayat (holy governance) for himself in these areas (Mojtahed Shabestari, 2004: 75–76).

Like Mojtahed-Shabestari, Eshkevari maintains that "the political authority of the Prophet was realized with the consent, support, and acceptance of the people, not through the exercise of one-sided authority from above (Eshkevari et al., 2006: 91). Eshkevari published a series of articles entitled "God's Sovereignty: The Biggest Lie in History" to highlight the fact that claims of divine sovereignty are not limited to Islam. Although many kings and empires have invoked God-appointed authority, these claims have never been supported by rational or clear evidence. He argues that none of the religious resources in Islam prove the divinity of the Prophet's rule of Medina. In other words, neither the Quran nor the Prophet himself claimed that he was appointed by God to establish an Islamic state (Eshkevari, 2009c). Eshkevari also emphasizes the tradition of criticizing the Prophet and Imam Ali regarding sociopolitical matters. He cites various cases of opposition factions challenging them over sociopolitical matters as evidence that their governance was not based on divine authority. In Eshkevari's view, the first and second Aqaba pacts were the popular source of the Prophet's political authority, a representation of the popular consent for his leadership (2010e; 2006: 90–91).

Divine Sovereignty and the Infallible Imams

Another religious intellectual who contributed to this debate was the late Mehdi Bazargan (1907–1995). Bazargan was appointed provisional prime minister by Khomeini after the 1979 revolution; but, together with his cabinet, he resigned after the hostage crisis at the United States embassy. Bazargan worked with Prime Minister Mohammad Mossadeq during the oil national-ization movement in 1950s, serving as the first Iranian head of the National Iranian Oil Company. Consistent with his political leanings, he offered a liberal-democratic understanding of political Islam. Bazargan's main agenda in his scholarly works was to reconcile the Quran with modernity. In one of his last publications, entitled "The Afterlife and God: The Aim of the Sacred Mission of the Prophets" (1992), Bazargan explicitly retreated from his earlier stance on the sociopolitical functions of religion (Yousefi Eshkevari, 2014). In contrast to Kadivar and Montazeri, Bazargan asserted that governance and prophecy were two disassociated matters. With the exception of a few who possessed political authority, prophets were not imbued with any sacred mis-sion to govern because "prophecy and kingdom or governance are two sepa-rate and independent functions" (quoted in Esmaeili, 2007: 348).

What distinguished Bazargan from other scholars was his frequent refer-ence to factual information about the Shiite infallible Imams. He contested the doctrine of divine sovereignty by analysing their thought and deeds and found that neither claimed divine right of political authority.

Bazargan quoted the third Imam, Imam Hussein, who challenged the Umayyad caliphate Yazid in 680 CE at Karbala. Imam Hussein, who is endowed with a special position in Shiite political thought and is a political icon of the Shiite school, represents a symbol of resistance. For Bazargan, Imam Hussein's resistance was spurred on by the oppressed masses, not by a desire to realize his divine right of governance. Bazargan maintained that "Imam Hussein's uprising, which was a totally defensive action aimed at pro-tecting Islam,. . . proved the fact that from the Imam's point of view, gover-nance belonged neither to Yazid, the caliphate, nor to the Imam, nor to the God. It belonged to the nation: it is the people's choice" (1995: 50).

Bazargan also referred to the peace agreement between Imam Hassan (625–669), the second Shiite Imam, and Muaviyah Ibn Abi Sufyan (602–680), the first caliph of the Umayyad dynasty, providing another example of Islam's adher-ence to popular sovereignty. He argued that had political leadership been a sacred and divine matter, Imam Hassan would have acted differently. Extending this line of reasoning, Bazargan asked whether the Prophet Mohammad would have compromised his prophecy by signing a peace agreement. Bazargan referred to an article in the peace agreement between Imam Hassan and Muaviyah, in which Muaviyah accepts the choice of his successor to be decided by the Muslim masses. For Bazargan, this episode demonstrated that Imam Hassan had faith in the people's right to choose their leader (Bazargan, 1995: 48–51). Imam Ali's acceptance of the people's insistence on his caliphate is highlighted as further evidence of the will of the people as the source of state authority. "It is very meaningful that when the people. . . requested Imam Ali to accept their allegiance and caliphate, he first refused but then he said that had you (people) not gathered and insisted, I would never have accepted this.. . . In other words he explicitly believed that sovereignty and the right to choose their ruler belonged to the Ummah" (Bazargan, quoted in Esmaeili, 2007: 349).

Non-jurisprudential Challenges

Ayatollah Khomeini, the architect of the doctrine of Velayat-e Faqih, was among the first group of students in the Qom seminary to study philosophy. He also taught philosophy in the Qom seminary, although the course was discontinued due to objections raised by other Ayatollahs. In spite of his philosophical propensity, both at the theoretical and empirical levels, his political doctrine of Velayat-e Faqih was based on jurisprudential reasoning. With the exception of the late Bazargan, all of the reformist scholars come from jurisprudential backgrounds. As such, they adopt the same methodological approach and the same Quranic verses, hadiths, and historical evidence used by proponents of the doctrine of Velayat-e Faqih. By highlighting Quranic verses and hadiths and exploring the tenuous historical background of the doctrine of Velayat-e Faqih, reformist scholars effectively question the religious validity of divine sovereignty. They provide different readings of the same Islamic sources in favour of popular sovereignty. However, the challenge posed to the notion of divine sovereignty is not confined to jurisprudential reasoning. Theological, philosophical, even non-religious reasoning have been marshalled to question the credibility of the doctrine of Velayat-e Faqih. There are two primary explanations for the importance of this non-jurisprudential reasoning.

First, this form of articulation is well received by the educated and upper-middle class. There is a rising trend among a significant portion of Iranian society today to eschew official interpretation of religion as a backlash to the state's version of Islam. However, this eschewal is not necessarily anti-religious or hostile towards the whole of Islam. This is why diverging religious approaches, such as non-jurisprudential and non-political attitudes, attracted a wide audience. If jurisprudential articulation against the doctrine sways the traditional religious cohort, the non-jurisprudential approach attracts audiences from among the non-religious, the less religious, and the educated.

A second important feature of the non-jurisprudential challenge to the doctrine of Velayat-e Faqih lies in the employment of civic reasoning. This approach neither expects its audience to accept certain principles of the faith nor restricts its argument to these principles. For example, while the jurisprudential approach insists that extracts from the Quran and hadiths are indisputable—which is why they provide different readings of these sources—the non-jurisprudential approach is based on the premise that it is not imperative for audiences to be guided by the Quran and hadiths. The argument for popular sovereignty is mostly articulated beyond the parameters of Quranic verses and hadiths. In addition, it should be mentioned that well-known scholars adopt this approach, adding to its currency in contemporary Iran. In this regard, Abdulkarim Soroush and Mojtahed-Shabestari, whose conceptualizations are elaborated below, are of particular importance to this debate.

Liberating Politics from Sanctity

Soroush's intellectual works cover a broad area spanning from philosophical to religious issues.[32] This section will focus on his challenge to the proclaimed sacred source of political power and support for popular sovereignty. As Soroush's religious-reformation discourse constitutes a key theme of this book, a concise explanation of his intellectual paradigm is critical. Soroush's intellectual project and theories have secularized various aspects of a believer's life. In the late 1980s, when composing his magnum opus *The Theoretical Expansion and Constriction of Shari'a*, Soroush conceptualized the separation of religion from religious knowledge, stating that whereas religion is a sacred and eternal phenomenon, human knowledge of religion is worldly and temporary. He further argued that a human understanding of religion is incomplete and imperfect (cited in Vahdat, 2004: 204), and, for this reason, no one can claim to possess an ultimate understanding of religion. In other words, all versions and understandings of religion, which have been offered in different times and places, are reflective of human knowledge and do not represent eternal, sacred, and error-free knowledge. Religious knowledge, according to Soroush, is contingent to other knowledge and sciences. Religious knowledge will change in accordance with the changes in knowledge that accrue from

---

32. Discussion centring on Soroush's thought includes Aliabadi, 2005; Esposito & Voll, 2001: 150–176; Ghamari-Tabrizi, 2008; Jahanbakhsh, 2001b: 140–171; Soroush, Sadri, & Sadri, 2000.

different times and places (Kamali, 1995; Soroush, 1994d). This articulation has served to disarm the ruling clergy in Iran, who expect the population to adhere strictly to the official version of religion.

The other area emphasized by Soroush is revelation, to which he adds a worldly dimension. In his *Expansion of Prophetic Experience,* Soroush sheds light on the human formation of revelation, arguing that revelation has been effected by the characteristics and personal history of the Prophet Mohammad's life. As a human being, the Prophet Mohammad's experiences were accidental; and, thus, the very experience of revelation in the Arabic culture and language is an historically accidental occurrence rather than an essential attribute of religion. Had the Prophet's life been different, the revelation experience may also have been different. However, Soroush insists that this understanding does not mean that revelation lacks sacred and eternal aspects (Soroush, 2006a). He mounts a similar argument regarding the holy text of the Quran, proposing a notion of *the intrinsic and contingent in religion.* Soroush maintains that the Quran reflects Arabic culture and that the history of the revelation era in its holy text is replete with the culture and events that marked the Prophet Mohammad's life. Thus, the message of the text is a substantial if not a literal interpretation. Soroush controversially categorizes jurisprudential principles and the Shari'a as an accidental dimension of the Quran (Hunter, 2009: 79; Soroush, 1998d).

Expanding this perspective to the sociopolitical realms, Soroush distinguishes two sets of values. The first set, which includes generic values such as justice, truth, humanity, and honesty, are classified as ultra-religious. In principal, these sets of values are universal; they are respected due to their very nature and are not necessarily derived from any one religion. But, according to Soroush, religion ought to endorse and promote them and its validity not to be questioned. The second set of values—outlawing usury, drinking wine, and issues surrounding the *hijab*—may vary from religion to religion (Soroush, 1996: 6–7). In Soroush's political thought, governments are responsible for materializing general values, rather than choosing to align with any specific religion (Soroush, 1996: 6–7).

Having provided a brief explanation of Soroush's intellectual vision, I will now examine his thought on the divine and popular source of state authority with occasional reference to his overall religious and intellectual paradigms. Soroush explicitly points out (a) that governance is a non-jurisprudential[33] and non-religious issue and (b) that any discussion

---

33. This fits with Soroush's general approach, which has brought him outright hostility not only from the ruling clergy but also from many traditional Ayatollahs. He promotes the notion that religion is not bounded to jurisprudence, arguing that the Shari'a is the legal framework and that jurisprudence is just a part of religion. This reasoning line is traceable in almost all of his writings.

about governance should take place either in a non-religious context or in non-jurisprudential contexts such as theology (Jahanbakhsh, 2001a: 21; Mottaqi, 2002: 48). Pointing to issues of the prophecy and Imamat, which fall within the theological rather than jurisprudential realm, Soroush maintains that "as a theory of state, the doctrine of Velayat-e Faqih ought to be discussed in theological rather than jurisprudential terms" (1996: 2). There is infrequent reference to the Quran, hadiths, and Islamic tradition in Soroush's core ideas about governance (Mottaqi, 2002: 48). Rather his focus is upon questioning the possibility of a reconciliation between Islam and democracy. While the main aims of Montazeri, Kadivar, and Eshkevari are to present a more democratic understanding of religious sources, Soroush sees these efforts as fruitless:

> We have put behind us a period in which some scholars, more in Arabic Islamic countries and less in our country, have sought to extract democracy from Islam.. . . Abul Ala Maududi and Bazargan were looking for this conceptualization. For example, they interpret Quranic references to consultation [shura] as parliament; and, when there is talk about allegiance [baya'at], they understand it as election.. . . We have come to a blest consensus, which proves that this is impossible and doomed to fail (2005b).

In an attempt to question the religious validity of the doctrine of Velayat-e Faqih as a practical notion of divine sovereignty, Soroush recruits a theological method. Similar to Haeri-Yazdi, Soroush investigates the concept of guardianship (velayat); but, he adopts a non-jurisprudential approach. He outlines two forms of guardianship, namely spiritual and political guardianship. Spiritual guardianship possesses a theosophical notion (irfan), based on a unique relationship between master and devotee. Soroush contends that in this notion of guardianship there is just submission; that is, master's order and devotee's obedience without question and without seeking explanation. The very nature of spiritual guardianship demands complete obedience and submission. Soroush further contends that this notion of guardianship can be set exclusively between two persons and can never be extended to the sociopolitical context.

For Soroush, the second notion of guardianship implies political leadership, where there is no such thing as complete obedience or submission. Imam Ali, the first Shiite Imam and the only one who led the Muslim world for five years (656–661 CE), exercised political guardianship—not spiritual guardianship—over Muslim society. Soroush furnishes a variety of examples showing that Imam Ali and other Shiite infallible Imams were criticized by their followers for their political decision-making. In many cases, they changed their minds following this criticism. For Soroush, the doctrine of Velayat-e Faqih does not have anything to do with the theosophical notion of guardianship: "Velayat-e Faqih does not resemble anything related to theosophical and spiritual guardianship. It is only the similarity of the term that has made some to associate this guardianship (meaning presidency and leadership) with the other notion of guardianship, which is exclusively suited to the friends of God [*uliya-e Allah*] and to those who are special before God" (Soroush, 1998c: 20). Finally, Soroush asserts that only a minority of Shiite jurists support the legitimacy and acceptability of the doctrine of Velayat-e Faqih (1998c: 10–20).

Soroush's intellectual work is strongly geared towards challenging the widespread misunderstanding that religion is synonymous with *fiqh* (jurisprudence) and the Shari'a. He consistently argues that, throughout history, Islamic civilization has been legal and jurisprudential rather than philosophical in orientation. Consequently, Muslims are generally of the opinion that the Shari'a is synonymous with Islam. Muslims feel obliged to concern themselves with the Shari'a in all aspects of their lives, including, for example, eating, drinking, and resting (Soroush, 2005b). However, jurisprudence intends only to outline the legal framework of the religion. By contrast, theology (*kalam*) and philosophy, Soroush asserts, are the core elements of religion. The faith of the believers comes first; it is then the responsibility of jurisprudence to articulate the details of the legal framework, the Shari'a. This endeavour, which is traceable in much of Soroush's work, has provoked a hostile response not only from the ruling clergy, but also from many of Iran's traditional jurists.

Soroush's political works purport that the doctrine of Velayat-e Faqih supports a jurisprudential but not a religious state. Soroush terms the current political system in Iran a "jurisprudential state" (*hukomat-e feqhi*), one in which the jurist, as ruler, makes sure that the jurisprudential regulations, as they appear in the Shari'a, are practiced by all subjects. This "sacrifices human rights for ideological purity" without enriching religion (quoted in Vakili, 2001: 159). He further argues that the Shari'a is simply an element of religion masquerading as religion in its totality. With reference to the well-known Quranic verse which states that there is no coercion in religion,[34] Soroush contends that faith must inherently be voluntarily. The state's

---

34. "There is no compulsion in religion. The right direction is henceforth distinct from error" [translated by Marmaduke Pickthall].

لَا إِكْرَاهَ فِي الدِّينِ قَد تَّبَيَّنَ الرُّشْدُ مِنَ الْغَيّ

responsibility is to provide a conducive environment in which society is not forced to be religious (Jahanbakhsh, 2001b: 153–154).

Soroush avoids resorting to the Quran, hadiths, or Islamic history when propagating popular sovereignty. He argues that the discussion surrounding governance should revolve around the principles of justice and human rights (Soroush et al., 2000: 131–133). To this end, he invokes the logic of civic reasoning—that is, the subjects' right to oversee their rulers. Before outlining his argument for popular sovereignty, Soroush investigates two questions pertinent to the state in a Muslim country: (a) Who has the right to govern? And (b) What is the best governing method? In Soroush's view, any answer to the latter question will determine the answer to the former. He builds a non-religious point of departure, directing the people as the only legitimate agency when appointing a ruler. He rigorously supports the notion that religion is of a duty-centred nature. In contrast to the modern world, in which human beings are rights-carriers, in the religious context human beings are duty-bound subjects (Soroush, 2000: 61–65). Since jurisprudential regulations are centred on duties rather than rights: "Jurisprudence is a duty-centred knowledge; but, it does not talk about rights.. . . I do not say jurisprudence lacks the concept of rights, but the duty is dominant rather than right" (Soroush, 2005b). Thus, human rights cannot all be derived from religion. Soroush argues that human rights ought to be seen as a non-jurisprudential and non-religious concern. One of these non-religious human rights principles is the right to oversee the ruler, for which Soroush does not attempt to find a religious basis. He states: "This right [to oversee the ruler] does not come from above: people possess this right because they are human beings. . . . [T]hey [people] can oversee their rulers (irrespective of whether they are religious rulers or non-religious rulers), and constantly investigate the political behaviour of their rulers" (Soroush, 1996: 5). Importantly, the right to oversee rulers provides subjects with the right to criticize and, if necessary, to dethrone them. The right to dethrone the ruler is, thus, integral to the right to appoint the ruler:

> If you have the right to oversee the government, it can easily be proved that you have the right to rule. It is insensate to tell someone that you have the right to dethrone a ruler but not the right to appoint a ruler. The right to appoint is prior to the right to dethrone (Soroush, 1996: 5–6).

In building his case for popular sovereignty, Soroush makes a distinction between values and methods. For Soroush, there are two further key questions about governance in a Muslim society: (a) What values should form the basis of government? And (b) What methods should be used to achieve these values? The second question, clearly a non-religious enquiry, refers to techniques: it is about management and accordingly falls into the scientific category. Soroush maintains that scientific-experimental questions are inherently non-religious. In cases where scientific issues are addressed by religion, it does not make them religious. As such, questions about governance and politics differ little from questions posed in the medical or engineering fields:

> If we ask "what should be done to have a successful state?" this question will be translated into questions such as how the education system should be instituted? How the country's economy should be managed? How the health and housing systems should operate?. . . Each and every one of these questions is a scientific question. Religion is not committed to and responsible for answering methodological and managerial questions. If we refer these questions to religion, we are making a mistake.. . . [T]hese aspects of governing have a rational nature. Wise men should get together and formulate arrangements for the managerial aspects of governance (Soroush, 1996: 6).

In an attempt to challenge the dominant political position of jurists, Soroush argues that jurisprudence is a science and, thus, incapable of providing answers to all issues of governance. And, similar to the other sciences, jurisprudence is bounded by the limitations of time and place (Soroush, 1994c: 2–16; 1998b: 2–9). He writes: "Jurisprudence is a production of humans and does not differ from other sciences and human productions.. . . It is knowledge consisting of conflictions and contradictions, truths and falsehoods, and certainty and uncertainty, which are all results of jurists' understandings. Thus, claiming perfectionism, excellence, and supremacy for this knowledge (or any other knowledge) is a false claim" (2006a: 155). He further suggests that not all answers to contemporary legal issues, let alone political, social, and economic matters, can be derived from Islamic jurisprudence.

Soroush argues that appreciation of the basic set of non-religious values is related to the nature of governance, not to its religious or non-religious features. For example, any given state ought to uphold justice, irrespective of whether that state is religious or non-religious. "If a state intends to succeed, it must be just. Just governance is, of course, confirmed by religion; but it does not earn its justice from religion" (Soroush, 1996: 7). However, in terms of religious values, Soroush incorporates a minimal role for government. In a religious society, the state may play an indirect role in fulfilling these sets of values. This indirect intervention by the state includes laying out a conducive environment for the fulfilment of these values by believers. He further argues that human beings have both primary and secondary needs. In a religious society, the state is responsible for fulfilling believers' primary needs and liberating believers from these concerns, so that "an opportunity to think and deliberate upon their secondary needs—including spiritual faith— is provided for believers" (Soroush, 1996: 10). Religious governments, there- fore, should not differ from non-religious governments, except in their goal of facilitating believers' opportunities to fulfil their religious values through their own voluntarily compliance.

In general, Soroush's intellectual project removes holiness and divinity from contemporary life in the Muslim world in general and Iran in particular. In other words, his main goal may be summarized as minimizing the sacred- ness of the religious features of life or at least adding a more worldly dimen- sion to areas dominated by religion. Soroush's political thought is inspired by this endeavour. Governance is perceived in completely non-religious terms, which leaves subjects to determine their political system based on civic reasoning. This is why, when discussing governance, he rarely refers to religious sources such as the Quran and hadiths (Jahanbakhsh, 2001b: 159). Highlighting the theosophical aspects of the concept of guardianship and the non-jurisprudential aspects of religion (faith and belief), Soroush refutes the doctrine of Velayat-e Faqih as a religious state. He describes it as essentially a jurisprudential state, which compels subjects to conform with the Shari'a at the cost of voluntary compliance with faith as dictated by personal conviction. As discussed above, Soroush builds his argument for popular sovereignty on the basis of the non-religious right of subjects to oversee rulers. Moreover, by creating a division between value and method, Soroush advocates for an indi- rect role for the state in religious societies to facilitate the fulfilment of reli- gious values. Appreciation of religious values, according to Soroush, does not automatically designate any specific form of state or governance. As methods of governance are non-religious issues, they ought to be dealt with through civic reasoning.

Finally, Soroush depicts the issue of governance as an entirely worldly matter. In contrast to other reformists such as Kadivar, Montazeri, and Eshkevari, he does not attempt to re-interpret religious sources or make any effort to present a democratic version of politics based on religion. Instead, he explicitly states that democracy is not extractable from Islamic holy texts (Jahanbakhsh, 2001b; Soroush, 2010b: 174–176). However, this approach does not locate him among those who subscribe to the notion of incompatibility between Islam and democracy. He maintains: "Democracy is a method of governance aiming to 'reduce management error' based on the principle of 'popular sovereignty'. Now you ask where these principles come from, we say that they are not extractable from principles of religion, although they are not inconsistent with it either" (Soroush, 2010b). As the ideal of popular sovereignty is achieved through civic reasoning, and Islam does not recommend any specific form of state, there is no conflict between Islam and popular sovereignty.

Popular Sovereignty: Islam's Essence

Soroush is not alone in challenging the notion of divine sovereignty in non-jurisprudential/non-religious terms. Mojtahed-Shabestari is another key figure who refutes the divinity of politics in Islam from a theological and philosophical standpoint. Mojtahed-Shabestari, an influential philosopher and Shi'a theologian, spent 18 years in the Qom seminary. He was appointed manager of the Islamic Centre in Hamburg in the 1970s and, after the 1979 revolution, served as a member of parliament for four years. He decided to avoid politics after his term in parliament, opting instead to teach at the Faculty of Theology and Religious Studies of the University of Tehran until 2006, when he was forced into retirement. Mojtahed-Shabestari advocates popular sovereignty as an appropriate and inevitable political choice to fulfil the very basic principles of Islam: justice and freedom. As discussed in an earlier section of this chapter, by adding a non-sacred dimension to religion, Soroush depicts governance as a completely non-religious issue to be dealt with based on civic reasoning. In keeping with this intellectual paradigm, the claim of divine sovereignty by jurists is rejected. Similarly, Mojtahed-Shabestari argues that governance is not a religious issue to be deliberated within a religious context: "Politics should not be based on faith and its scope should not be restricted by religion. In the contemporary world, Muslims may opt to eschew cases of politics and governance mentioned in the holy text and tradition. They may approach politics and governance as philosophical and scientific issues while at the same time not violating the core message of the holy text and tradition" (Mojtahed-Shabestari, 2004: 77). At no time does Mojtahed-Shabestari refer to the holy text or to Islamic tradition to refute the notion of divine sovereignty or substantiate the notion of popular sovereignty. Mojtahed-Shabestari objects to efforts to extract political ideas from jurisprudence as the latter's responsibility lies only in issuing religious decrees. A jurist's duty is thus to issue religious decrees, which address duties and not the rights of subjects. "Our jurisprudence totally lacks a rational and philosophical concept of political theory" (Mojtahed-Shabestari, 2001: 10–11). Like Soroush, he maintains that efforts to derive modern political notions such as democracy, freedom, and human rights from the Quran and the hadiths are misdirected and in vain (Mojtahed-Shabestari, 2001).

Another common ground between Soroush and Mojtahed-Shabestari, which distances them from Kadivar and Montazeri, is their depreciation of the status of the Shari'a. Mojtahed-Shabestari, highlighting the importance of individual–God relations without any intermediary, essentially minimizes the role of mediators by downplaying the importance of both behavioural mediators (the Shari'a) and human mediators (the jurists). Even revelation does not have primacy in this relationship. He states: "The core of Islamic faith. . . exists in the relationship between a human being and God, with or without revelation" (Mojtahed-Shabestari, 2008b). Yet, practicing the Shari'a is considered crucial by Iran's officially enforced version of religion, in which jurists play a prominent role not only in its sociopolitical dimensions but also in the individual practice of faith. Mojtahed-Shabestari proposes the concept of "religious experience", according to which Shari'a is a set of regulations that have been extracted from the holy text and tradition by jurists to express the faith. It is not, however, the core premise of religion. Insisting on the priority of faith over the Shari'a, Mojtahed-Shabestari maintains that based on their religious experience, every individual directly connects with God. Personal experience and interpretation of the message of God, thus, cannot be imposed (cited in Mortazavi & Manouchehri, 2004).

As religion is a personal relationship between the individual and God, An-Na'im asserts that the enforcement of the Shari'a by the state interrupts the key tradition of consensus, which guarantees the dynamic and creative development of the religion (An-Na'im, 2008: 16–20). As state intervention in religion "stands in direct contradiction to the true essence and spirit of religion", Mojtahed-Shabestari similarly argues that bogus guises of religiosity do little to benefit subjects' religious beliefs (2008: 168). From Mojtahed-Shabestari's standpoint, religious experience is always an incomplete process, thus requiring personal and political liberty for reinforcement. Attempts to master religious interpretation therefore impede the process of genuine understanding. (Mojtahed-Shabestari, 2000; 2005). To gain genuine religious experience, Muslims ought to be free of internal sensuality and external barriers (such as political dictatorships). Internal freedom, according to Mojtahed-Shabestari, is subject to external freedom. Religious experience, which is the essence of faith, can thus be compromised under an authoritarian political system. This suggests that a democratic political system is not only compatible with religion, but also crucial to maintaining genuine religious conviction in the Muslim world (Mojtahed Shabestari, 2000: 34–45; Mortazavi & Manouchehri, 2004; Vahdat, 2004: 215–216).

Mojtahed-Shabestari also proposes a hermeneutic approach to the Quran in order to inhibit state intervention in religion. To a large extent, he owes his standing in Iran to the introduction of hermeneutics. His work *Hermeneutics, the Book, and Tradition* invites Muslims to apply a new epistemological approach to reading the Quran and observing tradition. According to Mojtahed-Shabestari, there can be many readings of the Quran as each and every person approaches the text possessing pre-knowledge and presuppositions. Because each person's understanding of the text varies, a neutral reading is impossible. Mojtahed-Shabestari favours a "conversational correspondence" between text and reader, in which the reader's presuppositions may undergo change. The crucial point in Mojtahed-Shabestari's approach is that the reader's pre-knowledge and presuppositions are profoundly influenced by consciousness and cognition of the contemporary context. Thus, Mojtahed-Shabestari concludes that no individual reading of the holy text can ever claim full understanding because human consciousness and knowledge are always evolving (Mojtahed-Shabestari, 1996). "A distinctive aspect of God's word is its perpetual interpretative feature. No interpretation of God's word is the ultimate understanding.... [T]here should always be an open path for new interpretations" (Mojtahed-Shabestari & Kiderlen, 2007). In effect, state-espoused religion is a particular reading of religion imposed upon subjects and subverts the plural character of religious experience.

Mojtahed-Shabestari articulates a distinction between vertical and horizontal relations based on his notion of religious experience. Vertical, God–human relations are based on submission and obedience. By contrast, politics and human rights are matters based on human–human relations, which are of a horizontal nature. Thus, consent, agreement, and civic reasoning must be used to regulate these horizontal relations. This human–human relationship has significant implications for governance (Mojtahed-Shabestari, 2007b; Mortazavi & Manouchehri, 2004).

Mojtahed-Shabestari also agrees with Soroush that in Islamic history, jurisprudence has been the dominant feature of religion. However, his reading of history suggests that this knowledge has always been rational. "Reasoning *[ijtihad]* and issuing religious decrees *[efta]* were always resorted to observing rationality required by the situation of the age" (Mojtahed-Shabestari, 1999: 8). Dividing jurisprudential knowledge into three sections, he argues that jurists have maintained rationality in "worshipping" and "trading" matters, but not in "governance" issues. "The current general jurisprudential framework for worshipping and trading does not undermine a religious expedient nor a civic expedient. But, religious decrees [regarding political issues] are not congruent with these questions [contemporary political questions]: . . .

they do not respond to these questions.. . . . [T]hus, political jurisprudence has departed from its rational context" (Mojtahed-Shabestari, 1999: 8).

Like Soroush, he concludes that a democratic system cannot be extracted from jurisprudence. Issuing fatwas is not an effective solution. In order to realize the notion of popular sovereignty, he argues for a new conception of jurisprudence, according to which humans possess the right to determine their individual fates (Mojtahed-Shabestari, 2003).

Paralleling Soroush's theory of the expansion of prophetic experience, Mojtahed-Shabestari proposes that the Quran is but a human production of revelation and not the Revelation. The holy text grew out of the Prophet Mohammad's experience of revelation (Mojtahed-Shabestari, 2007a), and it is understood as a product of the Prophet Mohammad's personal religious experience.[35] The commands presented in the holy text were, thus, responses to the sociopolitical and cultural conditions of the revelation era and not eternal commands (Mojtahed-Shabestari, 2014). He states: "There are no timeless orders/prohibitions in the revelatory words, because both orders/prohibitions and human beings including the Prophet are ephemerally existent; thus, timeless commands and prohitions are impossible" (Mojtahed-Shabestari, 2003). Mojtahed-Shabestari further stresses that "[i]f there is a Quranic verse about a specific issue, it does not mean that it should always be practiced" (2008a). The political implications of this reasoning led him to argue that the political features of the holy text (Quran) and the hadiths were responses to the sociopolitical realities of the specific age of revelation. Explaining the sociopolitical context of the various commands alluded to in the Quran, Mojtahed-Shabestari concludes that adopting these commands is not particularly relevant in a differing sociopolitical context. As such, the notion of popular sovereignty and a democratic governance cannot be derived from a literal interpretation of the holy text. Mojtahed-Shabestari instead invites Muslims to understand the eternal message underpinning these commands and the essence of the holy text and traditions that are rooted in justice.

As explained earlier, Mojtahed-Shabestari sees the Prophet Mohammad's governance in Medina as a factual occurrence and as not integral to his prophetic mission. He maintains that in the revelation era, the essence of religion (justice) was manifested in the Prophet's political leadership. But this factual occurrence does not necessarily mean that religious leaders should possess political authority in the contemporary world. As such, the essence

---

35. Initially Mojtahed-Shabestari *publicized* this notion in an article entitled "Prophetic Reading of the World," published by *Madraseh* quarterly, which was banned following the publication of his article.

of religion can best be represented in the contemporary world through the principle of popular sovereignty and a democratic method of governance (Mojtahed-Shabestari, 1999).

Mojtahed-Shabestari maintains that the doctrine of divine sovereignty is not justifiable on the base of religious sources. Similar to Soroush, he articulates a non-religious foundation to argue for popular sovereignty, which sets him apart from scholars such as Montazeri, Kadivar, and Eshkevari, who adopt a religious approach to argue in favour of the compatibility of Islam and popular sovereignty. For Mojtahed-Shabestari, popular sovereignty is worthy of support, not because it is decreed by the Quran or tradition, but because it is the only plausible method of capturing the essence of religion. Through a hermeneutic reading of the holy text, he concludes that Islam does not prescribe any timeless form of state. Thus, it is the responsibility of human beings to articulate a viable political system capable of capturing the essence of religion, justice. In the contemporary world, human rationality advocates the establishment of a democratic political system as an appropriate way of meeting this goal.

In sum, the religious features of an Islamic state are evident in Iran's political structure and practice. The linchpin of these features is Velayat-e Faqih, a religio-political doctrine designed to effectively protect the Islamic veneer of the Iranian regime. The doctrine's chief function is to chain religion to politics in order to ensure the dominance of religion in the political sphere. This is why the doctrine begs crucial attention in any effort to challenge the authority of Iran's ruling clergy. Religious-reformation discourse pays particular attention to this conundrum. Not surprisingly, Velayat-e Faqih and divine sovereignty are central to the ongoing dispute between Iran's ruling clergy and religious reformist scholars.

There are similarities between the current religio-political debate in Iran and the historical experiences of secularizations in the Western countries, whereby the philosophers of contractarianism proposed the notion of popular sovereignty as an alternative to the proclaimed divine right of kings. In a similar vein, Iran's religious reformist scholars challenge the religious validity of divine sovereignty in favour of popular sovereignty. Casting serious doubt upon the religious justification for divine sovereignty, they offer popular sovereignty as a fully compatible political approach to Islam. Common among these scholars is their refutation of authoritarian readings of religion in politics and their downgrading of the role of religion in governance. Current religious-reformation discourse in particular subscribes to secularity while questioning the source of the Velayat-e Faqih's authority. Reformist scholars emphasize the role of popular will as

the source of authority rather than reducing their role to one of mere obedience. The mainstream contemporary literature surrounding secularism
is no longer engaged in the issue of divine or popular sovereignty. It is a
somewhat outdated topic in the mainstream debate surrounding secularism. However, as divine sovereignty underpins the Islamic state of Iran,
it requires particular attention in any scholarly or political effort to challenge the legitimacy of the Islamic state. By interrogating the religious justification of divine sovereignty, religious-reformation discourse effectively
destabilizes the linchpin of the Islamic state. On the other hand, providing
religious vindication for the notion of popular sovereignty establishes a
firm linchpin for the emergence of a secular state in the Muslim-majority
country of Iran.

Efforts to undermine the role of religion in the state are not confined to
debunking religious justification of divine sovereignty in favour of popular
sovereignty. Conflation of religion and the state is yet another area of conflict that the religious-reformation discourse addresses. The following two
chapters will aim to explain the religious justifications offered by reformist scholars to refute unification and promote the separation of religion
and state. Due to the unified system that prevails in contemporary Iran,
considerable effort is directed towards exposing the disadvantages of the
conflation of religion and state. Chapter 2 highlights this perspective by
employing theoretical argumentation and the lived realities of the Islamic
state of Iran.

2

Seeding Secularity

THE RISE OF A JURISPRUDENTIAL STATE

THE MODERN NOTION of state, a body vested with the power to impose law through force and coercion, was only imported into the Muslim world in the colonial era. When the Ottoman Empire collapsed after the cessation of World War I, polities that had been part of the Ummah under the Ottoman caliphate emerged as sovereign states. An-Na'im observes that it is precisely the coercive character of the state, in religious functions in particular, that contradicts the very nature of the Shari'a. Emphasizing the voluntary nature of the Shari'a, he states: "By its nature and purpose, Shari'a can only be freely observed by believers; its principles lose their religious authority and value when enforced by the state.. . . [C]oercive enforcement [of the Shari'a] promotes hypocrisy (*nifaq*), which is categorically and repeatedly condemned by the Quran" (2008: 4).

An-Na'im, alluding to the adverse consequences of confining the exercise of *ijtihad* to a specific group or institution, states that "knowing and upholding Shari'a is the permanent and inescapable responsibility of every Muslim.. . . [N]o human being or institution should control this process" (An-Na'im, 2008: 14). Indeed, restricting the practice of *ijtihad* to a specific group of Muslims or institution is likely to result in its exploitation for personal or political reasons. As modern states can only operate according to the officially established principles of law, and there are strong disagreements among and within different schools of Islamic jurisprudence, it is impossible to implement the Shari'a without prioritizing a single perspective to the detriment of the rest. This act of prioritization risks not only violating the fundamental plurality of Islam, but could force all Muslims to observe a single interpretation of the Shari'a in ways that, for some, may conflict with their personal beliefs (An-Na'im, 2008: 191). As well as violating the voluntary nature of faith, the religious claims of the state have the potential to transform religion into a tool designed to serve the political aspirations of the ruling clergy. An-Na'im insists that no state can govern effectively if it adheres exclusively to religious principles (1998: 39; 2008: 280).

Scrutiny of the lived experience of the Islamic state in Iran reinforces An-Na'im's thesis. Soon after the establishment of the Islamic state, the ruling clergy recognized the inherent contradiction between their Islamic political model and Islam itself. This chapter explores the extent to which the Islamic state serves religion, the degree to which Islam has grown to serve particular political ambitions, and the effects on faith of the state's prioritization of the exoteric layers of religion to the detriment of its esoteric dimensions. In addition it examines the shift from theocracy to Caesaropapism and *fiqh-ul maslaha*, and how the Islamic state of Iran has prioritized political interests over religious considerations.

The Shifting Trend in State–Religion Relations

Sociologists of religion have proposed various models describing the interaction between religious institutions and states. These models include the supremacy of church over state—theocracy as an obvious example of one extreme end of the spectrum—and the dominance of state over religion, which locates Erastianism and Caesaropapism at the other end (Panikkar, 1985; Robertson, 1987; Smith, 1970). Ostensibly, the Islamic Republic of Iran is a theocracy in which the clergy functions as a dominant political force. In reality however, state–religion relations in the post-revolutionary era have emulated a somewhat different model. Unlike Roman Catholicism, the lack of a unified hierarchical system in Islam has resulted in an ambiguous relationship between religion and state. This, then, begs the following questions: To what extent can the ruling clergy in Iran claim to represent religion? As one group among other representatives of religion, what are the religious credentials of the ruling clergy? Having posed these questions, the characterization of the Islamic Republic of Iran as a theocracy becomes problematic (Chehabi, 1991).

Due to its innovative structure, revolutionary character, and conflicting relationship with the West, the Islamic state of Iran has shifted strategies to overcome its various challenges. While the early years after the 1979 revolution were marked by the dominance of religion over politics, subsequent years saw a shift that gradually subordinated religious concerns to political considerations. This shift in priority may be traced through an analysis of politicians' religious standing and the policies they have implemented.[1] By promising to implement Islamic principles, Khomeini and his fellow clerics consolidated power and established the Islamic state. Khomeini, along with many other members of the clergy, possessed impressive theological credentials. Not only did he possess the highest of all religious positions (that of Grand Ayatollah),[2] but many others, including Montazeri, Taleghani, Beheshti, and Mousavi Ardebili, were considered mid-ranking in the religious sense. Their religious credibility thus enhanced their political credentials; but, with time, political power would enhance their religious credibility.[3] One outstanding example in this regard is the current Supreme Leader, Ayatollah Ali Khamanei. When Ayatollah Khomeini died in 1989, the ruling clergy could not immediately choose another clergyman to lead the country. The decision they made would have profound implications for state–religion relations in terms of whether they would stay loyal to the founding ideology of the political system or whether they would pursue a more pragmatic and politically driven course. In appointing Ali Khamanei, they implicitly chose the latter.

The Constitution stipulated two necessary qualifications for the position of Supreme Leader: robust religious competence (being Marja-e Taghlid) and political capability. While Ayatollah Khomeini had been fully qualified for the position in both political and religious terms, Khamanei, on the other hand, boasted the second qualification but was by no means qualified for the first.[4] It was only by way of a constitutional amendment made shortly after his appointment that Khamanei was allowed[5] to fill the vacancy left by Ayatollah

---

1. This argument may be raised about different issues on different occasions. For example, there have been many occasions on which religious consideration has taken priority over political consideration—and vice versa. But here the discussion is about the general trend of the interaction between religion and politics; thus, a level of generalization by overlooking exceptional cases is necessary.

2. As I explain in the following chapters, the majority of Grand Ayatollahs did not support the notion of political Islam. Khomeini possessed high religious credentials that brought him more publicity.

3. Ayatollah Mohammad Yazdi, the head of the Judiciary (1989–1999), explicitly argued that the political competence of the Supreme Leader entitled him to be the source of emulation, see Behrooz, 1996: 98–99.

4. There are officially five grades in the Shiite school for clergy: Seghatuleslam, Hujatuleslam; Hujatuleslam-e Valmuslemin, Ayatollah, and Grand Ayatollah. Khamanei was Hujatuleslam-e Valmuslemin, but he was called Ayatollah immediately after being appointed Supreme Leader. Nowadays, he is widely called Grand Ayatollah, but by no means is his religious knowledge and capability accepted.

5. The amended Constitution was endorsed through a referendum two months after Khamanei's appointment as Supreme Leader. Thus, clearly, his appointment was a violation of the enacted Constitution.

Khomeini (Milani, 1993: 367–369). While there were many high-ranking religious figures that would have made a suitable choice, the selection of Khamanei was a conscious decision of the ruling clergy, demonstrating the weight they accorded to political capability rather than religious clout (Chehabi, 1991; 1997; Gheissari & Nasr, 2006: 105–126; Roy, 2002). More than twenty years after his appointment as Supreme Leader, Khamanei's religious credentials remain tenuous.

Other positions filled by the clergy have followed a similar pattern. Today, those who hold senior political positions possess weaker religious credentials compared to those in the early years of the Islamic state. Clearly, the clerics' political status no longer depends on their religious credentials. As Oliver Roy observes: "Today there is not a single grand ayatollah in power" (2001: 180). For the large part, religious leaders who boast the highest ranks, even known supporters of the regime, do not hold official positions. The political resistance of 2009 emphasized the growing distance between the country's high-ranking religious leaders and the Islamic state, a split demonstrated when a considerable number of Grand Ayatollahs opted not to send congratulatory messages to President Ahmadinejad on the occasion of his second term. They also declined to meet Ahmadinejad during his visit to Qom in March 2010.[6]

This shifting trend is not confined to the ruling clergy alone. Subtle modifications to the policy-making processes and the political structure of Iran reflect the comprehensiveness of this ideological shift. In the context of the marriage of Islam and politics, however, this shift may have been unavoidable. In An Na'im's view, the notion of an Islamic state is a "dangerous illusion"; the state, as a political institution, is fundamentally incompatible with the nature of religion. The failure of an Islamic state, therefore, does not necessarily imply poor implementation, but rather demonstrates the impossibility of uniting these two institutions (An-Na'im, 2008: 280). An-Na'im further observes that self-styled Islamic states, such as Iran and Saudi Arabia, will be incapable of governing effectively if they steadfastly adhere to the regulations of the Shari'a as it is conventionally understood by Muslims (1998: 39; 2008: 280). Similarly, Eshkevari contends that there are some principles in Shari'a that are neither just nor rational in the context of the modern era (Eshkevari, 2009a; 2009d).

Soon after establishing the Islamic state, the ruling clergy realized that the multifarious realities of governance issues rendered the practice of many

6. He managed to meet only three Grand Ayatollahs: Noori Hamedani, Makareme Shirazi, and Sobhani. Others including Javadi Omoli, Vahid Khorasani, Safi Golpayegani, and Mousavi Ardebili refused to meet him.

religious precepts impossible (Arjomand, 1993). Recognition of this fact demanded prioritization; if religion and politics could not mutually coexist, either one or the other would need to take a dominant role in order for the Islamic state to operate. The contradiction between religious precepts and state function could have been mitigated by eschewing the responsibilities of governance in the modern era. But, opting for this course of action may have resulted in the emergence of a very radical and untimely politico-religious system, akin to that of the Taliban in Afghanistan. Instead, Khomeini and the ruling clergy pragmatically opted to overlook religious precepts in favour of political considerations, effectively sacrificing the very principles they purported to uphold. Hundreds of examples can be cited in which the ruling clergy in Iran ignored religious precepts and retreated from religious regulations and structures. Investigating the level of non-compliance with the Shari'a by the Islamic state, Mehran Tamadonfar has identified the non-observance of a significant number of religious principles by the ruling clergy. "They have found it increasingly impossible to govern by the Shari'ah. Motivated by self-preservation and intent on maintaining control, they have turned into self-appointed 'guardians of the community' and have abandoned the 'guardianship of Islam'" (Tamadonfar, 2001: 218). This is also evident in the many programs and policies that were implemented during the "pragmatist government" of President Hashemi-Rafsanjani (1989–1997).[7]

When the then president Khamanei claimed that the authority of the Islamic state could be exercised only within the framework of the sacred law, Khomeini reminded him that "a government in the form of the God-given, absolute mandate (*velayat-e motlaq*) was the most important of the divine commandments and has priority over all derivative divine commandments.. . . [It is] one of the primary commandments of Islam and has priority over all derivative commandments, even over prayer, fasting, and pilgrimage to Mecca" (cited in Arjomand, 1988: 182).

It is also worth noting the transformation of the Guardian Council's jurisdiction. Within this political structure, the Guardian Council, acting as a religious watchdog, has the authority to refuse and nullify any form of parliamentary legislation should they prove incompatible with Islamic principles. In the early years of the Islamic state, many parliamentary initiatives were rejected ostensibly due to their incompatibility with Islam.[8] Seven years after the founding of the Islamic state, in a bid to end the parliamentary

7. For further discussion, see Abrahamian, 2008: 182–185; Gheissari & Nasr, 2006b: 105–126; Niknam, 1999.

8. For a detailed explanation of these controversial cases, see Arjomand, 1993.

deadlocks that inevitably occurred, Khomeini established the "Council for the Determination of the Expedience of the Islamic State" (Majma-e Tashkhis-e Maslahat-e Nezam). Imbued with the authority to overlook Islamic precepts in the "interests of the state" and the power to override the Guardian Council's decisions, this new council became one example in a trend in Iran that essentially legislated Islam irrelevant and culminated in the hitherto unprecedented notion in Shiite jurisprudence that became known as *fiqh-ul maslaha*.

Fiqh-ul Maslaha

Compatibility between religious precepts and the challenges of time and space has been a key issue for religious scholars throughout Islamic history. Although matters of worship are relatively stable, the sociopolitical and economic dimensions of religious precepts are strongly shaped by circumstance. Indeed, one of the main responsibilities of religious scholars and jurists is to adjust Islamic precepts such that they may adapt to prevailing circumstances. Towards this end, there has been a general consensus regarding the two overarching categorizations of religious precepts: "constant precepts" and "variable precepts". As the terms suggest, while the former refers to those precepts which are applicable to all time and space, the latter represents those that should be adjusted to suit the time. Ayatollah Khomeini, however, went beyond the traditional categorization of constant and variable precepts by introducing *fiqh-ul maslaha* (expedient *fiqh*) within the Shiite jurisprudential faculty as a new means of adjusting religious precepts to contemporary circumstances, an innovation that had unprecedented impact on the lived experience of the Islamic state (Hashemi-Najafabadi, 2010).[9]

As discussed previously, the empirical obligation of the Islamic state to address governance-related issues led Khomeini to overlook religious precepts in favour of political considerations. As Iran's highest politico-religious authority, Khomeini justified this approach by acknowledging that many religious precepts were not applicable in the contemporary world. He stated:

> One of the extremely important issues in the current turbulent situation is the role of time and space in *ijtihad* and decision making. [The]

---

9. Graham Fuller, who stresses the importance of this empirical experience and its reflection in the conceptual evolvement of governance issues within a religious context, observes that being among the few countries wherein political Islam succeeded in forming a state, Iran's case is unique in that it offers more creative conceptualizations and reconceptualizations regarding governance and Islam than anything taking place elsewhere in the Muslim world (2003: 104).

government sets the practical doctrine of dealing with polytheism [and] heresy as well as domestic and international problems. And not only are [they] not soluble by these seminary debates, which take place in [a] theoretical framework, but [they] also take us to a deadlock which results in a seeming violation of the Constitution (Khomeini, 2006b: 217–218).

In short, justification was shaped by parliamentary expedience. In similar vein, he is repeatedly quoted as referring to the government as the most "religiously indispensable issue" (*oujab-e vajebat*), meaning that regime preservation was of the highest necessity (Yasuyuki, 2009). Governance, then, was considered the core element of Islam: all aspects of Islam were subordinate to the interests of the Islamic state; in the interests of preserving key goals, subsidiary aspirations could be changed or deliberately overlooked (Mahdavi, 2014: 33). When incompatibility arises, political considerations are prioritized over religious precepts. Accordingly, and perhaps paradoxically, it is in the interest of the Islamic state to clarify the necessity to either conform with or overlook religious precepts. Even fundamental religious mores such as worshipping are not excluded. According to Khomeini:

A government which is a branch of the Prophet Mohammad's absolute guardianship is one of the primary Islamic precepts and takes priority over all subsidiary precepts, even over praying, fasting and pilgrimage.... [I]f necessary, [a] governor can close or destroy mosques.... [T]he government can unilaterally terminate its religious agreements with the people if an agreement violates the expedience of the country or Islam. And [it] can abandon every precept—both worshipping and non-worshipping precepts—which is against the expedience of Islam (2006a: 170–171).

Essentially, Khomeini authorized the state to amend every religious precept based on perceived rational assessments of contemporary circumstances. The conceptual ramifications of Khomeini's revision for his original thought on state–religion relations included reconfiguration of the notion of Velayat-e Faqih as Velayat-e Motlagh-e Faqih (absolute guardianship of the jurist). Many scholars, who interpret this logical and pragmatist approach as a process of secularization—that is, as an inevitable outcome of an Islamic state— argue that the religious state in the modern world will inevitably lead to a process of self-secularization (Ashouri, 2011; Fereshtian, 2013; Hajjarian, 2001; Kazemi & Faraji, 2003; Kazemipur & Rezaei, 2003; Mohammadi, 2008: 279–331; Roy, 2007: 62–64; Salehpour, 1995; 1999; Vasigh, 2005: 11; Yasuyuki, 2009).

Saeed Hajjarian, a leading strategist in the Iranian reform movement who conceptualizes reconfiguration of state–religion relations in Khomeini's thought as an inevitable but constructive process, considers the latter's revision "a process of secularizing Shiite *fiqh*". Contending that for the first time the 1979 revolution gave birth to a nation-state in Iran, Hajjarian argues that modern states have a penchant for absolutism, a familiar experience of modern states which makes reconfiguration of the doctrine of Velayat-e Faqih comprehensible. For Hajjarian, in order to survive, a modern state ought to constantly make calculations, assess threats and opportunities, and analyse costs and benefits. The politics of expediency, he claims, is the key contributor to the survival of a modern state; a religious state is no exception in this regard. According to Hajjarian, this is exactly what occurred in post-revolutionary Iran. Arguing that in Shiite history the element of expediency had never played a significant role, Hajjarian asserts that the formation of the Islamic state imposed the politics of expediency on Shiite jurisprudence:

> In my opinion, the conflation of jurisprudence and the state apparatus, and the pre-eminence of the slogan "Our politics are the same as our religiosity" imposed the necessities and requisites of the political institution on the religious apparatus. States, in the modern age in particular, are the main agencies of secularization. Statesmen manage the affairs [of the country] in accordance with the conventional rationale. And, if there is a conflation of state institution and jurisprudence apparatus, this characteristic [of state institution] will be transferred to jurisprudence (Hajjarian, 2001: 94–95).

Hajjarian maintains that the survival of a state based on the doctrine of Velayat-e Faqih is conditional on the principle of expediency. This existential exigency led Khomeini to incorporate the principle of expediency into his theory of state. Hajjarian concludes:

> Despite its guise, according to which the establishment of a religious state based on the doctrine of Velayat-e Faqih seems contrary to the secularization process,. . . from a long-term perspective, a religious state in the modern age is the most important accelerator of the secularization process (Hajjarian, 2001: 79).[10]

---

10. Using the pseudonym Jahangir Salehpour, Hajjarian initially published his thesis as a series of articles in *Kiyan* magazine. Later, these articles were reprinted in a book titled *From the Sacred Witness to the Profane Witness: The Secularization of Religion in the Sphere of Politics*.

By employing this logic, Hajjarian espouses the notion of absolute guardianship of the jurist. However, he overlooks the fact that while Khomeini's idiosyncratic form of secularization intends to serve the expediency of the state, the latter may not necessarily comply with the nation's expediency. Any attempt to equate state expediency with the nation's expediency in an authoritarian regime could prove problematic. Furthermore, Hajjarian's thesis fails to note that decisions and policies are still made under the banner of religion. This is why a Valey-e Faqih expects blind obedience, even though his decisions and policies are made based upon rational calculations. Whereas in a secularized political space, decisions are open to dispute, Khomeini's doctrine sanctifies a Valey-e Faqih's decisions by attributing them to religion. Finally, one may argue that Khomeini articulated a selective secularization. While the Islamic state opts for expediency whenever it serves the state's interest, religious principles remain key instruments in the nation's politics. Thus, rather than being the cornerstone of politics, expediency is employed by the Islamic state as an additional instrument to facilitate its authoritarian excesses.

Khomeini implemented the notion of expediency-based *fiqh* both in the political structure of the Islamic state and in its administrative process. In February 1988, he ordered the establishment of the Council for the Determination of the Expedience of the Islamic State. Not only was this council added to the Constitution in the 1989 amendment, but the concept of Velayat-e Faqih in the Constitution was changed to Velayat-e Motlagh-e Faqih (absolute guardianship of the jurist). According to Khomeini's final articulation of absolute Velayat-e Faqih, one person has the ultimate authority over the decision-making process. Put simply, a Valey-e Faqih has the final word not only on all governance issues, but also regarding the necessity to either implement or abandon religious precepts. In effect, this is a totally authoritarian articulation of religion–state relations that favours political considerations. Rather than the enforcement of religious precepts, it stipulates that a person, a Valey-e Faqih, dictates the character of the religiosity of the Islamic state. In other words, the state is Islamic because it is pronounced Islamic by the Valey-e Faqih, not because it necessarily conforms to Islamic precepts.

Although Khomeini occupied a highly respected position in the Shiite clerical hierarchy, he was by no means the only senior religious authority. Many senior clerics did not agree with his religious and political thought. Because pluralism is an essential feature of the Shiite school, historically a single jurist had never claimed to represent the school in its entirety until the establishment of the Islamic state. The elevated political position of the Valey-e Faqih allowed him to prioritize his perspective over other senior jurists. Kadivar notes that this shift from pluralism towards a more monistic leadership has resulted in the dominance of political power over jurisprudence, and state power over religious precepts. "The authority of the state over *fiqh* subordinates Shari'a precepts and makes them submissive to political power, and subject to being floated along daily instabilities" (M. Kadivar, 2007a). In his view, religion is compromised when state and political interests take precedence and result in state control of religion, which leaves no space for genuine religious faith, spirituality, and passion (cited in Matsunaga, 2007: 326).

Fiqh-ul maslaha's acceptance within the traditional religious nexus is tenuous. According to Soroush, expedient *fiqh* was not taken seriously in the Qom seminary; and few conceptual works produced have examined this concept (2008a: 256). Not surprisingly, there were even some objections to expedient *fiqh* within the traditional cluster of the Shiite jurisprudential circle. One outstanding example was Ayatollah Montazeri, who explicitly objected to this rendition while agreeing with the doctrine of Velayat-e Faqih. He claimed that "[e]ven the Prophet Mohammad and the infallible [Imams] did not have absolute guardianship.. . . I do not believe in the absolute guardianship that the authorities added [to the Constitution] in the amendment and I did not vote for that" (Montazeri, 2006b).[11] Similarly, Kadivar, taking into account the fact that this approach departs from the established Islamic framework as well as from the widely accepted *ijtihad* method, outlines the lack of juristic support for Khomeini's approach:

> Many traditionalist *fuqaha* believe that there is no valid evidence in the Shari'a in support of the theory of the guardianship of the *fiqh*. The absolute authority/guardianship of the state over *fiqh* only has the endorsement of its progenitor and some of his students; it is not accepted among traditionalist *fuqaha'*. Traditional *fiqh* is very cautious and—unlike Ayatollah Khomeini—is neither of the view that interests or expediency can be clearly ascertained, nor that precepts based on interests or expediency can take precedence over all [of the] Shari'a precepts, especially the worship-related ones (2009: 59).

Kadivar further suggests that expedient *fiqh* does not provide a durable solution to the dilemma of incompatibility between Islamic precepts and the governance of the modern state. [I]t simply legitimizes contradictory legislation for a short period of time. Shari'a precepts will change at the level of practice, not at the level of religious validity. In other words, even when the state's

---

11. For a detailed explanation of Montazeri's jurisprudential objection to the doctrine of absolute Velayat-e Faqih, see Montazeri, 2000a.

expedient approach changes, the basic Islamic precepts will remain as default principles (M. Kadivar, 2009: 60). For example, pilgrimage to Mecca became a controversial issue when Iran converted a part of pilgrimage, "disavowal of infidels" (*beraat az moshrekin*), into a political occasion. In 1987, there was a clash between Shiite pilgrims and Saudi Arabian security forces, in which more than 400 people were killed. Following this incident, the Islamic state of Iran decided, based on the expedience of the time, to ban pilgrimage for three years. But, in effect, it did not mean that the jurisprudential principle of pilgrimage had altered. On another occasion in 1980, the Islamic state endorsed a bill introducing new regulations regarding the qualifications of land ownership within the limits of cities. But this did not necessarily mean that the jurisprudential precepts regarding ownership had changed.

Speaking more generally of the problematics behind the theory of expediency-based *fiqh*, Kadivar states that it is not reasonable to allow "the fate of the entire Shari'a ordinances—and, for that matter, the religion of Islam—to depend on the 'personal' understanding on the part of the ruling jurisprudent of the 'conditions of the time and place" (quoted in Matsunaga, 2007: 326). He further argues: "If assessing the expedient of the society and determining the requirements of time and place are rational, irreligious, and objective issues, why should these issues be conceded to a jurist?" (M. Kadivar, 2002a: 426). Finally, expediency-based *fiqh* should be challenged for exploiting religion. Put simply, decisions based on the rational assessment of circumstances cannot be tagged as "Islamic" without dangerous consequences. These decisions are made by the absolute authority of one person who is not free from error. Labelling state decisions with a religious tag will ultimately render religion—not government—responsible for policy failure.

Further research is imperative if one is to trace the record of expedient *fiqh* within contemporary Iran's political mosaic. One may argue that the Islamic state would never order people to abandon praying or fasting to comply with the expedience of the regime. However, Islamic precepts are not confined to clear-cut matters such as praying or fasting. When violation of the basic precepts is religiously justified, many issues are affected by the rubric of expediency. This is particularly evident in Khomeini's increasingly frequent insistence that the preservation of the Islamic state is the most important religious issue. In the aftermath of the 2009 presidential election, opposition leaders were advised to put an end to claims that challenged the election results because it threatened to jeopardize not simply the government but, more importantly, the Islamic state. The shooting of demonstrators and the commission of human rights abuses in prisons were similarly justified because they were committed with the aim of ensuring the survival of the

Islamic state. The application of expedient *fiqh* thus includes a range of issues that cover a much broader area and require independent research.

An authoritarian Islamic regime has emerged from the unification of religion and state to the detriment of each. Due to the jurisprudential roots of the doctrine of Velayat-e Faqih, which form the linchpin of the Constitution and support the dominant position of the clergy, *fiqh* claims supremacy over all other aspects of religion. One could argue that there is a conflation of state and *fiqh*, rather than of religion and state. Coupling *fiqh* with political power in Iran has arguably enhanced the power of *fiqh* at the expense of genuine religiosity. This predominance has galvanized reformist scholars to seek the separation of the religion and state in order to avoid one-dimensional religiosity and restore balance among the different dimensions of religion.

Fiqh *and the Spirit of Religiosity*

Ayatollah Khomeini's philosophical and mystical inclination was unique among traditional jurists.[12] As well as being one of the first students to study philosophy, he was among those who pioneered the teaching of philosophy at the Qom seminary. Moreover, he was one of the few high-ranking jurists who possessed theosophical inclinations. With this is mind, there is surprisingly little evidence of Khomeini's philosophical and theosophical inclinations in contemporary Iran's political structure, due in large part to his conceptualization of a jurisprudential doctrine of religion in politics. Ayatollah Khomeini led a revolution that resulted in the emergence of a jurisprudential state run by jurists, with the Shari'a, the main repository of *fiqh*, as the governing principle.

Although jurisprudence provides the framework for the practice of religion, it is not synonymous with religion. It only regulates religion's visible and exterior aspects—religious practices, for example. In essence, as the main concern of *fiqh* is the regulation of religious activities; an inner approach towards faith is only poorly represented. The political structure and practice of the Islamic state of Iran reflects this basic character of *fiqh* rather than the ethical and less visible aspects of religiosity. Throughout the last three decades, strenuous efforts have been made by the Islamic state to ensure the public visibility of religiosity. These efforts have included the reinforcement of compulsory *hijab*, obligatory prayer observance in the workplace, the official prohibition of eating and drinking in public during Ramadan, and various methods of rewarding those who effect a religious mien such as wearing

---

12. For further explanation of these features of Khomeini, see Abdo, 2001; Main, 1994.

a beard or wearing one's shirt outside of one's trousers. These are just a few examples of the hundreds of policies pursued by the state to promote the religiosity of the population publicly. State–religion unification is, in truth, unification of the state and *fiqh*. Thus, the current political system in Iran can be more accurately described by the term "jurisprudential state", rather than by the commonly used tags of "religious" or "Islamic" state.

When *fiqh* enjoys state support, it dominates the more subtle dimensions of religiosity—a dominance that will persist as long as religion remains confined within jurisprudence. The unification of religion and state has reduced Islam to *fiqh*, a phenomenon that has urged the reformists to reclaim the non-jurisprudential dimensions of Islam. In this regard, persuasive arguments have been mounted by Soroush and Mojtahed-Shabestari, who have challenged the dominance of *fiqh* from a theological/philosophical perspective. Other reformist jurists, Kadivar and Eshkevari, for example, have expressed their concern regarding hypocrisy, a topic I will address later in this chapter.

Concern over the dominance of *fiqh* constitutes a significant thread that runs through most of Soroush's intellectual works. Concurring with Moroccan philosopher Mohammed Abed Al Jabri (1936–2010), Soroush maintains that the dominance of *fiqh* is neither a new phenomenon nor one confined to contemporary Iran, for in contrast to the Greek philosophical civilization, Islamic civilization has historically been strongly jurisprudential (1997). Soroush points to the large number of jurists who have emerged throughout Islamic history, heavily outnumbering philosophers and theologians (2003). Having read the intellectual works of Muhammad Al-Ghazali (1059–1111), who expressed a similar concern (Cooper, 1998: 50–51), Soroush states: "According to him [Ghazali],. . . in his time, *fiqh* was so voluminous and so opulent that it did wrong to the other parts of Islam, especially ethics. For him, the essence of religiosity was ethics and morality.. . . [M]orality was suppressed under the pressure of law" (2010f).

For Soroush, religiosity is associated with faith and heartfelt credence (1996c: 2). As religiosity rests on the individual's religious experience, religious precepts have been designed to nurture these experiences. However, due to the highly subjective nature of faith, religious precepts cannot be universally effective for all believers. For example, while pilgrimage may stimulate one believer's personal religious experience, alms may work better for another. Without individual religious experience, Soroush argues, religion would only function as an empty melange of social rules (Soroush, 2006a: 161–179).

The two main dimensions of religiosity are outward practice (*amal*) and esoteric belief (*iman*). The current state of Iran can be described as symptomatic of the prioritization of outward practice over inner faith. Religious rituals and ceremonies take precedence, and *fiqh* is recognized as the core of religion. Accordingly, jurists serve as custodians of Shari'a and enjoy a prominent and privileged position in politics. Under these circumstances, the Islamic state is obliged to protect and implement the Shari'a even if it has to be done via coercive power (Jahanbakhsh, 2001b: 154). By labelling the current political system in Iran a "jurisprudential state", Soroush draws attention to the profound implications of the historical dominance of *fiqh* over other complex dimensions of religion. Not only does the dominance of *fiqh* compromise religion, but, when coupled with political power, it insists on enacting only the exoteric dimension of religion while suppressing the very heart of religiosity—esoteric belief (Soroush, 1994a: 13–15). In reinforcing the dominance of *fiqh*, the Islamic state of Iran undermines genuine religiosity by giving prominence to rituals and other ceremonial aspects of religion.

Similar to Soroush, Mojtahed-Shabestari objects to the unification of religion and state as it undermines genuine religiosity. The dominance of *fiqh* focuses on "God's orders and prohibitions". Throughout Islamic history, these orders and prohibitions have shaped religiosity for the masses, although theosophists have always offered a more spiritual understanding of religion. *Fiqh* has conceptualized these orders and prohibitions and allowed jurists to exercise a profound influence on the Muslim population (Mojtahed-Shabestari, 1999: 6).

Mojtahed-Shabestari attempts to resuscitate the spiritual aspects of Islam—mysticism, in particular. To this end, he identifies three levels of religiosity. The first includes religious ceremonies and practices such as worship, alms giving, and sociopolitical activities undertaken in the name of religion. At the second level are belief and conviction, including belief in monotheism, the Prophet Mohammad, the hereafter, and related issues. At the third level is the individual religious experience, which, in contrast to the two other levels, is totally individualistic and unique to each and every person. In Mojtahed-Shabestari's view, this is the very essence of religiosity. Without individual religious experience, rituals and ceremonies are little more than cultural traditions (Mojtahed-Shabestari, 1997: 118–119).

For Mojtahed-Shabestari, a "religious experience" entails a direct relationship between God and the believer. As such, the Shari'a and religious ceremonies do not enjoy a central place in this relationship. Mojtahed-Shabestari advances his argument by questioning the place of religious regulations in Islam. According to him, most of the effective social structures in place in the pre-Islamic Arabian Peninsula were incorporated by Islam. He states:

> The intervention of the holy book and Islamic traditions in legal aspects
> of familial, social, governmental, judicial and like issues in the Hejaz

did not intend to establish a legal [system] for these issues because relevant laws were enacted. . ... [T]hese interventions aimed to overcome the
barriers against monotheistic manners, barriers which, in some cases,
existed as law, custom or institution (Mojtahed-Shabestari, 1995: 297).

Significantly, Mojtahed-Shabestari disputes the use of religious revivalism to
characterize contemporary Islamic movements. He sees the latter as political
movements led by leaders employing religion to gain popular support. He states
that authentic religious revivalism must address the religious experiences of
believers by encouraging them to gain religious experience instead of accen-
tuating Islamic regulations and rituals (Mojtahed-Shabestari, 1997: 117–138).
With regard to the Islamic state of Iran, Mojtahed-Shabestari challenges the
common perception that practicing the Shari'a was initially an ultimate goal
for the Islamic state. As one who was involved in dissenting politics on the eve
of the 1979 revolution and for a short period thereafter, Mojtahed-Shabestari
argues that the Constitution of the Islamic Republic of Iran does not refer to the
implementation of Shari'a as the state's responsibility. The Constitution was
written based upon circumstances of time and place. It is neither a production
of *fiqh* nor of *ijtihad*. The claim that it is the state's duty to promote religious
precepts only emerged as an afterthought (Mojtahed-Shabestari, 2005: 21–53).

"Formal reading of Islam" (*Islam-e rasmi*) and "jurisprudential Islam"
(*Islam-e fiqahati*) are the two main terms that Mojtahed-Shabestari employs
to oppose the politicization of religion in Iran. In his view, the unification
of religion and state has resulted in an official reading of Islam, which pri-
oritizes *fiqh* over other key dimensions of religion. He states: "The content
and message of religion is an important issue. It is much richer and wider
than jurisprudential precepts. Dominance of *fiqh* over religion is equivalent
to emptying out the soul of religion and drying its gusto, its experience and
its message" (Mojtahed-Shabestari, 2005: 50). It is worth noting that neither
Soroush nor Mojtahed-Shabestari suggest that *fiqh* should be eliminated altogether. Soroush also recognizes the potential contribution of *fiqh* to the democratization process (2008d: 322–326). However, their emphasis on the mystical
dimension of Islam has resulted in some anxiety over the possible emergence
of another one-dimensional religion, one dominated by mysticism.

Islamic State and Fiqh

The view that there is no need to comply with entrenched religious practices such as praying and fasting, Islam without clergy (*Islam-e menhay-e
rohaniyat*), and the casting aside of *fiqh* has provoked some scholars to issue

warnings about the possibility of the emergence of a one-dimensional religion dominated by mysticism. Providing an insight into the diversity within *fiqh*, Kadivar claims that *fiqh* is neither a unified nor a well-bounded entity. It is beyond the scope of this book to delineate the various versions of *fiqh*; however, the diversity of jurisprudential ideas vis-à-vis *fiqh*'s political engagement is directly relevant to the current discussion. In terms of political involvement, Shiite *fiqh* has always incorporated widely diverse perspectives and conceptualizations (M. Kadivar, 1997; 1999a; Moussavi, 1992; Ridgeon, 2005: 198–199).

Criticizing the new wave of one-dimensional Islam, Kadivar allocates the bulk of his intellectual works to the task of questioning the jurisprudential authenticity of Iran's current political circumlocution. His main publications, *The Theories of State in Shiite Fiqh* and *Theocratic State,* include a detailed jurisprudential analysis which purports that the doctrine of Velayat-e Faqih is not only a constructed theory in Shiite tradition, but is also marginal to the contemporary Shiite school. Suggesting that the current anti-jurisprudential wave is a reaction to the misuse of *fiqh* by the Islamic state of Iran, he defends *fiqh* by shedding light on its diversity. Kadivar contests the presupposition that the Islamic state of Iran is representative of *fiqh*:

> The Islamic Republic [of Iran] is neither endorsed by the majority of jurists in terms of its governing methods nor is it supported by most religious individuals and Marja-e Taghlids in terms of its function.. . . [T]he number of dissidents among jurists and religious individuals is not less than among non-religious and seculars.. . . The Islamic Republic violates many fairly certain Islamic precepts: many Quranic verses are overlooked and many actions have been taken [by the Islamic Republic] which are clearly against the Prophet Mohammad's tradition (2010c).

Kadivar argues that although the ruling clergy claim to be jurists, it does not mean that they or the performance of the Islamic state genuinely represent *fiqh*. He further argues that the Iranian Islamic state was founded upon a marginal doctrine disseminated by jurists and has violated precepts of *fiqh* and Shari'a principles. Furthermore, the marriage of the religion and state in Iran has equipped a specific coterie of *fiqh* with the political authority to suppress traditional diversity within jurisprudential circles. Not surprisingly, the Islamic state is opposed by many jurists and religious scholars and individuals (Azimi, 2008: 418–419). Kadivar claims that this resistance is driven by the perception of the Islamic state as a symbol of religious dictatorship and not representative of *fiqh* (2010c). He contends that the most profound among the Islamic scholars have always insisted on the companionship of *fiqh* and mysticism.

Kadivar, while concurring with Soroush and Mojtahed-Shabestari regarding the dominance of *fiqh* in Islamic history, nevertheless points to the inevitability of this dominance (2010d). Like Mojtahed-Shabestari, Kadivar divides religiosity into three levels: Shari'a (Shariat), mystical path (*tarighat*), and truth (*haghighat*). In Kadivar's opinion, the majority of Muslims are not capable of taking the mystical path. He claims that most people remain in the first dimension (Shari'a): they rarely enter the second dimension, let alone the third. He further opines that mystical Islam will be accessible to relatively few people: "Each and every one of the three dimensions of religiosity is consonant with the intelligence of a certain cluster of population. Exclusive generalization and universalization of one dimension will result in the subversion of other dimensions" (M. Kadivar, 2010c).

Yet, his defence of *fiqh* does not mean that Kadivar subscribes to state-led *fiqh*. For him, morality and faith are two main aspects of religiosity that have been abandoned due to strong emphasis on an exoteric layer of religiosity. The main function of religion is to stimulate voluntary human evolution, something that cannot be achieved by state pressure and legal coercion. Kadivar insists that the state's promotion of religiosity will only result in the pretence of practicing religion; it will not lead to the strengthening of faith. In line with An-Na'im, he argues that religiosity cannot be promoted by state law. Thus, he concludes, if states seek to promote religiosity, the best strategy is to intervene as little as possible in religious matters (M. Kadivar, 2000a: 204–205; 2001a; 2003d; 2006d). Extending a non-interventionist approach to state–religion relations, Kadivar contests the current ruling clergy's qualifications to take charge of traditionally independent religious institutions:

> From compassionate Islam's point of view, states do not have the right to intervene in the religious institutions such as [electing] Marja-e Taghlid, [the activities of] the religious seminary, mosques, religious training, preaching and charity centres. Compassionate Islam is in conflict with governmental religion and strongly opposes converting the clergy, mosques, seminaries and Marja-e Taghlids into governmental bodies. Thus, independence of religious institutions from political institutions is one of the main pillars of compassionate Islam (2010b).

Although they approach the *fiqh* from different perspectives, reformist scholars unanimously oppose the unification of religion and state. Their concern is with safeguarding the esoteric layers of religion, one of the underlying motivations for religious secularity. A combination of the exoteric nature of *fiqh* and the jurisprudential features of the current political system promotes hypocrisy and threatens genuine religiosity.

Hypocrisy and the Unification of Religion and State

Various Quranic verses and hadiths denounce hypocrisy and enjoin believers to practice genuine religiosity.[13] Indeed, a major justification for the establishment of the Islamic state is the promotion of religiosity. This mandate assumes state intervention in religious matters, which may be variously achieved through persuasive/coercive and punitive policies. But, rather than enhancing the level of religiosity, state intervention has resulted in widespread hypocrisy, prompting reformist scholars to argue for a religiously neutral secular democratic state.

An-Na'im maintains that the enforcement of public policy necessitates granting governmental institutions and authorities the right to use coercive power (2008: 50–51). However, genuine religiosity is characterized by voluntary choice based upon personal pious intention. Thus, the implementation of the Shari'a as a form of state law underpinned by coercion stands in direct contradiction to the voluntary nature of religiosity (An-Na'im, 1998). Noting that hypocrisy is repeatedly condemned in the Quran, An-Na'im asserts that state intervention in religion entails hypocrisy and corruption (2008: 69). By contrast, separation of the institution of state from religious institutions "promotes possibilities of honest piety and diminishes the risks of hypocrisy among believers" (An-Na'im, 2008: 36). Three decades of the Islamic state in Iran have provided reformist Iranian scholars with a particular lived experience upon which to build their case for religious secularity.

Countless official and informal policies pertaining to Islam have been formulated in the post-revolutionary Islamic state of Iran. Many Shari'a principles have been legislated as laws and backed by the coercive power of the

---

13. For example, see the following Quranic verses: "O ye who believe! render not vain your almsgiving by reproach and injury, like him who spendeth his wealth only to be seen of men and believeth not in Allah and the last day" [translated by Marmaduke Pickthall].

يَا أَيُّهَا الَّذِينَ آمَنُواْ لَا تُبْطِلُواْ صَدَقَاتِكُم بِالْمَنِّ وَالأذَى كَالَّذِي يُنفِقُ مَالَهُ رِئَاء النَّاس وَلَا يُؤْمِنُ بِاللّهِ وَالْيَوْم الآخِر

"Lo! the hypocrites seek to beguile Allah, but it is he who beguileth them. When they stand up to worship they perform it languidly and to be seen of men, and are mindful of Allah but little" [translated by Marmaduke Pickthall].

إِنَّ الْمُنَافِقِينَ يُخَادِعُونَ اللَّه وَهُوَ خَادِعُهُمْ وَإِذَا قَامُواْ إِلَى الصَّلَاةِ قَامُواْ كُسَالَى يُرَآؤُونَ النَّاس وَلَا يَذْكُرُونَ اللَّه إِلَّا قَلِيلا

state. However, these policies are not entirely confined to the legal system. All social aspects of Iranian lives are expected to be religious—or, to be more precise, to appear religious. Due to the rentier character of Iran's state, its dominance of a quasi-command economy, unitary political system, and centralized administrative policy, it is well equipped to force people to conform to this expectation. To this end, the state's course of action extends to a very wide range of areas. In addition to controlling the appearance and behaviour of the populace, particularly in the public arenas, the state rewards religious gestures and penalizes non-religious—even neutral—gestures, the last two attracting harsh punishment. One example is the expectation that public servants are required to pray. This is usually an informal expectation; however, there is an official procedure in place to test the religious competence of the state employees, a procedure called *gozinesh* (choosing). A very commonly used term in post-revolutionary Iran, *gozinesh* refers to an important step in the official recruitment process whereby the applicant's knowledge of the Shari'a and Islamic principles is tested. It also used to be a university entrance requirement. The Islamic state has over time seen the departure from office of many professionals and skilled staff due to their weak knowledge of the Shari'a and of state-sponsored Islamic principles.

An-Na'im argues that "hypocrisy and corruption are the inevitable consequences of making subjective factors like religious faith and piety criteria for appointment and promotion in bureaucratic positions" (An-Na'im, 2008: 292). In Iran's case, the quality of the bureaucracy has been impacted by recruitment based on religious piety rather than on professional competence. The state's promotion and monitoring of religiosity has left many with only one option—that is, to pretend to be religious. Beyond governance concerns, this policy is unarguably unjust. Kadivar, who objects to the discriminatory nature of this process, states: "This choosing method [*gozinesh*] results in serious problems in terms of justice, specifically when youths are about to enter university or opt to be recruited" (2000a: 614). Kadivar, who considers hypocrisy an immediate result of "governmental religion" (*din-e dolati*), states that while committing sins, one can pretend to be religious to fulfil the requirements of governmental religion because the essence of such religion is of little consequence (M. Kadivar, 2003d). Evaluating the achievements of the Islamic state of Iran, Kadivar concludes that the Islamic state has not succeeded in increasing religiosity:

> Increasing religiosity in the country means the penetration of religious beliefs into the people's hearts and retrieving religious conscience. It does not mean pretension, guile, hypocrisy and belief in exoteric

religion. Thus, we can never say that the [1979] revolution has succeeded in this regard (M. Kadivar, 2000a: 615).

Distinguishing two different articulations of religion–politics relations
(i.e., "politicizing religion" and "religionizing politics"), Kadivar asserts
that while the Islamic revolution intended to make religion an influential force in the political sphere, religion has instead been subordinated to
politics (2000a: 622). Soroush terms this newly born phenomenon "official
Islam": only a specific interpretation of Islam[14] backed by political authority
is recognized in Iran. Similar to Kadivar, Soroush argues that religion has
become the basis of political power in the Islamic state:

> The main product of the [government] efforts to Islamize the society
> is the emergence of something named "official Islam". .. . [T]his is
> what I advised clergy about years ago and warned them that you should
> not back and possess power. You should be critical of power [holders]
> instead of providing religious justification for political stipulations.
> When captivated by the shortage of reasoning, you should not use
> power (2008a: 245).

For Soroush, an important outcome of official Islam is dual personality
disorder, a state or condition in which people learn how to live according
to the expected standards. They act differently according to public and
private arenas, a form of charade that undermines religiosity (Soroush,
2008a: 246). Referring to discrimination as an outcome of official Islam,
Soroush contends that there were three main discriminations in classical
fiqh: discrimination between slave/master, women/men, and Muslim/infi-
del. He attributes a new discrimination to *fiqh* since it has become coupled with political power: "Official Islam now decrees inequality between
insider and outsider. It sets filters like *gozinesh* for higher education, appro-
batory supervision [*nezarat-e estesvabi*] for the elections, and like settings to
deprive some people of their rights in civil society" (Soroush, 2008a: 250).
It is worth mentioning that Soroush promotes the notion of pluralism as a
social/historical actuality, as a religiously legitimate notion to defeat state
Islam (1999; 2000).

---

14. An important work by Soroush addresses the problems associated with the use of
religion as a political ideology. When religion is converted into political ideology, it will
inevitably set in place an official body to interpret religion (e.g., official interpreters), thus
restraining the development of religious knowledge. For Soroush, in contemporary Iran,
fiqh is a form of political platform, see Soroush, 1994b: 26; 1996a; Vakili, 2001.

Soroush discusses the impossibility of measuring the level of religiosity even by jurisprudential criteria. Living in the shadow of official Islam, many people opt not to express their true religious beliefs; for this reason, their genuine religiosity cannot be assessed. For Soroush, "this is the most serious disadvantage of official Islam" (2008a: 267). He refuses to characterize contemporary Iran as a genuinely religious society: coupling obedience with jurisprudential precepts cannot be perceived as representing religiosity. He further argues that while "humankind can be forced to profess religiosity, they cannot be forced to have faith within their hearts. Understanding religion and believing in it cannot be handed over or ordered by someone else" (Soroush, 2008d: 317).

Ethics are not only the central theme of some of Soroush's works (2004a), they are a constant thrust of his intellectual project. He raises the necessity of assessing the level of religiosity using ethical criteria. From an ethical standpoint, the current situation in Iran does not auger well for the promising future. Soroush argues that by no means does the social structure of the country promote moral values. He further observes: "*Gozinesh*, creating barriers to the recruitment process,. . . . eruption of violence, insincere and dishonest press and unaccountable authorities, are all against moral values.. . . [U]nfortunately hypocrisy and guileful manners are more compatible with our social structure than honesty and frankness" (Soroush, 2008a: 269). He also emphasizes that violence becomes the norm in this type of social structure wherein credence is prioritized over humanity, but humanity is beyond credence. Moreover, mankind is entitled to basic rights merely by dint of being human and not due to expressing a specific belief or faith (Soroush, 1995b). Contesting the categorization of people as religious, non-religious, holders of truth, or holders of falsehoods, Soroush argues that setting sociopolitical and individual rights based on these categorizations is not acceptable. All citizens, he maintains, possess equal rights (Soroush, 1998a: 27).

Soroush was supported by Ayatollah Montazeri in this regard. Montazeri asserted that since there are different understandings of the holy book and traditions, one should not impose one's understanding on others. He also maintained that the social rights of individuals should be protected regardless of different beliefs and understandings of religion (Montazeri, 2003: 229). Montazeri's fatwa directed towards the Baha'i is of great importance here. He was the first—and to date the only—Grand Ayatollah to acknowledge the Baha'i's rights as citizens of the country, although he insisted on his belief regarding the falseness of the Baha'i religion (H. A. Montazeri, 2008).

Similar to Kadivar and Soroush, Montazeri also contested the use of coercion by the state to make people practice the Shari'a. He wrote:

> Similar to faith, religious duties cannot be mandatory.. . . [T]here is a difference between mandating the performance of the Shari'a and persuasion of it by the state. If the state takes over [the responsibility of] practicing Shari'a, it won't solve the problem of people's obedience to these orders; in contrast, it may result in the evasion of religion and in hostility towards religiosity (2008: 142–143).

In sum, the Islamic state's claim to bear the responsibility for promoting religion has been contested. Reformist scholars point out the immanent conflict between genuine religiosity and the state's imposition of the Shari'a as an obligatory commitment. After three decades of the Islamic state, religiosity has not increased, if anything it has decreased.[15] The prevailing religious reformation discourses are partly a reaction to this paradoxical phenomenon. For reformist scholars, religious secularity and the emancipation of religion from the state is a means of promoting genuine religiosity.

It is widely recognized by the ruling clergy and reformists that the Islamic state in Iran has not succeeded in increasing the level of religiosity. One obvious sign was the explicit objection of the Supreme Leader to weak religiosity in the universities (Kian-Thiebaut, 1999). In the latest development in this regard, he targeted the universities again following the June 2009 election, which saw a state-sponsored Islamization campaign in the universities from 2009 onwards (M. A. Kadivar, 2014b). As this example shows, the ruling clerics' reaction to weak religiosity differs substantially from that of the reformist scholars. The state believes that greater state intervention in religious matters is required. Thus, for the ruling clergy, the problem does not stem from the conflict between the Islamic state and the promotion of religiosity.

Iran's experiment with the Islamic state demonstrates little advantage to a religiosity that, if anything, has been subordinated as a political instrument, circumstances that have provoked many religious scholars to reconceptualize state–religion relations. Although they agree with the ruling clergy that there are religious precepts that are not applicable in contemporary times, and that

---

15. Many researchers and surveys have explored the level of religiosity in contemporary Iran. See Abdi, 2009; Ghobadzadeh, 2004; Kazemipur & Goodarzi, 2009; Rafipoor, 1997; Zooalam, 2000.

a rational approach should be adopted to manage sociopolitical and economic matters (Eshkevari, 2010b; M. Kadivar, 2002a: 406407; Mojtahed-Shabestari, 2004: 192–208; Soroush, 2009e: 241–254), they are firmly opposed to the interventionist nature of the Islamic state. Reformist scholars instead promote a democratic secular articulation based on the mutually emancipative separation of religion and state.

3

Religious Rationale for
Separation

THE SEPARATION OF religion and state has been hotly debated within mainstream scholarship on secularism. Similarly, institutional separation of religion and state claims an important place within religious reformation discourse in Iran. However, there is an important difference between the two debates. In Iran, the unification of religion and state is a strong and well-established discourse in the politico-religious mosaic. By contrast, mainstream scholarship on the experiences of secularism in the West is built upon practiced cases of separation, offering descriptive, normative, and strategic conceptions of state–religion relations. In other words, the driving force behind the contemporary debate surrounding separation aims to outline more functional and effective models of separation. As the models of separation are inadequately studied topics in the literature, there is no controversy over the necessity for the separation of religion and state. Whereas in the West the necessity for separation is taken as given, the reformist discourse in Iran continues to focus on arguing for the necessity and justification of the separation of religion from state.

Current reformist discourse resonates with the discourse of the founding fathers of separation, John Locke (1632–1704) and Thomas Jefferson (1743–1826). Irrespective of their differences, the main thrust of their cases for separation in the West was to justify the necessity for the separation of religion and state. However, Iran's recent experience differs from the Western experiences of secularism. While the latter possesses political roots, religious rather than political concerns constitute the driving force behind religious secularity discourse in Iran. Scrutinizing the early religious views on the separation of religion and state, Witte Jr. traces the pursuance of the separationist approach not only in religious texts such as the Torah, the Bible, and the

New Testament, but also in the theological works of St. Augustine (354–430 CE) and Pope Gelasius (d. 496). For Witte, the early quests for the separation of religion and state aimed to protect religion from the corruptive force of worldly matters. He extends this logic to the founding era of the modern notion of the separation of state and church. In his view, John Locke, along with many founders of the American separationist movement, invoked separation to protect religion from the state (Witte Jr., 2006).[1] Similarly Chavura, who asserts that John Locke and Thomas Jefferson argued for the loosening of the state's coercive rights over religion, claims that "[i]f Locke's letter is the classic statement of separation of church and state then the nature of such separation is religious liberty. . . . Jefferson's preoccupation was ensuring that religion remained free and uncoerced" (Chavura, 2010: 41).

Unarguably, the early articulation of modern Western secularisms encompassed political theology, a fact evident in the works of the classic advocates of separation highlighted in Witte and Chavura's articles. By contrast, I suggest that although religious rationale played a small role in their argumentation, political persuasion represented the primary motive for separating state from church. I agree with Charles Taylor, who states that "the origin point of modern Western secularism was the Wars of Religion; or rather, the search in battle-fatigue and horror for a way out of them" (Taylor, 1998: 32). Classical scholars such as Locke, Montesquieu, and Rousseau frequently referred to religious texts and were called upon to reinterpret Christianity and its political dimension "from outside". In actual fact, while they built upon the religious reformation project laid down by Luther and Calvin, they did not explicitly advocate religious reformation so much as separation. Their project was political; religion featured in their argument only in relation to politics (Gencer, 2010; Nadon, 2014).

The extant literature does not suggest that any one monolithic experience characterized separation in the West. Contemporary scholarship detects varying origins of secularism in Western countries from which different patterns of separation have evolved.[2] Writing on "multiple histories of secularism," Hashemi, for example, distinguishes the Catholic tradition from the Protestant and Eastern Orthodox experiences (Hashemi, 2010: 328–329). Nonetheless, none of the different readings of the history of secularism depicts it as a religious discourse. Rather, the political inception of separationist discourse is a recurring motif. The scope of this book does not allow for a

---

1. For Witte, this is not the only reason for the separation, particularly in American history, but he depicts it as the main reason.

2. For example, see Beaufort, 2008; Monsma & Soper, 2009.

comprehensive investigation of the origins of the various separation patterns. However, it may do us well to subject the key founders of the notion of separation—Locke and Jefferson—to close scrutiny.

It has only been 45 years since John Dunn shed light on a widely forgotten aspect of Locke's work. In his pioneering work *The Political Thought of John Locke*, Dunn recalled the striking religious characteristics of Locke's work (Dunn, 1969).[3] The latter's personal religious conviction[4] (Marshall, 1994: 1–32) and the theological dimension of his work are beyond question. However, this neither makes him a religious scholar nor a Christian theologian. By and large, political philosophy forms the core of Locke's work. The separation of church and state is articulated in *A Letter Concerning Toleration* (1689), which appears to be a political treatise rather than a theological text. The context in which Locke develops the separation of church and state is of importance in this regard. In his early years, Locke, a proponent of an authoritarian state, refuted the notion of religious pluralism. However, political instability derived from religious conflict provoked a dramatic shift in his perspective.

Religious intolerance triggered the major catastrophe that defined the character of post-Reformation Europe. Zagorin points to the 16th century as the most intolerant period in Christian history: countless thousands of people of both sides perished in the civil and external religious wars waged between the Catholics and Protestants in the 16th and 17th centuries (Zagorin, 2003: 1–2). Similarly, Chadwick maintains that "[n]owhere in Europe was religious toleration thought compatible with civil stability, and the few lone Erasmian voices who advocated it were drowned in the general call for religious uniformity, whether Protestant or Catholic" (quoted in Madeley, 2003: 47). According to Nader Hashemi, "religious toleration and political stability were thought to be negatively correlated" (2014: 4). He notes that it was widely believed that an established religion and uniformity of religious practice in the public sphere were essential to attaining peace, order, and prosperity. The sum of this logic resulted in circumstances that saw Europe faced with an existential dilemma; in terms of England, in particular, an existential political crisis threatened to tear the country apart. This politico-religious turmoil in time gave birth to notions of religious tolerance and, by extension, to the separation of state from church. Thus, in the Anglo-American tradition, political secularism emerged as a solution to this existential problem (Hashemi, 2010: 331).

---

3. Since then, many scholars have explored the religious dimension of Locke's work. For example, see Harris, 1994; Marshall, 1994; Mitchell, 1990; Parker, 2004; Waldron, 2002.

4. See Marshall, 1994: 32.

John Locke proposed the separation of church and state in response to the above religio-political dilemma. In complete contrast to the dominant idea of the time, he established a positive correlation between religious tolerance and political stability. To this end, he separated the two realms of church and state: "We must above all distinguish between political and religious matters, and properly define the boundary between church and commonwealth" (Locke & Vernon, 2010: 6). For Locke, the commonwealth (state) was an association of people constituted solely for the purpose of preserving and promoting civil goods—that is, "life, liberty, physical integrity, and freedom from pain, as well as external possessions, such as land, money, the necessities of everyday life, and so on" (Locke & Vernon, 2010: 6–7). Locke maintained that the authority of the state was confined solely to the protection and promotion of these civic goods. It had no authority over the religious domain, which he saw as a "free and voluntary association" of people.

The purpose of religious association was to all intents and purposes the public worship of God and the attainment of eternal life. In Locke's view, no one was bound by nature to the church. People joined the church in the belief that they had found true religion of their own accord. The sole reason for an individual joining a church or sect was personal: the hope of salvation. Locke wrote (using the gendered pronoun peculiar to the time):

> If he finds anything wrong with its doctrine or unseemly in its ritual, he must have the same liberty to leave as he had to enter; no bonds can be indissoluble but those attached to the certain expectation of eternal life. It is from members so united, of their own accord and for this purpose, that a church is formed (Locke & Vernon, 2010: 9).

As evident in its title, Locke's *A Letter Concerning Toleration* aimed to develop a doctrine on religious toleration and, by extension, political stability. As Hashemi suggests: "Without. . . [his] solution, Europe would not know peace, prosperity or stability" (Hashemi, 2010: 331–332). Locke's ends were thus political rather than religious. By contrast, religious secularity in Iran stems from religion. It is part of a wider religious reformation process initiated by religious scholars.

In the United States, the separation model differed that pursued in Europe. Unlike Europe, there were no religious wars in 18th-century America. However, the European experience offered America a salutary lesson in eschewing established religion. There are two overarching sources in American history referring to the separation. One is the clause in the First Amendment pertaining to religion, which reads: "Congress shall make no law respecting an establishment of religion, or prohibiting the free exercise thereof". The other source lies in Thomas Jefferson's letter to the Danbury Baptist Association of Connecticut in which he uses a phrase that has become the quintessential image for American separatism: "a wall of separation between church and state". Both texts are of a political nature and by no means should be read as theological texts. A politician who lacked a theological background, Jefferson spoke from a purely political standpoint. As Huston asserts: "Jefferson's principal motive in writing the Danbury Baptist letter was to mount a political counterattack against his Federalist enemies" (1999: 776).

The significance of the phrase in Jefferson's letter, in which protection of religion from politics is emphasized, may provoke some to argue that Jefferson's wall of separation was "one directional" as it aimed to protect religion and the church from interference by the state (Davis, 2003). Having scrutinized the context in which the letter was written, Huston sheds new light on the religious aspect of the letter. During the presidential campaign of 1800, Jefferson was charged with being an atheist. The document from the Danbury Baptist Association provided him with a timely opportunity to launch a counterattack against this charge (Hutson & Jefferson, 1999: 781–782). The defensive nature of this letter may, therefore, provide an explanation for the emphasis on religious considerations. In short, it is difficult to view religious considerations within the American experience of separation as more than peripheral. The American separatist pattern was, in effect, rooted in political rather than theological discourse.

I would like briefly to suggest here that the anti-religious and anti-clerical features of the French early experience of separation make it unnecessary to explore the French case from this perspective. It is almost impossible to argue that the French separationist experience originated from a religious standpoint.

The above-mentioned cases represent only the pioneering patterns of the separation of church and state. As suggested earlier, there were many other patterns of separation in which religious considerations may have been of more importance than those investigated here. Furthermore, and as Witte emphasizes, the arguments proposed by the pioneering advocates of separation did include religious considerations to a varying extent (Witte Jr., 2006). In general, however, I will suggest that mainstream Western separatist patterns originated from political, rather than religious, discourse. In marked contrast, the genesis of the current secularity quest in Iran is rooted in religious discourse. Its leading proponents are religious scholars, who have included religion–state relations within their broader religious reformation project.

Without denying the political dimension and consequences of religious secularity, I argue that religious considerations and motivations claim a paramount position in the currently evolving secularity discourse in Iran. This feature distinguishes Iran's contemporary secularity-seeking discourse from that of its Western counterparts. It is this feature that justifies the use of the term "religious" as an adjective to secularity.

The ultimate goal of this chapter is to illustrate the disputes brought against an all-encompassing understanding of religion. Motivated by religious concerns, reformist scholars explain the incoherent nature of the Islamic state. As an alternative, they articulate a democratic solution based on the emancipation of religion from state. This chapter also discusses the ways by which reformist scholars contest unrealistic expectations of religion, in particular the employment of religion as a political instrument. The last part of this chapter proposes arguments to discharge religion in general—and *fiqh* in particular—from the responsibility of governance.

Religious Motivations

The Iranian religious secularity discourse is led by a group of religious intellectuals and clerics who split from the ruling clergy following the proposal of a democratic understating of religion–state relations. Rather than being political theorists, key figures of the religious secularity discourse tend in the main to be religious scholars; as such, a wide range of issues pertinent to Islam constitute the bulk of their intellectual work. A brief review of these figures will demonstrate that the quest for religious secularity is rooted in their religious, rather than political, concerns. Most scholars advocating religious secularity were educated in seminaries (e.g., Mojtahed-Shabestari, Kadivar, Eshkevari, and Haeri-e Yazdi). Eshkevari, formerly a cleric, was defrocked as a result of his reformist inclinations. Soroush is an exception in this regard; he studied at Alavi School in Tehran, one of the first schools to teach a combination of modern sciences and religious studies. He did, however, travel regularly to Qom to teach and participate in seminary discussions from 1988 to 1994.

Although there are records of political activism in the professional backgrounds of Iran's religious reformists, they were generally confined to the earlier part of their careers. For example, although Mojtahed-Shabestari and Eshkevari served as members in the first parliament of the Islamic state, they soon confined their activities to scholarly works. The highest official position held by Soroush was his membership of the Cultural Revolution Council. Since then, he has not held any official position within the ruling system of Iran. For the large part, these scholars have focused their efforts and built their reputations in the realm of religious scholarship rather than a political theory.

The push towards religious emancipation was precipitated by the revisionist writings of scholars such as Abulkarim Soroush, Masha-Allah Shamsul-Vaezine, Mohammad Mojtahed-Shabestari, and Mohammad Taqi Fazel-e Mayboudi, published in the late 1980s by the monthly journal *Kayhan-e Farhangi*. The *Kayhan-e Farhangi* editorial team also published a new magazine, *Kiyan*, in 1991, which provided them with a more relaxed platform to capture the interest of new scholars. *Kiyan*, and those who contributed to this emerging discourse, played a key role in Iran's political sphere. This monthly publication became hugely influential; the "*Kiyan* circle" was a popular tag used to explain this role in Iran's political developments after the second half of the 1990s (Jahanbakhsh, 2001b: 140–143; Kamrava & Dorraj, 2008: 423; Mirsepassi, 2010: 103–148; Soroush, 2007). By the late 1980s and early 1990s, Iran's revisionist religious scholars had become increasingly alarmed by the state's gradual shift towards prioritizing political considerations over religious principles. Concern over the exploitation of religion for political ends led reformist religious scholars to propose an alternative to expedient *fiqh*, one that would discharge religion from governmental responsibility.

Discharging Religion from Governance

The ruling clergy managed to conceptualize a pragmatist solution to the inherent contradiction between their religious claims and their political responsibility by centralizing power under a single figure—that is, a Valey-e Faqih—who would possess authority over both the political and religious domains. While some among the traditionalist clergy gradually distanced themselves from the ruling clergy (Keddie & Richard, 2003: 310–311),[5] other progressive scholars developed a new discourse designed to emancipate Islam from politics. They argued that due to the lack of religious basis for governance issues in the modern age, sociopolitical and economic matters should be entrusted to human beings. Thus, a collective decision-making mechanism and civic reasoning should prevail

---

5. An outstanding example in this regard is the resignation of Ayatollah Safi Golpayegani, the chairman of the Guardian Council, who is still in the circle of conservative Ayatollahs. Following several written exchanges with Khomeini, he resigned after complaining about the shifting policy of the Islamic state. Safi Golpayegani, who emphatically objected to the violation of Islamic precepts, did not agree with the solution of expedience. For further detail, see Arjomand, 1993; Salehpour, 1995.

over religious arrangements. Ironically, reformist scholars who employ the same jurisprudential reasoning as Khomeini, argue instead for the emancipation of religion from the state.

Kadivar divides Islamic precepts into four dimensions: (a) faith and belief, (b) morality, (c) worship, and (d) social transaction. The faith dimension addresses issues such as belief in God, Judgment Day, the Prophet Mohammad, and his mission. Ethical elements of Islamic teaching establish principles for self-purification and virtue. Worship includes praying, fasting, pilgrimage and alms rules, which together express Muslims' submission to God. Lastly, social transaction addresses sociopolitical issues. Naming this dimension "*fiqh* of social transaction" (*fiqh-e moamelati*), Kadivar states that it includes precepts related to civil law, commercial law, the penal code, and international law. As such, this category encompasses political issues as well.

The bulk of the Quran is composed of the first three dimensions. According to Kadivar's assessment, 98 percent of verses from the Quran address issues related to faith, morality, and worship: only 2 percent relate to social-transaction issues. He notes a similar pattern in the hadiths. Only 10 percent of infallibles' sayings and deeds are about sociopolitical issues (Kadivar, 2009: 65–66). Kadivar concludes that Islam does not specify any particular blueprint for political matters. In fact, it explicitly avoids providing economic, political, or policy prescriptions for civilizations across space and time (Kadivar, 2004; 2006b: 44).

The human capacity to accept the responsibility of decision-making is an important criterion for Muslim thinkers' categorizations of different approaches within the Muslim world. For example, Abou El Fadl distinguishes between puritans and moderates as follows: "Moderates believe that God entrusted humans with the power of reason and the ability to ascertain between right and wrong". By contrast, a puritan's trust in the capacity of human beings is not so vast. God's law is specific and detailed, and the human being is entrusted only with the ability to practice this law (2005: 276–277). Kadivar, who uses a similar criterion to categorize the different approaches to the holy text, claims that the fundamental disagreement between historical/traditional Islam and compassionate/intellectual Islam[6] revolves around *fiqh* of social transactions. For Kadivar, reason and rationality are integral to this disagreement. The epistemological approach of historical Islam denies the capabilities of human reasoning in the face of the multifaceted aspects

---

6. "Compassionate Islam", a label initiated by Kadivar to present his modern reading of Islam, is not well settled in the literature. Soroush (2011), for example, sees use of the phrase problematic.

of contemporary life.[7] Kadivar argues that historical Islam problematizes human reasoning in the following three essential areas: (a) The lack of ability to reason and to understand justice compels human beings to rely on sacred sources of law. The logical implication is that whatever is stated in a sacred context is just. It does not matter if some of these precepts do not seem just by the logic of human reasoning. (b) The notion that human legislation will lead to social disorder because it is incapable of achieving an all-embracing grasp of the true needs of human beings. Thus, the latter must inevitably submit to the Shari'a and to the sacred lawgiver if a genuine peaceful society is to be established. And (c) the inferiority of human reasoning in comparison with God's knowledge, which mandates the superiority of Shari'a law over man-made regulations (Kadivar, 2009: 51).

In contrast to this traditional understanding of Islam, Kadivar proposes a compassionate reading of Islam in which civic reasoning is an inherent dimension of religiosity. Accordingly, anti-rationalistic logic should be resisted from compassionate Islam's point of view. Kadivar adds that this does not mean that all religious precepts are explainable by rational reasoning. Distinguishing irrationality from anti-rationality, he claims that while some religious teachings appear irrational, they are not by any means anti-rational. In short, although some religious teachings may not be explainable by rational reasoning, it does not necessarily follow that they are in conflict with reason (Kadivar, 2010b).

According to Kadivar's reading of the Shari'a, each and every one of the non-worshipping precepts included three features in the revelation era: (a) they were deemed to be rational by the conventions of the time; (b) they were deemed to be just by the conventions of the time; and (c) they were deemed to offer the best solution when compared with alternative solutions proposed by other religions (Kadivar, 2006b: 44; 2009: 67). Thus, none of the non-worshipping precepts were considered unjust, tyrannical or anti-rational according to the norms of that era (Kadivar, 2002a: 427). Kadivar further argues that believers are not expected to comply with these historical non-worshipping precepts as purely devotional precepts. Unlike the worshipping precepts, this dimension of Islamic teaching is subject to understanding by rational reasoning, as was the case in the revelation era.

Eshkevari, who uses similar jurisprudential language to argue for the necessity of non-religious arrangements in the sociopolitical arenas, divides Islamic teachings into three domains: (a) teachings about worldview, (b) teachings about principles and values, and (c) precepts (*ahkam*). He contends that

---

7. For further discussion, see Javadi-e Amoli, 2002: 60; Mesbah-e Yazdi, 1997: 39–64.

the first and second domains of the Islamic teachings are eternal and valid in different circumstances. For example, with reference to belief in the existence of God, he states: "These [sorts] of statements are subject to be proved or disproved, but they are not subject to relativity.. . . . [I]f God exists, He always exists; and, if God does not exist, He never existed.. . . . [I]t cannot be said that God existed in the era of feudalism but not in the era of capitalism" (Eshkevari, 2000b: 327–328). Eshkevari divides the third domain of Islamic teachings (i.e., the precepts) into two categories: worshipping precepts and social precepts. Similar to the two aforementioned domains, worshipping precepts are fixed in different circumstances.[8] However, social precepts are inherently variable. They can never be eternal even if they are explicitly mentioned in the Quran (Eshkevari, 2000b: 227). Since the social precepts attributable to religious sources are not applicable in the modern age, contemporary sociopolitical matters cannot be regulated by religion.

He employs another jurisprudential principle to argue for the necessity of dealing with sociopolitical issues through civic reasoning: interdependence of precepts and subject matter. A guiding jurisprudential principle sanctions that the precepts follow the subject matter. When the subject matter changes, the jurisprudential precepts will change accordingly. Religious precepts address subject matter in the sociopolitical context; they are not just theoretical or general principles. No one, Eshkevari claims, can contest the fact that the sociopolitical arenas are mutable contexts. Since subject matter does not remain constant in different spaces and times, fixed religious precepts cannot therefore be universally applicable. For this reason, Eshkevari argues, it is inevitable that religious experts assess changes in the sociopolitical contexts and provide precepts appropriate for the contemporary subject matter (2010b; 2006: 164–167).

Another jurisprudential path to promote the necessity for the emancipation of the sociopolitical arenas from a rigid understanding of sacred texts scrutinizes the roots of the precepts in the revelation era. According to the widely accepted jurisprudential discourse, religious precepts of the revelation era were divided into two categories: (a) founding precepts *(ahkam-e taasisi)* and (b) endorsed precepts *(ahkam-e emzaiee)*. The first refers to precepts that were initiated by Islam and of which there is no record of their existence in the pre-Islamic era. The second set of precepts existed in the pre-Islamic Hejaz. Instead of changing all of the extant sociopolitical and economic

---

8. Obviously there are differences between these domains; but Eshkevari combines them here in terms of their validity in the contemporary world. For example, whereas worshipping issues are matters of devotion, the domain of worldview needs to be initially accepted through logical thought in the first place.

arrangements, Islam accepted many of the established pre-Islamic conventions in the sociopolitical and economic spheres (Eshkevari, 2010b; Haeri, 1996; Kadivar, 2003c; Lotfi, 1996; Mohaqhegh Damad, 2009).

According to Eshkevari, the Prophet Mohammad did not introduce new sociopolitical and economic structures; he approved the current structures as they were, perhaps with minor changes. Eshkevari argues that if the Prophet Mohammad had emerged in a different sociopolitical context, the Islamic social precepts may have been totally different. This suggests that these precepts are not intrinsic to Islam and can be altered under different circumstances (Eshkevari, 2000b: 230–232). He states:

> If the Prophet of Islam were alive now and wanted to complete his sacred mission under the current situation, he would take the same inevitable logical and rational approach towards the social norms, traditions, and mores.. . . [F]inally [he would] make creative and effective interaction with the contemporary era (Eshkevari, 2010b).

Soroush raises a similar point by noting that had Islam emerged in India or Rome, for example, it would have differed greatly from Arabic Islam. It has already found significant divergence in difference places (Soroush, 2006a: 64). Instead of authorizing a jurist to make decisions in the name of Islam, Eshkevari suggests that groups of professionals and experts should decide these matters based on the knowledge of the time and place, and that religious leaders should be included in this process. As well as doubting whether the current jurisprudential circle demonstrates the competence to take this path (Eshkevari, 2010a), he criticizes the literal interpretation of the Quran by jurists (2010b). Proposing justice as the underpinning element for sociopolitical matters, Eshkevari maintains that understanding justice in different times and places should be based on civic reasoning. Thus, justice and reasoning are required when assessing sociopolitical matters.

In arguing for the separation of religion from sociopolitical matters, Kadivar advocates for the abolition of all religious precepts that are not just and rational in the context of the conventions of time and place. Like Eshkevari, he subscribes to the notion that most of the social-transaction precepts (*fiqh-e Moamelati* [Kadivar's term]) are endorsed precepts. Islam accepted and practiced many of the pre-Islamic rules pertaining to sociopolitical matters in order to achieve justice (Kadivar, 2002a: 427). Thus, they are only valid insofar as they are seen to be just and rational according to contemporary conventions.

Departing from the traditional method of differentiating fixed and variable precepts, Kadivar proposes justice as a criterion for distinguishing said precepts. Civic reasoning and rationality should determine if a religious precept has been issued for every place and time or if it has been a variable precept that is no longer relevant. Unlike Eshkevari, Kadivar does not propose modifying these precepts; rather, he advocates disqualifying from practice those which are outdated. "Instead of variable precepts which are outdated, rational laws ought to be issued by the collective reasoning of people and these laws must not be attributed to religion" (Kadivar, 2002a: 429). As the revelation era was very different from the contemporary sociopolitical context, most social-transaction precepts can no longer be considered rational or just. This is why, compared with the other three dimensions of Islamic teachings (precepts pertaining to faith, morality, and worship), social-transaction precepts have undergone the most variation, rendering new legislation in this area justified.

One may argue that this rationality is similar to that of expediency in Khomeini's expedient *fiqh*, which authorizes the state to exercise legislative power over divine law. This notion is well summarized by Abou El Fadl, who, with reference to contemporary Islamic states, observes that "the disintegration of the role of the Ulama and their co-optation by the modern praetorian State, with its hybrid practices of secularism, has opened the door for the State to become the maker and enforcer of the Divine law" (2003: 33–34). But, contrary to expedient *fiqh*, Kadivar raises a fundamental objection. He argues that only God and the Prophet Mohammad hold law-making jurisdiction. No one—neither jurist nor a Valey-e Faqih—is authorized to issue religious precepts. Kadivar insists that "it is not admissible to issue civic commands and attribute them to religion and the Shari'a" (2002a: 429).

The mutable nature of sociopolitical and economic matters thus forms the bedrock of reformist discourse. This contextual approach is not, however, confined to scholars who propose jurisprudential justification for religious secularity. Scholars such as Mojtahed-Shabestari and Soroush, who adopt theological and philosophical perspectives, employ contextual reasoning when advocating for religious secularity. As I will explain later in this chapter, Mojtahed-Shabestari asserts that, from the beginning, religious precepts were responses to the sociopolitical challenges of the revelation era. However, as the questions of the contemporary world are completely different, the Quran and traditions should not be expected to provide humankind with answers. In contrast to Kadivar and Eshkevari, Mojtahed-Shabestari does not address the issue of fixed and variable precepts. When it comes to political matters, Islamic sources do not offer specific orders because Islamic teachings do not specifically address contemporary questions.

Similar to Eshkevari and Kadivar, Mojtahed-Shabestari maintains justice as the principal objective of Islam. Justice is the only overarching principle to be borrowed from Islam to manage sociopolitical matters. Mojtahed-Shabestari argues that there is a fundamental difference between the orders/prohibitions of God and those of the state. For a believer, while absolute submission to God's orders/prohibitions is required, it is rooted in discretionary trust. He states: "Being sure that there are matters of God's orders/prohibitions, a believer will obey them without. . . question.. . . State authority can never be the source of this submission" (Mojtahed-Shabestari, 2005: 180). Even if state authorities claim commitment to God's orders/prohibitions, this commitment and its consequences are human phenomena and are therefore not sacred. Thus, Islam cannot be held responsible for the sociopolitical matters determined by human beings (Mojtahed-Shabestari, 2005: 170–183).

In this respect, Mojtahed-Shabestari's view is close to that of Soroush, who adds a profane feature to the different layers of religion. As I explained briefly in chapter 1, the Quran is one of the layers discussed by Soroush in his elaboration of *the essentials and accidentals in religion*. This concept expresses the inherent contradiction between Islamic precepts and state responsibilities in the contemporary era.

Soroush argues that religions in general—and Islam in particular—possess both essential and accidental dimensions. The essential dimension is an integral feature of religion. In contrast, the accidental dimension, which includes most aspects of religion, may have been initially shaped in a different format. This is why amendments to accidental dimensions do not disadvantage religion. In the contemporary era, and under different circumstances, these dimensions may find varying formats. Soroush's articulation offers fertile ground for fundamental change in religion-oriented issues. He lists eight dimensions of religion as contingent:

1. Arabic language
2. Arabic culture
3. Concepts, notions, and theories that are used in the Quran
4. Historical occurrences alluded to in the Quran
5. The Quran's answers to questions raised by believers and their opponents
6. *Fiqh* and Shari'a
7. Distortions made by opponents of Islam
8. The capacities of the believers[9]

---

9. For a detailed explanation of these accidental dimensions of Islam, see Soroush, Mobasser, & Jahanbakhsh, 2009: 63–92.

Soroush maintains that the variability of precepts is not confined to socio-political matters. Significantly, the Shari'a, taken overall, is contingent. While Kadivar and Eshkevari regard worshipping precepts as fixed, Soroush presents them as part of a contingent dimension of religion. Building on the ideas of Shah Wali-ullah Dehlvi (1703–1762), Soroush argues that worshipping precepts may have been different had Islam emerged under different circumstances. He states:

> The precepts of Shari'ah, religious customs, the form and appearance of rites of worship and other rites, and the regulations pertaining to individual and social behaviour. . . [were] originally ordained on the basis of the lives and characteristics and the spiritual, social, geographical and historical circumstances of a particular generation of people, such that, had these circumstances been different, the customs, precepts and regulations would also have taken on a different form and shape.. . . There can be no doubt that the underlying contention is that most of the precepts of *fiqh* and even its basic tenets are accidentals. Even prayers and fasting have been made proportionate to what people can endure on average. If their endurance was much greater, the obligations may well have been more severe (Soroush et al., 2009: 88–89).

Soroush's proposition poses fundamental challenges to religious claims generated in the sociopolitical sphere. Although he does not directly address the political aspects of Islamic precepts, there are significant implications for the current discussion surrounding the contradiction between religious precepts and state responsibility. Religion is not bound to these precepts and will be preserved even if these precepts undergo total change; they were not fundamental to religion even in the revelation era let alone in the context of the contemporary world.

In short, the essential contradiction between the application of Islamic precepts and the responsibilities of state provided fertile ground for groups of religious scholars to advocate for the emancipation of religion from the state. Some scholars argued that the sociopolitical precepts of Islam are neither just nor rational according to conventions of contemporary time (Kadivar and Eshkevari). Others, such as Mojtahed-Shabestari and Soroush, suggest that the sociopolitical precepts of Islam were not a part of its essence from the beginning. In either case, it is agreed that Islamic precepts cannot effectively provide a contemporary state with the means for governance, a factor evident in the re-conceptualizations and practices of the Islamic state of Iran. The ruling clergy's claim to leadership based upon religious precepts is, therefore, highly questionable. Instead of implementing Islamic precepts, the unification of religion and state has facilitated the exploitation and abuse of religion. Using Islam as a rationale for state policies has resulted in religion being held responsible for policy errors and mistakes that are, in reality, a feature of governance; as such, the emancipation of religion from the dictates of state is imperative. Questioning the all-encompassing Islam of the Iranian state, religious reformation discourses continue to assert that this approach will create unrealistic expectations and ultimately disillusionment with religion.

Unrealistic Expectations of Religion

Islamic notions of the Seal of Prophethood and of Islam being the final religion have contributed to the widely held belief that Islam provides guidelines for all aspects of life and answers to every problem that assails humankind. This assumption played an important role in the emergence of political Islam, with "Islam is the solution" (al-Islam huwa al-hal) adopted as their main slogan by Islamic movements worldwide. Through the re-reading of religious sources, Islamic movements strove to find solutions to the myriad problems facing Muslims in the modern world (Fuller, 2003: 23–33; Martin & Barzegar, 2010: 1–13; Mulcahy, 2007; Nasr, 1996: 49–140; Roy, 2001: 35–42; Tibi, 2001: 84–145). The 1979 Islamic revolution was no exception. Indeed, the doctrine of Velayat-e Faqih was constructed based on the assumption that religion is capable of offering solutions to all challenges associated with governance in the modern age. Khomeini wrote:

> [T]he laws of the shari'ah embrace a diverse body of laws and regulation[s], which amounts to a complete social system. In this system of laws, all the needs of man have been met: his dealings with his neighbors, fellow citizens, and clan, as well as [with] children and relatives; the concerns of private and marital life; regulations concerning war and peace and interaction with other nations; penal and commercial law; and regulations pertaining to trade, industry and agriculture. . . . It is obvious, then, how much care Islam devotes to government and the political and economic relations of society, with [the] goal of creating conditions conducive to the production of morally upright and virtuous human beings. The Glorious Qur'an and the Sunnah contain all the laws and ordinances man needs in order to attain happiness and the perfection of his state (1981: 43–44).

Khomeini never abandoned this all-encompassing approach to Islam. As leader of the Islamic state, he faced many fundamental problems of governance when implementing Islamic precepts. However, he denied that these problems were reflective of religion's inability to solve contemporary issues. By introducing *fiqh-ul maslaha* he justified the breaching of religious precepts. This compromise, though of course in favour of the state, was depicted instead as a feature of religion—that is, Shiite *fiqh*. Khomeini who insisted on the capability of *fiqh* to address all issues in the modern world, stated: "*[F]iqh* is the authentic and comprehensive theory for administering human and society for the whole life. The principal goal is [to find out] how we want to apply the main principles of *fiqh* to individual and social behaviours and find answers to the problems" (Ruhollah Khomeini, 2006: 98).

The Islamic state of Iran has not hesitated to add "Islamization" as an overt prefix to each and every one of its programs. From the ruling clergy's view, the shortcomings of these programs are due to poor implementation. By contrast, poor governance has led reformists to re-conceptualize the notion of the inclusiveness of religion in general and *fiqh* in particular. The claim that religion provides answers to all issues pertaining to human life does not serve religion: it encourages unrealistic expectations of religion. Religious sources including the Quran and hadiths do not include specific sociopolitical directives. What have been put in place are human arrangements in the name of religion; and, these arrangements are not free from error. As such, religion ought not to be held responsible for governance failures.

The Hereafter: The Principal Mission of Religion

"Political Islam" refers, among other things, to an understanding of religion that is capable of administering Islamic society. Religion, according to this notion, is a framework not only for setting goals, but also for providing policies required for the governance of the state. Improving the socioeconomic and political standing of Muslims has become the core aim of political Islam. In this all-encompassing notion, religion is not confined to worship; it incorporates sociopolitical dimensions. As such, religion and religiously inspired leaders have the right and ability to lead and administer Muslim countries, an extravagant claim espoused by Islamic groups on the eve of the 1979 revolution (Akhavi, 1988; Dabashi, 1993; Esmaeili, 2007: 227–476; Richard, 1981; Taqavi, 2004: 67–136).

Religious intellectuals such as Ali Shariati and Mehdi Bazargan supported Khomeini and other politically motivated clerics who were disillusioned with the passivity of traditional religious leaders. For example, Ali Shariati maintained that religion addresses worldly issues as well as the hereafter and that an accurate practice of Islamic precepts will improve the standing of Muslims in this world (Esmaeili, 2007: 397). According to Shariati:

> Religion is an idea rooted in the worldview, anthropology, and sociology. . . which determines the social, national, and economic direction of human beings as well as value systems, social systems, lifestyle and utopia for individuals and society. . . . [I]t [religion] provides answers to [questions] such as how to live, what to do right now, what you must do, and what you should be (2009: 28–29).

On the eve of the 1979 revolution, it was widely perceived that an essential part of religion had been abandoned due to the non-interventionist approach of the traditional clergy. Thus, failure to comply with the sociopolitical precepts of Islam was seen as a major reason for Iran's pre-revolutionary problems. This belief continues to be propagated by the Islamic state in post-revolutionary Iran. In fact, a basic function of religion in post-revolutionary Iran was its perceived ability to provide remedies capable of addressing the country's socioeconomic and political problems. This is why the adjective "Islamic" is widely used to describe state policies and programs.

Reformation discourses, however, challenge this understanding of the function of religion. Disillusioned by the lived experience of the Islamic state, many religious scholars have re-conceptualized their earlier ideas regarding the function of religion. Mehdi Bazargan, the first prime minister in post-revolutionary Iran, is an outstanding example in this regard even though he supplemented religion with sociopolitical functions in the pre- and post-revolutionary eras (Jahanbakhsh, 2001b: 80–112; Rajaee, 2007: 74–83, 91–126; Taqavi, 2004: 66–77).

Following his lived experience of the Islamic state, Bazargan revised his early ideas[10] about the sociopolitical function of religion. In a speech delivered in 1992, he argued that setting worldly aims for religion contradicted the spirit of the teachings of the Quran and the Prophet Mohammad. Bazargan described the pre-revolutionary era in which the notions of "religion for a better world" or "religion for society" emerged as a reaction to ideas promulgated by the West, which blamed Islam for the country's backwardness. Believers with full confidence in Islam retaliated by introducing the axiom that Islam "includes the best moral, social and governmental precepts" (Bazargan,

---

10. Among his other publications, in 1969 Bazargan (1998) published a book titled *Bi'that va Idiolozhi*, in which he explicitly demonstrated Islamic precepts applicable to the state in the contemporary world.

1995: 47).[11] Bazargan asserted that this reading of Islam accorded with the intellectuals', the clerics' and the youthful cohort's inclinations to institute radical reform of the country's sociopolitical arena. As such, "a blessed marriage of religion and world happened" from which the Islamic Revolution emerged (Bazargan, 1995: 48).

Having declared that this reading of Islam was contradictory to the spirit of Islam, Bazargan introduced two ultimate goals for religion: God and the hereafter. Reviewing the Quran, he concluded that jurisprudential precepts accounted for only 2 percent of its content. By contrast, he argued, every page and verse of the Quran expressed "directly or indirectly, explicitly or implicitly concern about God and the hereafter" (Bazargan, 1995: 52). Bazargan continued, saying that the social precepts of the Quran aim to facilitate believers' devotion to God; and, if these precepts have impacted on the worldly lives of Muslims, it is only a subsidiary outcome, not the main goal. After scrutinizing the verses about alms, he asserted that they promise next-worldly rewards; the Quran, according to Bazargan, did not invite Muslims to give alms in order to achieve economic growth. According a sociopolitical function to religion, Bazargan listed seven disadvantages,[12] six of which were detrimental to religion. He stated:

> If worldly issues and their improvement are not pictured as a goal and responsibility of religion, religion won't be charged with deficiency and incompetence. It won't be said that [Islamic] principles and precepts do not include. . . the comprehensive and complete ground rules required for political, social and economic issues of the society (Bazargan, 1995: 54).

Bazargan concluded that from a religious point of view, there was no difference between governance and other material issues: "Islam and the Prophet have not taught us cooking, gardening, ranching and housekeeping. As [these issues] are left to us to be managed via employing our wisdom, experiences and skills,. . . economic, management and political issues are our responsibilities as well" (1995: 56).

Emancipating sociopolitical arenas from religious sanctity and entrusting these arenas to human reasoning is one of the key features of the evolving religious secularity. Similar to Bazargan, Mohsen Kadivar argues for the

---

11. Esposito and Voll (1996: 56–58) offer a similar argument, addressing one of the sources of the emergence of Islam as the solution.

12. For further explanation of these disadvantages, see Bazargan, 1995: 58–61.

necessity of managing sociopolitical matters through civic reasoning rather than religious sources. Kadivar contests the traditional understanding of Islam as all-encompassing. For him, human beings have spiritual needs that religion nourishes, and governance extends beyond this realm. He contends that even though human rationality is a principal element in Islam (Kadivar, 2010b), "religion is not established to organize politics, to manage our economy, and to shoulder management responsibility. We are capable of assuming these responsibilities. Human beings can deal with politics, the economy, and management by making use of human wisdom and experience" (Kadivar, 2005b).

Differentiating Religion from Political Ideology

Both Bazargan and Kadivar contest the perception that "Islam is the solution", particularly in the political realm. Along with Bazargan and Kadivar, Soroush upholds the notion that religion's role is to address next-worldly and spiritual issues. Viewing religion as a means of addressing worldly matters opens up the possibility of transforming religion into a political ideology. Soroush states: "If religion had put worldly matters aside, [religious] ideology would have been eliminated as well" (1996b: 5).

Soroush asserts that in reaction to the reformation in the West, Islamic scholars in the modern age ironically promoted the secularization of religion,[13] according to which worldly matters become the principal concern of Islam. Although the hereafter is not effaced from this Muslim worldview, it becomes subsidiary to worldly well-being. Twentieth-century reformers were of the opinion that making a better life in this world would lead to a better hereafter. Such an ideology, by focusing on worldly matters, furnished religion with sociopolitical functions (Soroush, 1996b: 7–8). Soroush, objecting to this articulation, argues that the main function of religion is to inform and lead human beings in issues pertaining to the hereafter (1994c: 12).

Addressing the subject of socioeconomic development in non-Islamic countries, Soroush maintained that there is no correlation between being Islamic and pro-development. It cannot be assumed that because a country is Muslim it should automatically be developed. Development and making a better life in this world are extra-religious issues that depend upon the ways in which governance is managed (Soroush, 1996a: 312–318). He contradicts

---

13. Soroush (2008b) used this term as the title of a speech he delivered in 1995.

his mentor, Ali Shariati, who is widely cited as the ideologue of modern political Islam in Iran.[14] Objecting to the employment of religion as a political pamphlet, Soroush enumerates six reasons why religion cannot function as a political ideology. These reasons include:

- The Prophet Mohammad never presented religion as an ideology; the Quran is not a codified book. The holy book is of an untidy order, and thus, Islam can never be confined to a specific framework.
- Religion is full of secrets and transcendental wonders. Clarity, lucidity, and precision, which are necessary features of an ideology, do not exist in religion.
- Religion is not established for a particular society or time. This is why it is eternal and everlasting. However, ideologies are formed to address a particular society in a particular time. Therefore, they are provisional.
- Ideology is only a theory for an establishment phase *(doran-e taasis)*, but religion is a theory for both the establishment and settlement phases *(doran-e esteghrar)*;
- Religion, as an ideological framework, will be reduced to its exoteric layer only—that is, the esoteric dimensions of religion will be abandoned.
- Finally, ideology aims to move in a particular political direction, and it will restrict religion to fit that direction (Soroush, 1993: 10–11).

In his *The Theoretical Expansion and Constriction of Shari'a*, Soroush argues that it is impossible to reach a single and ultimate understanding of Islam. However, transforming religion into a political ideology is to cast it in a definitive and fixed model. "The use of religion as a political tool also undermines the depth and complexity of religious understandings to the imperatives of a temporary political struggle" (cited in Vakili, 2001: 156).

Soroush's refutation of reducing religion to a political ideology brings him in line with the concerns of Bazargan and Kadivar, who maintain that genuine religion targets the hereafter and seeks next-worldly happiness. Soroush argues that worldly issues are religion's concern only as long as they serve next-worldly happiness. This does not mean that religion provides a plan of action for worldly matters, which is the case with political ideologies.

---

14. Shariati, who is known as the main ideologue of the Islamic revolution, converted Islam into a political ideology and played a leading role among the intellectuals and the educated. For a detailed explanation of his political thought and role in the 1979 revolution, see Abedi, 1986; Abrahamian, 2008: 143–149; Akhavi, 2013; Chatterjee, 2011; Dabashi, 1993: 103–146; Ghamari-Tabrizi, 2008; Mahdavi, 2014: 38–44; Rahnama, 1994; Rajaee, 2007: 131–140; Richard, 1981.

He further states: "Planning should include the economy, population, public education. . . all of which are the products of logical arrangements of human beings. Religion cannot replace rationality in these arenas" (Soroush, 2008d: 198). It goes without saying that a state's responsibility extends beyond religious issues. It includes a wide range of sociopolitical, economic, and cultural tasks that require planning. Dealing with these worldly matters entails a process of governance.

As suggested above, claiming that religion offers blueprints for a range of sociopolitical and economic issues gives rise to unrealistic expectations from religion. Furthermore, governance cannot be free from mistakes and failures. Therefore, labelling governance with religious tags may result in placing the blame on religion for governance failures. Emancipating Islam from both unrealistic expectations and false responsibility, religious secularity promotes the notion that Islam does not include a blueprint for governance. Due to the jurisprudential nature of the Islamic state in contemporary Iran, *fiqh* requires particular attention in this regard. For this reason, religion's inability to provide a blueprint for contemporary governance will now be discussed from two perspectives: religion in general and *fiqh* in particular.

Extra-Religious Nature of Governance

The ruling clergy's all-encompassing approach to religion is based on the premise that Islam fulfils all human needs, irrespective of whether they are worldly or other-worldly. They hold that religion addresses both the materialistic and spiritual needs of believers and provides them with instructions for governance (Haghighat, 2010: 49–50). In contrast, the religious secularity discourse maintains that Muslims cannot rely on religious sources such as the Quran, the hadiths, and Islamic history to manage governance and worldly affairs in the contemporary era. This limitation entails the necessity of employing non-religious sources and mechanisms. In this context, Mojtahed-Shabestari's commentary on the nature of religious knowledge and regulation significantly contributes to the religious-reformation discourse. It expounds the necessity of complementing religious sources with extra-religious sources (Sadri, 2001: 261). Mojtahed-Shabestari maintains that it is not the duty of prophets and the holy texts to provide clear guidelines on building social, political, and economic structures (2005: 158).

To elucidate his point, Mojtahed-Shabestari reviews the histories of other prophets and religions to further argue that changing sociopolitical and economic structures have never been the mission of religion. If a prophet such as Mohammad could manage to make significant changes in the sociopolitical structure of the day, it was a result of his personal engagement with political activities. The Prophet Mohammad indeed attained success in the sociopolitical spheres, but this engagement was entirely separate from his religious mission (Mojtahed-Shabestari, 1997: 126). Mojtahed-Shabestari divides the content of religious sources into two categories: fixed and variable. Broad principles such as justice and freedom fall within the fixed and everlasting category. Issues pertaining to the sociopolitical spheres are categorized as variable (Mojtahed-Shabestari, 1995: 297–300; 2003; Vahdat, 2000b: 38).

Mojtahed-Shabestari asserts that there is no contradiction between the nature of prophecy and the right of man to master his own destiny.[15] Prophets in the main have been cast as messengers rather than political rulers. "It should be said that each and every religion relegates the establishing of social organizations and the setting of goals for sociopolitical organizations to human beings" (Mojtahed-Shabestari, 2005: 219). Islam, then, should not be expected to provide instructions for governance in the contemporary world. *Fiqh*, theology, and theosophy constitute forms of knowledge, among others, which facilitate the religious experience. While the knowledge required for governance is absent from the holy book and from Islamic knowledge in general, the authorities of the Islamic state of Iran repeatedly promulgate Islamic sources as the cornerstone of the country's post-revolutionary political system. Mojtahed-Shabestari states:

> Development is a social goal that should be pursued by citizens of a given society through their own free will. (It is obvious that development has become inevitable in the contemporary world). [Muslims] should seek the required knowledge [for development] themselves or get it from the developed countries. The intervention of the [holy] book and traditions in the development of Muslim societies is just for setting the final moral goals of the development, which should not contradict the principles of the moral values of the book and traditions. All blueprints for development ought to be provided by modern sciences (1997: 89).

Mojtahed-Shabestari's argument is compelling given that it is based on his lived experience of the Islamic state of Iran. His challenge to the ruling clergy

---

15.   There is repeated reference to a principle that is rooted not only in an article in the Constitution of the Islamic Republic of Iran, but also in many Quranic verses. Article 56 of the Constitution reads: "Absolute sovereignty over the world and man belongs to God, and it is He Who has made man master of his own social destiny. No one can deprive man of this divine right, nor subordinate it to the vested interests of a particular individual or group".

scrutinizes the objective reality of the Islamic state. To this end, he argues that the macro-policies implemented by the Islamic state were formulated by a process of planning. These policies' failures and successes were neither derived from the holy book nor from Islamic traditions (Mojtahed-Shabestari, 2005: 194–195).

Mojtahed-Shabestari writes that civic reasoning early after the 1979 revolution resulted in the construction of a Constitution based on modern political philosophy and the social sciences (2005: 28). By contrast, religious sources can never provide clear instructions for constructing a modern political system: "Can we write a constitution in the contemporary world through accumulating tens of fatwas? Is the Constitution of the Islamic Republic of Iran a combination of fatwas or is it an outcome of fatwas?" (Mojtahed-Shabestari, 1998: 39). Mojtahed-Shabestari, who like Kadivar objects to labelling governance and policy issues as "Islamic," argues that simply applying Islamic tags does not make these agencies religious; furthermore, it is unacceptable to depict routine state governance as derived from Islamic precepts (Mojtahed-Shabestari, 2005: 25–27).

Irrespective of whether a state is religious or non-religious, it carries specific social, political, economic, and cultural responsibilities. Soroush argues that, in essence, the state's task in these arenas has little to do with religion. Branding these responsibilities as "Islamic" neither changes their nature nor the ways in which they ought to be approached. Soroush asserts that, like other states, the Islamic state is a human construction. Its religious title does not set it apart from other states except for its ostensible aim to be in the service of believers (1996c: 11). As governance is essentially an extra-religious endeavour, an Islamic state cannot be different from other states in terms of function or form.

Issues pertaining to public life such as education, economy, and health care require civic reasoning. In modern times, Soroush argues, religion cannot effectively manage these arenas; rather, the social sciences such as sociology, economics, and public administration comprise the more proper tools for governance (cited in Jahanbakhsh, 2001b: 157). The key issues regarding governance are the methods employed to attain the proposed goals. Soroush maintains that scientific-experimental issues are extra-religious (1996c: 6). Moreover, the engagement of religious sources in these matters does not obviate the need for other forms of knowledge. Responding to a question about two medical books written by infallible Imams,[16] Soroush maintains that these books were not written as part of the Imams' religious missions

16. *Teb-ul Sadeq* and *Teb-ul Reza* were respectively written by Imam Sadeq and Imam Reza.

(2008d: 275). Ibn Khaldūn, a medieval Islamic historian and philosopher, in his magnum opus *al-Muqaddima*, addressed the same issue and distinguished these aspects of religious sources from the Prophet's core message. He wrote: "The medicine mentioned in religious tradition is of the (Bedouin) type. It is in no way part of the divine revelation.. . . Muhammad was sent to teach us religious law. He was not sent to teach us medicine or any other ordinary matter (Ibn Khaldūn, Rosenthal, & Dawood, 2005: 387).

Pursuing the same path, Soroush insists that by no means does the existence of some scientific issues within religious sources suggest that Muslims should ignore modern science and solely rely upon religious sources to solve their contemporary problems. He further maintains that there is no difference between issues pertaining to governance and medical or engineering issues as they are all scientific and methodological matters, and cannot be considered the responsibility of religion (Soroush, 1996c: 6; 2006a: 65–67).

Fiqh *and Governance*

The centrality of *fiqh* in both the theory and practice of politics in post-revolutionary Iran has contributed to its centrality within the reformation discourses. Indeed, the ruling clergy has claimed the competency of *fiqh* to provide instruction on all governance-related issues. *Fiqh,* the most exterior layer of religion, includes more sociopolitical precepts than other dimensions of religion such as theology, philosophy, and morality. This is why jurisprudential precepts are the main sources of justification for those who argue that religion should dictate and govern public life (Soroush, 2008d: 253).

Fiqh, which is inherently about religious law, addresses the legal aspects of the individual and social lives of Muslims. The mandate of the jurists is to establish and constantly update Islamic law based on the Quran and the hadiths. The Shari'a is, therefore, the principal production of *fiqh.* However, both the doctrine of Velayat-e Faqih and the particular praxis of the Islamic state of Iran have expanded the functions and competency of *fiqh.* For example, in a message to the clergy about the future strategy of the Islamic state, Khomeini stated:

A jurist should possess perspicacity, intelligence and ingenuity to lead a big Islamic society. . . and should be manager and schemer.. . . Governance represents the practical features of *fiqh* to deal with all social, political, military and cultural problems. *Fiqh* is the authentic and comprehensive theory of administering humans and society from the cradle to the grave [for the whole life time] (2006: 98).

The unification of religion and governance in the Islamic state has in effect attempted to apply jurisprudential solutions to the country's sociopolitical and economic problems. Religious secularity, on the other hand, argues that *fiqh* cannot effectively manage and administer public life; jurists are not entitled to exercise political authority on the sole basis of their competence in *fiqh*.[17] Soroush locates the root of this misconception in notions of the "seal of prophethood" (*khatm-e nobowat*) and "accomplishment of religion" (*kamal-e din*).

Morteza Motahhari (1920–1979), a prominent ideologue of the Islamic revolution, argued that *fiqh* constitutes the eternality of Islam; as *fiqh* is dynamic and capable of addressing issues in different times and places via *ijtihad*, there is no need for a new prophet or a new religion (Motahhari, 1992: 40–56). For Soroush, this understanding of the notion of the finality of the prophethood comes partly from the dominance of *fiqh* in Islamic history. To counter this understanding, Soroush argues that the notion of finality is the seal of prophethood, not the seal of interpretation. In other words, after the Prophet Mohammad, no one possesses the authority to dictate their understanding of religion to others. "The message of the finality is that we perceive no understanding of religion as final. . . and no religious understanding should become official religion and unified with power" (Soroush, 2006a: 159). The notion of finality, according to Soroush, also means that there is no need for another prophet. This cannot be materialized except through the recognition of realistic expectations from religion (Soroush, 2006a: 155–159). Creating unrealistic expectations from religion will result in disappointment in Islam.

Distinguishing between accomplishment and inclusiveness, Soroush argues that the Quranic verse about the accomplishment of religion[18] does not mean that Islam includes answers to each and every issue.[19] Islam is complete in terms of its particular mission and purpose; but there are innumerable issues that are not mentioned in the Quran. This does not mean, however, that the Quran is imperfect; it is perfect, but only serves its particular aim. Soroush argues that by no means was religion established to teach

---

17. The next part of the current research will focus on explaining how religious reformation discourse challenges jurists' competency to exercise political authority.

18. "This day have I perfected your religion for you and completed my favour unto you, and have chosen for you as religion al-Islam".

الْيَوْمَ أَكْمَلْتُ لَكُمْ دِينَكُمْ وَأَتْمَمْتُ عَلَيْكُمْ نِعْمَتِي وَرَضِيتُ لَكُمُ الإِسْلَامَ دِيناً

Verse 5.3

19. Soroush (1998b) proposes the notion of minimalist religion, according to which it offers minimal guidance, not maximal, even in those areas wherein religion has its say. These sayings do not nullify the need to use extra-religious sources. See Soroush, 1998b.

men sciences that can be achieved through reasoning (Soroush, 1998b: 4–5; 2008d: 274–276). One of these sciences is *fiqh*, which does not differ from other knowledge produced by humans. And, while the Quran and hadiths are the main sources of *fiqh*, this does not make *fiqh* an all-encompassing body of knowledge.

Soroush maintains that *fiqh* is incapable of providing clear and complete solutions to governance in the contemporary world (1994c: 2–16; 1998b: 2–9). As a science produced by humans, *fiqh* is essentially speculative. And, since sciences are continuously evolving and unfinished, Soroush concludes that all sciences, including *fiqh*, are subject to deficient, mortal, and fleeting vagaries (cited in Boroujerdi, 1996: 167). In order to invalidate *fiqh*'s claim in the political sphere, Soroush claims that *fiqh* is only the science of law in an Islamic sense[20] and that issues pertaining to public life are much broader than legal issues. To this end, he writes:

> *Fiqh* is religious law; like extra-religious arenas and non-religious societies wherein there are legal systems to deal with worldly issues and disputes. . . . *[F]iqh* or law is responsible only for legal issues. Now we may ask are all social issues legal? Do we not have any other problems except legal problems? If we think that all social problems are legal, then *fiqh* will be the answer for all problems. . . . [B]ut it is evident that legal issues are just a small part of issues in life (Soroush, 1994c: 13).

Soroush further argues that contemporary legal issues cannot all be derived from Islamic *fiqh*, let alone prescriptions for political, social, and economic matters (2006a: 157–158). He emphasizes the significant difference between religious precepts and governance. *Fiqh* is responsible for issuing religious precepts, which is not the same as governing and addressing a country's sociopolitical and economic challenges. The complex nature of problems pertaining to contemporary public life renders them beyond *fiqh*'s ability to manage. Even full compliance with jurisprudential rules does not make a society prosperous. "For example, if 99 percent of marriages in a given society end in divorce, and couples divorce according to jurisprudential precepts, such a society is a jurisprudential society; but it is not a prosperous one" (Soroush, 1994c: 14).

Soroush observes that most issues pertaining to public life are non–legal-jurisprudential issues for which jurists cannot provide expertise. This is why jurisprudential texts, both in the contemporary world and in

---

20. Worshipping is one of the main areas addressed by *fiqh*. Obviously, here Soroush talks only about the social dimension of *fiqh*.

an historical framework, lack clear directions when addressing sociopolitical issues (Soroush, 1994c: 11–16; 1996a: 54–63). Similar to Kadivar and
Mojtahed-Shabestari, Soroush opposes the employment of "Islam" as a
tag for state policies. And, while one may argue that jurists use rational
methods to manage sociopolitical issues, Soroush contends that "dealing
with social and worldly issues through rational reasoning is a task which
is undertaken all over the world. There is no need to label it religious"
(Soroush, 1998b: 4).

As suggested above, *fiqh*–politics relations have captured the particular
attention of reformist scholars. Historically speaking, there have been strong
connections between *fiqh* and politics, whereas the issue of governance
has never attracted significant attention from a philosophical perspective
(Haghighat, 2010: 48). According to Soroush, governance is about rules and
regulations; by contrast, *fiqh* is charged with setting rules within a specifically religious context. This is why religious governance in Islamic history
has always been about *fiqh*. In Islamic history, not only have there been rare
philosophical discussions about governance, but these rare cases have always
been confined to scholarly circles (Soroush, 1996c: 2).

Mojtahed-Shabestari advances this point. For him, jurists rely only on
legal opinion and jurisprudential precepts and have never ventured into the
challenging terrain of sociopolitical philosophy. He explains how Islamic *fiqh*
lacks rational and philosophical thinking about governance: "In this intellectual framework [*fiqh,*] there is no place for a rational idea of politics. It is just
issuing fatwas. Exploratory analysis and rational reasoning do not have any
place in this framework" (Mojtahed-Shabestari, 2001: 9). Mojtahed-Shabestari
further states that political theories must be formulated through rational
and philosophical reasoning; jurisprudential precepts are about religious
responsibilities that require obedience. In his view, a *fiqh*-based state will
disadvantage both religion and politics. Religion is a benediction, a blessed
and peremptory discourse, not a discourse based on ideology or rational philosophy. If transformed into an ideology, religion loses its essential spirit
(Mojtahed-Shabestari, 1999: 13; 2001: 11).

Similar to Soroush, Mojtahed-Shabestari claims that the regulatory nature
of *fiqh* may mislead some to conclude that governance is a jurisprudential
issue. However, the main sources of *fiqh* (i.e., the Quran and traditions) do
not offer any framework and instruction in this regard. He further argues
that *fiqh* provides Muslims with instructions for a religious lifestyle; but there
is no religious or rational basis from which to expand this to the sociopolitical context (Mojtahed-Shabestari, 1998: 37–38). Insisting that most sociopolitical issues are modern phenomena and are not included in jurisprudential

sources, Mojtahed-Shabestari contends that issuing new fatwas about particular sets of social and political issues cannot lead to cognate relations between *fiqh* and politics, which are of a scientific and philosophical nature (Mojtahed-Shabestari, 1998: 31–33).

Responding to the claim that *fiqh* can provide solutions for all problems in contemporary Muslim countries, Mojtahed-Shabestari asserts that this notion denies the ability of human knowledge and its capacity to organize society (cited in Vahdat, 2000b: 40). Referring to the early Islamic era when a perceived dogmatic and ignorant group claimed that all living mechanisms and principles must be derived from the holy book and traditions, he argues that had Muslims submitted to this understanding, there would be no trace of Islamic civilization today (Mojtahed-Shabestari, 1996: 57). He is adamant that *fiqh* is incapable of governing a political system in the contemporary world. "Jurisprudential science cannot be the source of planning. It is a form of legal interpretation, which deals with the [holy] book and traditions. *Fiqh* can neither explain the realities of society nor provide mechanisms to make changes in society (Mojtahed-Shabestari, 1995: 300).

Due to its association with political power in contemporary Iran, *fiqh* faces fierce criticism from reformist scholars. However, there are some supportive voices within the reformation discourse, and Mohsen Kadivar's intellectual project is a good example in this regard. On the one hand, he attempts to shed light on the internal diversity of *fiqh*, in particular when it comes to *fiqh*–politics relations; on the other, he emphasizes the importance of *fiqh* in the religious context. For him, *fiqh* and the Shari'a are not only inseparable parts of religion, but are also the most visible dimension of Islam (Kadivar, 2010c). He invites reformist scholars to treat *fiqh* according to its intrinsic value, so as to locate it in its authentic place within the sociopolitical context.

Compared to other reformist scholars, Kadivar provides a more detailed analysis of the sociopolitical standing of *fiqh*, postulating that since laws should not contradict religious principles in an Islamic country, the principal role of *fiqh* in the sociopolitical sphere is in the process of legislation. This, of course, does not mean that members of parliament should be jurists; only legislations inherently related to religion should be assessed from a jurisprudential perspective (Kadivar, 2003b).

Kadivar elaborates on various mechanisms for this monitoring process, all of which differ from the autocratic method adopted by the Islamic state. However, he does not clarify how any possible contradiction between religious principles and the people's will should be resolved. For example, does *fiqh* have the right to veto legislation in contradictory cases? Nonetheless,

Kadivar joins other reformist scholars in their attempts to defuse the exaggerated capability of *fiqh*. He directly challenges Ayatollah Khomeini from a jurisprudential perspective:

> It is said that *fiqh* is capable of answering all of the problems [that men deal with] from the cradle to the grave. [It is said that] all political, economic, cultural and military dilemmas can be solved by *fiqh*. This claim is too extravagant. This kind of *fiqh* is not born; basically, it is impossible to have such a *fiqh*. This is just an illusion. If successful, *fiqh* can only solve legal issues within religious jurisdiction (Kadivar, 2010d).

In contrast to Soroush and Mojtahed-Shabestari, Kadivar is not of the opinion that *fiqh* is equivalent to a science of law. However, he proposes that *fiqh* has distinct connotations of law. It correlates significantly with other social sciences and humanities, supplying them with legal branches such as constitutional law, the law of commerce, and civil and criminal law. Nevertheless, *fiqh* does not obviate the need for other social sciences. Kadivar, providing the example that commercial law does not eliminate the need for economics, adds that an economic planning task could never be delegated to business lawyers alone (2010d).

For Kadivar, science and expertise are key features of compassionate Islam. Religious piety and *fiqh* cannot effectively replace other forms of knowledge. He sees the social sciences as playing the most important role in leading a society and by no means considers *fiqh* sufficiently competent to represent these sciences. Emphasizing the recent campaign mounted by the Islamic state against the social sciences,[21] Kadivar states that the defiant attitude of the ruling clergy towards the social sciences is anti-Islamic and is at best rooted in ignorance (2010b).

Jurisprudential protocol demands that in the process of issuing fatwas, jurists should address the general principles surrounding an issue rather than focus on specific cases. When asked about specific cases, jurists invariably respond very generally without directly mentioning the particular case.

---

21. Universities made an effective contribution to the post-election protests in 2009. The state reacted by launching a campaign against the humanities at the universities, particularly the social sciences. One of the key reformists, Saeed Hajjarian, was forced to confess that he had cooperated with Western philosophers to launch a colourful revolution in Iran. Khamanei, the supreme leader, made a speech against the humanities and their curricula in Iran's universities, accusing them of copying Western countries' curricula. The campaign to revise the humanities and social sciences, which started both as an official policy and a media campaign, is on-going.

As a result, the application of these guidelines for specific cases is left to the emulators (Montazeri, 2006a: 31). Kadivar, who employs this protocol to challenge the misplacement of *fiqh* in the current political structure, argues that from a jurisprudential viewpoint, most of the issues pertaining to the political sphere and state administration are of a case-by-case nature. Therefore, he concludes, jurists should not directly intervene by providing answers or plans appertaining to political cases and administrative decisions. Moreover, becoming a learned jurist is a lifetime commitment that leaves little time for an aspirant to achieve competence in the political sphere. For this reason, the knowledge of learned jurists about political issues may well be limited (Kadivar, 2002b; 2003b).

Ayatollah Montazeri's effort to revise his early political thought provides a good example of the ways in which reformist ideas have expanded to include the traditional segment of the religious strata. The application of the doctrine of absolute Velayat-e Faqih channels enormous power into the hands of one single person, the Supreme Leader. The outcome of this autocratic articulation provoked Ayatollah Montazeri to revise his early thought on the roles of jurists in the Islamic state. Initially a pioneer advocate of the political competence of *fiqh*, Montazeri ultimately promoted the constraint of jurist authority on religious issues. His later works paid particular attention to despotism, signalling much of his concern vis-à-vis the *fiqh*-interventionist approach.

Abandoning his early idea about the necessity for Velayat-e Faqih to supervise all state powers, Montazeri provided jurisprudential justification for the necessity of the segregation of powers. As explained in chapter 1, Montazeri saw citizens as the sources of state authority. He furthered this concept by suggesting that people could either opt for the segregation of powers or the empowerment of one jurist to exercise authority over the main segments of governance: issuing fatwas (legislature), sitting in judgment (judiciary), and administration (executive). As the fulfilment of the ultimate goals of Islam in the sociopolitical sphere is the main concern, subjects could choose between different formulas (Montazeri, 2006a).[22] Contrary to other reformists who adamantly rejected the political leadership of Kadivar, Soroush, and Mojtahed-Shabestari, Montazeri considered it a viable option if the people opted for it.

---

22. In Montazeri's early writings, the sociopolitical dimensions of Islam necessitated the political leadership of jurists. For further discussion, see Kadivar, 2010d; Montazeri, 2000d: 55–78.

The people may, therefore, entrust all three segments of governance to a jurist. But, from Montazeri's perspective, experience and civic reasoning suggest that this articulation leads to despotism and corruption (Montazeri, 2008: 13–14). Referring to a variety of hadiths, Montazeri argued for the necessity of delegating tasks in public life to more knowledgeable people. Those who aspired to administer the country should be sufficiently competent to shoulder such a responsibility.

Montazeri introduced a new notion of religious emulation to invalidate the justification for jurists' authority over emulators in the sociopolitical spheres. He deemed fatwas issued by Marja-e Taghlid non-obligatory for his emulators unless they were personally assured of the accuracy of each fatwa (Kadivar, 2010d; Montazeri, 2008: 14). Through this innovative understanding of fatwas, Montazeri transformed the devotional nature of jurist–emulator relations into a rational articulation. The jurisprudential principal of the emulation did not necessitate obedience to jurists specifically in the sociopolitical sphere wherein *fiqh* may not demonstrate high competence. This led Montazeri to confine the authority of Velayat-e Faqih to religious matters. In support of his opinion, he stated:

He [Valey-e Faqih] cannot interfere in all affairs, particularly the ones that fall outside his area of expertise, such as complex economic issues, or issues of foreign policy and international relations.. . . The most important point to be highlighted is that Islam is for the separation of powers and does not recognize the concentration of power in the hand[s] of a fallible human being (quoted in Abdo, 2001: 11).

As a high-ranking member of the most traditional cluster of jurists in the Shiite school, Ayatollah Montazeri maintained his preference for jurists' sociopolitical engagement. However, as explained earlier, he introduced certain restrictions upon their roles. It goes without saying that Montazeri's understanding of *fiqh*'s sociopolitical engagement was not exactly progressive. However, considering his distinguished position within the very traditional segment of the religious nexus, as well as his political-scholarly background,[23] his revisionist approach underpins the far-reaching reform that is taking place

---

23. Both politically and scholarly he had a pioneering role in promoting the doctrine of Velayat-e Faqih. He played a key role in the inclusion of the doctrine in the Constitution; and some say that it was he who suggested this inclusion. In terms of scholarly works, he produced more work than Khomeini. For example, he published four volumes on the doctrine, which provide more detailed discussions of the concept than Khomeini's one volume book.

today within the religious context in Iran. It is an indication of the widespread anxiety within the religious nexus over state–religion relations.

The jurisprudential nature of the Islamic state represents a distinguishing characteristic of the contemporary political system of Iran. *Fiqh* is the exclusive territory of clerics. Because *fiqh* is depicted as capable of offering directions for governance, clerics are accorded a unique position to assume the leadership of the country. In other words, clerics are considered the most learned people when it comes to jurisprudential principles, which provide direction for leading the country. They are the most eligible group for political leadership solely because of their competence in *fiqh*. This simple logic has had a formative impact on Iran's post-revolutionary political mosaic. The omnipresence of the clergy in Iran's sociopolitical and economic spheres has led to a fundamental change in clergy–state relations. Furthermore, the simultaneous claim to political and religious authority by a single cleric (i.e., Valey-e Faqih) has merged religion and state into one single institution. The details of this unique setting, the negative impacts it has had on both religion and the clergy, and the critiques of the clergy's direct political leadership are discussed in the following chapters.

4

Political Construction of Clericalism

THE HEGEMONIC NATURE of the ruling clergy is the most distinctive feature of Iran's political system. Along with other characteristics, the clergy's exclusive right to rule the country mandates its non-secular nature. Iran is one of the rare examples wherein religious leaders directly assume political leadership. Distinguishing between constitutional theocracy and pure theocracy, Hirschl asserts that "in a pure theocracy the supreme religious leader is also the highest political leader" (2010: 2). According to this distinction, the Islamic state envisioned by the Prophet Mohammad in the early seventh century, and its emulation in Mahdist Sudan of the late 19th century, are two examples of a pure theocracy. Insofar as Iran's ruling clergy claim both political and religious authority, one could also categorize Iran as a pure theocracy.

The doctrine of Velayat-e Faqih grants superior authority—both in the political and religious realms—to a cleric solely because of his religious credentials. The ultimate authority of the Valey-e Faqih in political procedures is beyond question: it has been repeatedly proven that the Valey-e Faqih can override all political authority and procedures.[1] However, exercising supreme authority over the religious domain is somewhat controversial: establishing a hierarchical structure and setting a supreme authority among Shiite clerics contradicts the founding principles of Shiite jurisprudence. This may explain why the ruling clergy have established supreme authority over the religious strata only gradually.

---

1. In Iran's political lexicon, the term *hukm-e kukomati* (governmental decree) implies the supreme authority of the Valey-e Faqih, according to which he can veto decisions made by other political bodies beyond the legal procedure.

The ruling clergy are not the sole representatives of religion. Other clerics favour alternative politico-religious discourses. On the eve of the 1979 revolution, Khomeini's political discourse did not enjoy the support of the country's senior clerics, the established Marja-e Taghlids. Accordingly, in the post-revolutionary era the majority of the senior clerics remains apolitical, opting not to support the clergy's political leadership, an approach that is still popular among the traditional circle of the religious strata. For this group, a new generation of clerics should be included—that is, those who adhere to the reformist discourse. Disillusioned by the authoritarian excesses of the Islamic state, a group of clerics and lay religious intellectuals, who supported the establishment of the Islamic state in the 1970s and later contributed to its institutionalization in the 1980s, have re-conceptualized the notion of the clergy's political leadership.

As discussed in chapter 2, there has been a discernible shift in state–religion relations in post-revolutionary Iran. While the early years after the 1979 revolution were marked by the dominance of religion over politics, subsequent years have seen a shift to the supremacy of politics over religion. Nowadays, the ruling clergy in general, and the Valey-e Faqih in particular (Ayatollah Khamanei), do not have the highest credentials within the clerical establishment. This is why the ruling clergy's efforts to claim superior authority over the broader religious strata are deeply contested to say the very least.

In the Islamic state of Iran, the ruling clergy may claim neither sole representation of religion nor superior religious credentials. However, membership to the institution of the clergy, rather than blood, ethnicity, or the vote of the people, is the main justification for their exclusive power in Iran's political mosaic. This specifically places Iran's politico-religious structure among the rare cases of pure theocracy. By comparing this with the pre-secular Western experiences, we will see the extreme rareness of this characteristic—that is, the conflation of religious and political authority.

Pope–Emperor Relations

Western pre-secular history has witnessed the complex relations between Popes and emperors. As Logan points out, these relations were a central theme of medieval history (2002: 72). Despite their various vicissitudes, the broad generalization may be made that there have always been two separate institutions of clergy and kingk. In short, the two did not merge under politico-religious institution. Because of their power and influence, a complex interaction prevailed among Popes and kings.

Constantine's reign (306–337), which was unquestionably a turning point for Christianity, saw the emergence of the church as a key power in the political sphere. The development of the Edict of Milan in 313 CE not only allowed Christians to practice their religion freely, but also mandated the return of confiscated property of the church. Throughout his rule, Constantine supported the church financially, built basilicas, granted privileges to the clergy (such as tax exemption), promoted Christians to high office, and returned property confiscated during the Diocletian persecution (Cruz & Gerberding, 2004: 55–56). These privileges aside, the early centuries of the papacy were dominated by the secular power of emperors. It was only in 751 CE that, for the first time, a Pope was involved in anointing a monarch. This took place when a Frankish bishop not only crowned Pepin the Short (714–768), but also anointed him with holy chrism. The forged alliance between the Pope and the Charlemagne dynasty in the mid-eighth century not only marked a milestone in Pope–emperor relations; it marked the beginning of a political turning point. Henceforth, the office of the king found a sacramental element in the church, which then bestowed the king with functions, duties, and responsibilities in exchange for his support of the church. As Logan suggests, the precedent for this was seeded by Pepin's anointment by the bishop in 751 (2002: 72; Ullmann, 1972: 46–48).

The major turn took place in the Gregorian age, in the 11th century. In accordance with the "Hildebrandine Reform", Pope Gregory VII reconceptualized the supremacy of Pope over emperor. Prior to the Gregorian era, emperors traditionally appointed bishops and indirectly the Pope; in 1075, however, a Roman synod, after attacking lay investiture, announced that "[i]f anyone receive a bishopric or abbey from the hands of a lay person, he shall not be considered a bishop or abbot.. . . [L]ikewise, if an emperor, king, duke, margrave or anyone vested with secular power presumes to invest a person to bishoprics or other ecclesiastical offices, he shall likewise be condemned" (quoted in Logan, 2002: 113). In 1076, Pope Gregory VII issued a Dictatus Papae (a Pope's dictations to a secretary), which included twenty-seven unprecedented statements concerning papal power. The main thrust of this statement was the establishment of the supremacy of Pope over emperor. Article 12 of the statement even delineated a Pope's right to dethrone an emperor (Collins, 2009: 213; Gaudemet, 2003: 470; Morrison, 2003: 735).

Pope Gregory VII's efforts to institutionalize the church's supremacy resulted in a bitter battle between the Pope and King Henry IV. The conflict did not end in the Pope's favour; however, the Pope's theological justification paved the way for the greater influence of church over empire. It seeded the notion of divine sovereignty in the Christian world, a formulation proposed as a theological framework a few years later by the French abbot Bernard of Clairvaux (1090–1153),[2] who argued that both temporal power and spiritual authority were uniquely combined in the Pope. Bernard proposed the notion of "the two swords", which became the commonly accepted medieval metaphor expressing supremacy of religious authority over the secular and the notion that both secular and spiritual power belonged to the Pope. The Pope would exercise spiritual power while temporal power would be handed to a secular person to wield according to the will of the Pope. In Bernard's view, temporal power should be the domain of a king because it was not the function of the Pope to descend to trivial activities (Ullmann, 1972: 117–118). Pope Boniface VIII (1294–1303) gave the theory of "the two swords" its final formulation:

> And we are taught by evangelical words that in this power of his are two swords, namely spiritual and temporal.. . . Therefore, each is in the power of the Church, that is, a spiritual and a material sword. But the latter, indeed, must be exercised for the Church, the former by the Church.. . . [I]t is necessary that a sword be under a sword and that temporal authority be subject to spiritual power. It is necessary that we confess the more clearly that spiritual power precedes any earthly power both in dignity and nobility, as spiritual matters themselves excel the temporal (cited in Denzinger, 1957: 187).

Worldly power was only emancipated from religious authority in the 17th–18th centuries. Three patterns in the history of Pope–emperor relations can be generalized. Whereas early centuries of Christianity saw the supremacy of emperor over Pope, from the mid-eighth century the notion of supremacy of Pope over emperor emerged. As Wood points out: "[F]ar more prevalent in. . . modern history has been the supremacy of state over church" (1967: 262).

This generalization by no means denies the fluctuations that occurred in Pope–emperor relations. A closer look reveals that these relations ultimately rested on the power of both parties. The king's higher power would require the obedience of Pope to king; conversely, the Pope's greater

---

2. This notion is in general known through the classic statement of St. Thomas Aquinas, who offered a scholarly-theological formulation of the supremacy of church over state. He wrote: "The highest aim of mankind is eternal happiness. To this chief aim of mankind all earthly aims must be subordinated. This chief aim cannot be realized through human direction alone but must obtain divine assistance which is only to be obtained through the Church. Therefore, the State, through which earthly aims are obtained, must be subordinated to the Church. Church and State are as two swords which God has given to Christendom for protection; both of these, however, are given by him to the pope and the temporal sword by him handed to the rulers of the State" (quoted in Bates, 1945: 140).

strength would lead to his authority over the king. As such, medieval history is replete with emperors' influence over Popes' appointments and vice versa. One outstanding example was the relationship between Pope Gregory VII and King Henry IV, in which conflict between the two led to the excommunication of the latter by the former. Unable to defeat the Pope, Henry sought his forgiveness. When he went to seek the Pope's pardon at a castle in Canossa, northern Italy, Gregory VII kept him waiting for three days, barefoot in midwinter, outside the castle gates. Soon, however, the power relations were reversed. Within a few years, Henry IV marched on Rome and installed a new Pope. Gregory VII fled to Monte Casino and, later, to Salerno, where he died in exile on May 25, 1085 (Logan, 2002: 112–115; Ullmann, 1972: 92–105). Despite the almost constant shifts in the power struggle between emperor and pope, the separate identity of these two institutions survived throughout Western-Christian history. When Henry IV took Rome, he appointed a new Pope rather than declare himself Pope. Conversely, at the peak of their prosperity, neither Gregory VII nor Boniface VIII proclaimed kingship.[3]

In contrast to the Western experience, the two institutions have merged into one in contemporary Iran. When Khomeini toppled Mohammad Reza Shah in 1979, as one of the country's leading religious leaders[4] he then gained the highest political status as well. The institution of Velayat-e Faqih is, in essence, the unification of kingship and spiritual authority. In other words, as a Valey-e Faqih, a cleric assumes both supreme political and religious authority simultaneously. This is why Kadivar argues that the doctrine of Velayat-e Faqih is based on the notion of the philosopher-king (2003b). The point that

---

3. The history of state–clergy relations in the Islamic context is highly diverse. It is too complex to be neatly summarized here and requires comprehensive research. For this reason, I rely upon An-Na'im's study, which concludes that except for during the Prophet Mohammad's governance, there has never been conflation of the two authorities of religion and state (An-Na'im, 2008). Similarly, Abou El Fadl observes it as an historical fact that neither Sunni nor Shiite jurists, prior to the modern age, ever assumed direct rule in the political sphere (2003: 33). In the contemporary Muslim world, Iran's clerical establishment does not have any parallel. Saudi Arabia might be the most known Islamic state next to the Islamic state of Iran. However, state and Ulama are not merged in Saudi Arabia. From the time of its ousting in 1932, Saudi's political system was formed based on the coalition of a political leader, Muhammad ibn Saud and a religious leader, Muhammad ibn Abd-al-Wahhab. Until now, this distance remains intact. For further discussion, see Kechichian, 1986.

4. As noted earlier, there is no hierarchical structure within the Islamic context: no single cleric may claim superior authority over others. It needs, of course, to be noted that a dimension of the doctrine of Velayat-e Faqih aims to establish this hierarchical structure. This issue will be explained later in chapter 6.

I wish to emphasize here is that it is a rare setting in which the institution of kingship/political leadership is merged with Marjaiat (religious leadership).

An Enduring Apolitical Tradition

Prior to the articulation of the doctrine of Velayat-e Faqih, the notion of the clergy's direct governance was never part of the mainstream Shiite politico-religious discourse. Indeed, no serious conceptual or practical effort was invested to this end. Scrutiny of the Constitutional Revolution (1906–1911) will provide some insight into the clergy's political leadership in contemporary Iran. The Constitutional Revolution marked a milestone that distinguished the pre-modern from the modern epoch in Iran's political history, for not only did it introduce new political notions, but it also posed vital questions pertinent to Shiite political philosophy (Feirahi, 2010: 363). This had an impact upon the clergy's conceptual articulations of politics as well as on their practical engagement with politics. It represented a new phase of Shiite political engagement, which led to the reformation of religious thought (Derakhsheh, 2001a: 192). The clergy's reaction to the Constitutional Revolution was diverse and marked by strong disagreement. For example, a leading cleric, Shaykh Fazlollah Nuri (1843–1909), was executed with the approval of his peers.[5]

Generally, there were two mainstream clerical groups, divided in terms of their stance towards the Constitutional Revolution. Neither had built their position based on the clergy's right to assume political authority. However, this does not mean that such an idea did not exist. For some it was considered an unrealized utopia, a fact evident in the writings of the main proponent of parliament. Alameh Mohammad Hussein Naeini supported the parliamentary system not because it was the desired system for Shi'a, but because it was plausible at the time and superior to the system of absolute monarchy. Naeini declared that he favoured this option because there was neither an infallible Imam nor a pious person who could serve as ruler (Derakhsheh, 2001a: 199).

However, the outcome of the Constitutional Revolution did not please the clergy: many senior clerics who contributed to the Constitutional Revolution later regretted having lent their support. Displeasure with the outcome of the Constitutional Revolution and the need to safeguard Islam against the West led to the establishment of the Qom seminary in 1921 (Feirahi, 2010: 366). And, while this was to play a significant role in Iran's future politico-religious aggregate, at the time it led to the domination of an apolitical discourse

---

5. For a detailed explanation of the disputes between clerics during the Constitutional Revolution, see Arjomand, 1981; Bayat, 1991: 161–183; Boozari, 2011: 45–98.

within the religious strata. Sheikh Abdul Karim Haeri-Yazdi (1852–1936), the founder of the Qom seminary, firmly avoided politics. He migrated from Iran to Najaf and later Karbala to distance himself from the clergy's involvement in the Constitutional Revolution (Derakhsheh, 2001a: 219). Haeri-Yazdi's entire career was marked by only two political activities. On one occasion, he sided with other clerics when they asked Reza Shah to abandon the idea of republicanism; on another, he sent a telegram to Reza Shah in which he protested against the law banning the *hijab* (Haeri, 1985: 189). His unchallenged influence in Iran's Shiite world dissuaded politically motivated clerics from claiming a space in mainstream religious discourse.

Haeri-Yazdi's apolitical stance aligned with Reza Shah's repressive policies and top-down secularization programs to bring about an era of silence. There was no precedent for the clergy's political engagement, let alone the possibility of their political dominance. Seyyed Hassan Modarres (1870–1931), a politically active cleric in the Reza Shah era,[6] was also a member of parliament. His slogan, "Our politics are the same as our religiosity", is widely used by Iran's ruling clergy today to justify the unification of religion and state. However, Modarres never called for an Islamic state. He was loyal to constitutionalism and his main political efforts were channelled towards resisting Reza Shah's dictatorship in support of constitutionalism. Although he insisted on the practice of the Shari'a and the need for compliance with all legislation imbued with Islamic principles, he never suggested that the clergy should possess political authority based on their religious competence. As he was not a senior cleric within the religious strata, he did not adopt a determinative position in the mainstream religious discourse.

When Ayatollah Haeri-Yazdi died in 1936, Ayatollah Seyyed Hossein Tabatabai Broujerdi (1875–1961) emerged as the leading figure in Iran's Shiite clerical establishment.[7] Similar to his predecessor, Broujerdi maintained unrivalled dominance over the religious strata, believing that religious sources such as the Quran and hadiths lacked sufficient evidence to justify the clergy's political authority. However, Broujerdi maintained that there

6. It should, of course, be mentioned that there were some occasions upon which a few other clerics clashed with Reza Shah, but it was not their constant approach to politics. One example was the Gauharshad uprising of 1935. For further evidence of clashes between the clergy and Reza Shah, see Amini, 2003; Basirat-Manesh, 2007.

7. Shiite history, both in practice and conceptual terms, has recorded a pluralistic structure among the clerics. It has only been over the last two centuries that an informal hierarchical structure has been established in practice. Although on many occasions there have been one or a few predominant clerics in practice, as Amanat explains, there are significant jurisprudential implications for establishing the authority of a cleric over other clerics. For a detailed explanation, see Amanat, 1988; Moussavi, 1994.

were rational bases upon which to argue that religion and politics could not be separated. This led him to opt for a supervisory role of the clergy over sociopolitical affairs (Kadivar, 1997: 20–21). Although on many occasions Broujerdi was strongly urged by politically active clerics to oppose the secularization policies of Mohammad Reza Shah, he never engaged in politics. An apolitical discourse prevailed under his leadership. This does not mean, however, that political discourse was missing altogether from the religious strata. There were clergy who were actively involved in politics, although they did not hold prominent religious credentials.

Political Engagement: A Marginal Discourse

Khomeini was not the first cleric to take part in politics in contemporary Iran; importantly, however, he was the first among senior clerics to advocate for political leadership. Because of his senior position within Iran's religious establishment, Khomeini's political discourse made an impact on the religious mainstream for which lower-ranking politically active clerics had been striving and failed to achieve. This applied equally to all clerics who entered politics prior to the emergence of Khomeini's Velayat-e Faqih; Sheikh Mohammad Khiabani Tabrizi (1880–1920), Seyyed Hassan Modarres (1870–1937), Sheikh Mohammad Bafqi (1875–1945), Ayatollah Kashani (1881–1962), and Navab-Safavi (1924–1956), among others. Ayatollah Kashani and Mojtaba Navab-Safavi are two examples worthy of closer investigation.

It is worth noting that Kashani and Navab-Safavi did not advocate for the religious right of the clergy to assume political leadership. Like Modarres, Seyyed Abolghasem Kashani was more of a political activist than a religious scholar. Resisting colonization and British policies in the Middle East formed the main thrust of his engagement with politics. His initial political activity took place in Iraq where, as a soldier, he fought against the British during the World War II, becoming a wanted man as a result. He managed to escape to Iran, where he actively contributed to the liberation of Iran's oil industry from British control. Later, in 1953, Kashani served as parliamentary speaker, falling short of raising the idea of an Islamic state or the political leadership of clerics. His political engagement was not rooted in a religious scholarly framework, but rather in the political framework of the day. Furthermore, his shifting political position, evident particularly in his support for the 1953 coup and adherence to the monarchy, suggests that he was not influential within the religious establishment. He was more strongly perceived as a political activist among clerics. In the words of Ayatollah Khomeini:

In the era of Kashani–Mossadeq, politics was the principal [factor].
The political dimensions of the [oil nationalization] movement were
weighty. I wrote and told Kashani that he should pay attention to the
religious dimensions. But he either could not or did not want [to do so].
Instead of reinforcing religious dimensions and prioritizing religious
dimensions over political dimensions, Kashani became a politician.
He became parliamentary speaker which was a mistake. I told him to
work for religion, not to be a politician (2006b: 268).

Mojtaba Navab-Safavi was the first cleric in Iran's contemporary history to propose the notion of an Islamic State (*hukoomat-e eslami*). While Navab-Safavi
published a rudimentary Constitution for the Islamic state, his thought
was not well received within the religious strata, possibly because he was a
younger cleric with limited religious credentials. One could therefore argue
that he was not sufficiently prominent to be included in a study about Shiite
political thought. However, his radical approach played a key role in paving
the way for Ayatollah Khomeini's revolutionary discourse. He established a
terrorist group known as the Fadaeian-e Islam (Devotees of Islam),[8] members
of which assassinated a number of secular Iranian intellectuals and politicians. The group was active from 1940 to 1955, when Navab-Safavi and other
Fadaeian-e Islam leaders were executed. The most notable contribution of
Navab-Safavi and his group to Iran-Shiite political discourse was their role in
initiating a utopian vision of an Islamic state (Behdad, 1997: 40).

The main document showcasing Navab-Safavi's political thought was a
90-page pamphlet titled *Barnamey-e Enqhelabi-e Fadaeian-e Islam* (The revolutionary program of devotees of Islam), which included his views on a wide
range of sociopolitical issues: economic and welfare issues; women's position
in an Islamic society; instructions for cultural management of society (radio/
television, cinema, publications, entertainment); international relations; and
guidelines for different ministers of the administration. Despite his junior
religious credentials,[9] Navab-Safavi included recommendations for clergy
and religious seminaries. He called upon senior clerics to reform the educational system and economic structure and to introduce a monitoring system
within the religious seminaries (Hadad-Adel, 2004). Significantly, nowhere

---

8. For further discussion about this militant group, see Khosroshahi, 2000; Sealy,
2011: 65–78.

9. Navab-Safavi was just 26 when he wrote this pamphlet. He "neither received any formal training beyond a high school education (and a technical one at that), except for his
short stint in Najaf; nor was he ever engaged in any intellectual endeavours". See Behdad,
1997: 52.

in this pamphlet or in his other writings did Navab-Safavi recommend the political leadership of the clergy, which further throws into relief the peculiarity of Ayatollah Khomeini's doctrine of Velayat-e Faqih.

Senior clerics, specifically Marja-e Taghlids,[10] play essential roles in promoting religious discourses. A review of Iran's contemporary politico-religious history shows that a religious discourse stands little chance of succeeding unless it originated with or is supported by senior clerics, particularly by a Marja-e Taghlid (Farati, 2004: 217–219). Not only did Kashani and Navab-Safavi fail to attract support from Ayatollah Broujerdi, the most eminent Marja-e Taghlid, but there were tensions between the two of them and Ayatollah Broujerdi.[11] This goes some way towards explaining why their ideas did not become part of the mainstream discourse within the religious establishment. Dominance of the apolitical elite eliminated any possibility of serious political engagement by the clergy within the religious establishment. When Sheikh Mohammad Bafqi objected to the entrance of female members of Reza Shah's family to the mosque without *hijab*, Reza Shah responded by personally going to Qom, where he assaulted and humiliated Bafqi. The people of Qom were incensed to the point of uprising. Although Bafqi was his bursar, Ayatollah Broujerdi abandoned him, sending a letter to the Shah explaining that Bafqi's action had been personal and had nothing to do with *hawza*. He then issued a fatwa to ease the tension in Qom:

> Speaking about and discussing the occurrence involving Sheikh Mohammad Taghi Bafqi is against enlightening Sharia and is utterly *haram*.. . . [B]y no means should those who are my students engage in this occurrence (quoted in Amini, 2003: 164).

In short, the apolitical attitudes of both Haeri-Yazdi and Broujerdi effectively prevented the rise of political discourse in the Qom seminary prior to the 1960s. However, both clerics played a major role in re-structuring the Shiite seminaries. Their reforms led to the emergence of a new generation of clerics, who fuelled the future clerical active sociopolitical engagement (Algar, 1988: 267–268).[12] As suggested above, the political engagement of clerics was limited to exceptional cases and never fully supported by the dominant religious discourse. As such, the notion of clerics holding political

---

10. For a discussion of the history of Marja-e Taghlids' position in the Shiite world, see Amanat, 1988: 98–132; Moussavi, 1985.

11. For example, see Montazeri, 2000b: 138–140.

12. For a detailed explanation of the reforms implemented by Grand Ayatollahs Haeri-Yazdi and Broujerdi, see Abbas, 2009; Ranjbar, 2003; Rohbakhsh, 2001.

leadership is highly unprecedented. Traditionally, senior clerics have not supported the activities of political clerics. In this context, Ayatollah Khomeini's
religio-political discourse represents a milestone not only in Iran's political
history, but also in Shiite political history. However, this discourse emerged
following a process of conceptual and empirical evolvement[13] within the political and religious domains.

The Clergy's Political Leadership in Khomeini's Thought

The idea of direct rule by the clergy existed in Ayatollah Khomeini's
politico-religious thought before his political practice. Although Ayatollah
Khomeini refused direct political leadership of the clergy in the first years
after the victory of the 1979 revolution, he had nevertheless proposed the
doctrine of Velayat-e Faqih earlier in 1971. The term "velayat-e faqih"[14] had
appeared even earlier in 1943 in his first main politico-religious work titled
Kashf Al-Asrar (Secrets unveiled), which was not only a systematic critique of
an anti-religious tract, but also a critique of the secular policy of the Pahlavi
monarch (Mahdavi, 2014: 28). In this book, Ayatollah Khomeini expanded
the clergy's authority beyond religious affairs by outlining their sociopolitical
and economic responsibilities.[15] His concept was similar to the notion raised
in the slogan "Islam is the solution", which would be widely used by Islamic
movements in the Middle East for decades to come. Ayatollah Khomeini
maintained that God, as the law-giver, provided instructions for each and
every aspect of the lives of humankind, which could be applied irrespective of time and space (1944: 8). From Khomeini's point of view, this left the
clergy with the unavoidable responsibility of extracting Islamic precepts for

13. Kadivar, who scrutinizes both Khomeini's practice and thinking, distinguishes four
different stages in his thought and actions. He refers to the first phase (1941–1964) as the
"Qom Era", a period during which Khomeini subscribed to the notion of jurists' supervision of the ruler. He was constitutionalist at this time. Calling the second phase the "Najaf
Era" (1961–1977), Kadivar claims that Khomeini shifted his thought towards the notion of
the generic appointment of jurists. Kadivar refers to Khomeini's thought during the revolution as the "Paris Era", the time when Khomeini advocated for people's right to appoint
their ruler. Khomeini was democratic and republican during this phase. The final phase
in Khomeini's thought, Kadivar maintains, was the "Tehran Era", when Khomeini introduced the notion of Velayat-e Motlagh-e Faqih. For details of Kadivar's categorization of
Khomeini's thought, see Kadivar, 2000a.

14. While the term has a long history in Shiite thought, it is mostly used to refer to the
religious authority of the clergy over specific affairs.

15. For detailed account of Khomeini's political views in this book, see Martin, 1993.

issues pertaining to the sociopolitical and economic arenas. However, while Khomeini expanded the clergy's authority, he by no means proposed replacing the monarchy with an Islamic state under clerical leadership. He unambiguously expressed his support for the tradition of the clergy's cooperation with kings:

> They [the *fuqahd*] have not opposed existing unsatisfactory arrangements, and have not wished to undermine the government. Up till now, if the "ulama" have opposed a particular sultan, their dissatisfaction has been with that person on the grounds that they found that his existence was contrary to the interests of the country. Till now this group has not opposed the fundamental principle of the sultanate. On the contrary, many of the great "ulama" co-operated with the government in the administration of the country (quoted in Martin, 1993: 35–36).

Although the young Khomeini urged the clergy to actively engage in politics, he did not argue for the clergy's right to assume the position of political ruler. Adhering to the principles of a constitutional monarchy,[16] he sought a supervisory role for clergy within the state. Khomeini argued that the state should be skilled in jurisprudence, but not necessarily led by jurists: "We do not say that the king must be a jurist or that he must know *moghadam-e vajeb* [a subject taught in the seminaries]. The king must be a military man, but he should not violate *fiqh* which is the formal law of the country.. . . [C]lergy's supervision can facilitate the enforcement of the country's law" (Khomeini, 1944: 232–233). Ayatollah Khomeini did not offer a clear mechanism for the jurists' supervision over legislative and executive bodies, which is explicitly mentioned in his *Kashf al-Asrar.* He only discussed the founding of an assembly that would consist of just clerics who would make sure that an appropriate person was appointed King. In sum, despite his employment of the term *velayat-e faqih,* in the 1940s Ayatollah Khomeini did not promote direct political leadership for the clergy.[17]

---

16. Scrutinizing the thought of Khomeini, Millward shows that Khomeini defended constitutional monarchy until 1963. See William Millward, "The Islamic Political Theory and Vocabulary of Ayatollah Khomeini, 1941–1963". Paper delivered at the Middle East Studies Association Conference, Salt Lake City, Utah, 1970, cited in Keddie, 1980: 541.

17. There is a counter-argument which claims that Ayatollah Khomeini believed in the right of jurists to possess political authority; but, due to the changing circumstances, he did not raise this in his book. See Derakhsheh, 2001b: 215.

The first significant religious uprising swept Iran in 1963.[18] Led by Ayatollah Khomeini, the people were mobilized against the White Revolution program; but ultimately the uprising failed, resulting in Khomeini's exile to Turkey. However, this event not only seeded the 1979 revolution, but also marked a significant shift in Ayatollah Khomeini's politico-religious thought. In effect, it signalled the birth of a new Khomeini (Goudarzi, Jawan, & Ahmad, 2009: 77; Harmon, 2005: 41).

Khomeini's second major political work, which he wrote in Turkey in 1964 and entitled *Tahrir al-Wasilah* (A clarification of questions), evinced a radical political repositioning. He called on believers to distance themselves from *taghut* (oppressive government) and explicitly declared it *haram* for clerics to cooperate with the regime (Derakhsheh, 2001b: 216). The most distinguishing feature of Khomeini's thought in this book was his statement on the rights and responsibility of clergy to assume political leadership:

> In the absence of the twelfth Imam, jurists, who are entitled to issue fatwas and act as judges, are representing the Hidden Imam in terms of political and other issues of Ummah. These jurists possess all of the authority which belongs to the Hidden Imam except for primary jihad (2008: 474, 483).[19]

By the late 1960s, Khomeini's political thought was characterized by a delineated, clear conceptual framework. He gave 13 lectures in Najaf between January 20, 1970, and February 8, 1970, which were later published as a book entitled *Islamic Government: Governance of the Jurist.*[20] As evident in the title, the clergy's political authority was the linchpin of Khomeini's doctrine. This was in line with the Shiite traditional approach in terms of focusing on the characteristics of the ruler rather than on providing a detailed outline of the methods of governance. From Khomeini's point of view, legal knowledge was the most important attribute of the ruler:

---

18. For further discussion surrounding this uprising, see Bakhash, 1990: 27–35; Harmon, 2005: 34–42.

19. In the Islamic context, "secondary Jihad" refers to the defending position when Muslims' territory is attacked. "Primary jihad" is a war initiated by Muslims to expand the Islamic world.

20. For discussion on the historical context of the emergence of the idea of the Islamic state, see Chehabi & Schirazi, 2012.

The qualifications required for a ruler are derived from the nature of Islamic governance. Along with general qualifications such as being sane and wise, there are two principal qualifications, i.e., justice and knowledge of law.. . . . Since the Islamic state is the reign of law, it is necessary for a ruler to know the law. From an Islamic standpoint, knowing the law and justice are the principle conditions, and other things [qualifications] are secondary.. . . If one does not know law-related issues, he is not eligible to be ruler.. . . If kings adhere to Islam, they ought to respect jurists' will and adopt laws and precepts from jurists to practice. In this case, jurists are the actual rulers. Therefore, sovereignty ought to be handed to jurists and not to those who have to follow jurists due to their ignorance of knowledge of the law (1976: 58–61).

The doctrine of Velayat-e Faqih grants political authority exclusively to the clergy. Khomeini explicitly claimed that all other political systems, specifically constitutionalism, were illegitimate and unacceptable from a religious point of view. As explained in earlier chapters with reference to placing jurists as representatives of the Hidden Imam in the OCCULTATION ERA, Khomeini argued that jurists possess the same religious and political authority over Muslims as the Prophet Mohammad and the infallible Imams. As mainstream Shiite tradition subscribes to the notion that governance exclusively belonged to the infallible Imams, a Muslim's responsibility is to wait for the Hidden Imam to return and establish just government. Challenging the apolitical jurisprudential tradition, Khomeini wrote:

From the time of the Lesser Occultation[21] down to the present (a period of more than twelve centuries that may continue for hundreds of millennia if it is not appropriate for the Occulted Imām to manifest himself), is it proper that the laws of Islam be cast aside and remain unexecuted, so that everyone acts as he pleases and anarchy prevails? Were the laws that the Prophet of Islam labored so hard for twenty-three years to set forth, promulgate, and execute valid only for a limited period of time? Was everything pertaining to Islam meant to be abandoned after the Lesser Occultation? Anyone who believes so,

---

21. The term "Lesser Occultation" (Ghaybat-e Soghra) refers to a period of approximately 70 years when the 12th Imam disappeared from the physical plane but remained in communication with his followers through four deputies. Upon the death of the fourth deputy in 941 CE, no successor was named and the Greater Occultation (Ghaybat-e Kubrah) began and continues to this day. See As-sadr, 1980; Hussain, 1982.

or voices such a belief, is worse situated than the person who believes
and proclaims that Islam has been superseded or abrogated by another
supposed revelation (2005: 37).

Khomeini emphasized that it was the right and responsibility of the clergy to
ensure implementation of the Shari'a by assuming political leadership. He
addressed the issue of governance again in his five-volume book entitled *Kitab
al-Bay*, which was published in the early 1970s. Although many ideas in this
book echo those of his earlier works on the Islamic state, an important difference is the expansion of the authority of the ruler (jurist). Khomeini explicitly
states in this book that the political authority of the Valey-e Faqih should be
supported by other jurists: "If one of the jurists succeeded in establishing a
state it is *vajeb* for other jurists to obey him" (Khomeini, 2006a: 466).

   The major thrust of Khomeini's works in the pre-revolutionary era was the
implementation of the Shari'a. However, this changed with the course of time,
when he undertook the responsibility of leading the state. As head of government, Khomeini shifted his focus from the implementation of the Shari'a to
the preservation of the Islamic state. *Fiqh al-maslaha*, or expedient *fiqh*, was
the religious articulation of this shift (as explained in detail in chapter 2).
The rationalization of absolute clerical hegemony may be seen as the ultimate
articulation of Khomeini's political doctrine. The Valey-e Faqih possesses
supreme authority both in a political area and the religious area. This includes
overshadowing other clerics' differing interpretations of the Shari'a.

   As discussed earlier, the practice of the doctrine of Velayat-e Faqih led
Khomeini to prioritize stability of the state's adherence to the Shari'a. This
was conceptualized in his political thought via the absolute authority of the
Valey-e Faqih (Velayat-e Motlagh-e Faqih). While the evolution of Khomeini's
thought may be traced over the course of four decades (from the 1940s to
the 1980s), his practical political engagement is characterized by extreme
fluctuation.

Khomeini's Shifting Political Stance

Khomeini's political stance does not accurately reflect the evolution of his
conceptual ideas, a pattern that is constant with his entire politico-religious
life. Prior to 1963, Khomeini did not directly engage in politics. He had, however, long promoted the political engagement of the clergy. As noted above,
he subscribed to this idea as early as *Kashf al-Asrar* in 1943. He saw political
engagement as the religious responsibility of the clergy while simultaneously
eschewing politics. During these years, clerics including Ayatollah Kashani

and Navab-Safavi became directly involved in politics; but there is no record of Khomeini's public support for their engagement. Any support he afforded their pursuits remained in the private sphere. He continued to enjoy a close relationship with Ayatollah Kashani and, as Bager Moin states, "was a frequent visitor to Kashani and admired his courage and stamina" (1999: 64). While he did not publicly object to Navab-Safavi's execution in 1955, Navab-Safavi's widow claimed that her husband used to attend Khomeini's talks and was helped by Khomeini on several occasions to escape the security forces (Algar, 1988: 129).

The evidence suggests that Khomeini neither initiated political movement in the 1940s and 1950s nor publicly sided with politically active clerics. Algar offers one explanation for this detached attitude—that is, that despite Khomeini's belief in political engagement, he respected Ayatollah Broujerdi. Solidarity within the religious establishment was very important to Khomeini, and for this reason he did not want to be seen as a dissenting voice within the religious hierarchy (Algar, 1988: 279–280). Furthermore, Khomeini may have learnt a lesson from other politically active clerics who were not supported by Ayatollah Broujerdi. He knew that any political discourse stood little chance of becoming effective within the religious strata as long as Ayatollah Broujerdi and his apolitical discourse prevailed. This could explain why Ayatollah Broujerdi's death was concurrent with a marked a shift in Khomeini's politico-religious life (Harmon, 2005: 37). Under circumstances in which there was no single, prominent religious leader within Iran's Shiite strata, Khomeini's political engagement from the early 1960s onwards made him not only an important political figure, but also established his position as a prominent religious leader. The riots that erupted in June 1963 and culminated in Khomeini's exile to Turkey facilitated his departure from the notion that the incumbent political structure and constitutionalism could accommodate religious concerns.

Khomeini thus augmented clerical political authority from the late 1960s onwards. Furthermore, he claimed that clerics had singularly led the 1979 revolution. On the eve of the revolution, he announced that:

> Iran's recent, sacred movement. . . is one hundred percent Islamic. It was founded by the able hand of the clerics alone, and with the support of the great, Islamic nation. It was and is directed, individually or jointly, by the leadership of the clerical community. Since this 15-year-old movement is Islamic, it continues and shall continue without the interference of others in the leadership, which belongs to the clerical community (quoted in Bakhash, 1990: 48).

By contrast, in the early years after the 1979 revolution, he denied the clergy the right to occupy political positions. On the eve of the revolution, there was no record of Khomeini's support for the clergy's right to exercise political authority. In the months leading up to the revolution, reporters streamed into Khomeini's headquarters in exile (in Neauphle-le-Chateau, France), wanting to know what character of Iran the head of the anti-Shah movement would establish. Khomeini gave over 120 interviews in Paris (Bakhash, 1990: 49), but never at any time did he refer to the religious right of the clergy to possess political leadership. Many wanted to know if Khomeini himself was the person to lead the state. However, at the time he refuted any such possibility: "Neither my age nor my inclination and position would allow me to occupy a post in the new government" (quoted in Schirazi, 1997: 24). When an NBC correspondent asked him if he would consider leading the state, Khomeini repeated clearly that he would not accept any political position: "I will not have any position in the future government. I will not be the President or the Prime Minister. I will be some sort of supervisor of their activities. I will give them guidance. If I see some deviation or mistake, I will remind them how to correct it" (quoted in Sciolino, 2000: 51). Khomeini's stance, however, was not confined to his own role in Iran's future. For him, clerics should, in toto, avoid political positions. A few months before the overthrow of the monarchy, Khomeini stated in an interview with Reuters in Paris on October 29, 1978, that "[c]lerics themselves will not hold power in the government. They will exercise supervision over those who are in charge of governance and will give them guidance. The [Islamic] government will be based on the people's vote and will be under public surveillance and assessment" (1983: 30).

These claims persisted after his return to the country following 15 years in exile. Despite many requests that he should reside in the capital city of Tehran, Khomeini moved to the religious capital city of Qom. As he had promised in Paris, he did not accept any political position. He appointed a lay man, Mehdi Bazargan, as prime minister of the interim government. He even signed and approved the first proposed draft of the new Constitution in which there was neither explicit nor implicit reference to the clergy's political leadership in general or to the notion of Velayat-e Faqih in particular. This draft was largely prepared on the eve of the revolution.[22] He reviewed the final draft and sought amendments;[23] but neither Velayat-e Faqih nor any other

---

22. For a discussion of the process of writing the Constitution and the debates to which its various articles gave rise, see Chehabi & Schirazi, 2012; Katouzian, 2002.

23. He asked for three specific amendments including (1) only a Shiite male could be president (to be added to the Constitution); (2) the form of the flag; and (3) the rights of religious minority groups. For further discussion, see Sahabi, 2010: 4.

privileged position for the clergy were among them. Khomeini insisted upon enacting this draft without referendum. Naser Katouzian, a member of the committee responsible for drafting the Constitution, notes that during the submission of the draft to Khomeini, the latter asked for it to be approved as soon as possible: "Imam [Khomeini] asked that it not be put to the people because it would take time.. . . [He said] I want this law to be endorsed soon so that I can return to my scholarly life" (2002: 125).

Khomeini's statements and political stance have since been viewed as a surreptitious strategy to gain political power. Islamists have been accused of "hijacking democracy", using a "one vote, one man, one time" strategy to gain power. Once attained, they overthrew the democratic system (Esposito & Voll, 1996: 171). This view has been extended to the Islamist electoral participation in Turkey and Algeria and to Hamas in Palestine. For example, in the Turkish case it was claimed that the AKP had a hidden agenda to establish yet another Islamic state in the Muslim world. Or was this simply justification for the coup d'état launched in Algeria in 1992? This concern has once again been raised following recent political uprisings in the Arab world (from 2011 onwards) and the electoral rise of Islamic groups such as the Muslim Brotherhood in Egypt and Al-Nahda in Tunisia.

Such theories seem particularly problematic when one considers the actual events that took place in early post-revolutionary Iran, for not only did Khomeini appoint a lay person as the country's first prime minister, but he also prevented clerics from standing for presidential election. This explains why the first two presidents of the Islamic Republic of Iran, Abul Hassan Banisadr and Mohammad Ali Rajaee were not clerics, even though a cleric would have been in a strong position to win the election. Banisadr was subsequently ousted from the presidency and Rajaee was killed in a terrorist attack. Only after the latter incident did Khomeini agree to the candidature of a cleric (i.e., Khamanei). In retrospect, however, it is hard to see these events as deliberate machinations aimed at elevating a cleric to the presidential office.[24]

Scrutiny of scholarly works by Khomeini's key proponents underscores this claim.[25] For example, when Ayatollah Mohammad Hosseini Beheshti, the

---

24. It is important to mention that the issue of the clergy's political authority was not confined to the presidential office. However, the case of presidency is a good example to scrutinize the process that led to the dominance of the clergy over the political structure.

25. Khomeini's suggestion to call the new political system "Islamic Republic" proves his departure from the notion of an Islamic government that he held at the juncture of the 1979 revolution. This frequently gives rise to heated debate between reformists and hardliners in Iran today. Where reformists insist on the republican feature of the system, hardliners emphasise the Islamic feature. Ayatollah Mesbah-Yazdi, a leading conservative

first judiciary chief of the Islamic Republic (1980–1981), spoke of an Islamic state, he did not mean rule by the clergy (Derakhsheh, 1999: 74). For Beheshti, the primary aim of forming an Islamic state was to pursue the interests of the nation, not to hand over political authority to a specific person or group (Khosro-Shahi, 1992). Morteza Motahhari, a key ideologue of the Islamic revolution, advocated the supervisory role of clergy (Derakhsheh, 1999: 78). Distinguishing between an Islamic state and a clerical state, Motahhari stated that by no means did the term "Islamic state" suggest the right of clergy to rule the country (Motahhari, 1993: 86–88). For him, Velayat-e Faqih had only a supervisory role:

> Velayat-e Faqih does not mean that a jurist becomes the head of state and rules [the country]. In an Islamic country. . . a jurist possesses the role of an ideologue not the position of ruler. The responsibility of an ideologue is to supervise correct application of said ideology (Motahhari, 1993: 85).[26]

Thus, the idea of a privileged position for the clergy in Iran's post-revolutionary political system was neither dominant in conceptual discourse nor evident in the political conduct of key religious figures in the 1979 revolution. As Esposito and Voll correctly observe, Khomeini's earlier conceptual articulation, in which everything was under the control of a cleric (i.e., a Valey-e Faqih), was widely and somewhat surprisingly overlooked (Esposito & Voll, 1996: 62). The dominant discourse on the eve of the revolution and immediately following corresponded to Khomeini's articulation in the 1940s and not that of the 1970s. In time, however, the position of the clergy strengthened. Within a few years of the revolution, the highest executive, judiciary, and legislative positions were occupied by clergy. This shift led to an even more powerful position for the clergy in the political structure, compared to that articulated in Khomeini's doctrine of Velayat-e Faqih. As explained in chapter 2, this shift was facilitated by the transformation of the doctrine Velayat-e Faqih into Velayat-e Motlagh-e Faqih.

---

theorist, argues that Khomeini used the term "Islamic Republic" in contradiction to the monarchy. He states: "The regime is called Republic in the political literature but it is not Republic in a way which is used in the West. A democratic republic is a system in which everything and all authority are handed to the people and [everything] is subsidiary to the whim of the people and their vote. It [Western republic] is not of an Islamic nature" (Mesbah-Yazdi, 2005).

26. For further discussion of Motahhari's political thought, see Davari, 2005: 121–160; Shimamoto, 2006.

Institutionalizing the Power of the Clergy

The power shift towards the clerical establishment was heralded by the moment when the first draft of the Constitution was set aside and a new draft was proposed by the Assembly of Experts in 1980.[27] Whereas the first draft did not include any privileged position for the clergy, the notion of Velayat-e Faqih formed the linchpin of the new system. As historian Elton L. Daniel observes, the new Constitution generally sought to completely Islamize the state according to Khomeini's earlier conceptual framework (2001: 15). Accordingly, the clergy were granted not only the highest political positions, but also many other privileges in the new political structure. This marked a significant turning point in post-revolutionary Iran that led to the current dominant political discourse, in which the clerics' right to possess political authority is beyond question. The introduction of the Constitution, which explicitly recognizes a cleric as a political leader, reads as follows:

> In keeping with the principles of governance and the perpetual necessity of leadership, the Constitution provides for the establishment of leadership by a holy person possessing the necessary qualifications and recognized as leader by the people (this is in accordance with the saying 'the direction of affairs is in the hands of Ulama [learned] concerning God; they are trustworthy in matters pertaining to what He permits and forbids). Such leadership will prevent any deviation by the various organs of the state from their essential Islamic duties.

The number of positions allotted to the clergy is limited to five by the Constitution. The positions are, however, the most powerful. They include Supreme Leader, Chief of the Supreme Court, Prosecutor-General, Chief of Judiciary, and six members of the Guardian Council. The positions of the Chief of Judiciary and members of the Guardian Council are appointed by the Supreme Leader. According to Article 110, the authority of the Supreme Leader extends to appointments, dismissals, and the acceptance of the resignation of (a) jurists of the Guardian Council, (b) chief of the judiciary, (c) the head of the radio and television networks, (d) the Chief of Staff of the Armed Forces, (e) the chief commander of the Islamic Revolution Guards Corps, and (f) the senior commanders of the armed forces.[28] Although it is not mentioned in

---

27. For a detailed explanation of this shift, see Saffari, 1993.

28. These are specific cases mentioned in the Constitution. But, in practice, the Supreme Leader's authority goes well beyond these specific cases. His power and consequent

the Constitution, all 86 members of the Assembly of Experts must be clerics according to the assembly's housekeeping by-law.[29]

The clergy's role in Iran's political sphere goes well beyond the positions mentioned specifically in the Constitution and other legislation. For example, a Friday Imam, a leader who possesses enormous power to influence local issues, is appointed for each and every city. Almost all state organizations include a cultural branch, which is generally led by a cleric. Every university has an office that represents the Supreme Leader, filled without exception by clerics. Furthermore, a set of religious courses designed by clerics are included in all university curricula, and all students, irrespective of their field of study, are expected to study them. Another institution led by the clergy is the Sazeman-e Aghidati Siyasi (Political and Ideological Organization), a powerful division within the armed forces, including the country's army and the Islamic Revolutionary Guard Corps (IRGC). The clergy is omnipresent in the country's political mosaic.

In 1981, Khomeini stated that the presence of clerics in administrative positions was ineluctable. He claimed that this was a temporary phenomenon and that clerics would return to their mosques and seminaries when they were no longer needed (quoted in Bazargan, 1984: 49). More than three decades after this promise, not only have clerics remained in the administration, they have expanded their presence further into the sociopolitical and economic spheres. Today they are embedded in almost all of the key governmental organizations, as well as in many other mid-level administrative positions throughout the country. For many clerics, religious leadership is no longer their primary responsibility. Many no longer engage in the clergy's traditional functions such as preaching or conducting prayers. Even if a change in the political system were to occur, it would be difficult to remove clerics from their positions in state agencies and return them to the seminaries and mosques.

Any discussion of clerics returning to mosques and seminaries has been totally marginalized in the official political lexicon. However,

---

intervention in different areas has increased over the course of time. A more stable and established political system has resulted in more centralized power.

29. The Assembly of Experts is responsible for monitoring the Supreme Leader's performance; but they are mostly the Friday Imams of different cities who are appointed by the Supreme Leader. Moreover, candidates need to be approved by the Guardian Council, which is also controlled by the Supreme Leader. Thus, there is a vicious circle. In addition, members of the assembly are indirectly appointed by the Supreme Leader. This is why there is no record of their critique of the Supreme Leader. For further discussion, see Kadivar, 2001c.

counter-arguments exist in the traditional cluster[30] of the Shiite world. Although the ruling clergy have sought to suppress any dissenting ideas, counter-discourses do exist. They have survived particularly within the traditional cluster of the religious strata. Ayatollah Khomeini was the exception among Marja-e Taghlids who subscribed to a clerical establishment. The other established Marja-e Taghlid who engaged in politics in the turbulent years of the revolution, Ayatollah Shariatmadari, explicitly resisted the clergy's direct political leadership. There is a devotional relationship between believers and the traditional cluster of religious leaders. Regardless of the scale of their religious knowledge, religious intellectuals lack religious authority over believers. By contrast, a fatwa issued by a Marja-e Taghlid is religiously indispensible for his emulators. Thus, their political standing is of huge importance, particularly when the Islamic state is not led by a Marja-e Taghlid. This explains the Islamic state's effort to gain the support of Marja-e Taghlids or at the very least their quietude in cases where they do not agree with the Islamic state. This was particularly evident in Khamanei's efforts to gain Marja-e Taghlids' support during the political unrest in 2009. The next chapter aims to explicate the resistance to clericalism by traditional religious leaders, who objected to the clerical establishment in many ways. By maintaining their apolitical approach, many senior clerics resorted to passive methods in their bid to resist clericalism. Others, adopting a more aggressive approach, actively resisted the clerical establishment. Due to its problematic nature, the clerical state model has not been emulated by other Shiite-dominated countries such as Iraq and Lebanon. In these countries, political and religious leaders have not embraced the notion of clericalism.

---

30. By "traditional cluster", I mean those thinkers who are entirely trained in religious seminaries and carry out primarily religious rituals—those known as Mojtaheds, or Marja-e Taghlid at the higher level. There is a new generation of clergy who are trained not only in seminaries, but also in the ways of Western-style universities. The members of this new generation do not restrict themselves to traditional religious functions. They teach at universities or work in administration. Religiously speaking, the traditional cluster possesses stronger spiritual influence over habitual believers.

5

Clerics against Clericalism

IT IS A common misunderstanding that Ayatollah Khomeini represented mainstream Iranian religious discourse on the eve of the 1979 revolution. In actual fact, his discourse was not popular among the most prominent Ayatollahs in the Shiite world—neither in Iran nor in other Shiite sites such as Iraq and Lebanon (Menashri, 1980). However, Khomeini enjoyed two parallel advantages: First, the highest-ranking clerics, Marja-e Taghlids,[1] remained loyal to the traditional quietist approach. As Khomeini's discourse was deemed political rather than religious, the majority of Marja-e Taghlids kept a neutral stance on his politico-religious discourse. This quietist approach provided Khomeini with the particular space needed to promote his discourse.[2] Second, Khomeini trained a new generation of clerics on his discourse who were supported by religious strata. By the time of the 1979 revolution, Khomeini's disciples from the 1950s and 1960s had gained midlevel religious credibility. Their contribution to the emerging politico-religious discourse saved Khomeini's discourse from seminary opposition.

---

1. The notion is literarily translate as "source of emulation" or "religious reference" and refers to highest-ranking authority of Twelver Shiism. Marja-e Taghlid's words and deeds serve as a guide for those members of the community unable to exercise independent reasoning (ijtihad). They are believed by other clerics and lay believers to be superior in learning and the most authoritative religious scholars of their day. The process of selecting Marja-e Taghlids has never been formalised and they usually emerge and are gradually accepted by consensus. For further discussion see, Momen, 1985: 203–206, and Oxford Islamic Studies Online.

2. It should be taken into consideration that since Khomeini's discourse was new and heated compared with orthodox discourse, it attracted much higher attention in the media and in the public space. This significantly contributed to his elevation to his Marja-e Taghlid position. For a detailed explanation of how Khomeini's political activities contributed to his religious credibility, see Khalaji, 2006: 25–27.

Three decades after the revolution, the Islamic state has spawned a new generation of high-ranking clerics who unconditionally subscribe to the politico-religious discourse constituted by Khomeini. Ayatollahs including Mesbah-Yazdi, Makarem-e Shirazi, Nouri Hamedani, Javadi-e Amuli, Sobhani, and Safi-Golpayegani, to name but a few, are now senior clerics driving the Islamic state.[3] Ayatollah Mesbah-Yazdi, President Ahamadinejad's spiritual mentor, argues that because the notion of Velayat-e Faqih is a core Islamic principle, opposing it "is like opposing the holy Imams and is equal to becoming an infidel" (Mesbah-Yazdi, 2011). Instructively, the most outstanding Ayatollahs of the traditional cluster had never supported the clergy's political leadership. This group included the most eminent Marja-e Taghlids of Khomeini's time, but also the Grand Ayatollah Sistani, the last remaining member of that eminent generation.

Despite the ruling clergy's efforts to mobilize clerics in support of their political discourse, political quietism has continued to be the mainstream discourse among senior clerics. There are, however, instances of active resistance against the clerical establishment by some Marja-e Taghlids, some of which led to political conflict between the ruling clergy and the Marja-e Taghlids. In the case of Ayatollahs Shariatmadari and Montazeri, the conflict was not just confined to scholarly debate, but actually resulted in a power struggle. Marjaiat has always been a transnational institution in the Shiite world; therefore, in my concluding section of this chapter, I examine precisely why the idea of the clergy's political leadership was met with clerical opposition not just within Iran's borders, but in other majority Shiite countries as well.

Passive Resistance: Loyalty to Political Quietism

Prior to the 1960s, Ayatollah Broujerdi had managed to establish himself as a single authority within the Shiite strata. His death in 1961 left the Qom seminary in chaos as it struggled to unify Marjaiat. There were a few candidates who could replace his now vacant leadership,[4] but none stood uncontested. Three

---

3. These clerics enjoy the widespread support of the Islamic state, which advocates for their religious credibility. But they are far from reaching the eminent position of a Marja-e Taghlid, like Grand Ayatollahs Sistani and Montazeri, for example.

4. There is no official process of nominating and appointing a Mojtahed as the main Marja-e Taghlid. It is an informal process. A Marja-e Taghlid may assume the position gradually through recognition by believers and other Marja-e Taghlids. For example, when the Grand Ayatollah Haeri-Yazdi died, there were other Mojtaheds in Qom who could have potentially replaced him. But, Ayatollah Broujerdi moved to Qom from Broujerd, and they all made way for him.

Ayatollahs, including Marashi-Najafi (1897–1990), Golpayegani (1899–1993), and Shariatmadari (1906–1986), were the most outstanding of the candidates. Religiously speaking, Khomeini had yet to establish a sufficiently solid reputation to be considered as Marja-e Taghlid.[5] None of the three aforementioned Marja-e Taghlids subscribed to the notion of clergy's political leadership; however, as I will explain later, only Shariatmadari raised explicit objections to Khomeini's political leadership. Both Marashi-Najafi and Golpayegani retained their quietist political positions, opting to avoid publicly spelling out their dissatisfaction with the clergy's political leadership. Other senior clerics such as the Grand Ayatollahs Araki (1894–1994) and Khoei (1899–1992) also fell into this category. As the most prominent Marja-e Taghlid in the current Shiite world, Grand Ayatollah Sistani (b. 1930) continues to maintain his quietist standpoint. As Cole notes, the most eminent Shiite religious leaders have managed to survive both Khomeini's theocracy and Saddam's dictatorship precisely because of their quietism (Cole, 2006: 25).

Political quietism embodies the passive nature of the aforementioned Marja-e Taghlids' approach. However, as Rahimi argues, the Shiite clergy's approach should not be reduced to a simplistic dichotomy between quietism and activism; there are in fact a range of approaches that fall within this spectrum. Throughout Shiite history, the clergy have shifted their attitudes in response to varying situations.[6] Hence, quietism varies at the levels of the aforementioned Marja-e Taghlids. Despite the importance of the clergy's political leadership in post-revolutionary Iran, the topic of governance is conspicuously absent from the scholarly works of many of these Marja-e Taghlids.[7] Ayatollahs Marashi, Golpayegani, and Araki have overlooked the issue of governance and an Islamic state, and there is no record of their position on the clergy's political leadership in general and on the doctrine of Velayat-e Faqih in particular. This was also the case for the Ayatollahs who lived before them. There is some evidence in the scholarly works and political stances of Ayatollahs Khoei and Sistani that reveal their objection

---

5. According to the enacted law, the Marja-e Taghlid possessed a form of immunity from prosecution and execution. When he was arrested after the 1963 riots, there was talk that he might be executed. In order to protect Khomeini, Ayatollahs Shariatmadari, Marashi, and Milani called him Marja-e Taghlid (Montazeri, 2000b: 236–237).

6. For some examples of the shifting attitudes of the clergy in different circumstances, see Rahimi, 2008: 2–4.

7. One may argue that non-partisanship is a traditional principle among Ayatollahs. In the 2009 presidential election and its aftermath, there were many requests from Marja-e Taghlids to take positions. These requests were made by both hardliners and the Green Movement. But, many among them opted to remain neutral.

to the notion of clergy's political leadership: this difference may be attributed to their location in Iraq, which keeps them safely outside the Islamic Republic's jurisdiction.

Gleave's comparison of the jurisprudential foundations of Khomeini and Khoei's works on jurist authority concludes that Khoei's concept of *ijtihad* and Marjaiat is less overtly political. For Khoei, a jurist has limited responsibility and authority within the sphere of governance issues (Gleave, 2002). The notion of Velayat-e Faqih, in Khoei's view, is confined to issuing fatwas, to judgement, and Hisbiyah[8] matters (Kadivar, 2000a: 101–105; Khalaji, 2006: 14; Mohammad Hadi, 1998: 179). Authority vis-à-vis Hisbiyah matters was restricted to supervision of the financial affairs of those unable to protect their own interests (e.g., minors, orphans, and the mentally infirm) and the administration of religious endowments. Governance was not a part of Hisbiyah matters. For Ayatollah Khoei, there was no authentic place for the clergy in the political sphere during the OCCULTATION ERA (Khoei, 1998: 16). Ayatollah Khoei stated:

> There is no evidence to prove Velayat-e Faqih in the OCCULTATION ERA because this Velayat [guardianship] was specified for the Prophet and the infallible Imams. [Jurist authority] over judgment and fatwa is evident in the *revayats* [religious quotations]; but, jurists do not have the right to take control of possession of minors, incapables and incompetents [the mentally infirm]. Hisbiyah matters are the exception because a jurist has authority over these matters (quoted in Karbalaie, 2001: 325).

However, the current politico-religious dynamism in Iraq has placed pressure on religious leaders to directly involve themselves in the political arena. Even still, Ayatollah Ali Sistani's political thought and occasional direct engagement in daily political issues leans generally towards the quietist approach, though there has been a shift from the total quietism of Saddam's time towards the semi-activism of the post-Saddam era. Yet, it is still far from the Iran-style political activism adopted by Khomeini and the Iranian ruling clergy (Rahimi, 2005: 13–14; 2012: 64–65).

Due to the weak institutional structure, it is impossible to determine precisely the number of followers of Marja-e Taghlids. However, Ayatollah Sistani is widely cited as the most prominent living Marja-e Taghlid in the Shiite world. It is estimated that some 80 percent of Shiite believers emulate Ayatollah Sistani. This provides him with a high degree of sociopolitical influence (Khalaji,

---

8. Hisbiyah refers to non-litigious matters such as religious endowments, safeguarding the wealth of a mission person, the orphans, and the divorcees.

2006: 7; Terhalle, 2007: 78). Sistani has used his influence in Iraqi politics on more than one occasion, though he has acted in a strictly advisory role. Advising the government on referendums and constitutional matters, settling tensions generated by Muqtada al-Sadr's radical militia, and efforts to calm Shi'a–Sunni tensions are among Sistani's direct engagements with politics. For Sistani, Iran's experience of clericalism has not been a successful one. In 2006, he commented to a visiting scholar: "Even if I must be wiped out, I will not let the experience of Iran be repeated in Iraq" (quoted in Cole, 2006: 8).

One may argue that the concept of popular sovereignty is central to Sistani's political thought. This is evident both in his occasional involvement in Iraq's politics and in his fatwas. In his first major fatwa after the fall of Saddam on 28 June 2003, Sistani rejected the American plan to appoint a committee to draft a new Constitution. Rather than advocating Khomeini's concept of divine sovereignty, he promoted popular sovereignty, insisting that those who draft the new Constitution would first have to be elected by the people. He further stated that a draft Constitution should then be submitted to a national referendum (Cole, 2006: 10–11). A year after Saddam's fall, "there [was] growing concern in certain quarters that Sistani—born, raised and partly educated in Iran—shows signs of Persian hubris that might lead to an Iraqi version of Iran's Islamic Republic" (Gerecht, 2004). To date, however, Sistani's scholarly works and political engagement have proven these concerns wrong. Unlike other Iraqi Shiite political groups such as the Islamic Supreme Council of Iraq (ISCI) and the Islamic Dawa Party, Sistani discourages the clergy's participation in state institutions (Khalaji, 2006: 17; Rahimi, 2005: 14). Sistani is opposed to the expansion of an Iranian-style clerical establishment in Iraq; on one occasion, Sistani explicitly refuted the religious foundation of the clergy's right to political authority. Responding to an *istifta* (a religious question by an emulator) concerning Velayat-e Faqih, Sistani replied:

> Velayat-e Faqih, in terms of only Hisbiyah matters as commonly understood by jurists is evident for all jurists who are qualified to be Marja-e Taghlid. But, when [it comes to] public issues to which the social order is linked, there are other conditions, one of which is the acceptance of the jurist by believers. [Believers' acceptance] is required for both the jurist and the conditions according to which his Velayat [authority] is to be applied (2005).

Evidently, Sistani differentiates religious from political authority; for him, the clergy's religious authority does not automatically extend to their political leadership unless it is accompanied by the people's consent.

Active Resistance: Campaigning for an Apolitical Stance

As the prominent leader of the 1979 revolution, Khomeini gained not only a lofty political reputation, but also enhanced his religious credentials. In the course of leading the revolution, many shifted their emulation to him as Marja-e Taghlid. Achieving political power with the victory of the revolution, Khomeini's religious credentials were reinforced by most senior religious leaders' apoliticism. In short, by adhering to quietism they did not pose a political threat.[9] There were others, however, including dissident religious leaders and intellectuals, who actively resisted the clerical establishment. These religious objections have posed serious challenges to the clergy's political authority across more than three decades.

Despite Khomeini's seemingly unchallengeable power, there were some senior religious leaders actively opposed the clergy's political leadership shortly after the 1979 revolution (Rahimi, 2012: 56–59). More than launching a discursive threat, however, their opposition led to political instability. Their discourse departs from quietism in two ways—first, by opting not to keep silent and launching a political battle against the ruling clergy and, second, by adhering to the supervisory role of the clergy. Ayatollah Seyyed Kazem Shariatmadari, one of the three preeminent Marja-e Taghlids after Ayatollah Broujerdi's demise, opposed the incorporation of the doctrine of Velayat-e Faqih into the constitution, arguing that the clergy should not assume political leadership:

> In Islam, there is no decree that states that the Ulema must intervene in matters of state.. . . [I]t is not for the Ulema to involve themselves in politics. That is for the government.. . . [W]e must simply advise the government when what they do is contrary to Islam.. . . [I]t is the duty of the government to govern. There should be no direct interference from spiritual leaders (quoted in Hiro, 1985: 117).[10]

Ayatollah Shariatmadari was the most influential dissident clergy at the time, (Kadivar, 2014a: 361) and enjoyed widespread support in the Azerbaijan,

9. For example, Ayatollah Sistani did not take any position either in favour of or against the 2009 political instability in Iran. This, of course, deprived the Islamic state of his support, which could have greatly benefited the ruling clergy due to his enormous number of emulators in Iran—but, at the same time, neither did Sistani fuel instability.

10. For a detailed discussion of the differences between Khomeini and Shariatmadari on politico-religious issues, see Menashri, 1980.

Gilan, and Zanjan provinces; his opposition to Khomeini resulted in political instability more particularly in Azerbaijan (Akhavi, 1980: 168). On one occasion, his supporters took control of Tabriz, the capital city of Azerbaijan. The Islamic state accused Ayatollah Shariatmadari of planning a coup d'état and terrorizing Khomeini. After confessing on state television in 1982, Ayatollah Shariatmadari was kept under house arrest for a few years. In 1986, the Islamic state announced that he had passed away. Instructively, no funeral or memorial ceremony was held in his honour.[11]

Like Shariatmadari, Ayatollah Hassan Qomi (1911–2007), a Grand Ayatollah of Mashhad, objected to the clergy's political leadership. In 1981, when it became obvious that clerics were consolidating their power, he observed: "The real cleric does not want power.. . . [H]e does not approve of those clerics who govern us. The real task of the clergy is to advise and enlighten the people" (quoted in Chehabi, 1991: 82). Ayatollah Qomi was also detained under house arrest until a few years before his death in 2007. Other Ayatollahs such as Mohammad Shirazi, Mohammad Rowhani, and Reza Sadr, who disagreed with notions of the clergy's political leadership, were suppressed by the ruling clergy. A more recent case is Ayatollah Seyyed Hossein Kazemeyni-Boroujerdi, who was imprisoned in 2006.

It is worth noting that advocates of quietism and active objectors to the clerical establishment have avoided addressing issues of governance in their scholarly works. In effect, active objection is a form of political opposition to the ruling clergy rather than a jurisprudential challenge to the clergy's political leadership. As such, they do not propose any alternative to clerical political leadership other than reverting to the traditional paradigm of state–religion relations. For example, Kazemeyni-Boroujerdi explicitly labels political religion "mock religion" and claims to stand for traditional religion (in his words, "true religion") (Bruno, 2008; Esfandiari, 2006; Kazemeini-Boroujerdi, 2008). Another group of religious leaders offer a well-structured theoretical framework of the clergy's status in the political system. In contrast to the apolitical discourse of some of their peers, they continue to support clerical political authority albeit with some amendments to Khomeini's model.

---

11. This was one occasion upon which Ayatollah Golpayegani, another Marja-e Taghlid, expressed his dissatisfaction with the Islamic state by sending a letter to Khomeini complaining about the way in which Shariatmadari had been treated (Kadivar, 2013b; Montazeri, 2000b: 927).

Ummah: Heirs to the Hidden Imam's Political Authority

According to the doctrine of Velayat-e Faqih, the clergy possess political authority because of their religious credentials. And yet for Khomeini, the role of the people was of importance as well. Take, for example, Khomeini's widely quoted reminder that "the criterion is the vote of the people" (*mizan ray-e mellat ast*).[12] However, in the post-Khomeini era, a new generation of ideologues have explicitly undermined the significance of the popular vote in their conceptual articulations of the doctrine of Velayat-e Faqih.[13] Ayatollah Makarem-e Shirazi, for example, states: "[I]f avoiding people's votes and election provide enemies with pretext of damaging the reputation of the Islamic state, people's votes can be referred to only as a subsidiary [element]" (quoted in Kadivar, 1997: 90). By contrast, some religious scholars have switched emphasis to the people's vote. Lebanese scholar Muhammad Jawad al-Moghniya (1904–1979), who argued that the fallibility of jurists necessitates restriction of the jurists' authority in the political sphere, agreed with Khomeini that an Islamic state ought to be formed to fulfil the sociopolitical dimensions of Islam.[14] Moghniya, on the other hand, asserted that a state will be Islamic if its laws are based upon the Quran and *sunna* (tradition), not because of the clergy's political leadership. It would therefore not be necessary for an Islamic state to be led by a jurist. In other words, any state which applies Islamic principles is an Islamic state regardless of its leadership (Kadivar, 1997: 167–171). In line with the quietist approach, Moghniya argued that the clergy have only two forms of authority: issuing fatwa and forming judgment, neither of which warrant clerical leadership of the state (Akhavi, 1996: 243). He further stated that there is no difference between laymen and clerics in terms of their competence in political matters. A cleric who is interested in political leadership ought to seek the people's vote. "We do not know any other method except seeking the public vote" (quoted in Kadivar, 1997: 170). According to Moghniya, an Islamic state is a necessary political

---

12. As is evident so far, Khomeini's discourse includes many paradoxes. As I suggest in chapter 1, the doctrine of Velayat-e Faqih was founded based upon divine sovereignty. One explanation for these statements, which refer to the importance of the people's role, could be Khomeini's popularity. He enjoyed unique popularity; thus, both divine and popular sovereignty would place him in the leadership position. Hence, for him there was no contradiction between people's willingness and divine articulation.

13. For example, see Javadi-e Amoli, 1989; Mesbah-e Yazdi, 1999.

14. He believed that politics is the nerve of life. In his view, those who try to separate politics from Islam are trying to separate it from its nature (Akhavi, 1996).

formulation from a religious point of view; this religious standing does not however secure a privileged position for the clergy in the Islamic state.

Lebanese scholar Mohammad Mehdi Shams al-Din (1936–2001) attached significance to the concept of popular sovereignty by arguing that the formation of an Islamic state requires the people's consent. For Shams al-Din, forming an Islamic state is not a religious obligation and in the OCCULTATION ERA, no one possesses the divine right to assume political leadership. As such, the clergy do not represent the Hidden Imam in political matters. After the Prophet Mohammad and the infallible Imams, political authority was transferred to the Ummah (the people), enabling them to select their political leaders and the political system they favoured. Thus, it is the right of any Muslim community to decide on a structure of government, irrespective of whether it is an Islamic structure or not. Shams al-Din supported the Islamic state in Iran not because he agreed with the religious foundation of the clerical establishment but because, in his view, it was founded based upon popular will (Jadallah, 2013: 10–21; Kadivar & Kamali-Ardakani, 2004: 67–69; Mneimneh, 2009: 46–47). The clergy cannot, he argued, claim any privileged position in the political sphere. He saw them as equal to the lay person, given that jurisprudential knowledge is not a prerequisite for leading a state (Kadivar, 1997: 172).

The centrality of the popular sovereignty in the political thought of both Moghniya and Shams al-Din led Kadivar to characterize their ideas as an independent political doctrine within the Shiite faculty. He refers to their political thought as the "elected Islamic state" (Kadivar, 1997: 27). This, however, somewhat diminishes the nuances of their thought: Shams al-Din recognized the legitimacy of a non-Islamic state if it was based on the people's will; Moghniya believed that forming of an Islamic state is a religious obligation and therefore beyond the will of the people.

Given the complex Shiite status in Lebanon, it seems surprising that Shams al-Din and Moghniya highlighted the role of the people in determining the country's political system. As the Shi'a do not constitute a majority in Lebanon, one would expect Lebanese scholars to emphasize elements such as divine sovereignly, which will afford them a better chance of mobilizing the Shiite population. The situation in Iran was the reverse: the country's Shi'a demography was enough to provide Khomeini with widespread support, and therefore the notion of popular sovereignty would not have disadvantaged his doctrine, at least not at the time; Khomeini's doctrine, however, did not give equal weight to the people's role. In this light, Ayatollah Salehi-Najafabadi's interpretation, in which the people are the central determinant of the political system, was rather unconventional.

Representing the People, Not the Hidden Imam

Central to the doctrine of Velayat-e Faqih is the clergy's divine right to undermine the people's will. The Quran explicitly states that most people are uncomprehending and unreasonable.[15] These verses are generally used as the religious foundation for questioning the majority opinion. Ayatollah Nematollah Salehi-Najafabadi (1923–2006), a lesser-known Iranian scholar, opted to avoid generalizing these verses. He argued that attributing ignorance to the people is confined to matters such as Judgment Day and is not relevant to current political matters (cited in Moussavi, 1992: 103–104). Salehi-Najafabadi highlighted that Khomeini and Imam Ali were two outstanding examples in Shiite history in which Velayat, in the sense of political leadership, was materialized through the people's will (cited in Akhavi, 1996: 245–248).

Questioning the religious justification for the clergy's political authority,[16] Salehi-Najafabadi argued that the clergy do not represent the Hidden Imam in the OCCULTATION ERA and, thus, cannot claim political authority. Associating Velayat (authority) with Vekalat (representation), Salehi-Najafabadi argued that the clergy represent the people and not the Hidden Imam in the political sphere. Hence, their political authority ought to be based upon majority opinion. Being a Mojtahed is not required of a ruler. In this line of thought, Salehi-Najafabadi detached political leadership from religion (Salehi-Najafabadi, 1984: 23–24). Salehi-Najafabadi's articulation resembled

---

15. For example, see the following Quranic verses:

"They question thee as if thou couldst be well informed thereof. Say: knowledge thereof is with Allah only, but most of mankind know not" (7:187; trans. Marmaduke Pickthall)

يَسْأَلُونَكَ كَأَنَّكَ حَفِيٌّ عَنْهَا قُلْ إِنَّمَا عِلْمُهَا عِندَ اللّه وَلَكِنَّ أَكْثَرَ النَّاسِ لَا يَعْلَمُونَ

"Allah hath not appointed anything in the nature of a *bahirah* or a *sa'ibah* or a *wasilah* or a *hami*, but those who disbelieve invent a lie against Allah. Most of them have no sense (5:103; trans. Marmaduke Pickthall]

مَا جَعَلَ الله مِن بَحِيرَةٍ وَلَا سَائِبَةٍ وَلَا وَصِيلَةٍ وَلَا حَامٍ وَلَكِنَّ الَّذِينَ كَفَرُواْ يَفْتَرُونَ عَلَى اللّه الْكَذِبَ وَأَكْثَرُهُمْ لَا يَعْقِلُونَ

16. A narrative by Umar Ibn Hanzalah was the key religious source used by Khomeini and other proponents of the clergy's political authority. Umar Ibn Hanzaleh said: "I asked Imam al Sadiq whether it was permissible for two Shi'a, who had a disagreement concerning a debt or a legacy, to seek the verdict of the ruler or judge. He replied: 'Anyone, who has recourse to the ruler or judge, whether his case is just or unjust, has in reality had recourse to *taghut* [oppressive government]. . ..'" Umar ibn Hanzalah then asked: "What should these two Shi'a do then, under such circumstances?" Imam al Sadiq answered: "They must seek out one of you who narrate our tradition; who is versed in what is permissible and what is forbidden; who is well acquainted with our laws and ordinances, and accept him as judge and arbiter, for I appoint him as judge over you" (Khomeini, 2005, 79). Salehi-Najafabadi questions the authenticity of this narrative. For detailed discussion, see Baik-Mohammadian, 2007: 85–86.

the doctrine of social contract, according to which government is a consequence of a contract between people and ruler (Akhavi, 1996: 248). However,
his employment of Velayat-e Faqih was problematic. One would argue that
his usage of the concept is understandable in view of the dominance of the
Velayat-e Faqih discourse at the time his book was published. He may have
been obliged to use language similar to Khomeini's discourse. Furthermore,
he confined his ideas to scholarly circles and was reluctant to publicly criticize
the clergy's political leadership. This may explain why he was not detained by
the Islamic state in contrast to such figures as the Ayatollahs Shariatmadari,
Qomi, and Montazeri.

The contribution of scholars such as Moghniya, Shams ad-Din, and
Salehi-Najafabadi are by and large theoretical analyses, as they did not examine the Islamic state of Iran in empirical terms. But the lived experience of
the clerical establishment has provided a new source of empirical evidence for
a generation of scholars who are opposed to the clergy's political leadership.
Like Moghniya, Shams al-Din, and Salehi-Najafabadi, Ayatollah Montazeri
highlighted the role of the people while promoting the clergy's strong presence in the political sphere. Along with jurisprudential sources, Montazeri
made good use of empirical evidence to set specific restrictions for clerical
authority in the political sphere. His personal contribution to the formation of
the Islamic Republic of Iran was invaluable inasmuch as it reified his critique
of the clergy's privileged political status.

Restricting the Clergy's Political Authority

For Ayatollah Montazeri, religious piety allows the clergy to be effective
political leaders as long as they have the people's consent. However, without the people's consent the clergy's religious credentials do not justify their
privileged status in the political sphere. Revising his earlier ideas, Ayatollah
Montazeri described the lack of legislative experience of clerics as an important shortcoming of the members of the Constituent Assembly. The possibility of the emergence of a new dictatorship[17] was central to the decision
to include the Velayat-e Faqih in the Constitution (Movahedi-Savoji, 2011;
Parliament, 1989). Ayatollahs Beheshti and Montazeri played key roles in setting aside the early draft of the Constitution in which the clergy were not

17. Another justification for granting political authority to the clergy was the ideological
nature of the revolution. It was suggested that similar to the former Soviet Union, the ruler
should act as an ideologue. The ultimate political power should be handed to someone of
superior religious knowledge (Kadivar, 2011b).

granted special privileges. In the early draft of the Constitution, the president was accorded significant power, a condition that provoked Ayatollahs Beheshti and Montazeri to advocate the clergy's political leadership as a counterbalancing force. Ayatollah Montazeri wrote:

> There was still a lot of fear with respect to the vestiges of despotism in the executive branch. . .. Due to too much devotion to Imam Khomeini, a divine and eternal image of him had been ingrained in the minds of the Experts.. . . Hence, the Experts, by and large, tried to weaken the executive branch and to make an innocuous entity out of it, instead opting to invest all power in the position of leadership, which was then occupied by Ayatollah Khomeini. As such, there was little concern for future problems that this kind of approach might bring. The problem intensified when the revision of the Constitution coincided with the departure of Imam Khomeini from this world (quoted in Abdo, 2001: 17).

For the proponents of the clergy's political authority, immense power vested with a single person such as a president could have facilitated the emergence of a new dictatorship in post-revolutionary Iran. However, the same logic should have prevented them from granting a single person—in their case, a jurist—immense executive power. Due to the religious nature of the clergy, however, it was argued that power in the hands of the clergy could not lead to a dictatorship. In session 32 of the Constituent Assembly, Ayatollah Jaafar Sobhani maintained appointing a just jurist as leader would prevent the possibility of a dictatorship; as in Iran's distant and contemporary history, the presence of a jurist has always worked against the force of dictatorship. This explains his suggestion that the sentence "In order to secure freedom and to prevent dictatorship" be added to the article pertaining to the Velayat-e Faqih (Movahedi-Savoji, 2011). Defending the clergy's privileged status in the Constitution, Ayatollah Montazeri highlighted the imperative of preempting the rise of dictatorship. As the prayer Imam, Montazeri stated in a Friday sermon in December 1979:

> Whoever holds the power would necessarily lean [towards] autocracy and dictatorship. Thus, the law should be articulated in a way to prevent dictatorship. In the first draft of the Constitution the president enjoyed widespread authority while being subject to minimum qualification. All three branches of the government were to be controlled by the president. Dictatorship comes from these branches. We obstructed

these three ways of dictatorship by handing the control of all three branches [of government] to the elected ruler [Valey-e Faqih] (quoted in Kadivar, 2011b).

The religious qualifications of the clergy were thought to eliminate the possibility of the clergy's political authority degrading into a dictatorship. The basic qualifications of a just jurist, which commanded him to prioritize religious goals over all other matters, were deemed sufficient. It was argued that being just should be the key qualification of the jurist; if the ruler of an Islamic state, a Valey-e Faqih in Iran's case, inclined towards dictatorship, he would have lost this basic qualification. This may be true from a religious standpoint, but as subsequent developments proved, politics in practice can complicate matters. Upon this realization, Ayatollah Montazeri, formerly the key advocate of the clergy's political leadership in the Constituent Assembly,[18] revised his thought on clerical political authority.

In 1979, the whole debate surrounding the ultimate power of a cleric was overshadowed by the charismatic presence of Ayatollah Khomeini. It was difficult to imagine or discuss the possibility of dictatorship in the presence of such a figure. There was, in effect, de facto Velayat-e Faqih and the Constituent Assembly had legalized it. As noted later by Ayatollah Montazeri, a divine and eternal image of Khomeini was ingrained in the minds of the members of the Constituent Assembly, and this reinforced the underlying faith in the impossibility of dictatorship by a cleric.

Establishing the Assembly of Experts to appoint and monitor the Valey-e Faqih was seen as the best insurance against potential dictatorship by the Valey-e Faqih. This appointment process was perceived as delegating the position to an elected figure (indirectly elected by the subjects) and also subjecting this figure to surveillance. This was evident in the responses of Ayatollah Montazeri and others, including Ayatollah Beheshti, to critics. However, subsequent politico-religious developments have revealed that not only did the Valey-e Faqih system incline towards authoritarian rule, but that the Assembly of Experts has become transformed into a body that glorifies the Valey-e Faqih rather than oversees him.[19] Even minor criticism of the Valey-e Faqih within the assembly is not

18. Ayatollah Montazeri was also president of the Constituent Assembly. Along with Ayatollah Beheshti (1928–1981), who was then the vice president of the assembly, he played a prominent role in adding the notion of Velayat-e Faqih to the Constituent Assembly.

19. See Ehteshami & Zweiri, 2006. Also, for details of the failure of the main mission of the Assembly of Experts, see Montazeri, 2003: 193–199. Interestingly, the chairman of the Assembly of Experts provides a strange definition of overseeing Valey-e Faqih by claiming that the overseeing role of the assembly meant protecting the Supreme Leader. He even advanced the old argument that monitoring the role of the assembly was just monitoring

tolerated. A notable example is Hashemi-Rafsanjani, the former chairman of the assembly, who lost his position when he refused to second the Valey-e Faqih's endorsement of the controversial 2009 election.

While at the time of drafting the Constitution Ayatollah Montazeri clearly distinguished the clergy from laymen by their aptitude for justice, the actual implementation of the doctrine of Velayat-e Faqih was enough to convince him that there is indeed no difference between the lay and the cleric in terms of political power. In his latest articulation, Montazeri affirmed that clerics like laymen are prone to corruption and misuse of power. He wrote: "From a rational as well as religious point of view, running the issue of the country ought not to be confined to traditional methods. We should understand that the risk of dictatorship and corruption is associated with the imperium of an infallible jurist as well as of a layman" (Montazeri, 2008: 30).

Montazeri's writings included significant detail in addressing the role of clergy in the judiciary, army, legislation, and executive body. He introduced the strongest restrictions on the role of clergy in the sociopolitical and economic spheres. Ayatollah Montazeri invalidated the ruling clergy's claim to possess exclusive political authority from various angles. The most significant point made by Montazeri was his ground-breaking fatwa about religious emulation (*taghlid*), which in 2003 introduced a new notion of religious emulation to invalidate jurists' authority over emulators. Specifically, he deemed fatwas issued by Marja-e Taghlids not obligatory for emulators unless they were personally assured of the accuracy of each fatwa. Through this innovative understanding of fatwa, Montazeri transformed the devotional nature of jurist–emulator relations into a rational exercise (Kadivar, 2010d; Montazeri, 2006a: 80; 2008: 14). Thus, the jurisprudential principal of emulation no longer necessitated uncritical obedience to jurists, particularly in the sociopolitical sphere, wherein *fiqh* may not necessarily demonstrate high competence.

Montazeri recognized that the intervention of the clergy in different aspects of Iranian sociopolitical life had led to the erosion of the clergy's religious authority (2003: 161). By and large, this erosion of religious authority was rooted in the clergy's lack of competence in non-jurisprudential arenas. Montazeri, confining the political role of the clergy to a supervisory position, built his argument upon a simple but critical point: sociopolitical capacities require skills in the relevant

---

the continuation of the qualification, not the performance, of the Supreme Leader. There was a report by a conservative weekly magazine saying that Khamenei has specifically ordered the Assembly of Experts not to adopt a monitoring role on the conduct of the Supreme Leader (BBC, 2012).

fields. He attributed religious precepts[20] along with rational justifications for experts to manage sociopolitical affairs. As Montazeri played a key role in conceptualizing and materializing the doctrine of the Velayat-e Faqih, not surprisingly he confined many of his revisionist arguments to issues restricting the authority of Velayat-e Faqih; occasionally, however, he did address the clergy's role in other capacities. For example, Montazeri objected to the fact that all of the members of the Assembly of Experts were clerics. He argued that jurisprudential knowledge (*fiqahat*) was only one among other qualifications of the Valey-e Faqih. Thus, members of the Assembly of Experts are not necessarily qualified to appoint a Valey-e Faqih. Montazeri wrote:

> Many of them [members of the Assembly of Experts] are only equipped with seminary knowledge and are not sufficiently engaged with the press and news. They are unaware of political issues and events in the country. Under these circumstances, those who are learned and expert in social and political issues, want to know how persons with such limited qualifications can choose the leader of the country (2007: 292–294).

Montazeri argued that only two positions in an Islamic state require clerical qualifications: Velayat-e Faqih and judgement. In line with his revised position, Montazeri proposed a somewhat more democratic mechanism than that practiced in the current political structure. After the Constitution was amended in 1989, the Chief of the Judiciary was appointed by the Supreme Leader. Montazeri opposed this amendment, deeming the original arrangement more appropriate. According to the original Constitution, the judiciary was led by five jurists, three of whom were elected by judges. He argued that the amendment made the system vulnerable to despotism. Instead of being appointed by the Supreme Leader, Montazeri contended that the chief of the judiciary should be selected by senior judges. However, he advocated, as he had earlier, a robust jurisprudential knowledge within the judiciary, privileging the clergy for their religious capability. Montazeri stated: "According to most of the Shiite jurists including Imam Khomeini, a judge should be qualified to be *mojtahed* in addition to qualifications such as possessing judicial skills and being just. Judgement by a non-*mojtahed* is religiously vain (*batel*)" (2003: 426).

---

20. Montazeri referred to few hadiths, mostly those of infallible Imams. For details of these hadiths, see Montazeri, 2003: 502–503; 2008: 31–34.

Montazeri maintained that the Islamic nature of Iran necessitated the supervision of a just jurist possessing a learned understanding of Islam over the country's management. Similarly, each sociopolitical arena ought to be led by those skilled in the relevant field. He resolved this seeming contradiction via the demotion of the clergy to a supervisory role. Montazeri asserted that only the Islamic aspects of governance should be the domain of clerical authority. Thus, there was neither religious justification nor a rational basis for clergy in general and Valey-e Faqih in particular to dictate non-religious matters. The clergy's role was to ensure that the Islamic dimension of policy-making was secured and that the general direction of the political system did not contradict Islamic teachings (Montazeri, 2003: 39, 592; 2008: 29–34). Montazeri reconceptualized the Velayat-e Faqih (rule of the Islamic jurist) into Velayat-e Fiqh (rule of Islamic jurisprudence), arguing that the ultimate goal was to maintain the integrity of Islamic principles rather than the political leadership of the clergy:

> Velayat-e Faqih is the rule of jurisprudence, not rule of [a] jurist. It means custodianship of God's commands over men's social behavior.. . . A just jurist, who is expert and proficient in Islamic issues, should supervise the process of leading the country in order to make sure that Islamic precepts are not violated.. . . Religion and rationality never permit the handing over of decision-making pertinent to complicated social, political, economic, military and international relations to a man whose specialty is only jurisprudence (Montazeri, 2003: 371).

Not only did he call for confining the authority of the Valey-e Faqih to religious matters,[21] he also urged changing the lifetime tenure of Valey-e Faqih to a limited period. As explained in detail in the first chapter, from Montazeri's perspective, as the authority of Valey-e Faqih is rooted in the subjects' consent, he thus ought to be accountable to the people.

Consistent with the view of scholars such as Salehi-Najafabadi, Shams al-Din, and Moghniya, Montazeri prioritized and privileged the position of the people in the Islamic state. In Montazeri's view, the religious competency of the clergy accorded them a privileged place in the sociopolitical sphere. However, the people's will must remain central to the privileges accorded to clerics. While this privilege is confined to religious matters, Montazeri's argument falls short

---

21. From Montazeri's point of view, these issues included appointing Friday Imams, the head of pilgrimage office, and announcing fasting dates along with general monitoring of the Islamic direction of legislation and policy-making (Montazeri, 2003: 284–285).

of drawing a clear line between religious and non-religious matters. Placing this within Montazeri's overarching notion that Islam incorporates sociopolitical dimensions, one could readily envision the possibility of expanding the spectrum of religious matters to all sociopolitical issues, as is the case with the current political practice in Iran. The scope of religion in Iran has been broadened to provide justification for the clergy's intervention in all sociopolitical issues. Furthermore, Montazeri did not explicate whether the clergy should enjoy the right of veto in religious matters. What would happen if experts in sociopolitical issues promoted policies that are deemed to have violated religious principles? The assumption is that religious principles should be prioritized, which ultimately gives the clergy's authority the upper hand in governance.

Evaluating Montazeri's ideas through a democratic lens is problematic, particularly when promoting a model of secularity. However, the contribution of his scholarship to the formation of religious secularity is unquestionable. It is worth noting that his students have formed the bulk of the religious secularity discourse. Mohsen Kadivar, Hadi Ghabel, Fazel Maybodi, and Emad al-Din Baghi are some examples of clerics who have contributed significantly to the reformist scholarship that promotes religious secularity. In addition, Montazeri belonged to the most traditional circle of the religious strata. His followers not only included educated, religious people, but many habitual believers. His quasi-democratic ideas appealed to the most religious layer of society; in many ways, his influence among traditional jurists was ground-breaking. This refers not only to his definition of state–people relations within the framework of a social contract and his enormous work in the field of human rights, but also to his religious fatwas urging Muslims to rise up against the clergy's political leadership. After the Islamic state's violent suppression of the protests following the 2009 presidential election, Montazeri issued a series of fatwas in which he urged believers to rebel against the Islamic state. He overtly referred to Ayatollah Khamanei as *ja'er* (unjust and oppressive). Montazeri invited the people to take action against what he saw as religiously illegitimate rule by clergy:

> [Unjust leaders'] authority is not legitimate in any way. If they remain in their position by using force, fraud or forgery, then the people must express their opinion regarding the illegitimacy and unpopularity [of the rulers], and remove them from their position in the least harmful and most effective way (2010: 404–405).

This fatwa marked a turning point in Montazeri's thought. Stressing its importance, Soroush describes it as a ground-breaking development in both

Shiite and Sunnite political history. Soroush argues outright revolt against a ruler is not supported by mainstream Islamic political thought. Throughout Islamic history, jurists have proven extremely reluctant to provide believers with religious justification to revolt against a ruler (Soroush, 2009c). As an example of this, Ghazali did not see revolt against a ruler as an option from a religious perspective: "Enforcing change by the use of force by any subject against his ruler is not an option because this only serves to stir up turmoil and arouse evil, leading to greater danger" (quoted in Ghazali & Farouk-Alli, 2010: 34). Ghazali allowed for the criticism of a ruler verbally as long as it did not lead to general upheaval. Ghazali and Farouk-Alli's historical review led them to conclude, "Permission in this regard reached such a stage that some legal scholars even began regarding perseverance in the face of the injustice of the ruler as a branch of faith" (2010:34–35). As a Marja-e Taghlid against a backdrop of this tradition, Montazeri's authorization of revolt against the Islamic state is highly unprecedented.

Iran's ruling clergy failed to export Islamic revolution to the rest of the Muslim world. Certainly, the Shiite basis of Iran's Islamic state and its political model has been a major obstacle to accomplishing this goal. However, closer scrutiny reveals that Sunni–Shi'a division is not the only reason for the weak Islamic state model within the Muslim world. Iran's ruling clergy has also failed to export their notion of clerical state to Iraq and Lebanon, two major Shiite countries. One may give many different reasons for this unfulfilled aspiration; however, I suggest that senior clerics in Iraq and Lebanon have rejected the idea of political leadership by the clergy. The ruling clergy seized political power and institutionalized the clerical establishment in Iran. However, their politico-religious discourse failed to gain support of the senior religious leaders of the Shiite world, which hindered the expansion of the clerical establishment.

The Clerical Political System: Resisted and Rejected

There is no major or respected entity within the Shiite or Sunnite worlds beyond Iran that subscribes to a political system based on the clergy's political leadership. In the Shiite world this is particularly significant in view of the close connection between the different Shiite sites.[22] Qom in Iran and Najaf in Iraq have been the two main Shiite centres of learning. Najaf has traditionally been the major hub for Shiite religious learning, while Qom's

---

22. For further discussion about the connections between Iran and Lebanon, see Chehabi & Abisaab, 2006.

religious education structure was only formed in 1921. In the contemporary world, there has never been a senior Ayatollah who has not trained in these centres. In the past, Najaf was the more prominent of the two, and for this reason all Iranian Marja-e Taghlids undertook the main part of their training in Najaf. This is also true about the training of Lebanese Grand Ayatollahs such as Imam Mousa-Sadr, Muhammad Hussein Fadl-Allah, Mohammad Mehdi Shams al-Din, and Mohammed Jawad Moghniya. Moreover, many high-ranking Ayatollahs in Iraq including Akhund Khurasani, Mahmoud Shahroudi, Khoei, and Sistani originally came from Iran.[23] Hence, because of this close Shiite clerical association, the stances adopted by Shiite clerics and scholars in Iraq and Lebanon are of great importance.

Iran's experience in terms of a clerical political rule has set a precedent for other Shiite-majority countries. Both Iraq and Lebanon have experienced tremendous political shifts over the last few decades. To be sure, political Islam and the Shiite clergy have been significant contributors to these political shifts. However, senior clerics in these states have never attempted to assume political leadership on the grounds of their religious credentials. The strategy adopted by the ISCI, the most powerful Shiite party in the post-Saddam era, is a good example. It was founded and led by Iraqi clerics,[24] but has never advocated political leadership by the clergy. The Islamic Dawa Party in Iraq has worked towards the institutionalization of non-clerical leadership within the Party (Rodger Shanahan, 2004: 947). Cole concludes from his investigation of the Ayatollahs' position in the post-Saddam era that the principles of

---

23. This has changed during the last few decades. Saddam's oppressive policy in Iraq coincided with the reign of the Islamic state in Iran, during which Qom received great support from the state. This may change the Shiite setting in the future. Currently, Grand Ayatollah Sistani is the most high-ranking Ayatollah in the Shiite world. Many new Ayatollahs are being trained in Qom; and, while not at the same level as the Grand Ayatollah Sistani, in the near future they may constitute a new generation of high-ranking Ayatollahs. It should, of course, be taken into consideration that in the long term, post-Saddam Najaf may regain its traditional preeminent position. For example, Vali Naser suggests that compared with the pre-2003 era, now "many more Iranians recognize Ayatollah Sistani as their religious leader and turn their religious taxes over to him. Although largely cynical about their own clerical leaders, many Iranians have embraced the revival of Shiite identity and culture in Iraq." See Nasr, 2006: 63; Shams al-Din, 1999.

24. The ISCI was founded in 1982 in close association with the Islamic Republic of Iran in order to overthrow Iraq's Saddam Hussein. Always headed by clergy, its first leader was Hashemi-Shahroudi, who was Iran's chief of judiciary from 1999 to 2009. This is further proof of the close association of the Shiite clergy beyond the nation-state border, which was, of course, a problematic issue during the eight-year war between Iran and Iraq. Despite this war, however, transnational relations between the Shiite clergy remained untouched. From 1986 onwards, the ISCI has been led by the al-Hakim family: Ayatollah Mohammed Baqir al-Hakim (1939–2003), Abdul Aziz al-Hakim (1953–2009), and Ammar al-Hakim (1971–), respectively.

popular sovereignty have been invoked by the most prominent religious leaders of Iraq. The clerical state is markedly absent from their discourse (2006).

Lebanon's Constitution, political system, and diverse religious ethnic
society make little space for Iran's model of clerical rule, a fact that both of
the main Shiite political groups, Hezbollah and the Amal movement, have
long acknowledged. Although the establishment of an Islamic state was an
ideal of the Hezbollah leadership (Badran, 2009: 53–59; Byers, 2003: 21–23;
Saad-Ghorayeb, 2002: 64–65), "Nasrallah and his colleagues have repeatedly
declared that the prospects for establishing a state based on Islamic rule will
probably never exist in Lebanon" (Norton, 2007: 158). The Amal movement
has long embraced a secular political system. Amal's non-clerical leaders, who
actively participate in the electoral process, abandoned radical policies from
the 1980s onwards. Instead of the ruling Iranian clergy, they are inspired by
the lay figures of Iran's revolution such as Ali Shariati and Mehdi Bazargan
(Norton, 2007: 29–30; R. Shanahan, 2005).

John Esposito sheds light on the wide political diversity within the Muslim
world. His term "silenced majority" effectively debunks the image of most
Muslims as extremists. Extremists only constitute a minority of Muslims
and are not necessarily more religious than their fellow Muslims (Esposito &
Mogahed, 2007: ix). Borrowing Esposito's term, this chapter argues that in
the Shiite context, there is a "silenced majority" within the religious establishment, while the minority who subscribe to the clergy's political leadership have portrayed themselves as the sole representatives of Islam in Iran.
Khomeini's vociferous political discourse, the regional and international
impacts of the revolution, and, more importantly, the oppressive policies of
the ruling clergy have silenced the apolitical and quietist attitudes of the
preeminent Marja-e Taghlids. Taking advantage of the quietist approach of
the majority of Marja-e Taghlids, the ruling clergy has been able to suppress
the few attempts to resist its political leadership. The Iranian state's political system based on the clergy's political leadership has been rejected by
eminent Shiite leaders. Devotional relations between these religious leaders
and habitual believers are of significant importance in a long-term perspective. These religious leaders will play a pivotal role in the interplay of religion and politics in a prospective post-Islamic state of the country. Many do
not actively contribute to the religious secularity discourse, but their apolitical approach will contribute to the evolution of religious secularity over the
course of time.

Iran's religious intellectuals have played a leading role in the evolution of
religious secularity and resisting the legitimacy of the clergy's political leadership. They have articulated the religious secularity discourse as an alternative

to the clerical Islamic state. They have undermined not only the clergy's polit-ical authority, but also its religious authority. Although the main bulk of the religious secularity discourse has crystallized in post-revolutionary Iran, in particular from the late 1980s onward, its roots can be traced back to the pre-revolutionary era, when Ali Shariati popularized the concept of "Islam without clergy".

6

Clerical Hegemony

CONTRADICTIONS AND PARADOXES

RELIGIOUS INTELLECTUALS ARE the main drivers of a discourse that refuses to accord privilege to the clergy in sociopolitical life. The term "religious intellectuals" describes scholars who are not religious leaders in the conventional sense, but who place religion at the centre of their scholarly works. Jahanbakhsh defines them as "individuals who are committed to religion, but who do not necessarily belong to the religious establishment. They are aware of science and of the sociocultural problems resulting from economic change. Their major concern is to prove that what they judge to be true religion is not irrelevant to the modern changing world" (2001b: 51). Soroush, who coined the term in the mid-1980s, outlines the core characteristics of religious intellectuals (2010e: 251–336),[1] as follows: They are differentiated from secular intellectuals by way of their religious convictions, and from the clergy by their use of both religious and extra-religious sources to offer a modern understanding of religion. Thus, while an individual may receive training in a seminary and dress in the style of the clergy, he may also be considered a religious intellectual due to his adherence to extra-religious sources. Scholars such as Mojtahed-Shabestari, Kadivar, and Eshkevari are good examples in this regard.[2]

The concept of religious intellectualism has been subjected to considerable controversy in contemporary Iranian scholarly circles, where it has faced objections from both secular and religious scholars. Secular scholars

---

1. For details of these characteristics in the English language, see Jahanbakhsh, 2004.

2. For further explanation of the religious intellectuals and reformist clerics' subscription to this group, see Boroujerdi, 1996: 99–131; Jahanbakhsh, 2004; Kamrava, 2008: 122–132; Kazemi, 2008; Pedram, 2003; Yousefi Eshkevari, 2014.

including Seyed Javad Tabatabaei, Mohammad Reza Nikfar, and Aramesh Doostar assert that religiosity and intellectuality are two distinctive, non-cohesive, oxymoronic phenomena. As the logic goes, intellectualism requires absolute commitment to rationality, whereas religiosity demands slavish adherence to specific principles that cannot be questioned (Nikfar, 2003; Tabatabaei, 2007). Religious scholars (e.g., Seyyed Hossein Nasr) criticize religious intellectuals for merging Islam with modernism. More conservative religious scholars (e.g. Ayatollah Javadi-Amoli and Mesbah-Yazdi) criticize them for their diversion from Islamic tradition. Irrespective of the contested nature of the concept of religious intellectualism, there remains a group in Iran's scholarly circle who distance themselves from both traditional religious leaders and secular intellectuals. They may not claim devotional authority over habitual believers, but they do claim formative influence over the educated and youthful cohort.

Objections to the clergy's political leadership from within the traditional circle are voiced solely by other clerics and are confined to the political authority of the clergy. Importantly, there have been no constructive alternatives to the clerical establishment proposed by the traditional circle despite their criticisms. By contrast, the reformist discourse is led by religious intellectuals, including lay religious scholars and reformist clerics, who challenge the clergy's religious and political authority. Some branches of religious intellectualism have even extended their challenge to questioning the very basis of the clergy in Islamic history.

This chapter explores the arguments advanced by religious intellectuals, the leading proponents of religious secularity. Although the concept of religious intellectualism is relatively new due to the main bulk of their work emerging in the post-revolutionary era, it is worth noting that similar arguments existed in the pre-revolutionary era. After providing a brief explanation of the emergence of the religious intellectuals and their fluctuating relations with clergy, this chapter elaborates on the notion of "Islam without clergy", a notion proposed by pioneering religious intellectual Ali Shariati.

This is a way of critique of the clergy's internal structure, including its limitations in the sociopolitical realm and dangerous conflation of religious and political authority. Paying specific attention to Velayat-e Faqih, this chapter highlights the intrinsic inconsistency between Velayat-e Faqih and the decentralized structure of the clergy and Marjaiat. The concluding discussion examines the lived experience of the Islamic state. Focus is upon the manner in which the clergy's political leadership has undermined the reputation of the clerics and their traditional democratic-pluralistic structure.

The Clergy: A Genuine Class in Islam?

As part of his modernization program, Reza Khan established the first university in Iran in 1934. He subsequently sent students abroad to study new sciences. His ousting in 1941 coincided with the emergence of a new generation that, while trained in the Western-style education system, possessed strong religious convictions. A number of Iranian scholars—Bazargan and Sahabi, for example—have provided scientific explanations for Islamic teachings in an attempt to prove the compatibility of Islam and modern science.[3] Their innovative approach offered a timely interpretation of Islam that appealed to the country's youth. As well, they were welcomed by the clergy in Qom, particularly by the politicized clerics (Eshkevari, 2011d). It was this informal coalition between the religious intellectuals and politicized clerics that played a significant role in the events leading up to the 1979 revolution.

This friendly relationship between the religious intellectuals and the clergy, however, was short-lived. The very existence of religious intellectualism, which espoused the ability of the layman to possess religious knowledge, undermined the clergy's monopoly of religious wisdom. Generations of religious intellectuals with backgrounds in science and social science held unorthodox interpretations of religion, which engendered long-lasting tension within the clergy. This tension can be traced back as far as the pre-revolutionary era when Shariati questioned the historical authenticity of the clergy as a class within Islam. Shariati represented the second generation of religious intellectuals who approached Islam from a modern and scientific perspective; but, unlike the first generation (e.g., Bazargan and Sahabi), he used social science concepts to introduce an ideological Islam (Derakhsheh, 2002).

Shariati opposed an apolitical form of Islam that was confined to seminaries, funerals, and mourning rituals. He blamed the clergy for what he argued was mass consent to oppression. According to Shariati, the ruling class—the wealthy, holders of power, and the clergy—formed a triangular structure of economic power, political oppression, and inner justification—what he called the "trinity of oppression", or "gold, coercion and deception". "They possess economic authority, political authority and religious authority.

---

3. For example, using his educational background in biology, Ezatullah Sahabi (1930–2011) published two books entitled *Creation of Mankind in the Quran* and *Quran and Evolution* in which he tried to prove the compatibility of evolution theory with Quranic verses. Mehdi Bazargan (1897–1994) took the leading role in provoking a scientific approach to religious sources, particularly the Quran. Books such as *Thermodynamic in Life* (1954), *The Mission and Evolution* (1967), and *Monotheism, Nature and Evolution*, to name but a few, are among these efforts.

It did not matter if they were in peace or in war. Their peace or conflict was about reigning over people not for people" (Shariati, 2011: 128).

In Shariati's view, the sociopolitical function of the clergy after Shiism became the official religion during the Safavid dynasty (1501–1736 AD) was to legitimize oppression (Ghamari-Tabrizi, 2004: 511). The solution, for Shariati, lay in their elimination. To this end, he developed the doctrine of "Islam without clergy" (*Islam-e menhaye rohaniayt*):

> Doctor [Mossadegh] developed the doctrine of "economy without oil" in order to achieve the independence of the [oil nationalization] movement.. . . . Fortunately nowadays the doctrine of "Islam without clergy" is realized. As an outcome of this achievement, Islam has been released from its Middle Ages–style narrow framework.. . . [A] free Islam has stepped out of the sanctuaries and seminary chambers into life, thought, consciousness, action and dynamism instead of being confined to mourning ceremonies (Shariati, 2000: 7).

Shariati argued for the elimination of all mediating forces between God and humankind, establishing instead a direct relationship with the creator. He maintained that "there is no formal organization of clergy in Islam. Various positions of the clergy are not recognized in Islam and the acceptance of faith, as well as the performing of religious rituals by believers, are not subject to supervision and intercession by any official authority" (Shariati, 2009: 24). This is why, Shariati argued, the clergy as a class is neither rooted in Islamic history in general nor in Shiite history in particular. In short, he states that the clergy was imported from Christianity and has in actuality no real place in Islam (quoted in Razmjoo, 1994: 37–47).

Despite his notable contribution to the 1979 revolution, Shariati's notions vis-à-vis the clergy placed him among the clergy's most hated opponents.[4] In the 1970s, senior clerics who did not take a position against Shariati were rare.[5] Requesting the imprisonment and possible execution of Shariati, Ayatollah Ansari-Qomi called upon the imperial government, the people, and the clergy to condemn him as a terrorist and saboteur. The Ayatollah wrote: "During the past 1,000 years, the histories of Islam and Shi'a Islam have never, nor

---

4. Soroush (2006a) maintains that the opinions of all groups about Shariati have varied over time. The clergy is the one group that has always hated Shariati as a threat to Islam.

5. Ayatollah Khomeini resisted his followers' requests to take a position against Shariati. It seems that he had political considerations due to the pivotal role that Shariati played in mobilizing educated people against the Shah.

ever will, encounter a more dangerous, dreadful and bolder enemy than Ali Shariati" (quoted in Rahnama, 2000: 271). Ayatollah Motahhari became embroiled in a debate with Shariati, which resulted in the issuing of fatwas by Ayatollah Ruhani and Ayatollah Tabatabaie-Qomi, declaring Hosseiniyeh Ershad's[6] talks and publications *haram*.[7]

Eshkevari correctly points out that before the 1979 revolution, the clergy's only weapon was excommunication. After claiming political authority in post-revolutionary Iran, however, the clergy were now equipped with the tools necessary to more effectively manage their opponents (2011d). This explains the decline in frequency and severity of challenges to the clergy's legitimacy in the post-revolutionary era. However, there was one exceptional case that provoked a severe reaction from the ruling clergy. In the relatively open atmosphere of the reformist era, Hashem Aghajari, a history professor at Tarbiat Modares University, expounded upon Shariati's view of the clergy. In his seminal lecture "Islamic Protestantism and Shariati", Aghajari highlighted the similarities between the current clerical establishment in Iran and Christianity before the Protestant Reformation (Sukidi, 2005: 407). Just as Protestantism in the West sought to rescue Christianity from the clergy and the hierarchy of the church, so Aghajari urged that an Islamic Protestantism was indispensible for liberating Islam and Iranian Muslims from the political and religious domination of the ruling clergy (Savyon, 2002). Echoing Shariati, Aghajari stated:

> We [Muslims] do not need mediators between us and God. We do not need mediators to understand God's holy book. Did the Prophet speak to the people directly? We don't need to go to the clergy: each person is his own clergy.. . . In Islam, we never had a class of clergy; some clerical titles were created as recently as 50 or 60 years ago. Where did we have a clerical class in the Safavid dynasty? [Today's titles for Islamic clergy] are like the Church hierarchy—bishops, cardinals, priests. This type of hierarchy in [contemporary Shiite Islam] is an emulation of the Church (2002b).

Aghajari's position gave rise to heated debate, with some even comparing him to Martin Luther.[8] To a large extent, this was not because he raised an original

---

6. For Hosseiniyeh Ershad and its importance to Iran's politico-religious history, see Chehabi, 1990: 203–210; Rahnama, 2000: 226–242.

7. For a detailed explanation of the clergy's confrontation with Shariati, see Haidari, 2008; Rahnama, 2000: 246–260.

8. See Sukidi, 2005. In contrast, Alatas objects to this comparison, declaring that Luther is an inappropriate model for Muslim revivalists (2007: 514–517).

doctrine, but because of the circumstances under which he reintroduced an earlier argument. The ruling clergy's reaction was severe, to say the least. Aghajari was convicted of apostasy and sentenced to death in November 2002. It was only after major campaigns and an outcry from both inside and outside Iran that the charge was dropped and his sentence commuted to three years in prison, two years of probation, and a five-year suspension of social rights (including a ban on teaching in universities). Although Aghajari was not executed, the ruling clergy nonetheless made an example of him for other religious intellectuals. For the most part, they succeeded. Today a line of direct attack against the clergy's authenticity is totally lacking from the religious intellectual discourse. However, this does not mean that the occurrence had no impact on the clergy's religious authority. Although the political authority of the clergy is the prime target of advocates for religious secularity in contemporary Iran, the clergy's religious authority has not been totally omitted from the discourse.

Governmental Incompetence

In post-revolutionary Iran, the threat of clerical retaliation has all but silenced questions of legitimacy put forward by the reformist discourse. As a result, religious intellectuals have been forced to adopt more subtle methods of undermining the clergy's authority. This has seen dissent channeled into diverse areas and embedded deeply within theological discussion. For example, scholars, including Mojtahed-Shabestari and Soroush, argue that jurisprudence is simply an exoteric dimension of religion, the implication being that while the clergy may claim authority over jurisprudence, the more esoteric and essential aspects of religion remain outside of their competence.

Religious intellectuals have also subjected specific details of the clerical establishment to scrutiny, such as the seminaries' curricula and the financial livelihoods of the clergy. Furthermore, contributions to the discussion from within the clergy are an added advantage of the religious secularity discourse. And while clerics such as Kadivar and Mojtahed-Shabestari have been the architects of these challenges, Ayatollah Montazeri could also be included in this category when one considers his rationalized articulation of emulation.

The more subtle, implicit, and sectarian features of the challenges to the clergy's authority in post-revolutionary Iran, along with the tactical retreats of their critics, have denied the ruling clergy sufficient justification for eliminating dissent. As a result, critics of the clergy have managed to survive by advancing their arguments in increments. With the passage of time, the post-revolutionary challenge to the clergy's authority is reaching a similar point to that of Shariati's in the 1970s. However, in contrast to Shariati's challenge, contemporary discourse offers a well-built challenge rooted in theological discussion and clerical contribution.

In the Western experiences, the clergy's religious and political authority was challenged in two different phases. In the 16th century, Protestantism provided an occasion to challenge the religious authority of the clergy by destabilizing the sole right of the Catholic Church to speak for religion. The political power of the church and its clergy was undermined during the secularization process of the 17th and 18th centuries through the Glorious Revolution in Britain (1688) and the French Revolution (1789–1799). In the contemporary Islamic world, religious secularity challenges the religious and political authorities of the clergy simultaneously. From this perspective, resemblance to the histories of Protestantism and secularism becomes clear.

As noted earlier, the current challenge to both the religious and political authority of the clergy is built upon theological and empirical questions surrounding clerical hegemony in the politico-religious sphere. Religious knowledge, combined with connections to—and understanding of—the structure and function of the religious establishment, has positioned religious reformists to effectively challenge the internal shortcomings of the clergy. In particular, the clergy's internal establishment has been scrutinized to prove the incompetence of the clergy to assume sociopolitical responsibility. The training of the clergy and their financial livelihoods are two dimensions used by reformist religious scholars to challenge the political and religious authority of the establishment.

Shortcomings of the Hawza *Educational System*

The Shiite seminary system differs significantly from the modern university system. One essential difference is the absence of centralization: seminaries are based on the teachings of distinguished jurists. Every Marja-e Taghlid and senior cleric runs his own seminary (*hawza*) without formal connection to other seminaries or an overarching supervisory institution. Teachers at the seminaries establish the ability of students (*talabeh*)[9] to reach the different clerical grades such as Hojat-ul Eslam or Ayatollah. There is no office to administer exams and issue graduation certificates to students.[10] One could expect that the lack of a centralized system would provide an appropriate

---

9. Students in seminaries are referred to as *talabeh,* an Arabic word meaning "one who seeks knowledge".

10. In recent years, particularly after Khomeini's demise, considerable efforts have been made by the government to take control of seminaries via developing different institutions in Qom as well as by institutionalizing religious rituals such as establishing the

context for innovation, leading to a more dynamic educational atmosphere. But, this has not been the case. Educational systems in religious seminaries have been unable to keep pace with developments in the contemporary world. Religious beliefs and traditions have muffled any attempts to effect change. One example may be found in the history of teaching philosophy at the Qom seminary. Ayatollah Khomeini and Alameh Tabatabai,[11] who pioneered the teaching of philosophy at Qom, were pressured by other teachers in the seminary as well as by the then-highest figure in the Shiite world, Grand Ayatollah Broujerdi, to discontinue teaching philosophy (Gerami & Emami, 2002: 113; Montazeri, 1991: 254). Under these circumstances, teaching methods, curricula, and textbooks in Shiite seminaries have remained unchanged for decades and in some cases even centuries.

Outdated textbooks and teaching methods have stimulated criticism of the clerical education system. As training in *hawza* does not encompass contemporary issues, clerics from this system are not sufficiently equipped to lead believers into the modern age. Kadivar claims that Shiite seminaries are not able to address questions pertaining to modern life (Kadivar, 2000a: 560–561). Calling upon *hawza* to revise the main textbooks, Kadivar argues that relying on books that are 400 years old is not acceptable:

Why the emphasis on teaching *Moalem-e Asoul* which was written in the 16th century? Is it not right that there have been many changes in jurisprudence knowledge—in terms of newly emerging issues and reasoning methods—from the time of *Sharh-e Lomma*, which was written five hundred years ago? Why should rationality belonging to the 15th century, which is very controversial, be taught [in seminaries]? What is the problem with teaching from textbooks based on contemporary issues and knowledge?. . . Unfortunately, most of the textbooks [of seminaries]. . . are not fit to remain in [the] *hawza* educational system (1992: 9–10).[12]

Headquarter of Prayers (1990) and the Centre to Manage the Affairs of Mosques (1989). For detailed information about these efforts, see Khalaji, 2008.

11. Allameh Seyyed Muhammad Hossein Tabatabai (1892–1981), an exception among the clergy, focused on teaching philosophy and interpretation of the Quran rather than *fiqh*. That is why he was never appointed to a senior position in the religious strata. Grand Ayatollah Khoei said that Tabatabai sacrificed himself for the Quran, whereas he could have been a Marja-e Taghlid and could have gained high social status (Soroush, 1996a: 13).

12. Khalid Sindawi (2007) lists the main textbooks taught in *hawza*. A brief review of this list proves the lack of new books in *hawza*'s curricula.

Compared to the university, Soroush claims that there is a determination in *hawza* to hallow textbooks used in seminaries. While questions are supposedly welcomed in *hawza*, Soroush claims that the adverse reaction to new ideas make it virtually impossible for both external scholars and those of *hawza* to adopt a critical stance. To demonstrate, Soroush highlights the extremely hostile *hawza* reaction to Ayatollah Salehi-Najafabadi when he published his unorthodox reading of the early years of Islamic history.[13] Soroush protests against the hallowing of textbooks by *hawza*, arguing that, because much theological thought is accepted uncritically by *hawza*, this has led to its decadence and ignorance: "God, Prophet or infallible Imams are not the ones who are located in *hawza*. They [seminaries lecturers] are jurists, Ulama and theologians, who are human and fallible. Whatever they produce is human-made and profane. Thus, the holiness of the Quran and hadiths is not transferred to their knowledge and science" (Soroush, 1996a: 30–31).

Hawza have employed a traditional metaphor—*shobha* (uncertainty)— to curse critical questions. Shiite seminaries commonly curse questions addressing the accepted principles of religion as *shobha*: "When a question is called *shobha* it will lose its very basic characteristic. The main characteristic of a question is [the fact] that it requires your research. . . but *shobha* means that it is a sinister question, which ought to be repressed in any possible way" (Soroush, 1996a: 34). Khalaji claims that the concept of *shobha* has provided the clergy with the excuse to curse the very basis of modern thinking. For the clergy, modernity is a set of *shobha* aiming to destroy believers' faith. Not surprisingly, the traditional basis of understanding religious texts in *hawza* has remained untouched (2008: 27–30). Mehdi Khalaji maintains that the clergy have created an "epistemological crisis" by failing to offer a critical review of modernity from an Islamic standpoint. An essential difference between university and *hawza* education is the restriction on debate. Debate in *hawza* is confined to certain basic principles: no person may extend his questions to areas conceived of as holy (Soroush, 1996a: 23). And yet, scientific development hinges on having the liberty to ask questions.

Because the education offered in *hawza* is dominated by *fiqh*, the clergy are often incapable of managing complicated sociopolitical and economic issues in the contemporary world. Other dimensions of religion, such as theology, philosophy, and ethics, are also excluded from *hawza* curricula. *Fiqh* has gained

13. While he was a respected scholar in *hawza*, after publishing his book entitled *Shahid-e Javid* (The eternal martyr), Salehi-Najafabadi suffered from severe *hawza* hostility. His book criticised the Shiite understanding of Imam Hussein's martyrdom at Karbala. For further discussion about this book and the difficulties that the author faced following its publication, see Siegel, 2001.

dominance over religion in post-revolutionary Iran, in large part because it circumscribes the clergy's knowledge (Soroush, 2011). They have little or no knowledge of other sciences or dimensions of religion. In Soroush's view, this deficit is rooted in the *hawza* educational system in which emulation (*taghlid*) is a core concept. It aims to establish a special relationship between believers and the clergy, in which the believers are expected to submit to the clerics' fatwas unquestioningly (Soroush, 1996a: 5–7). As interpretation, philosophy, and theology are not included in *hawza* formal curricula, it has been unable to produce distinguished interpreters or theologians. Soroush further asserts that those of the clergy who move away from *fiqh* to theology or philosophy are not welcomed with esteemed status (1996a: 13–14).

Like Soroush, Kadivar considers the dominance of *fiqh* to be a significant hindrance for *hawza*. Providing fresh insight into the teaching records of the Qom seminary, Kadivar points out that while approximately 75 subjects related to *fiqh* were offered in Qom between 1990 and 1992, only two philosophy, one theosophy, and two interpretation subjects were available. He concludes that of all the subjects, less than 1 percent were non-jurisprudential in orientation (Kadivar, 1992: 11; 2008: 423). One way to reform *hawza*, in Kadivar's view, is to transform *hawza* from a university of *fiqh* to a university of Islamic studies. He further argues that expecting seminaries to train clerics who are qualified to accept sociopolitical responsibility is unreasonable:

> Responsibilities which are abdicated to the universities, social scientists, and management and planning authorities ought not to be expected from *hawza*. This is an expectation for which there is no preparation in *hawza* programs. It is better if we [in *hawza*] focus solely on areas of study which are closely related to religion. . .. Otherwise, neither the main tasks of *hawza* will be accomplished nor will good leaders for the country be produced (Kadivar, 2008: 413).

For the most part, the clergy obtain their professional qualifications from *hawza*.[14] But, reformist religious scholars, after scrutinizing the institution's educational system, are starting to question the competency of the ruling clergy to claim sociopolitical leadership. Awareness of the one-dimensional

14. Over the last two decades, receiving university degrees has become a fashion among the clergy. This is why new universities (e.g., Mofid and Baqir-ul Uloom) were established in Qom. Also, many clerics enroll in universities at the same time they are studying in *hawza*. New titles such as "Doctor Ayatollah" and "Hujatuleslam-e Valmuslemin Doctor" are the outcome of this trend. For a detailed explanation of this new phenomenon, see Khalaji, 2008: 25–27; Ramazan-Narjesi, 2002.

nature of the clergy's qualifications has emboldened the campaign to challenge the clergy's claim to represent religion. Although *hawza* structure is scrutinized from various points of view, the most essential challenges posed by reformist religious scholars are outdated teaching material and *fiqh*-dominated education. Both issues reify the clergy's lack of competence to assume political leadership. Reformist religious discourse further scrutinizes the clergy's perceived conflict of interest in terms of their religious and political capacity. This has involved examination of the clergy's financial livelihoods and the link between their income and religious function.

The Clergy's Financial Livelihoods

The main source of the clergy's income is derived from their religious capacity. The shared income constitutes an essential feature that qualifies them as a professional group, members of which share a collective identity and common interests. This has prompted reformists to question the clergy's qualification to speak for religion. Compared to the university system, the term "tuition" (*shahriyya*) has a totally different meaning in *hawza*, wherein it refers to the stipend paid by *hawza* to seminary students. As seminary students are required to devote their time to the study of religion, their accommodation, food, and basic needs are paid for by monthly stipends. The *shahriyya* for students who are married may be higher than that for those who are single, and the amount varies based on the reputation of the Marja-e Taghlid who runs the seminary. When a Marja-e Taghlid has a large following, he will be able to collect more religious taxes,[15] accept more students, and pay them a higher stipend. This works in a circular fashion, causing an increase in popularity and, by extension, an increase in religious tax from his followers.

When the clergy leave *hawza*, equipped with jurisprudential knowledge alone, they are not prepared for any specific profession. Performing religious functions is the only way they can make a living. This includes acting as prayer Imams and preaching at religious ceremonies. However, their main source of income is the *sahm-e Imam* (Imam's share),[16] which is directly paid to clerics by believers.

---

15. There is no organized system for collecting religious taxes. It is paid voluntarily and every person freely chooses a Marja-e Taghlid to pay his/her religious taxes. For more information, see Khalaji, 2006: 6–7.

16. *Sahm-e Imam* is a part of *khoms* (one-fifth of net income), the obligation of believers in Shiism to pay to their Marja-e Taghlid. *Khoms* is divided into six portions to be spent on expenditure for God, the prophet, Imams, and charitable activities. The expenditure for the Imam is called *sahm-e Imam*. For the history of *sahm-e Imam* in the Shiite school, see Calder, 1982b.

Just as the authenticity of the institution of clergy was scrutinized, their financial livelihoods was also subjected to criticism in the pre-revolutionary era by Ayatollah Morteza Motahhari, who was himself a cleric and highly respected by his peers. Motahhari's popularity protected him and kept the issue relatively benign in pre-revolutionary Iran; however, when Soroush, a layman, raised the same issue in post-revolutionary Iran, he was met with hostility from the ruling clergy.

In 1962, Ayatollah Motahhari published an article entitled "Fundamental Problem for the Organization of the Clergy"[17] in which he argued that the financial livelihoods of the clergy had a subversive impact on their roles as religious leaders. His main concern was reforming religion to suit the conventions of time and space. Motahhari, who wrote, "*Sahm-e Imam* is the chief reason for all problems" (2010: 285), further argued that due to their financial dependence upon the masses (believers), the Shiite clergy were deprived of the ability to reform religion as necessary. He pointed out that the Sunnite clergy were financially dependent upon their government and thus lacked the power to challenge the state in political terms. Financial independence from the government, on the other hand, allowed the Shiite clergy to occupy an autonomous position in the political sphere. Despite this leverage, however, the Shiite clergy suffered another setback referred to as *avamzadeghi* (common-struckness). Motahhari maintained that "[r]elying on people, Shiite clergy are able to stand up against the state's tyranny, but [they] are weak and unable to combat people's [wrong] ideas and opinions which are formed upon ignorance" (2010: 302). To support his argument, Motahhari provided some examples of senior clerics who had been forced to abandon innovation. When Grand Ayatollah Broujerdi decided to send a few students to the West to learn the English language and propagate Islam in those countries, a group of his influential emulators travelled from Tehran to Qom to present him with an ultimatum to overturn his decision. They argued that believers do not pay *sahm-e Imam* to be spent in infidels' lands. The project was abandoned because it threatened to jeopardize the function of the seminary (Motahhari, 2010: 305–306). Grand Ayatollah Broujerdi had openly objected to the clergy succumbing to people's desires. According to Motahhari, Broujerdi claimed that this changed his thinking:

When I became a Marja-e Taghlid, I first acknowledge that *ijtihad* is my responsibility and that people will apply my reasoning; when

---

17. For the English version of this paper, see Motahhari, Arshad, & Dabashi, 2000. Shimamoto (2006) also provides a useful summary of the article.

I issue a fatwa they will practice it. But in the course of some fatwas that contradicted the inclinations and tastes of the ordinary people, I realized that this was not the case (quoted in Motahhari, 2010: 305).

Motahhari noted that there were no clergy as a class in early Islamic history. "The Prophet or infallible Imams never ordered a person or several persons to end their careers to solely pursue activities such as issuing fatwas, teaching, leading prayers and preaching, all of which are clergy's responsibilities at the present time (Motahhari, 2010: 294). Unlike Shariati, who concluded from this that there was no place for the clergy in Islam, Motahhari argued that different circumstances in the contemporary world necessitated the focus of the clergy as a distinguished group of people who devote their lives to learning, teaching, and leading religious affairs. As such, it made sense that their livelihoods were drawn from an alternate source—and, indeed, Motahhari did not have any problem with believers constituting the major financial source of the clergy's livelihoods. What he saw as the core problem was the mechanism through which *sahm-e Imam* was transferred from believers to the clergy. Because their livelihoods are derived directly from the people, clerics are compelled to tailor their thoughts accordingly. In an attempt to address this dilemma, Motahhari suggested the formation of a central fund that would collect religious payments and taxes and redistribute them among clerics according to a well-organized bookkeeping system. Direct payment from the people would be eliminated.

Although widely discussed, Motahhari's suggestion never led to changes in the clergy's financial livelihoods. In fact, the establishment of an Islamic state encouraged further dependence on government funds and substantially improved the living standards of the clergy. In addition to the *sahm-e Imam*, *hawza* and different religious organizations were now allocated a share of the government budget. It is now common for the clergy and their families to engage in economic activities, with some enjoying direct control of a number of institutions: Astan-e Gods-e Razavi, Bonyad-e Panezda-e Khordad, and Bonyad-e Mostazafan va Janbazan are just a few examples. All organizations are tax-exempt and are not subject to auditing (Ganji, 2011; Khalaji, 2008: 22–24).

Motahhari was killed in 1979 in a terrorist attack. As one of the main ideologues of the Islamic state, he continues to be considered an iconic figure by the ruling clergy. Drawing upon Motahhari's credibility, Soroush broached the subject of the clergy's livelihoods as part of his reformist discourse in the post-revolutionary era. On the anniversary of Motahhari's martyrdom in 1994, Soroush published a paper entitled "Liberty and Clergy", in which he subscribed to Motahhari's concerns and elaborated further on the problematic nature of the clergy's financial livelihoods. Soroush extended Motahhari's argument by asserting that the problem is not solely related to the transfer of funds from the people to the clergy, but that any link between the clerics' religious status and their financial livelihood is inherently problematic.

Soroush goes beyond distinguishing between Shiite and Sunni clergy by claiming that religion is the main source of livelihood for the clergy of both sects. If speaking the truth is associated with the particular interest of a given group, there is no guarantee that the truth will be safeguarded in the face of personal interest. Though it may be that exceptional persons can remain loyal to the truth when there is conflict of interest, Soroush argues that the world is full of average people, and no one can ensure that all clerics are beyond corruption.

Soroush distinguishes the clergy's position from other professions, arguing that there are valuation methods that can be used for other professions. For example, practitioners are not only evaluated by members of their relevant scientific circle, but by the impact of their services. Shared interests among members of any profession may tempt those involved to act dishonestly; however, external and institutional safeguards encourage them to make decisions beyond their narrowed interests. No comparable safeguard exists for the clergy. According to Soroush, the abstract nature of clerical work (Soroush, 1995a: 2–5) and the sacredness of clerics' service diminish the likelihood of supervisory control of their work (Soroush, 1996a: 30–33). Thus, it is the very nature of clerical work that makes financial incentives for their services problematic.

Soroush also draws upon intra-religious sources to support his argument, quoting prominent religious scholars who have expressed similar concerns. He argues to the effect that "[i]f religion becomes the source of livelihoods and [a channel through which] to pursue legitimate or illegitimate interests, religious life will suffer irreparable damage. This has been the observation and concern of many religious leaders" (1995a: 6).

Soroush distinguishes himself from Motahhari by arguing that the problem is not one of accepting money from the people either directly or indirectly. The essential problem is making a living from religion. "The coupling of religion with a profession is the chief problem, not for the clergy but for religion" (Soroush, 1995c: 30). As Soroush sees it, Motahhari's notion of a central fund would not necessarily solve the problem. "There should not be any overt or covert or individual or collective connection between religiosity and the religious knowledge of a person and his worldly interests" (1995a: 10). Therefore, unless they pay for their education and earn their financial livelihoods through a profession distinct from their religious role, the problem cannot be solved. Religion is a matter of love and passion, not of business. Soroush further adds that if the clergy's position is detached from worldly interests, the number of clerics will be reduced, and those who follow this path will be more passionate about religion and exercise genuine devotion to their religious role.

The clergy did not react to Souroush's challenge to religious principle as harshly as they had previously to critiques from their own class. Both Shariati (in the pre-revolutionary era) and Aghajari (after the revolution) were excommunicated. In the case of Shariati, excommunication was effected at the religious strata as the clergy lacked political power. In Aghajari's case, a judicial procedure was established, and he narrowly missed execution.

Nevertheless, Souroush had raised a subject that was absolutely taboo, and drawing upon Motahhari's writing did not save him from trouble. He experienced a severe backlash from the ruling clergy. Scathing criticism of his work was published in conservative newspapers and voiced during Friday prayer meetings. During lectures delivered at Isfahan University and the University of Tehran in 1992, Soroush was physically attacked by Basij militia and seminary students. Following these attacks, Soroush ceased delivering public orations. The following year (1993), he was not offered a teaching position at a single university in Tehran. He managed with difficulty to facilitate one teaching course at Tehran University (Soroush, 2009a: 47). While it may not be the case that all this transpired because of one paper, the coincidence should not be overlooked. The most interesting aspect was the Supreme Leader's intervention. Over time, Soroush formulated many theories about various dimensions of religion that posed formidable challenges to the orthodox view. But none provoked Ayatollah Khamanei's direct response. Khamanei viewed Soroush's work on the clergy's financial livelihoods as part of a U.S. conspiracy, a similar reaction to the critiques against the clergy during Reza Khan's reign (1925–1941). Khamanei described it as "unjust", "oppressive", and a "violation of the truth" (Khamanei, 1995).

In response to his critics, Soroush published another paper in *Kiyan* in 1995. Although initially *Kiyan* invited scholars to contribute to the debate by submitting balanced arguments to be included in the next issue, they later announced unexpectedly that the subject would be excluded from future issues (Ghoochani, 2007). Historically, Soroush played a leading role in opening new areas of debate. As a highly original scholar, his papers tend to be followed by a flow of writings in response. His ideas have been expanded upon by reformist religious scholars and translated into more colloquial language by reformist journalists. In this way, his ideas have slowly disseminated from scholarly circles to the general population.

No prominent reformist scholars have published articles on the clergy's financial livelihoods. Kadivar addressed the issue only in a nuanced way by quoting verses from the Quran that he claimed explicitly prohibit the existence of a financial relationship between the Prophet and believers. A code of conduct required the Prophet to offer his religion and guidance free of charge. He further argued that all prophets had professions apart from religion and that prophecy was not a career from which to reap financial security. Kadivar further maintained that "[p]ropagation which is driven by the financial interests of the propagator will not capture the heart. It will not raise consciousness. . . and, in a practical sense, it will not succeed. Religion is not a source of livelihood" (2001d). Kadivar, however, confined his argument to prophets: he neither directly addressed the contemporary era nor the financial livelihoods of the clergy.

The reformist clergy have strongly driven the religious reformation discourse in contemporary Iran. Although scholars such as Ayatollah Montazeri, Mojtahed-Shabestari, Kadivar, and Eshkevari are members of the clergy and share common interests with the clergy, they are not entirely dissuaded from touching upon taboo topics. However, they must walk a fine line. The ruling clergy's harsh treatment of Shariati, Aghajari, and Soroush serves as a glaring lesson to reformist scholars.

Eighteen years after the publication of Soroush's paper, the subject is still taboo within the Islamic state. To date, no one has yet broached the subject. Prominent religious scholars such as Soroush, Kadivar, and Eshkevari have been driven into self-imposed exile. From there, they seize every opportunity to challenge the ruling clergy and, best of all, the Supreme Leader. Two distinctive examples are Soroush's open letter to the Supreme Leader Ayatollah Khamanei and Kadivar's 43-page letter to Hashemi-Rafsanjani, the former head of the Assembly of Experts. Soroush, who triggered a bitter dispute by directly targeting Ayatollah Khamanei, predicted that the opposition would soon celebrate the "downfall of religious dictatorship" (Soroush, 2009d). Adopting a similar approach, Kadivar urged the Assembly of Experts to impeach the Supreme Leader, basing his argument on constitutional articles and jurisprudential principles (Kadivar, 2010a).

These exiled religious scholars have tended to downplay theological and jurisprudential arguments and are more outspokenly critical of the malfunction of the Islamic state and clerical corruption. However, it would be too simplistic to state that their sharp focus on daily politics is superficial. As discussed in chapter 1, the ruling clergy's claim that "sovereignty in an Islamic country solely belongs to the clergy" has been challenged for many years. Their arguments expand challenges outside of the internal establishment of the clergy by highlighting the intrinsic conflict between the political leadership of the clergy and the principles of the Shiite faculty. This critique exposes the ways in which the ruling clergy violate their own traditional conventions and the fundamental Shiite principles.

A Decentralized Structure

An important concern expressed by reformist scholars involves the clergy's autonomy. Both conservatives and reformists alike single out independence as a distinguishing feature of the clergy. The latter's autonomy, however, is not confined to independence from the state. Rather, since Shiite jurisprudence is not organized around a centralized power structure, clerics enjoy an interior independence from one another. A few days before his death, the fourth special deputy of the Twelfth Imam, Ali ibn Muhammad Samari (d. 941 CE), claimed to be the last deputy of the Hidden Imam (Aghajari, 2002a: 61). Up to the current time, this claim defines the decentralized character of the Shiite denomination of Islam. Theoretically, both religious and political authority are centralized around the Hidden Imam; however, as the Hidden Imam is not currently in a position of authority and has not appointed any person to act on his behalf, Shiism lacks both a religious and political foundation upon which to establish an overarching authority.

It is only recently that the clergy have tried to establish an informal structure of leadership. Upon investigating these efforts, Abbas Amanat concluded that there are conceptual obstacles inherent in Shiism that make it problematic to set a criterion for the superiority of one cleric over the others. Linking this obstacle to the notion of the Hidden Imam, he argues: "The inescapable presence of the Hidden Imam made any attempt towards theoretical elaboration of a supreme authority a matter of controversy and conflict. The theological grounds for the designation of leadership, therefore, remained inherently limited" (1988: 99). Amanat emphasizes *a'lamiyat* (superiority in knowledge), a notion proposed by some leading Shiite scholars to distinguish eminent clerics by giving them informal authority over the rest. However, the criterion for measuring *a'lamiyat* remains problematic. The fact that the Shiite clergy have never succeeded in developing a standard criterion to distinguish superiority in knowledge has led the Shiite school to be inherently pluralistic in structure. Moreover, the evolution of *ijtihad,* and the inclusion of reasoning as a source of Shiite *ijtihad,* have played a supplementary role in institutionalizing a decentralized setting in Shiite jurisprudence. Each and every cleric is allowed to issue fatwas upon his reasoning of religious sources. There is no upper criterion to prove superiority of one line of reasoning over another.

In sum, the notion of the Hidden Imam and the open gates of *ijtihad* in Shiism make it problematic to conceptualize a supreme authority. However, efforts over the last two centuries have resulted in the establishment of an informal clerical hierarchy on a few occasions. The first cleric to emerge as an eminent Marja-e Taghlid was Sheikh Morteza Ansari (1781–1864), who was perceived as the first effective model of Marjaiat in Shiite history (Mottahedeh, 2000: 211; Moussavi, 1985: 45). In the course of time, Ayatollah Broujerdi was also acknowledged as an eminent Marja-e Taghlid. However, by no means does this suggest that other clerics were denied the opportunity to adopt an independent path. One outstanding example is Navab-Safavi, a young cleric with no religious credentials who undermined Ayatollah Broujerdi's authority by his militant-political actions.[18]

Marjaiat—Velayat Conflict

In the Shiite school, the decentralized nature of the clergy granted clerics autonomy from the state and from a superior clerical authority. But, as Roy points out, the traditional clerical structure faced a deep crisis after the establishment of the Islamic state in 1979 (1999: 208–212). The formation of the Islamic state by Khomeini undermined both the clergy's interior independence and autonomy from the state. As has been suggested throughout this book, Khomeini was not only revolutionary in the political arena, but also in a religious context. He introduced many initiatives to the Shiite faculty; the clergy's interior independence was not excluded from this. Khomeini's main book on the doctrine of Velayat-e Faqih does not discuss the authority of Valey-e Faqih over other clerics in a substantive way. Thus, when there is disagreement between Valey-e Faqih and one or more of the other Marja-e Taghlids it is not clear who should take precedence. What are the criteria, procedures, and justifications for ruling in favour of the Velayat-e Faqih over those of other Marja-e Taghlids? This is never adequately addressed. However, in another book, *Kitab al-Bay* (The Book of Business Transactions), Khomeini briefly implies the superiority of the Valey-e Faqih over other Marja-e Taghlids: "If one of the jurists succeeded in establishing [the Islamic] state it is *vajeb* [religiously indispensible] for other jurists to conform to him" (2006: 466). Khomeini's reluctance to expand this part of his doctrine is understandable. In view of the traditional pluralistic character of the clergy,

---

18. Navab-Safavi and his comrades overtly confronted Ayatollah Broujerdi, their political activities in Qom interrupting *hawza*'s routine education process. For further information, see Farati, 2004; Montazeri, 2000a: 139–146.

the apolitical sensibility of senior clerics in Qom and Najaf, and the residence of senior clerics, including Ayatollahs Khoei and Sistani, outside of the Islamic state's jurisdiction, ruling clergy have found it problematic to establish a central religious authority.

Khomeini's preeminent position within both the religious and political spheres minimized the possibility of tension between his status as the Valey-e Faqih and other Marja-e Taghlids. However, the subject sparked controversy following his death in 1989, which was soon accompanied by a constitutional amendment that saw a power shift in favour of the Valey-e Faqih. According to the original Constitution, a Valey-e Faqih should be a Marja-e Taghlid; but this was removed following the amendment. As suggested in chapter 2, when Khamanei was appointed the Valey-e Faqih in 1989, he was not even an Ayatollah, let alone a Marja-e Taghlid. It was obvious then that Khamanei was not able to extend his authority over the religious domain in general and over the Marja-e Taghlids in particular. The ruling clergy elevated his clerical ranking overnight and began referring to Khamanei as "Ayatollah" immediately after his appointment as Valey-e Faqih.

Khamanei's appointment made relations between Marjaiat (source of emulation) and Velayat (political leadership) a controversial issue. Highlighting the complex nature of governance in the contemporary world, the proponents of the Islamic state argue for the necessity of a centralized authority in the politico-religious arena. They claim that because the state is led by a jurist, other jurists ought to obey the political and religious commands issued by the Valey-e Faqih. But, while this directive may seem simple, it becomes complicated when the core function of Marjaiat is taken into consideration. Claiming authority over a religious domain contradicts the basic foundations of Shiite belief. When a Marja-e Taghlid issues a fatwa, he is relaying God's command, and his emulators truly believe that it is *God's command* (Eshkevari, 2000a: 48, emphasis added). At the sociopolitical level, however, this can prove very problematic. In Hajjarian's words, it "can lead to 'delinquent religious deeds' *[amal shari-e mojremaneh]*" (2007: 520). For example, Marja-e Taghlids interpret the end of Ramadan (fasting month) differently. If Marja-e Taghlids and the Valey-e Faqih give different dates for believers to break their fasts, believers are caught between violating the law or their faith. There have been similar problems regarding tax. Some Marja-e Taghlids encourage believers to avoid paying taxes to the state, a fatwa that cannot be broken even if the Valey-e Faqih issues a contradictory fatwa (Eshkevari, 2000a: 36).

The ruling clergy have proposed two ways of rationalizing the supremacy of the Valey-e Faqih over the Marja-e Taghlids. The first line of reasoning proceeds thus: In their time, the Prophet and the infallible Imams possessed supreme authority over both the political and religious realms. Therefore, it is reasonable to assume that the Valey-e Faqih enjoys authority over both the political and religious domains. From this viewpoint, the right to issue fatwas belongs ultimately to the Valey-e Faqih; other Marja-e Taghlids may only issue fatwas after first gaining his permission (Ansari, 1999: 40–48; Hashemi-Shahroudi, 1998: 29; Mohmmadi-Gilani, 1993: 120). Mirbagheri suggests further that the relationship between Marjaiat and the political leadership is the same as that between management and experts. It is impossible for a single person to surpass experts in various areas. A Valey-e Faqih should enjoy superiority of management, and experts should come under his supervision. Thus, Mirbagheri argues: "Marjaiat is a specialized position, which needs to be under the supremacy of a just Valey-e Faqih and his surveillance" (quoted in Amo-Shahi, 1999: 35).

The second line of reasoning involves confining the authority of the Marja-e Taghlids to the private sphere. This approach urges Marja-e Taghlids not to issue fatwas pertaining to sociopolitical issues. The argument suggests that while a Marja-e Taghlid should be sufficiently competent to preach on individual matters, he may not have adequate knowledge to espouse complicated sociopolitical and economic issues (Mohammadi-Rayshahri, 2004: 37). Thus, Marjaiat and political leadership occupy separate areas of jurisdiction. Regarding individual issues, Marja-e Taghlids may issue different fatwas and their emulators may opt to follow their fatwas. When it comes to sociopolitical issues, however, the Valey-e Faqih's command reifies his superiority (Mesbah-Yazdi, 1999: 29–37). Obedience to the Valey-e Faqih is compulsory for all believers, including Marja-e Taghlids: "People cannot emulate any Marja-e Taghlid but the leader [Valey-e Faqih]. Emulating other Marja-e Taghlids is confined to individual issues" (Hadavi-Tehrani, 1998b: 144). All sociopolitical and economic issues are the responsibility of the Islamic state, which mandates the superiority of Valey-e Faqih. Ayatollah Hadavi-Tehrani, distinguishing between a fatwa and a *hukm* (decree), argues that a fatwa is reasoning based on religious sources, whereas for a decree, the temporal circumstances ought to be taken into consideration along with the religious sources. Hadavi-Tehrani contends that a fatwa issued by a Marja-e Taghlid is obligatory for his emulators only, whereas decrees issued by the Valey-e Faqih are obligatory for everyone, including other Marja-e Taghlids. Thus, obedience to the Valey-e Faqih is religiously indispensable for everyone, including Marja-e Taghlids (Hadavi-Tehrani, 1998a: 161–163). The authority of the Valey-e Faqih over Marjaiat is not confined to restricting their right to issue fatwas. It has even been suggested that a Valey-e Faqih possesses the right to oust a Marja-e Taghlid (Amo-Shahi, 1999: 28).

It cannot be said that the aspirations of the ruling clergy to establish supremacy of the Valey-e Faqih over Marjaiat have been wholly achieved. The ruling clergy's interference in Marjaiat affairs continues to give rise to religious concern. Reformist scholars agree with the ruling clergy that there is conflict between Marjaiat and Velayat under the current politico-religious setting that has its roots in the contradictory nature of two institutions, namely the state and Marjaiat. As An-Na'im posits, political authority and religious authority are of two different natures (2008: 49) in the modern world, given that the institution of the nation-state requires a centralized and hierarchical structure. Due to its pluralistic nature, however, Shiite jurisprudence contradicts the establishment of a centralized authority. Thus, conflation of the two authorities is highly problematic. In order to fit within the modern reality of the nation-state, the nature of Marjaiat, as it has been known for centuries, would have to be changed. However, there is another way to resolve the conflict without completely undermining Marjaiat—that is, the separation of the two institutions.

Regarding the religious secularity discourse, the issue is neither the hierarchical structure of the state nor the pluralistic institution of the clergy, but the conflation of these institutions. As Eshkevari argues, the incorporation of the clergy into the governmental domain has generated a contradiction between the institutions of state and Marjaiat (2000: 30). By taking over state control, the ruling clergy claim to be in charge of religion. In order to resolve Marjaiat–Velayat conflict, neither state nor Marjaiat need to change their character. Rather, the state could allow both religion and the clergy to be managed according to long-established tradition. These two institutions perform different functions and should not be merged as one. As Kadivar points out:

> State and religion are two [autonomous] institutions: both are necessary [for society]; but they have different functions. It is better to keep these institutions as two separate institutions and not to try to combine them into one single institution. If religious institutions (*hawza*, mosques, clergy, Marja-e Taghlids). . . and political institutions (state, government and their forces) conflate, the religious institution will suffer damage. . . [because] politics will misuse religion (1998: 17).

For Kadivar, another reason that mandates the necessity for the separation of Marjaiat from the state is the impossibility of finding a single person qualified to lead both institutions. Scholarly involvement in religious issues will not leave any time for a Marja-e Taghlid to gain sufficient qualifications for leading the country. Similarly, the volume of sociopolitical and economic challenges confronting a political leader will leave him little time to fully comprehend complicated religious issues (Kadivar, 1998: 17).

Hashem Aghajari also argues that the institutions of Marjaiat and the state should be kept separate. Conflation of these institutions will compromise the autonomy of Marjaiat and undermine its fundamental Shiite structure (Aghajari, 2000a). The religious sphere is one of pluralism, diversity, and disagreement; the state is underpinned by coercion. It is neither desirable nor possible to merge the two institutions into one politico-religious body (Velayat-e Faqih). Aghajari argues that when religion is coupled with political power, it will gravitate towards monopoly and authoritarianism because of the coercive powers of the state (2000b: 15).

Before the establishment of the Islamic state, there was some form of division of labour between Marjaiat and the king. While king was the political authority, Marjaiat held religious authority. This came to an end upon the establishment of the Islamic state. Under the current circumstances, either Marjaiat should adhere to the state or vice versa. In Eshkevari's view, both options are problematic. Given the principles, structure, and relations embedded within the institution of Marjaiat, it cannot be ruled by the state. On the other hand, Valey-e Faqih, and other political positions held by the ruling clergy, claim to represent Islam and speak for religion. Thus, there is no reason for the ruling clergy (the state) to obey Marjaiat in either political or religious matters.[19] As Eshkevari asks: Even if the state agrees to adhere to Marjaiat, which one of the Marja-e Taghlids should be chosen, and by what criteria? He also contests the proposal that Marja-e Taghlids should confine their fatwas to individual or private issues, this suggestion contradicting the widely accepted notion that religion is for the private sphere alone. Thus, it is not a legitimate expectation for religious leaders to confine their fatwas to individual issues. Eshkevari concludes that a supervisory role of Marjaiat, while maintaining a certain distance from executive politics, would be the most suitable option for solving Marjaiat–Velayat conflict. However, the procedure of this monitoring position and its empirical mechanism have been left unspecified. In Eshkevari's view, this is the vital element missing from the discourse of the proponents of a monitory role for Marjaiat (2000).

---

19. This was exactly Khomeini's argument when he drew the necessity of the clergy's direct political leadership from the necessity of practicing the Shari'a. He argues that governance is about practising Islamic law. Thus, a ruler should know Islamic law or should adhere to the edicts of a jurist who knows the Shari'a. He concluded that if the ruler ought to listen to a jurist, why should not a jurist be the ruler directly.

In sum, both conservatives and reformists acknowledge Marjaiat–Velayat contradiction. However, their solutions differ significantly. For the ruling clergy, the solution lies in the supremacy of the Velayat over Marjaiat. In contrast, reformist scholars highlight the adverse consequences of a state-controlled Marjaiat. For them, the solution lies in the emancipation of Marjaiat from the state.

Religious Remuneration

Further to Marjaiat–Velayat conflict, there are financial implications related to the impact of the Islamic state on the clergy. The main factor driving the clergy's independence from the state has always been its source of income. In contrast to Sunni clergy, Shiite clergy can claim independence from political states, given that their financial sources are derived from religious taxes, namely *khums* and *zakat*. As deputies of the Hidden Imam, Marja-e Taghlids collect religious taxes. With an Islamic state in place, led by a Valey-e Faqih, these taxes must be surrendered to the Islamic state. This was a part of Khomeini's doctrine: Religious taxes become a means of contributing to the establishment of an Islamic state in the OCCULTATION ERA. A section of the doctrine of Velayat-e Faqih reads as follows:

> *Khums* is a huge source of income that accrues to the treasury and represents one item in the budget.. . . It is obvious that such a huge income serves the purpose of administering the Islamic state and meeting all its financial needs.. . . [T]he purpose for the imposition of such a tax is not merely the upkeep of the Sayyids or the religious scholars, but on the contrary, something far more significant—namely, meeting the financial needs of the great organs and institutions of government (Khomeini, 2005: 38–39).

Khomeini claimed that because the Prophet's authority was delegated to the Valey-e Faqih, religious taxes would have been paid to him in the OCCULTATION ERA (2006: 496). But, when serving as Valey-e Faqih in the Islamic Republic of Iran, Khomeini backtracked on his own jurisprudence. He did not make any effort to practice this part of the doctrine and did not ask believers to pay their religious taxes to the Valey-e Faqih instead of to their own Marja-e Taghlids (Fereshtian, 2013). Shortly after the establishment of the Islamic state, he issued the following order: "Do not make changes to the people's relations with the clergy. Religious taxes and payments should be managed as they used to be: Marja-e Taghlids have always spent [them] on expenditure

pertaining to *hawza* affairs and religious matters, based on their priorities"
(quoted in Yazdi, 1987: 85–86). Furthermore, in his will, Khomeini asked that
the remaining money in his account, which had been collected as religious
payment, be sent to *hawza* (Eshkevari, 2000a: 43). Khomeini's shift in stance,
however, has not been replicated by the ruling clergy. At a roundtable meeting
in 1995, two senior members of the ruling clergy, Ayatollahs and former chiefs
of the judiciary Yazdi and Hasehmi-Shahroudi, stressed the necessity of paying
religious taxes to Velayat-e Faqih. Ayatollah Mohammad Yazdi stated:

> When there is no Islamic state, all qualified jurists are somehow rulers
> and can collect *khums;* but, when one of the jurists becomes ruler and
> takes over the Islamic society, other qualified clerics become jurists,
> not rulers. They are not caliphs; thus, they cannot collect *khums* unless
> they have permission from the Islamic ruler (1995: 36).

From a reformist perspective, efforts to centralize religious payments under
the control of the Valey-e Faqih would seriously compromise the clergy's
financial autonomy. Losing their financial autonomy from the state threatens their capacity to act freely, particularly in the political sphere. Placing
this in a broader context, Kadivar argues that it is the people's decision to pay
their religious taxes to every qualified jurist. The centralist approach, according to which religious taxes ought to be paid to Valey-e Faqih, jeopardizes
Marjaiat's financial autonomy. Kadivar, who maintains that this is an outright violation of the opinion of the majority of Marja-e Taghlids (1998: 19),
overlooks the fact that the independence of Marjaiat contradicts the nature of
the Islamic state. Pointing out this contradiction, Eshkevari argues that due
to its jurisprudential-religious character, the Islamic state may claim authority not just over social, political, and economic matters, but also over religious issues. As it is a just jurist (Valey-e Faqih) who leads the state, religious
issues come under his authority. Eshkevari further claims that the affairs of
government cannot be managed by the pluralistic traditions that have ruled
hawza for many centuries:

> Calling upon people to give their [religious] payments to the Supreme
> Leader [Valey-e Faqih] at the present time is a correct and sensible state-
> ment from a governmental point of view. There is no reason to have
> billions of *tomans* [Iranian currency] sent to [*hawzas* in] Najaf, Qom,
> Tehran and Mashhad. . . so that they [Marja-e Taghlids] can spend this
> money on their own programs without any regulation (2000: 48).

Having said this, reformist discourse does not suggest breaking long-lasting Marjaiat tradition. Rather, it advocates retaining the autonomy of the clergy. To this end, the state should terminate its religious claims.

The imposed supremacy of Velayat-e Faqih over Marja-e Taghlids did not succeed in clarifying Marjaiat–Velayat relations or the issue of religious payments. Despite the ruling clergy's powerful position, a pluralistic setting is still the mainstream discourse within Shiite jurisprudence. Several issues have made it difficult for the ruling clergy to master this situation, including (a) the traditional pluralistic feature of the clergy, (b) Shiite jurisprudential principles, (c) the voluntary nature of both emulation and religious payments, (d) the non-transparent process of cash flow between emulators and Marja-e Taghlids, and (e) continuation of the apolitical approach by the most eminent Marja-e Taghlids.

Despite the issue's importance, Khomeini neither expanded this part of his doctrine (supremacy of the Valey-e Faqih over Marja-e Taghlids) nor made any move to practice it. Due to his low religious rank, Khamanei, Khomeini's successor, was denied supremacy over Marja-e Taghlids in the post-Khomeini era. The state has, however, adopted an interventionist approach towards the clergy, interrupting the internal process, structure, and function of the clergy. This has provoked calls for the institutional separation of state and clergy in order to rescue the clergy from the Islamic state.

The dishonouring of the opponent Marja-e Taghlids, the defrocking of dissident clerics, and, more gravely, interruption of the very democratic process of preferment to Marjaiat level have collectively proven disadvantageous to the clergy since the establishment of the Islamic state.

Dealing with Dissident Clerics

As discussed above, the position of Marjaiat has always been an informal and totally democratic procedure. While other statuses within the clergy are subject to confirmation by a senior cleric, Marjaiat is achieved only through believers' gradual increase in confidence. Religious credibility and financial power are directly related to a cleric's level of public support. Approval of other clerics is important as well, as they may refer people to a given Marja-e Taghlid. There is no institution or senior cleric to appoint a cleric to the position of Marja-e Taghlid, nor is there a procedure in place for removing a Marja-e Taghlid from his position.[20]

---

20. Borghei explains how Ayatollah Golpayegani lost his chance to replace Ayatollah Broujerdi in 1961 by issuing an unorthodox fatwa about usury. Yet, there was no official statement claiming that he was not eligible for the position, see Borghei, 1992: 43–44.

The ruling clergy have had to contend with this process on more than one occasion. In 1982, Grand Ayatollah Shariatmadari opposed the inclusion of Velayat-e Faqih in the Constitution and the clergy's direct political leadership. He was charged with being involved in a plot to assassinate Khomeini. The political assault on Shariatmadari was harsh, but the religious basis of the ruling clergy's reaction was unprecedented. For the first time in Shiite history, a Marja-e Taghlid was disqualified from Marjaiat by his fellow clerics. The Society of the Lecturers of Qom Seminary (JMHEQ)[21] made the following announcement:

> Due to our religious duty we have to announce that he [Ayatollah Shariatmadari] has lost his qualifications to be a Marja-e Taghlid. [This announcement] addresses those believers who are uncertain and hesitant. This [announcement] lets them know their duty so that they will not blemish Islam and the revolution through their emulation (quoted in Mohammadi-Rayshahri, 2004: 306).

However, the JMHEQ does not enjoy the same degree of religious authority as a Marja-e Taghlid. Therefore, there was basis for Shariatmadari's followers to change their emulation in response to this announcement.[22]

On another occasion, following the controversial presidential election of 2009, some senior clerics, including Ayatollahs Montazeri, Sanei, Dastghaib, and Bayat-Zanjani, overtly sided with opposition groups. Not only did they not respond to the Valey-e Faqih's call to withdraw their objection, but they also provided religious justification for the opposition groups. While Ayatollah Sanei was the emerging Marja-e Taghlid, Ayatollah Montazeri had for a long time been one of the most eminent Marja-e Taghlids. When Ayatollah Montazeri died in December 2009, it was expected that his emulators would choose Ayatollah Sanei as their Marja-e Taghlid due to their intellectual connections.[23] In an apparent reaction to this expectation, the JMHEQ issued

---

21. The JMHEQ was the first and only clerical institution secretly founded in 1961 by a group of junior clerics in Qom. The members of this society, who were students of Khomeini, effectively spread his politico-religious discourse. They campaigned for the expansion of Khomeini's followers amongst seminary students as well as amongst ordinary people as the source of emulation in the 1960s and 1970s. The society has been an influential actor in Iran's politico-religious mosaic and has controlled the Qom seminary and its political activities. It systematically supports conservatism obedient to the Supreme Leader, see Kholdi, 2010; Princeton, 2009.

22. Born in Azerbaijan, almost all of my own family and relatives maintained their emulation to Ayatollah Shariatmadari.

23. As a jurisprudential principle, emulation of a dead Marja-e Taghlid is not acceptable. When a Marja-e Taghlid dies, his emulators seek a new Marja-e Taghlid.

a second announcement in January 2010, this time disqualifying Ayatollah Sanei. The announcement was very short but surprising in its rarity: "In response to frequent questions by believers, after various meetings and investigations over the last year, JMHEQ came to the conclusion that he [Ayatollah Sanei] lacked the necessary qualifications to act as a Marja-e Taghlid" (JMHEQ, 2010). A few months later, Basij militia attacked Sanei's office, and some in Qom sought to defrock Ayatollahs Sanei and Bayat-Zanjani. Organized attacks on the Ghab mosque in Shiraz, where Ayatollah Dastghaib was based, as well as attacks on Ayatollah Montazeri's residence in Qom, were further acts perpetrated to dishonour the dissident clerics. Each of these assaults on highly respected clerics was organized and carried out under a religious banner.

The Islamic state also initiated a legal-institutional procedure to undermine dissident clerics. In June 1980, Khomeini ordered the establishment of a special court to be known as the Special Clerical Court (SCC). This court, which works directly under Valey-e Faqih supervision, functions outside of the judicial system. So far, it has proven to be a loyal supporter of the Valey-e Faqih by targeting dissident clerics. It has the authority to both imprison and defrock clerics.[24] Those defrocked by this court include Eshkevari, Hadi Ghabel, Arash Honarvar-e Shojaei, and Ahamad-Reza Ahmadpour. Other leading reformist clerics, including Mohsen Kadivar and Abdulah Noori, were imprisoned by the order of the SCC. Furthermore, petitions were submitted by hardliners to the SCC in the last three years—in the aftermath of the 2009 election—demanding the defrocking of Khatami, Karroubi, and Mousavi-Khoeiniha, three eminent opposition clerics. As well as dishonouring dissident clerics, the Islamic state has also intervened in the clergy's internal procedures by lavishing favour on clerics who were allied to the Islamic state. The most important case in this regard was the elevation of Ayatollah Khamanei to the status of Marja-e Taghlid at the expense of the traditional and firmly rooted procedure of a cleric having to earn respect and reputation as a Marja-e Taghlid.

Politicizing the Preferment to Marjaiat

By appointing Khamanei Valey-e Faqih, the ruling clergy violated the 1989 Constitution. According to the enacted Constitution, being a Marja-e Taghlid was a key qualification for appointment as a Valey-e Faqih. But by no means could Khamanei claim religious credibility to be a Marja-e

---

24. For a detailed explanation of its procedure and authority, see Princeton, 2011.

Taghlid. The ruling clergy solved this problem by removing the require-ment of Marjaiat from the Constitution. At the time of his appointment, Khamanei's religious credentials were too weak to support his candidacy for Marjaiat: however, this situation changed over the course of time. The four most eminent Marja-e Taghlids died a few years after Khamanei's appointment: Ayatollah Marashi-Najafi (d. 1989), Ayatollah Khoei (d. 1992), Ayatollah Golpayegani (d. 1993), and Ayatollah Araki (d. 1994). These Marja-e Taghlids neither took a stand against the clerical establishment, nor did they undermine Khamanei's authority. They remained loyal to the traditional political quietism, eschewing the doctrine of Velayat-e Faqih and the clerical establishment.

The death in 1994 of the last eminent Marja-e Taghlid, Ayatollah Araki, left the Qom seminary without an eminent cleric eligible to be known as a Marja-e Taghlid. This situation offered the ruling clergy an opportunity to make their move (Rahimi, 2012: 59–61). As Gieling suggests, the Islamic state was motivated primarily by a desire to ensure that the institution of Marjaiat came under state control. This would eliminate competition or intervention in state affairs by Marja-e Taghlids (1997: 781). In an announce-ment delivered in December 1994, the JMHEQ introduced seven clerics as Marja-e Taghlids. This initiative was unprecedented and contrary to the traditionally democratic and meritocratic procedure of the Marjaiat institu-tion. Khamanei's name, of course, was included on the list while more emi-nent clerics, including Ayatollahs Montazeri, Tabatabai-Qomi, and Sistani, were excluded.

Objections to the inclusion of Khamanei in the list prompted him to announce that he would only be Marja-e Taghlid for foreign emulators and not for those who resided in the country. Over the years, Khamanei has care-fully avoided implementing these plans.[25] In this particular case, he planned to establish his Marjaiat in two distinct steps. Dividing emulators based on their nationality had neither traditional nor theological precedence in Shiite history: Marjaiat is and always has been transnational (Behrooz, 1996: 99). Khamanei's announcement was seen as a retreat; while objections were widely withdrawn, the feeling that drove the objections—about his religious credentials to be a Marja-e Taghlid—persisted. In effect, he was not qualified to be a Marja-e Taghlid, neither for Iranian nor for non-Iranian Shiite emulators. By making this announcement, Khamanei deflected public attention from the issue of his suitability, while at the same time acting as a Marja-e Taghlid. While Khamanei

---

25. For a detailed discussion of Khamanei's personality and his role in Iran's domestic and international politics, see Sadjadpour, 2009.

had not sought *ijtihad* permission[26] from any distinguished Marja-e Taghlid,[27] he nonetheless began issuing fatwas and collecting religious payments. Less than a year after his announcement, he initiated a fatwa council to investigate religious questions sought by emulators. This council was responsible for providing Khamanei with advice on issuing fatwas. With the passage of time, criticism of his qualifications to become a Marja-e Taghlid abated.[28] The next strategic move by the ruling clergy was to promote the seniority of Khamanei over other Marja-e Taghlids by proclaiming him a Marjaiat-e Amm (supreme source of emulation).[29]

Khamanei's Marjaiat was a sensitive case, but was not the only time the ruling clergy intervened in the clergy's internal procedures to promote their political aspirations. This form of intervention both compromised the clergy's autonomy and undermined the credibility of the religious establishment by privileging unqualified clerics. Promoting one's own Marjaiat would require

---

26. A cleric's competence to conduct *ijtihad* is confirmed by a senior Ayatollah. When a cleric acquires enough knowledge, his teacher issues verbal or written permission called "*ijtihad* permission". This is an informal process and the credibility of the *ijtihad* permission is associated with the credibility of the cleric who gives permission. A cleric may get permission from several senior clerics, and this will add to his credibility. This is why clerics' biographies often include a section listing the names of those who issued *ijtihad* permission to them.

27. Members of the ruling clergy, including Ayatollahs Janati, Lankarani, Hashemi-Shahroudi, Rasti-Kashani, and Meshkini, confirmed Khamanei's *ijtihad* capability, but they did not have sufficient religious credentials themselves. Furthermore, the language used in these confirmations was unorthodox. Clerics who issue *ijtihad* permission are usually masters; but the language used in the *ijtihad* permissions for Khamanei was obsequious.

28. This does not mean that questions surrounding his qualification to conduct *ijtihad* ceased. Ayatollah Montazeri, for example, kept questioning Khamanei's qualifications; there was informal news about a radical comment made by Ayatollah Shabiri-Zanjani. In October 2010, Shabiri-Zanjani was approached to issue *ijtihad* permission for Khamanei's son. In response, Shabiri-Zanjani asked if the *ijtihad* permission was for Khamanei or his son? This suggests that Shabiri-Zanjani still did not accept Khamanei's basic qualifications to issue fatwas (DaneshjooNews, 2010).

29. This was not officially announced by the ruling clergy, but it was evident in the propaganda campaign conducted before the trip. Furthermore, Ayatollah Golpayegani, the head of Khamanei's office, recently announced the establishment of a center in Qom to investigate jurisprudential issues. He did not clarify the specific function of the center and its relations with other Marja-e Taghlids; however, it was evident in his announcement that it was another effort by Khamanei to establish his supervision over Marja-e Taghlids and over the matter of issuing fatwas. For further information, see Mohammadi-Golpayegani, 2011. Further evidence of this claim is provided by Ayatollah Azari-Qomi, who recalled a meeting with Khamanei during which Khamanei talked about his expectation of JMHQ to introduce a single Marja-e Taghlid instead of seven names. Azari-Qomi believed that Khamanei meant that he alone should be introduced as the Marja-e Taghlid. For more detailed information, see Montazeri, 2000b: 722–723.

massive intervention in the clergy's internal affairs. In the process of achieving this goal, many changes and arrangements would have to be made in
the religious domain. This is why some apolitical and conservative clerics
expressed concerns over Khamanei's elevation to Marjaiat.

One outstanding example was Ayatollah Ahmad Azari-Qomi, who wrote
a letter to President Khatami a few years after the JMHEQ's announcement.
As a member of the JMHEQ, Azari-Qomi revealed confidential details of
the JMHEQ's announcement and questioned Khamanei's qualifications
for Marja-e Taghlid. He claimed that the normal procedure for making the
announcement was not followed and that many members of society were
forced to support the inclusion of Khamanei on the list. In his letter to the
president, Azari-Qomi informed him of the establishment of a department
in the Ministry of Intelligence and National Security specifically created to
advocate Khamanei's Marjaiat and prevent the ascension of other Marja-e
Taghlids. Azari-Qomi, who had been a member of the conservative ruling
clergy, clearly had access to crucial information. He also highlighted other
cases in which the ruling clergy had used their political leverage to undermine dissident clerics. After publishing his letter, Azari-Qomi was ousted
from his membership of the JMHEQ and kept under house arrest until his
death in 1999 (Kadivar, 2013a; 2014c; Menashri, 2001: 22–32).

A even more serious and overt challenge came from the spiritual leader
of the reformist scholars, the late Ayatollah Montazeri. Having anticipated
the events that were to unfold, he referred to the constitutional amendments and argued that Marjaiat *was* a separate institution from the political
leadership. In other words, the position of Velayat-e Faqih was now only
a political position, not a religious one. Applauding Marjaiat's autonomy,
Montazeri expressed his concern over the state's intervention in clerical matters: "Misusing the excuse of protecting the Islamic state, unfortunately, brings this strong citadel [Marjaiat] down.. . . [T]he enemies of
Islam and the clergy should not throw the sanctity of *hawza*, the clergy and
Marjaiat into disrepute by spending billions of *tomans* [Iranian currency]
in the way that the authorities [ruling clergy] have done" (2003: 384). Under
the current circumstances, he suggested, the clergy would soon be state
employees and *hawza* would lose its autonomy, its spiritual focus, and its
reputation among believers. Alarmed by the preparations for Khamanei's
Marjaiat, Montazeri wrote a letter to him a few months before the JMHEQ's
announcement:

> Shiite Marjaiat has always been an independent, spiritual power. It is
> better if this independence is not compromised by you.. . . For the sake

of Islam, *hawza* and yourself, I recommend your office to announce [the following]: since he [Khamanei] carries many responsibilities and the task of leading the country, [he] cannot answer religious questions. From now on, no answer will be provided for the religious questions. Scholarly and religious inquiries, as well as religious payments, ought to be handled by *hawza* as they used to be (2000a: 758–759).

Echoing the words of Azari-Qomi, Montazeri questioned the process of announcing Khamanei as Marja-e Taghlid. Commenting on the role of the country's intelligence service and other governmental organizations in promoting Khamanei as Marjaiat, he exposed Iranian delegations to countries such as Lebanon, India, and Pakistan to promote Khamanei's Marjaiat among Shiite populations abroad. A storm erupted when Montazeri made a public speech objecting to Khamanei's Marjaiat, accusing the latter of unjustified intervention in *hawza*. Montazeri questioned Khamanei's qualifications for political leadership as well as for Marjaiat. He said: "Mr. Khamanei, disregarding [political] leadership, why Marjaiat? You are not at the level of Marjaiat? I warned him [Khamanei] earlier". Montazeri alleged that Khamanei's name was included on the JMHEQ's list through the intervention of the security services and that these interventions denigrated the institution of Marjaiat.

Montazeri's public speech resulted in attacks organized by both the Basij militia and seminary students. He was subsequently unable to run his course in *hawza*. His office and house were attacked and occupied for a period of time, and he was finally placed under house arrest from 1997 until 2002. Maligning Khamanei had come at a high cost. Although Montazeri's criticism occurred at the beginning of the reformist era, the hard-liners did not allow anyone to support his argument. However, there were signs that some reformist scholars had criticized the promotion of Khamanei to Marjaiat. For example, without mentioning Khamanei by name, Mohsen Kadivar wrote:

If political power and propaganda machines convert a layman into a jurist and a normal jurist into a Marja-e Taghlid, the religious community will face serious problems. Science and religion will be victimized by political power. The best articulation is to maintain *hawza* autonomy, to strengthen its foundation and avoid state intervention in *hawza* procedures.... Political power should not be allowed to support promotion to Marjaiat. People should be able to freely choose their Marja-e Taghlids. Security, martial and disciplinary forces should seriously avoid any intervention in issues pertaining to *ijtihad* and emulation (1998: 19).

Recalling the list offered by the JMHEQ, Kadivar maintained that this intervention by the ruling clergy could cause deep anxiety among religious people and leaders and that Marja-e Taghlids unanimously agreed that the state should not intervene in issues of Marjaiat. When a government organization announces seven names of Marja-e Taghlid, does this mean that people cannot emulate other Marja-e Taghlids? Kadivar also notes that the names of the most eminent Marja-e Taghlids in Najaf and Qom were not included on the list. These controversies have provoked reformist scholars to urge the clergy to retreat from political leadership in order to regain their religious reputation.

Clergy's Spiritual Reputation

In part, the notion of religious secularity is based on restoring the clergy's reputation, which, from a reformist point of view, has been tarnished by their direct engagement in politics. Before the establishment of the Islamic state, the clergy had never exercised coercive or oppressive force in its relations with the population. Its financial privilege acted to strengthen the bond between the clerics and their people: the former enjoyed spiritual authority rooted in their religious standing and frugal lifestyles. Traditionally autonomous from the political process, the clergy have in the past been critical of the state. Free from concern vis-à-vis the empirical implications of the task of governance, they denounced the state from an idealist position. Thus, while the state was held responsible for any and all failures, the clergy's reputation remained intact. A well-known statement by Shariati summarizes this reality: "Not a single cleric has ever signed a shameful contract" (2009: 394). The fact is, the clergy were never in a position to sign contracts. Had they held political positions during the colonial era, this may not have been the case.

After the 1979 revolution, the clergy held political positions; thus, they had to make decisions pertaining to domestic and international politics. They signed thousands of agreements and contracts with many countries, so much so that concern arose vis-à-vis whether they in fact served the national interest. An outstanding example lies in Iran's current relations with China and Russia. There is a widely held view that the ruling clergy gives too many concessions to China and Russia, acting against the national interest to continue their ideological conflict with the West. One readily finds commentary on opposition websites criticizing Iran's agreements with China and Russia,[30] along with

---

30. Even the conservative website *Baztab* recently published a report about the concessions given by the ruling clergy to China (Moatamedi, 2012).

allegations that the ruling clergy grant these concessions to ensure their survival. Such allegations were made real by the demonstration organized by the government in 2009 on the anniversary of the Iran hostage crisis. While official speakers were urging demonstrators to chant "Down with America" and "Down with the UK", protestors were replying "Down with China" and "Down with Russia".

The political leadership of the clergy in post-revolutionary Iran has severely damaged the reputations of the clerics, as they have become involved in financial, moral, and political corruption. In contrast to the pre-revolutionary era, today's clerics are wealthy and live lavish lifestyles. Concomitant with the increase in their material affluence has been a decline in their spiritual authority, which Kadivar asserts, has been squandered for political power. There is a general consensus among reformist scholars that the clergy's reputation became tarnished after the establishment of the Islamic state (Eshkevari, 2000a; 2010c; 2011a; Kadivar, 2000c: 2; 2001b; Montazeri, 2010: 260, 430; Rabiee, 2001: 161–164; Rafi-pour, 2003; Soroush, 2011). Montazeri believed that, as the clergy are not skilled in management and governance, they have failed to capitalize on the opportunities that became available to them after the 1979 revolution. This failure has led to the weakening of the clergy's spiritual authority (2003: 160–161).

Clerics who are not members of the ruling clergy have generally remained silent regarding the damage to Islam. Recognizing this silence, Montazeri urged Marja-e Taghlids to denounce the Islamic state's violent reaction to the post-election protest in 2009. In a message addressed to the Marja-e Taghlids, he stated that the ruling clergy's brutal suppression of the uprising took place in the name of religion. Reminding them of their religious responsibility to protect Islam, he wrote:

> On these occasions [protests after the 2009 presidential election], oppression, violation of rights and misdeeds were inflicted [on the people] in the name of religion with the approval of a minority of clergy.. . . [Now] people wonder if this oppression and violation of rights contradicts Islam, why respected Marja-e Taghlids and Ulama, who are the guardians of religion. . . do not overtly object to these heretics and wrongdoers.. . . [If] Marja-e Taghlids keep quiet, people will think that the clergy and Marja-e Taghlids endorse this wrongdoing (2010: 431–434).

As discussed in chapter 1, Montazeri steadfastly maintained his adherence to the notion of Velayat-e Faqih, but his concern for the clergy's reputation led him to urge the clergy to distance themselves from political power. Guided by this concern, he supported Ayatollah Sistani's objection to the clergy's political leadership in Iraq: "The clergy must keep themselves as far as possible from executive roles and from the centres of power so as not to compromise its role as the spiritual guide of the population" (Montazeri, quoted in Rafat, 2007).

As discussed previously, while the JMHEQ intervenes in purely religious matters such as introducing Marja-e Taghlids, it sides with the political factions as well. For example, in the 1997 presidential election it urged the people to vote for Nategh-Nouri, although 70 percent of voters supported his competitor, Khatami. The JMHEQ's unpopular political positions have negatively impacted on its religious credibility, a situation made worse when political views are expressed from a religious standpoint. Kadivar warned the clerics not to misuse their religious affiliation. No cleric may equate his political attitude with religion and impute heresy to the political opposition. Similarly, Mojtahed-Shabestari asserts that there should be a clear-cut distinction between God, political power, and coercion. If a society fails to differentiate between these spheres, the notion of God will lose its sanctity, and coercion will become hallowed (Mojtahed-Shabestari, 2006). The conflation of religion and political positions poses a big risk for the clerical establishment, a prospect that prompted Kadivar to urge the clergy to distance themselves from day-to-day politics (2000c: 4–5). He argues that an uncorrupted political process avoids the conversion of religion into an instrument of political power by politicians and power holders (Kadivar, 1998).

Kadivar observed the misuse of religion during the 1997 presidential election when conservative clerics and clerical organizations announced that voting for the conservative candidate Nategh-Nouri was a religious responsibility. Conversely, those who voted for the reformist candidate, Khatami, were accused of acting against God and the Prophet (Kadivar, 2000c: 6–7). Kadivar maintained that when members of the clergy run for office and contribute to day-to-day politics, they should then be treated as lay citizens in the sociopolitical sphere. In other words, clerics ought to stand in an equal position to laymen when they seek political positions. Under such circumstances, clerics (a) should not claim any privileges because of their religious affiliation and (b) should not be allowed to voice their political views under a religious banner (Kadivar, 2011a). Kadivar, who approaches the privileged position of the clergy in public life from a human-rights perspective, sees this privileging as fuelling one of the major conflicts between human rights and traditional Islam. He argues that there is no religious justification for proclaiming the exclusive right of clergy in the public sphere (Kadivar, 2007a).

There are moral implications associated with the clergy's continued political leadership. As suggested in chapter 4, Islamist groups, particularly Khomeini and his followers, never discussed clerical rule on the eve of the revolution. In fact, they actively denied any plan to elevate the political status of clerics. Recalling these denials, Eshkevari urges the ruling clergy to honour their promise, arguing that the establishment of an Islamic state has not served the genuine interests of the clergy. Among other reasons, protecting the clergy's reputation is of significant importance as it mandates the ruling clergy to honour their preservation of time-honoured moral values (Eshkevari, 2000a: 23–27).

Many scholars believe that the ruling clergy have betrayed religion, irrespective of the fact that they owe all of their worldly belongings—including their political power—to religion. A widely quoted sentence of Ayatollah Montazeri affirms this point: "I hoped that. . . the authorities would be brave enough to announce that this state is neither Islamic nor a republic" (Montazeri, 2010: 424). Soroush, approaching this point from a different perspective, describes Shariati's notion of "Islam without clergy" as "wishful thinking". Rather, "I want to say that Shariati made a mistake. The future of Iran was not "Islam without clergy", but "clergy without Islam" (Soroush, 2006b).

Religious reformation discourse has come to a similar conclusion as that reached by Shariati in the pre-revolutionary era. Shariati questioned the authenticity of the clergy as a class in Islam from an historical perspective. Today, reformist discourse stands in the same position but instead adopts theological arguments. As noted in chapter 1, Mojtahed-Shabestari advocates building a direct relationship between God and believers. He minimizes the role of mediators in human–God relations by downplaying the importance of both human mediators (the clergy) and behavioural mediators (the Shari'a) (Mojtahed-Shabestari, 2008b). In advancing the same concept, Soroush argues that the notion of a mediator between God and believer was imported from Christianity and that, in Islam, no one may claim privileged mediation between God and believers (2005a: 23–24). In Soroush's view, this unique feature of Islam implies a strong affinity between Islam and secularization. He states that secularization removes the authority of clerics from public life. For purposes of prayer, worship, marriage, divorce, and other rituals, it is not necessary to have someone acting as a mediator. "There is absolutely no single religious practice [in Islam] in which you need the presence of a cleric" (2008c). After scrutinizing the different connotations and practices of secularism, Soroush claims that many aspects of secularism are embedded in Islamic teachings. For example, in the Western Judeo-Christian world, the desire for worldliness was an important part of secularization: but, the same notion is already embedded in Islamic teachings, which means, paradoxically, that there is no need to fight for it (Soroush, 2008c).[31]

Insisting on the profound place of politics in the Islamic reformation project, Soroush states that the most controversial issue in contemporary Iran is political secularism. This controversy involves the role of the clergy in the political sphere: Is political leadership a secular matter, or is it the right of the clergy to assume political leadership? Confronting the current politico-religious structure of the Islamic state, Soroush maintains that the clergy may not claim any right in the political arena due to their religious affiliation. He states: "Those who are superior in terms of religiosity do not possess any right to claim superiority in the political sphere. In other words, clerics and religious people may not enjoy any privileges in areas related to the leadership and political affairs" (Soroush, 2004c: 71). Depriving the clergy of privilege in the political sphere conforms with secular principles according to which all citizens, irrespective of religious affiliation and religious credentials, are placed on an equal footing when competing for political leadership.

The clergy's absolute privilege in the political sphere is unique to the Islamic state of Iran. The country's politico-legal structure and its jurisprudential framework not only grant the highest authority to a cleric but discriminate in favour of the clergy in almost all political procedures and positions. The dominance of the clergy in the political sphere has encouraged some scholars to declare Iran a clerical state, rather than Islamic per se. Kadivar states that approximately 80 percent of political power has been handed to the clerics in Iran's political system (2000c: 2). Similarly, Eshkevari, who contests the methods of applying the doctrine of Velayat-e Faqih, observes that the doctrine could be applied without transforming the "Islamic Republic" into a "Clerical Republic" (2000: 24).

The clergy's direct political leadership marks a major departure from Shiite history. This divergence has not only generated conflict over the long-lasting traditions within the institution of the clergy, but also contradicts the jurisprudential principles and pluralistic character of the Shiite school. The outcome has been the merging of political and religious leadership; and, the politico-religious position of the Velayat-e Faqih mirrors this conflation. The Valey-e Faqih simultaneously claims both the highest political and

---

31. Soroush, who offers six meaning of secularism, argues that most of these meanings are not only compatible with Islamic teachings, but are also embedded in Islam's history. For more information, see Soroush, 2004b; 2010d. Analysing the Quran from a secular perspective, Akhtar similarly asserts that Islam inherently encompasses some dimensions of secularity, specifically its worldliness. For further discussion, see Akhtar, 2008.

religious authority, and this has inflicted significant damage on both spheres of Iranian life.

This chapter highlights another dimension of the notion of religious secularity: urging the clergy to retreat from their political positions. The reformist scholars' call for a solely jurisprudential position for the clergy is rooted in three arguments. First, reformist scholars provide a useful insight into the clergy's internal setting. Having scrutinized the internal structure of the clergy and the clerics' educational backgrounds, reformist scholars argue that the clergy lack sufficient qualifications to skilfully execute the responsibility of political leadership. The reformist scholars suggest confining the responsibilities of the clergy to their area of expertise in *fiqh* so as to preserve their credibility.

Second, the clergy's political authority has led to conflict between religious and governmental institutions. This contradiction, which has been called Marjaiat–Velayat conflict, cannot be resolved unless the state jettisons its religious claims. The reformist scholars purport that retaining of Marjaiat autonomy by giving religious authority to Marja-e Taghlids and abandoning the proclaimed religious authority of the supreme leader is the most logical way to settle the conflict.

Third, the lived experience of the clerical establishment in Iran has provided reformist scholars with concrete examples of the dangers associated with the clergy assuming political leadership. There is a consensus among reformist scholars that direct political leadership by the clergy has tarnished the clergy's reputation, a consensus rooted not only in the clergy's mismanagement of the sociopolitical sphere, but also in the Islamic state's intervention in the clergy's internal matters. This is evident in the dishonouring of dissident clerics and in the interrupting of the democratic process of preferment to the level of Marjaiat. Religious secularity is, thus, very much a scholarly effort aimed at regaining the clergy's credibility and retaining their traditional autonomy from the state.

Conclusion

THE PAST FEW decades of the 20th century saw "Islamism" and "political Islam" commonly associated with anti-modernism, violence, fundamentalism, fanaticism, and, of course, the Islamic state. The rise of political Islam spawned a hostile attitude towards secularism in much of the Muslim world. In many countries, religious forces succeeded in mobilizing the Muslim masses to resist the secularization processes initially undertaken by the colonial West and sustained by postcolonial authoritarian states (Ghobadzadeh & Rahim, 2012). Within this milieu, the "Islamic state" and "authoritarian secularism" emerged as two mutually exclusive paradigms available to Muslim majority countries. Although the new millennium coincided with the peak of radical Islamism, subsequent years have witnessed a shift in the direction of political Islam. "Islamism", rather than being simply a byword for radicalism, has become a far more nuanced and contested notion. Provoked by negative and extreme depictions of Islam, moderate voices of the Muslim world have gained increasing prominence. Promulgations of more moderate versions of political Islam have been demonstrated by the Turkish Justice and Development Party (AKP) and other mainstream Islamist groups, including Tunisia's An Nadha.

Along with the concept of Islamism, the notion of secularism has also been deeply contested. Secularism is no longer presented as a universal paradigm; indeed, its multiple forms are enjoying growing recognition. The contested natures of both notions—Islamism and secularism—would seem to invalidate the conceptualization of a dichotomy between the two. Rather, a broad dynamic spectrum exists between two extreme possibilities. Political Islam, seen in this way, no longer signifies fundamentalism, fanaticism, terrorism, and an Islamic state; and, secularity does not stand in direct opposition to religion and Islam. This emerging global Muslim discourse is not confined solely to the heartland of Islam in the Middle East and North Africa. A similar trend is traceable in the Muslim countries of South East Asia and among the Muslim diasporas.[1] Nowadays, both Sunni and Shiite sects are embracing moderate versions of political Islam.

New visions of political Islam have adopted a middle ground, or *wasatiyyah*, position that rejects both dogmatic secularism and radical Islamism. This book provides a detailed analysis of a scholarly discourse in Iran that transcends the religious/secular dichotomy and examines the possibility of reconciling Islam with an inclusive secular democratic state. Iran's political experience is of particular significance given the nine decades in which it has witnessed both an authoritarian secular state and an Islamic state. Shiite religious leaders have a long history of exposure to modern political concepts. Early in the 20th century, Iran's Shiite leaders were embroiled in the Constitutional Revolution, and they pioneered the integration of religious articulation with modern political thought in the Muslim world. The Iranian revolution of 1979, and the subsequent establishment of an Islamic state, inspired other Islamic movements. Today, despite its myriad shortcomings, Iran's clerical Islamic state is considered a political model by conservative Islamists. However, this particular model has been challenged by the emerging discourse of religious secularity, the foundations of which rest upon two main components: (1) repudiating the Islamic state by invalidating its religious foundations, and (2) offering an Islamic rationale for an inclusive secular democratic state.

Repudiating the Clerical Islamic State

The key religious features of the Islamic state of Iran are divine sovereignty, unification of the institutions of religion and state, and the clergy's exclusive right to political leadership. Religious-secularity discourse targets these features. Drawing upon identical Quranic verses and hadiths, scholars, including Ayatollah Montazeri and Kadivar, pose a serious internal challenge to the proclaimed divine sovereignty of the foundation of the Islamic state. While they agree with the ruling clergy that the Prophet Mohammad and the Shiite infallible Imams possessed divine political authority, they refuse to extend this right to jurists in the OCCULTATION ERA.

Other scholars, including Haeri-Yazdi, Eshkevari, and Bazargan, repudiate the historical background of divine sovereignty in the Shiite tradition. They reject the unification of religion and state on the grounds that unification

---

1. See (Elson, 2013; Hosen, 2013; Künkler, 2013; Moustafa, 2014; Rahim, 2013; Roy, 2013a; Seo, 2012).

ultimately serves the political interests of those in power to the detriment of religion, evident in the prioritization of governance over religious precepts by the Islamic state of Iran. Even though the Islamic state was established upon the rationale of implementing Shari'a, Iran's ruling clergy repeatedly discount Islamic principles in the interests of the state.

Additionally, the creation of the Islamic state has seen widespread hypocrisy and the prioritization of the exoteric layers of religion (*fiqh*). The imposition of Shari'a on believers has not only perverted its voluntarily nature, but has also engendered religious hypocrisy, a trait strongly denounced in the Quran and hadiths. The jurisprudential character of the Islamic state of Iran also privileges the exoteric layers of religion to the detriment of genuine religiosity.

Furthermore, the clergy's direct political leadership has tarnished their credibility, undermined their traditional decentralized structure, and threatened their autonomy from the state. The clergy's claim to direct political leadership faces two principal challenges: first, the clergy are neither trained to assume the responsibility of governance, nor have their seminaries equipped them with the requisite skills for dealing with the complexities of governance. Limited to jurisprudential knowledge, the seminary education system has failed to provide the comprehensive religious knowledge (let alone the general knowledge) required to manage modern sociopolitical issues.

Second, clerical political leadership is a recent phenomenon; it has been resisted by many within the Shiite faculty, who regard it contrary to the basic principles and traditions of Shiite jurisprudence. Velayat-e Faqih, the linchpin of the Islamic state, violates the decentralized nature of Marjaiat. By claiming superior authority over both the religious and political domains, Velayat-e Faqih subverts an important principle of the Shiite sect; that is, the idea that the Hidden Imam alone possesses superior authority over all believers, Marja-e Taghlids included.

Pluralism has always been a defining character of the clergy. However, emboldened by political power, Iran's ruling clergy have persecuted those within their circle who do not subscribe to their politico-religious ideology. Not only has this persecution taken many forms, it has become an established pattern since the inception of the Islamic state. The persecution of Grand Ayatollahs Shariatmadari, Montazeri, Qomi, Azari-Qomi, and Sanei—to name but a few—has not only been justified under banner of Islam, but has been arguably more severe compared to the persecution of the clergy during the Pahlavi era.

Another notable development since the establishment of the Islamic state has been the interruption of the democratic process due to the preference afforded at the level of Marjaiat. Khamanei, the current Supreme Leader, makes an excellent example. For centuries, Marja-e Taghlids' reputations have been built upon public veneration. A jurist reaches Marjaiat level as a result not only of his great jurisprudential knowledge, but also of his piety and spiritual reputation. Khamanei lacked these basic requirements, both intellectually and spiritually: his premature elevation to Marjaiat was ensured by political leverage. Today, his Marjaiat status is widely propagated by the Islamic state and efforts are being made to position him as the most eminent Marja-e Taghlid. The nature of Khamanei's elevation has not only eroded the status of other Marja-e Taghlids, but also tarnished the reputation of the clergy. Their possession of political power has exposed the clergy to political, financial, and ethical corruption; their reputations have been further tarnished by failures in the sociopolitical and economic realms.

Promoting the Secular Democratic State

Another component of the religious secularity discourse is its justification of the secular democratic state on religious grounds. Popular sovereignty finds support in the Quranic verses *Al-Shura* 42:38 and *Al-Imran* 3:159. The case for popular sovereignty can be further made by looking at the early years of Islamic history. The Aqaba pact reached between the Prophet Mohammad and the leaders of Medina formed the foundation of the Prophet's governance of the region. It served as an example of the popular basis of his political authority. The historical conduct of Shiite Imams offers further sources for popular sovereignty. When Imam Ali, the first Shiite Imam, agreed to become caliph, he explicitly acknowledged the role of the people, claiming that he would have never accepted the position had there been no insistence by the people.[2] Imam Hassan, the second Shiite Imam, signed a peace contract with Muaviyah Ibn Abi Sufyan, the first caliph of the Umayyad dynasty, in large part taking the issue of the next caliph to the people. It can be easily argued that had Imams Ali and Hassan assumed divine political authority, they would not have deemed endorsement by the people necessary.

The essential nature of justice in Islamic teachings further provides a rationale for popular sovereignty. Islamic scripts do not offer any timeless model of state; rather, they emphasize the necessity for justice in the

---

2. "if people had not come to me and supporters had not exhausted the argument and if there had been no pledge of Allah with the learned to the effect that they should not acquiesce in the gluttony of the oppressor and the hunger of the oppressed, I would have cast the rope of Caliphate on its own shoulders, and would have given the last one the same treatment as to the first one" (Sharif al-Radi & Jafery, 1984: 58).

sociopolitical sphere. The holy texts have left believers to develop a political system that captures the essence of religion—that is, justice. In the contemporary world, a democratic political system based upon popular sovereignty makes "the most compelling claim to legitimacy and moral virtue" (Abou El Fadl, 2003: 7). As Abou El Fadl asserts, it offers a potential system for promoting justice (2003: 10).

An-Na'im contends that the democratic secular state offers a conducive environment for believers to observe their beliefs (An-Na'im, 2008). Religious experience is a voluntarily choice based upon the personal relationship between God and believer. Human beings (jurists) or organizations (state) may not claim a mediatory role in this relation. Islam offers fertile ground for secularity; as Soroush notes, all religious rituals in Islam can be performed without clergy. Their presence is not required for prayer, fasting, or marriage and burial ceremonies. The religious dictates of the Islamic state, which impose a specific understanding of religion upon all believers, stifle genuine religiosity. Similar to the Islamic state, authoritarian secular states limit the right to religious freedom in their attempts to control religion. By contrast, a democratic Muslim state based on religious secularity is not only compatible with religion, but allows for genuine religiosity to flourish in the Muslim world.

According to Abou El Fadl, the holy texts uphold the importance of human competency in determining the appropriate solution to worldly matters (2003: 276–277). An outstanding example is the Prophet Mohammad's saying: "You know best about the affairs of your world".[3] It is logical that as religion does not provide a blueprint for managing sociopolitical and economic matters, these areas ought to be entrusted those competent in handling such matters.

The solution to conflict between the state and Marjaiat, on the one hand, and plural elements within the institution of clergy, on the other, may be found in the secular democratic state. Religious secularity, acknowledging the limitations of the state in the religious domain, concedes that it is neither feasible nor desirable for a state to be in charge of the religious realm. It is able to respect the traditional autonomy of the Marja-e Taghlids, who in turn administer the clergy and manage the religious establishments. Thus,

---

3. "The story of the pollination of the date-palm trees describes how, when the Prophet (peace and blessings of Allah be upon him) migrated to Madeenah, he saw the people there pollinating the date-palm trees by hand, and he said to them, "If you do not do this, it should still be fine". So they did not do it, and the crop failed, producing only bad dates. He passed by them and said, "What is wrong with your date-palms?" They said, "You told us such-and-such". He said, "You know best about the affairs of your world". (Reported by Muslim, 4358). See also Abdul-Rahman, 2007: 107.

religious secularity is the discourse that best facilitates the ongoing process of negotiation and reconciliation required to mediate complex and potentially conflicting elements.

Religious Secularity: An Unfolding Discourse

The location of the boundaries between religion and state and the form of their separation are currently of major interest to mainstream Western scholarship. Generally speaking, whereas models such as the French *laïcité* that suppress religion have been subject to wide criticism, religion-friendly models such as passive secularism (Kuru, 2009) are held in high regard. As such, religious secularity, which contests the Islamic state and promotes the secular democratic state, is of tremendous importance, given that it promotes a religion-friendly model of secularity that, importantly, is rooted in Islamic teachings. The contemporary quest for the separation of religion and state in Iran is part of the greater discourse of religious reformation:

- The leading proponents of the religious secularity discourse are religious scholars. State–religion relations are a part of their religious reformation project. The bulk of their work scrutinizes different religious issues not limited to political matters.
- Protecting the integrity of Islam is the basic principle that underpins the quest for religious secularity. As Casanova reminds us, secularism in the West was aimed at emancipating state and economy from religion (2006). By contrast, religious secularity is oriented towards the emancipation of religion from the state.
- The quest for religious secularity is paradigmatic given that it is rooted in Islamic teachings. The Quran, hadiths, and Islamic tradition and history are the main sources used within a theological and jurisprudential framework to challenge the unification of religion and state.
- Finally, anti-clericalism was one of the distinguishing features of the secularization process in Western Christendom, particularly in the European countries.[4] By contrast, the emerging model of secularity in Iran is not anti-clerical. Reformist scholars have made clear distinction between the ruling clergy and other clerics who do not subscribe to the ruling politico-religious discourse.[5] Reformist scholars hope to gain the support

---

4. For a detailed discussion of anti-clericalism in Europe, see Aston & Cragoe, 2000; Halperin, 1947; McGinness, 2004; Sánchez, 1972.

5. For example, see (Eshkevari, 2011b, 2011c; Ghabel, 2005; Kadivar, 2000c, 2005a).

of senior clerics in their struggle with the ruling clergy. An outstanding example in this regard is Soroush's open letter to the Marja-e Taghlids, in which he urged them to leave Iran for Iraq in order to be able to freely criticize the clerical establishment (Soroush, 2010a).

Iranian religious secularity is emerging in a context that corresponds loosely to the French and Turkish experiences. France's and Turkey's early experiences of secularism were formed in direct response to hegemonic religious forces. Religious secularity in Iran is in many respects a backlash against such forces—or, more precisely, against specific religious groups who establish hegemony in the religious and political domains. However, in contrast to the French and Turkish experiences, this discourse is by no means anti-religious. Religious secularity is based on an intimate connection with religion. Charles Taylor has called for the decentring of attention from religion in debates about secularity (Taylor, 2009). The argument advanced by this book pushes the boundaries of Taylor's suggestion by proposing not only the possibility of the coexistence of religion and secularity, but the need to recognise the religious roots of an emerging model of secularity in the Muslim world and, with that, the reductive nature of the secular/religious dichotomy.

In the European Judeo-Christian experience, secularization was a comprehensive project that led to several dualisms, the most important of which were the worldliness/next-worldliness and science/religion dichotomies. Islam, which is a worldly religion, has not experienced the conflict with science as seen in the Christian world. It accepts that science has its own logic and regulation. As Soroush argues, in the Muslim world, politics is the main area that needs to be secularized (Soroush, 2008c). Religious secularity, arguing the necessity for civic reasoning in the sociopolitical arenas, represents this effort.

Religious secularity, a discourse confined to the political arena, does not incorporate other dimensions of secularization. For example, it neither promotes the marginalization of religiosity nor the privatization of religion. Although the Iranian people remain deeply religious, recent surveys show that they distance themselves from political Islam in the form of an Islamic state. The popularity of the religious reformation discourse of the Green and reformist movements demonstrates its influence in the political arena. Due to the strong religious character of the country, its people respond readily to the religious discourse championed by the reformist scholars. In fact, their religious quest for the detachment of religion from the state has proven to be more popular than the secular voices[6] that objected to the clerical establishment from the outset of the establishment of the Islamic Republic of Iran. Thus, there is room to trace the influence of this scholarly discourse at the societal and political levels.

While religious secularity is very much a response to the excesses of the authoritarian secular state and the Islamic state, it is not a finished project. As Laclau and Mouffe argue, discourses are constantly in flux (cited in Jørgensen & Phillips, 2002: 25). Under the current circumstances, religious secularity pursues two primary aims: (1) to challenge the dominance of radical Islam in Iran's official political lexicon and (2) to establish a religious argument for the acceptance of secularity in the Muslim world. Secularism in the Muslim world is bound up with colonialism, Westernization, and anti-religious policies. In a general sense, it suggests "acting against God" and "ruining religion". The peculiarity of secularism is evident in the lack of a defining word for it in the Arabic, Turkish, and Persian languages. In Iran, for example, the term "secularism", as it appears in English, is commonly used. Efforts to provide a Persian substitute such as *orfigeraei, do'niageraei, dahri,* and *gitigeraei* have not been generally accepted. The term "secularity" as used in this book, is no exception. I have faced this very problem trying to find a Persian word to describe the concept of "religious secularity". Religious secularity offers only Islamic justification for the acceptance of a secular democratic state: it is not a violation but a prerequisite for genuine religiosity.

This book sets the ground for further research into the challenges and possibilities associated with the implementation of religious secularity. In post–Islamic state Iran, the issue of religion will certainly remain topical. Further comparative studies tracing this trend in other Muslim countries— both Shi'a and Sunni majorities—will serve as fruitful contributions to the scholarship.

---

6. A fact that confirms the conceptual articulation by Wolterstorff, who argues that in a religious society, religious reasoning works better than secular reasoning. John Rawls, proposing the notion of "overlapping consensus", urges believers to advocate their ideas through secular reasoning. By contrast, Wolterstorff promotes the usage of religious reasoning in a religious society. For further discussion, see Audi & Wolterstorff, 1997: 67–120; Rawls, 1993: 133–172.

Bibliography

Abdi, A. (2009). Farhang-e Umoomi: Hal va Ayandeh [Public culture: Now and future]. In A. Abdi & M. Goodarzi (Eds.), *Cultural changes in Iran* (pp. 17–78). Tehran: Nashr-e Elm.

Abdi, A., & Goudarzi, M. (2009). *Tahavolat-e farhangi dar Iran* [Cultural changes in Iran]. Tehran: Elm.

Abdo, G. (2001). Re-thinking the Islamic Republic: A conversation with Ayatollah Hossein Ali Montazeri. *Middle East Journal, 55*(1), 9.

Abdul-Rahman, M. S. (2007). *Islam: Questions and answers—basis for jurisprudence and Islamic rulings.* London: MSA Publication.

Abed Al Jabri, M., & Khalaji, M. (1997). Danesh-e fiqh, bonyad-e raveshshenakhti-e Arabi-Islami [The knowledge of fiqh: Methodological foundation of the Arabic-Islamic rationality]. *Naghd o Nazar, 4*(12), 114–140.

Abedi, M. (1986). Ali Shariati: The architect of the 1979 Islamic revolution of Iran. *Iranian Studies, 19*(4), 229–234.

Abisaab, R. J. (2004). *Converting Persia religion and power in the Safavid empire.* New York: I.B. Tauris.

Abou El Fadl, K. (2002). The place of tolerance in Islam. In K. Abou El Fadl, J. Cohen, & I. Lague (Eds.), *The place of tolerance in Islam* (pp. 3–26). Boston: Beacon Press.

Abou El Fadl, K. (2003). Islam and the challenge of democratic commitment. *Fordham International Law Journal, 27*(1), 4.

Abou El Fadl, K. (2005). *The great theft: Wrestling Islam from the extremists.* New York: HarperCollins.

Abou El Fadl, K., Cohen, J., & Chasman, D. (2004). *Islam and the challenge of democracy.* Princeton, NJ: Princeton University Press.

Abrahamian, E. (1982). *Iran between two revolutions.* Princeton, NJ: Princeton University Press.

Abrahamian, E. (2008). *A history of modern Iran.* New York: Cambridge University Press.

Abu Zayd, N. (2004). *Islam, Muslims and the west: Religion and secularism; from polarization to negotiation.* Retrieved May 20, 2010, from Initiatives of Change, http://www.nl.iofc.org/print/22865.

Abu Zayd, N. (2006). *Reformation of Islamic thought: A critical historical analysis.* Amsterdam: Amsterdam University Press.

Abu Zayd, N., & Eshkevari, H. Y. (2005). *Naghd-e tafakor-e dini* [A critique of religious discourse] (H. Yousefi Eshkevari & M. Javaher Kalam, Trans.). Tehran: Yadavaran.

Abu Zayd, N., & Nelson, E. R. (2004). *Voice of an exile: Reflections on Islam.* Westport, CN: Praeger.

Adelkhah, F. (2000). *Being modern in Iran.* New York: Columbia University Press.

Afary, J. (2013). The place of Shi'i clerics in the first Iranian constitution. *Critical Research on Religion Critical Research on Religion, 1*(3), 327–346.

AFP. (2009). Iran daily slams Rafsanjani querying of election result. In *Agence France-Presse (AFP)*, July 18, 2009. Retrieved Augutst 20, 2010, from http://www.timesofmalta.com/articles/view/20090719/world-news/iran-daily-slams-rafsanjani-querying-of-election-result.265775.

AFP. (2010). Iran opposition leader vows to keep up vote protest. In *Agence France-Presse (AFP)*, June 19, 2010. Retrieved June 24, 2010, from http://www.google.com/hostednews/afp/article/ALeqM5i-dyT6Wkcs2gfFbF3aKcmwVezwxQ.

Aghajari, H. (2000a). Dolat-e dini va na din-e doulati [Religious governmental and not a governmental religion]. *Asr-e Ma, 7*(174).

Aghajari, H. (2000b). Tafkik-e nahad-e din va nahad-e doulat [The separation of the institution of religion and the state]. *Baztab-e Andishe, 1*(5), 14–19.

Aghajari, H. (2002a). Farayand-e tahavol va takamol-e andisheh va raftar-e aleman va faqihan Shiie Imami [The process and evolvement of the thoughts and conducts of Imami Shiite Ulama and jurists]. *Aftab, 3*(20), 60–65.

Aghajari, H. (2002b). Islamic Protestantism. In *Faith: The Journal of the International League of Religious Socialists.* Vol. 3. Retrieved August 8, 2010, from http://ilrs.org/faith/aghajaritext.html.

Ahdar, R. (2013). Is secularism neutral? *Ratio Juris, 26*(3), 404–429.

Aienevan, S., Aghajari, H., Rahmati, M. K., & Moftakhari, H. (2010). Tahvolhay-e dini asr-e Safavi va naghsh-e aleman-e Ameli: Motalaeh moredi-e Mohaghegh Karaki va Shahid Thani [Religious transitions of Safavids era and the role of Amili Ulama: The cases of Mohaghegh Karaki and Shahid Thani]. *Jostarhay-e Tarikhi, 1*(2), 1–18.

Akbarzadeh, S. (2014). The Arab revolution is bad news for Iran. In A. Saikal & A. Acharya (Eds.), *Democracy and reform in the Middle East and Asia: Social protest and authoritarian rule after the Arab Spring* (pp. 105–120). London: I.B.Tauris.

Akhavi, S. (1980). *Religion and politics in contemporary Iran: Clergy–state relations in the Pahlavi period.* Albany: State University of New York Press.

Akhavi, S. (1988). Islam, politics and society in the thought of Ayatullah Khomeini, Ayatullah Taliqani and Ali Shariati. *Middle Eastern Studies, 24*(4), 404–431.

Akhavi, S. (1996). Contending discourses in Shi'i law on the doctrine of Wilayat al-Faqih. *Iranian Studies, 29*(4), 229–268.

Akhavi, S. (2008). The thought and role of Ayatollah Hossein'ali Montazeri in the politics of post-1979 Iran. *Iranian Studies, 41*(5), 645–666.

Akhavi, S. (2013). Ali Shari'ati. In J. L. Esposito & E. E. Shahin (Eds.), *The Oxford handbook of Islam and politics* (pp. 169–179). New York: Oxford University Press.

Akhtar, S. (2008). *The Quran and the secular mind: A philosophy of Islam.* London: Routledge.

Alatas, S. F. (2007). Contemporary Muslim revival: The case of "Protestant Islam". *Muslim World, 97*(3), 508–520.

Alatas, S. F. (2010). Rejecting Islamism and the need for concepts from within the Islamic tradition. In R. C. Martin & A. Barzegar (Eds.), *Islamism: Contested perspectives on political Islam* (pp. 87–92). Stanford, CA: Stanford University Press.

Al-e Ghafur, S. M. (2007). *Jaygah-e siasi-e alem-e dini dar do maktabe Akhbari va Usuli* [The political position of clergy in the two Akhbari and Usuli schools]. Qom: Boustan-e ketab.

Algar, H. (1969). *Religion and state in Iran, 1785–1906: The role of the ulama in the Qajar period.* Berkeley: University of California Press.

Algar, H. (1972). The oppositional role of the Ulama in twentieth-century Iran. In N. R. Keddie (Ed.), *Scholars, saints, and Sufis: Muslim religious institutions in the Middle East since 1500* (pp. 231–255). Berkeley: University of California Press.

Algar, H. (1988). Imam Khomeini, 1902–1962: The pre-revolutionary years. In E. Burke, I. M. Lapidus & E. Abrahamian (Eds.), *Islam, politics, and social movements* (pp. 263–288). Berkeley: University of California Press.

Al-Ghannouchi, R. (2000). Secularism in the Arab Maghreb. In A. Tamimi & J. L. Esposito (Eds.), *Islam and secularism in the Middle East* (pp. 97–123). London: Hurst.

Al-Ghannouchi, R. (2013). The state and religion in the fundamentals of Islam and contemporary interpretation. *Contemporary Arab Affairs, 6*(2), 164–171. doi: 10.1 080/17550912.2013.783184.

Al-Ghannouchi, R., & Bouazza, B. (2011). Ghanouchi says, "I'm no Khomeini" (interview). *Associate Press* (January 3, 2011). Retrived June 23, 2012, from http://www. foxnews.com/world/2011/01/30/tunisian-islamist-party-leader-returns-home/

Aliabadi, A. M. (2005). *Abdolkarim Soroush and the discourse of Islamic revivalism.* Published Ph.D. diss., New School University, New York. ProQuest dissertations & theses full text dataset. Retrieved from http://ezproxy.library.usyd.edu. au/login?url=http://search.proquest.com/docview/305347221?accountid=14757. (305347221).

Alizadeh, A. (2009). Neither theocracy nor secularism? Politics in Iran. *Radical Philosophy* (158), 2–10.

Aljazeera. (2014). *Foreign leaders hail Tunisia's constitution.* Retrieved February 20, 2014, from http://www.aljazeera.com/news/africa/2014/02/foreign-leaders-hail-tunisia-constitution-201427144047687702.html.

Amanat, A. (1988). In between the madrasa and the marketplace: The designation of clerical leadership in modern Shi'ism. In S. A. Arjomand (Ed.), *Authority and political culture in Shi'ism* (pp. 98–132). Albany: State University of New York Press.

Amini, D. (2003). *Chaleshhay-e rohaniyat ba Reza Shah* [Clergy's conflict with Reza Shah]. Tehran: Sepas.

Amo-Shahi, M. (1999). Rabbet-e Marjaiat va rahbari dar nazariyeh Velayat-e Faqih [The relations between leadership and Marjaiat in the doctrine of Velayat-e Faqih]. *Daneshgah-e Islami,* 3(11), 23–47.

An-Na'im, A. A. (1998). Shari'a and positive legislation: Is an Islamic state possible or viable? *Yearbook of Islamic and Middle Eatern Law,* 5 (1), 29–41.

An-Na'im, A. A. (2008). *Islam and the secular state: Negotiating the future of Shari`a.* Cambridge, MA: Harvard University Press.

An-Na'im, A. A. (2009). Islam and the secular state. In *Rethinking the secular* (Vol. 1, pp. 12–17). Pluralism working paper. Netherlands: Promoting Pluralism Knowledge Program.

An-Na'im, A. A. (2010). Islam and secularism. In L. E. Cady & E. S. Hurd (Eds.), *Comparative secularisms in a global age* (pp. 217–228). New York: Palgrave Macmillan.

An-Na'im, A. A., & Baderin, M. A. (2010). *Islam and human rights: Selected essays of Abdullahi An-Na'im.* Surrey: Ashgate.

Ansari, H. (1999). *Marjaiat va Rahbari: Tafkik ya Vahdat?* [Marjaiat and leadership: Segregation or unity?]. Tehran: Moasseh Tanzim va Nashre Asare Imam.

Arasteh, A. R. (1962). *Education and social awakening in Iran.* Leiden: E.J. Brill.

Arjomand, S. A. (1981). The Ulama's traditionalist opposition to parliamentarianism: 1907–1909. *Middle Eastern Studies,* 17(2), 174–190.

Arjomand, S. A. (1988). *The turban for the crown: The Islamic revolution in Iran.* New York: Oxford University Press.

Arjomand, S. A. (1993). Shi'ite jurisprudence and constitution-making in the Islamic Republic of Iran. In M. E. Marty & R. S. Appleby (Eds.), *Fundamentalisms and the state: Remaking polities, economies, and militance* (pp. 88–109). Chicago: University of Chicago Press.

Arjomand, S. A. (2009). *After Khomeini: Iran under his successors.* New York: Oxford University Press.

Arkoun, M. (2006). *Islam: To reform or to subvert?* London: Saqi Essentials.

Arkoun, M. (2008). *Positive moderate secularism and negative extremist secularism.* Retrieved December 14, 2009, from http://www.arabphilosophers.com/Arabic/aphilosophers/acontemporary/acontemporary-names/Muhammad_Arakoun/Arabic_Material/Secularism_Moderate_and_Extrimist.htm.

Armajani, J. (2004). *Dynamic Islam: Liberal Muslim perspectives in a transnational age.* New York: University Press of America.

Armstrong, K. (2000). *The battle for God.* New York: Alfred A. Knopf.

Ashouri, D. (2011). Creeping secularism. *Comparative Studies of South Asia, Africa and the Middle East, 31*(1), 46–52.

Ashraf, A., & Banuazizi, A. (2001). Iran's tortuous path toward "Islamic liberalism". *International Journal of Politics, Culture, and Society, 15*(2), 237–256.

As-sadr, M. B. (1980). *An inquiry concerning Al-Mahdi.* Tehran: World Organization for Islamic Services.

Assyaukanie, L. (2009). *Islam and the secular state in Indonesia.* Singapore: Institute of Southeast Asian Studies.

Aston, N., & Cragoe, M. (2000). *Anticlericalism in Britain, c. 1500–1914.* Phoenix Mill, UK: Sutton.

Atabaki, T., & Zürcher, E. J. (2004). *Men of order: Authoritarian modernization under Ataturk and Reza Shah.* London: I.B. Tauris.

Audi, R., & Wolterstorff, N. (1997). *Religion in the public square: The place of religious convictions in political debate.* Lanham, MD: Rowman & Littlefield.

Azimi, F. (2008). *The quest for democracy in Iran: A century of struggle against authoritarian rule.* Cambridge, MA: Harvard University Press.

Badran, T. (2009). Hezbollah's agenda in Lebanon. *Current Trends in Islamist Ideology, 8,* 52–67.

Baik-Mohammadian, N. (2007). Daghdagh-e Ayatollah Salehi-Najafabadi: Javab porseshhay-e jadid [Ayatollah Salehi-Najafabadi's concern: Answering new questions]. *Cheshm Andaz-e Iran, 9*(47), 83–91.

Baker, R. W. (2003). *Islam without fear: Egypt and the new Islamists.* Cambridge, MA: Harvard University Press.

Bakhash, S. (1990). *The reign of the Ayatollahs: Iran and the Islamic revolution.* New York: Basic Books.

Baran, Z. (2010). *Torn country: Turkey between secularism and Islamism.* Stanford, CA: Hoover Institution Press.

Bashiriyeh, H. (2009). *Jameh shenasi-e siyasi: Naghsh-e niroohay-e ejtemaei dar zendegi siasi* [Political sociology: The role social forces in political life]. Tehran: Nashr-e Nay.

Basirat-Manesh, H. (2007). *Ulama va regime Reza Shah* [Clergy and Reza Shah's reign]. Tehran: Chap o Nashr-e Uroj.

Basmenji, K. (2005). *Tehran blues: How Iranian youth rebelled against Iran's founding fathers.* London: Saqi.

Bates, M. S. (1945). *Religious liberty: An inquiry.* New York: Harper & Bros.

Baum, G. (2009). *The theology of Tariq Ramadan: A Catholic perspective.* Notre Dame, IN: University of Notre Dame Press.

Bayat, A. (1997). *Street politics: Poor people's movements in Iran.* New York: Columbia University Press.

Bayat, A. (2007). *Making Islam democratic: Social movements and the post-Islamist turn.* Stanford, CA: Stanford University Press.

Bayat, M. (1991). *Iran's first revolution: Shi'ism and the constitutional revolution of 1905–1909.* New York: Oxford University Press.

Bazargan, M. (1984). *Enghelab-e Iran dar do marhaleh* [Iranian revolution in two phases]. Tehran: Mazaheri.

Bazargan, M. (1995). Akherat va khoda: Hadaf-e bathat-e anbia [The afterlife and God: The aim of the sacred mission of the prophets]. *Kiyan*, *5*(28), 46–61.

Bazargan, M. (1998). Ba'ithat va ideolozhi [Prophetic mission and ideology]. In M. Bazargan (Ed.), *Ba'ithat 1* (pp. 233–384). Tehran: Ghalam.

BBC. (2012). The leader said he would not accept the assembly's intervention in details. In *BBC Persian*, February 18, 2012. Retrieved February 9, 2013, from http://www.bbc.co.uk/persian/iran/2012/02/120218_l39_khobregan_khamenei_supervision.shtml.

Beaufort, F. D. (2008). *Separation of church and state in Europe: With views on Sweden, Norway, the Netherlands, Belgium, France, Spain, Italy, Slovenia and Greece.* Brussels: European Liberal Forum.

Behdad, S. (1997). Islamic utopia in pre-revolutionary Iran: Navvab Safavi and the Fada'ian-e Eslam. *Middle Eastern Studies*, *33*(1), 40–65.

Behrooz, M. (1996). The Islamic state and the crisis of Marja'iyat in Iran. *Comparative Studies of South Asia Africa and the Middle East* (16), 93–100.

Behrooz, M. (1996). The Islamic state and the crisis of Marja'iyat in Iran. *Comparative Studies of South Asia Africa and the Middle East* (16), 93–100.

Benard, C., & Khalilzad, Z. (1979). Secularization, industrialization, and Khomeini's Islamic Republic. *Political Science Quarterly*, *94*(2), 229–241.

Berger, P. L. (1997). Epistemological modesty: An interview with Peter Berger. *The Christian century*, *114*(30), 972.

Berger, P. L. (1999). *The desecularization of the world: Resurgent religion and world politics.* Washington, DC: Ethics and Public Policy Center.

Berger, P. L., Davie, G., & Fokas, E. (2008). *Religious America, secular Europe? A theme and variations.* Aldershot: Ashgate.

Berg-Sørensen, A. (2013). *Contesting secularism: Comparative perspectives.* England: Ashgate.

Berman, B., Bhargava, R., & Laliberté, A. (2013). *Secular states and religious diversity.* Seattle: University of Washington Press.

Bertram, C. (2004). *Routledge philosophy guidebook to Rousseau and the social contract.* New York: Routledge.

Beyer, P. (2013). Questioning the secular/religious divide in a post-Westphalian world. *International Sociology*, *28*(6), 663–679. doi: 10.1177/0268580913507070.

Bhargava, R. (1998). What is secularism for? In R. Bhargava (Ed.), *Secularism and its critics* (pp. 486–542). Delhi: Oxford University Press.

Bhargava, R. (2009). Political secularism: Why is it needed and what can be learned from its Indian version? In G. B. Levey & T. Modood (Eds.), *Secularism, religion and multicultural citizenship* (pp. 88–103). New York: Cambridge University Press.

Bhargava, R. (2013). Reimagining secularism: Respect, domination and principled distance. *Economic and Political Weekly*, 48(50), 79–92.

Boozari, A. (2011). *Shi'i jurisprudence and constitution: Revolution in Iran*. New York: Palgrave Macmillan.

Borghei, M. (1992). Iran's religious establishment: The dialectics of politicization. *Iran: Political culture in the Islamic Republic* (pp. 39–55). London: Routledge.

Borji, Y. (2006). *Velayat-e Faqih dar andisheh faqihan* [Velayat-e Faqih in jurists' thought]. Tehran: Samt.

Boroujerdi, M. (1996). *Iranian intellectuals and the West: The tormented triumph of nativism*. Syracuse, NY: Syracuse University Press.

Browers, M., & Kurzman, C. (2004). *An Islamic reformation?* Lanham, MD: Lexington Books.

Brown, C. G., & Snape, M. F. (2010). *Secularization in the Christian world*. Farnham, UK: Ashgate.

Bruce, S. (2002). *God is dead: Secularization in the West*. Malden, MA: Blackwell.

Brumberg, D. (2001). *Reinventing Khomeini: The struggle for reform in Iran*. Chicago: University of Chicago Press.

Bruno, G. (2008). Religion and politics in Iran. *Council on Foreign Relations (June 19, 2008)*. Retrieved July 20, 2010, from http://www.cfr.org/iran/religion-politics-iran/p16599.

Bukovansky, M. (2002). *Legitimacy and power politics: The American and French Revolutions in international political culture*. Princeton, NJ: Princeton University Press.

Burgat, F. (2003). *Face to face with political Islam*. London: I.B. Tauris.

Butler, J., Mendieta, E., & VanAntwerpen, J. (2011). *The power of religion in the public sphere*. New York: Columbia University Press.

Byers, A. (2003). *Lebanon's Hezbollah*. New York: Rosen.

Cady, L. E., & Hurd, E. S. (2010). *Comparative secularisms in a global age*. New York: Palgrave Macmillan.

Calder, N. (1982a). Accommodation and revolution in Imami Shi'i jurisprudence: Khumayni and the classical tradition. *Middle Eastern Studies*, 18(1), 3–20.

Calder, N. (1982b). Khums in Imami Shii jurisprudence, from the tenth to the sixteenth century A.D. *Bulletin of the School of Oriental and African Studies*, 45(1), 39–47.

Calhoun, C. J., Juergensmeyer, M., & VanAntwerpen, J. (2011). *Rethinking secularism*. Oxford: Oxford University Press.

Casanova, J. (1994). *Public religions in the modern world*. Chicago: University of Chicago Press.

Casanova, J. (2003). Beyond European and American exceptionalisms: Towards a global perspective. In G. Davie, L. Woodhead & P. Heelas (Eds.), *Predicting religion: Christian, secular, and alternative futures.* Farnham, UK: Ashgate.

Casanova, J. (2006). Rethinking secularization: A global comparative perspective. *Hedgehog Review, 8*(1/2), 7–22.

Casanova, J. (2009). The secular and secularisms. *Social Research: An International Quarterly, 76*(4), 1049–1066.

Casanova, J. (2011). The secular, secularizations, secularisms. In C. J. Calhoun, M. Juergensmeyer, & J. VanAntwerpen (Eds.), *Rethinking secularism* (pp. 54–74). Oxford: Oxford University Press.

Cavatorta, F., & Merone, F. (2013). Moderation through exclusion? The journey of the Tunisian Ennahda from fundamentalist to conservative party. *Democratization, 20*(5), 857–875. doi: 10.1080/13510347.2013.801255.

Chatterjee, K. (2011). *Ali Shari'ati and the shaping of political Islam in Iran.* New York: Palgrave Macmillan.

Chaves, M. (1994). Secularization as declining religious authority. *Social Forces, 72*(3), 749–774.

Chavura, S. (2010). The separation of religion and state: Context and meaning. *Nebula* (7), 37–46.

Chehabi, H. E. (1990). *Iranian politics and religious modernism: The liberation movement of Iran under the Shah and Khomeini.* Ithaca, NY: Cornell University Press.

Chehabi, H. E. (1991). Religion and politics in Iran: How theocratic is the Islamic Republic? *Daedalus, 120*(3), 69–91.

Chehabi, H. E. (1997). Eighteen years later. *Harvard International Review, 19* (2), 28–31.

Chehabi, H. E., & Abisaab, R. J. (2006). *Distant relations: Iran and Lebanon in the last 500 years.* London: The Centre for Lebanese Studies.

Chehabi, H. E., & Schirazi, A. (2012). The Islamic Republic of Iran. *Journal of Persianate Studies, 5*(2), 175–204.

Cinar, A. (2005). *Modernity, Islam, and secularism in Turkey: Bodies, places, and time.* Minneapolis: University of Minnesota Press.

Cizre, U. (2008). *Secular and Islamic politics in Turkey: The making of the Justice and Development Party.* New York: Routledge.

Cole, J. (1985). Shi'i clerics in Iraq and Iran, 1722–1780: The Akhbari-Usuli conflict reconsidered. *Iranian Studies, 18*(1), 3–34.

Cole, J. R. I. (2006). *The Ayatollahs and democracy in Iraq.* Amsterdam: Amsterdam University Press.

Collins, R. (2009). *Keepers of the keys of heaven: A history of the papacy.* New York: Basic Books.

Cooper, J. (1998). The limits of the sacred: The epistemology of 'Abd al-karim Soroush. In J. Cooper, R. L. Nettler, & M. Mahmoud (Eds.), *Islam and modernity: Muslim intellectuals respond* (pp. 38–56). London: I.B. Tauris.

Cronin, S. (2003). *The making of modern Iran: State and society under Riza Shah, 1921–1941.* New York: Routledge.

Cruz, J. A. H. M., & Gerberding, R. (2004). *Medieval worlds: An introduction to European history, 300–1492.* Boston: Houghton Mifflin.

Dabashi, H. (1993). *Theology of discontent: The ideological foundations of the Islamic Revolution in Iran.* New York: New York University Press.

Dalmasso, E., & Cavatorta, F. (2013). Democracy, civil liberties and the role of religion after the Arab awakening: Constitutional reforms in Tunisia and Morocco. *Mediterranean Politics, 18*(2), 225–241. doi: 10.1080/13629395.2013.799341.

DaneshjooNews. (2010). Kalaf-e sardar ghom-e marjaiat [A confusing skein of Marjaiat]. Retrieved November 23, 2011, from http://www.daneshjoonews.com/vijeh/3618-1389-07-25-22-20-57.html.

Daniel, E. L. (2001). *The history of Iran.* Westport, CN: Greenwood Press.

Davari, M. T. (2005). *The political thought of Ayatullah Murtaza Mutahhari: An Iranian theoretician of the Islamic state.* London: Routledge.

Davie, G. (2000). *Religion in modern Europe: A memory mutates.* Oxford: Oxford University Press.

Davis, D. H. (2003). Thomas Jefferson and the "wall of separation" metaphor. *A Journal of Church and State, 45*(1), 5–14.

Denzinger, H. (1957). *The sources of Catholic dogma.* St. Louis, MO: Herder.

Derakhsheh, J. (1999). Nazariy-e hokumat dar andisheh-e siasi-e ulamay-e Shi'a Iran: 1320–1357 [State theories in the political thought of Iranian Shiite Ulama: 1941–1979]. *Faslnam-e Pazhoheshi-e Daneshgah-e Imam Sadeq* (10), 65–86.

Derakhsheh, J. (2001a). Jostari dar tafakor-e siasi-e ulamay-e shi'a az mashrotiyat ta 1320 [An inquiry about the political thought of Shiite Ulama between the Constitutional Revolution and 1320]. *Imam Sadeq Quarterly, 7*(13 & 14), 189–224.

Derakhsheh, J. (2001b). Tabar shenasi-e nazaryeh-e hukoumat dar andisheh Imam Khomeini [Roots of state theory in the political thought of Imam Khomeini] *Ulom-e siasi* [Political Science], *4*(13), 206–225.

Derakhsheh, J. (2002). Sakhtar Shenasi-e Fekr Dini Dar Iran-e Moaaser ba Takid bar Roykardhay-e Roshanfekri [A study of religious thought in the contemporary Iran with special focus on intellectualism]. *Imam Sadeq Quarterly 5*(20), 67–90.

Dobbelaere, K. (1984). Secularization theories and sociological paradigms: Convergences and divergences. *Social Compass, 31*(2–3), 199–219. doi: 10.1177/003776868403100205.

Dobbelaere, K. (1999). Towards an integrated perspective of the processes related to the descriptive concept of secularization. *Sociology of Religion, 60*(3), 229–247.

Dobbelaere, K. (2002). *Secularization: An analysis at three levels.* New York: P.I.E.-Peter Lang.

Dressler, M. (2010). Public-private distinctions, the Alevi question, and the heads-
    carf: Turkish secularism revisited. In L. E. Cady & E. S. Hurd (Eds.), *Comparative
    secularisms in a global age* (pp. 121–142). New York. Palgrave Macmillan.

Dunn, J. (1969). *The political thought of John Locke: An historical account of the
    argument of the "Two Treatises of Government"*. London: Cambridge University
    Press.

Eftekhari, A. (2004). Sharie sazi ghodrat-e siasi [Legitimizing political power].
    Faslnameh Motaeat-e Rahbordi, 7(2), 275–298.

Ehteshami, A. (2002). *After Khomeini: The Iranian second republic.*
    New York: Routledge.

Ehteshami, A., & Zweiri, M. (2006). *Understanding Iran's Assembly of Experts.*
    Durham, UK: Durham University.

Elson, R. E. (2013). Two failed attempts to Islamize the Indonesian constitution.
    Journal of Social Issues in Southeast Asia, 28(3), 379.

Engineer, A. A. (2006). Islam and secularism. In I. M. Abu-Rabi (Ed.), *The
    Blackwell companion to contemporary Islamic thought* (pp. 338–344). Malden,
    MA: Blackwell.

Esfandiari, G. (2006). Outspoken Ayatollah alleges official persecution. In *Radio
    Liberty*. Retrieved June 12, 2011, from http://www.rferl.org/content/arti
    cle/1071839.html.

Eshkevari, H. Y. (2000a). Hawza va hokumat: Bist sal pas az edgham [Hawza
    and state: Twenty years after unification]. In M. Ghochani (Ed.), *Din-e dou-
    lat: Doulat-e dini* [Religious government: Governmental religion] (pp. 22–53).
    Tehran: Saraei.

Eshkevari, H. Y. (2000b). Hoghoug va jonbesh-e zanan [Women's rights and wom-
    en's movement]. In M. A. Zakariaee (Ed.), *Conferanc-e berlin: Khedmat ya khiya-
    nat* [Berlin's conference: Service or treason] (pp. 226–234). Tehran: Terh-e No.

Eshkevari, H. Y. (2009a). Din, hokoumat va secularism [Religion, state, and secu-
    larism]. In *Jonbeshe Rahe Sabz (Jaras)* (September 10, 2009). Retrieved August
    17, 2010, from http://www.rahesabz.net/story/2506/

Eshkevari, H. Y. (2009b). *Farbehi din va khoroj az korsi-e akhlagh, maanaviyat va edalat*
    [Wealthy religion and abandonment of ethics, spirituality, and justice]. Retrieved
    May 5, 2010, from http://talash-online.com/neshrye/matn_29_0_172.html.

Eshkevari, H. Y. (2009c). *Hakemyat Khoda: Bozorgtarin doroghe tarikh* [God's sov-
    ereignty: The biggest lie in history]. Retrieved April 3, 2010, from http://youse
    fieshkevari.com/?p=658.

Eshkevari, H. Y. (2009d). *Pasokh be chand porsesh* [Answer to some questions].
    Retrieved November 20, 2011, from http://www.rahesabz.net/story/2647.

Eshkevari, H. Y. (2010a). *Fiqh, ekhtelafat-e fiqhi va tagheer paziri-e ahkam* [*Fiqh,
    jurisprudential disagreements, and variability of commandments*]. Retrieved
    November 5, 2010, from http://yousefieshkevari.com/enteshar/?p=1322.

Eshkevari, H. Y. (2010b). *Hughogh-e bashar va ahkam-e ejtemaie-e Islam* [Human rights and Islamic social commandments]. Retrieved December 10, 2010, from http://yousefieshkevari.com/enteshar/?p=751.

Eshkevari, H. Y. (2010c). Latme jomhuri-e Islamic be etebar-e din va rohaniyat [The brunt of the Islamic Republic to the reputation of religion and clergy]. Retrieved October 9, 2011, from http://yousefieshkevari.com/?p=1491.

Eshkevari, H. Y. (2010d). Mashroiyat-e ghodrat [Power legitimacy]. *Talash, 8*(33), 89–96.

Eshkevari, H. Y. (2010e). *Zist-e momenan-e dar hukumat-e orfi* [Religious life in a secular state]. Retrieved November 18, 2010, from http://yousefieshkevari.com/enteshar/?p=777.

Eshkevari, H. Y. (2011a). *Mohammad Reza Mahdavi or Mohammad Reza Pahlavi?* Retrieved December 6, 2011, from http://yousefieshkevari.com/?p=2132.

Eshkevari, H. Y. (2011b). *Morori bar tarikh-e hawz-e Qom az manzar-e eslah talabi* [A review of the history of Qom seminary from a reformist perspective]. Retrieved November 12, 2011, from http://yousefieshkevari.com/?p=1995.

Eshkevari, H. Y. (2011c). *Naghsh-e doganeh-e ruhaniat dar jomhouri Islami* [Double role of clergy in the Islamic Republic]. Retrieved December 21, 2011, from http://yousefieshkevari.com/?p=2287.

Eshkevari, H. Y. (2011d). *Roshanfekran-e Dini va Tahavolat-e Hoziya Qom* [Religious intellectuals and intellectual developments in Qom seminary]. Retrieved August 03, 2011, from http://www.rahesabz.net/story/40510.

Eshkevari, H. Y., Mir-Hosseini, Z., & Tapper, R. (2006). *Islam and democracy in Iran: Eshkevari and the quest for reform.* London: I.B. Tauris.

Esmaeili, H. R. (2007). *Din va siyasat dar andishe siyasi moaaser* [Religion and politics in contemporary political thought]. Tehran: Pajoheshkade Motaleate Farhangi va Ejtemaei.

Esposito, J. L. (1990). *The Iranian revolution: Its global impact.* Miami: Florida International University Press.

Esposito, J. L. (1997). *Political Islam: Revolution, radicalism, or reform?* Boulder, CO: Lynne Rienner Publishers.

Esposito, J. L. (2000). Islam and secularism in the twenty-first century. In J. L. Esposito & A. Tamimi (Eds.), *Islam and secularism in the Middle East* (pp. 1–12). New York: New York University Press.

Esposito, J. L. (2011). *Can we find a way to bring some understanding here today?* Retrieved January 12, 2012, from http://www.unitedforchange.com/events/united-we-stand/videos.

Esposito, J. L., & Mogahed, D. (2007). *Who speaks for Islam? What a billion Muslims really think.* New York: Gallup Press.

Esposito, J. L., & Tamimi, A. (2000). *Islam and secularism in the Middle East.* New York: New York University Press.

Esposito, J. L., & Voll, J. O. (1996). *Islam and democracy.* New York: Oxford University Press.

Esposito, J. L., & Voll, J. O. (2001). *Makers of contemporary Islam.* New York: Oxford University Press.

Farati, A. (2004). Radicalism Islamic dar Iran-e Moaser [Islamic radicalism in contemporary Iran]. *Panezdah-e Khordad, 15*(2), 207–242.

Farzaneh, M. M. (2010). Shi'ite clerical authority and modern politics: Muhammad Kazim Khurasani of Najaf and his support of the Iranian Constitutional Revolution of 1906–1911. Ph.D. diss., University of California, Santa Barbara. ProQuest dissertations & theses full text database. Retrieved from http://ezproxy.library.usyd.edu.au/login?url=http://search.proquest.com/docview/814800678?accountid=14757. (814800678).

Fatah, T. (2008). *Chasing a mirage: The tragic illusion of an Islamic state.* Mississauga, Ont: John Wiley & Sons Canada.

Feirahi, D. (2005). Mabani Fiqih Mashrotehkhahi az didghahe Akhund Khurasani [Jurisprudential foundations of the constitutionalism: Akhund Khurasani's perspectives]. In T. University (Ed.), *Barrasi mabani-e fekri va ejtemaei Mashrotiyat Iran* [Review: Intellectual and social foundations of Iran's constitutionalism] (pp. 192–214). Tehran: Tehran University.

Feirahi, D. (2010). *Din va dolat dar asr-e modern: Dolat-e Islamic va tolidat-e fekr-e siyasi* [Religion and state in the modern age: Islamic state and development of political thought]. Tehran: Rokhdad-e No.

Fereshtian, H. (2013). *Secularism-e penhan dar tajrob-e Jomhouri-e Islami* [Hidden secularism in the experience of the Islamic Republic]. Retrieved December 12, 2013, from http://www.rahesabz.net/story/66043/

Filali-Ansary, A. (2003). Muslims and democracy. In L. J. Diamond, M. F. Plattner, & D. Brumberg (Eds.), *Islam and democracy in the Middle East* (pp. 193–207). Baltimore, MD: Johns Hopkins University Press.

Fuller, G. E. (2003). *The future of political Islam.* New York: Palgrave.

Ganji, A. (2011). *Imam zaman, godrat, servat* [The 12th Shia Imam, power, wealth]. Retrieved October 14, 2011, from http://www.akbarganji.org/?p=69&langswitch_lang=fa&page=4.

Gaudemet, J. (2003). Gregorian reform. *New Catholic Encyclopedia* (2nd ed., Vol. 6, pp. 468–473). Detroit: Gale.

Gencer, B. (2010). Sovereignty and the separation of powers in John Locke. *European Legacy, 15*(3), 323–339.

Gerami, M. A., & Emami, J. (2002). *Khaterat-e Ayatollah Mohammad Ali Gerami* [Memories of Ayatollah Mohammad Ali Gerami]. Tehran: Markaz-e Asnad-e Engelab-e Islami.

Gerecht, R. M. (2004). *The standoff with Iraqi Shiites over direct elections.* Retrieved June 17, 2011, from the American Enterprise Institute (AEI), http://www.aei.

org/issue/foreign-and-defense-policy/regional/middle-east-and-north-africa/
the-standoff-with-iraqi-shiites-over-direct-elections/

Gerges, F. A. (2013). The Islamist moment: From Islamic state to civil Islam?
Political Science Quarterly, 128(3), 389–426. doi: 10.1002/polq.12075.

Ghabel, H. (2005). Ruhaniat va azmoon-e ghodrat [Clergy and appraisal of power].
Eghbal (166), 1–3.

Ghabel, H. (2011). Akhund Khurasani va naghsh-e ruhaniyat dar hokumat [Akhund
Khurasani and clergy's role in the state]. Retrived February 17, 2012, from http://
www.rahesabz.net/story/8522.

Ghamari-Tabrizi, B. (2004). Contentious public religion: Two conceptions of Islam
in revolutionary Iran: Ali Shari`ati and Abdolkarim Soroush. *International
Sociology, 19*(4), 504–523.

Ghamari-Tabrizi, B. (2008). *Islam and dissent in postrevolutionary Iran: Abdolkarim
Soroush, religious politics and democratic reform.* New York: I.B. Tauris.

Ghazali, M., & Farouk-Alli, A. (2010). *Within the boundaries of Islam: A study on
Bid`ah.* Kuala Lumpur: Islamic Book Trust.

Gheissari, A., & Nasr, S. V. R. (2006). *Democracy in Iran: History and the quest for
liberty.* New York: Oxford University Press.

Ghobadzadeh, N. (2002). *A study of people's divergence from ruling system in the second
decade of the Islamic revolution* [Revayati asib shenakhti az gosast-e nezam va
mardom dar dahyeh dovvom-e enghelab]. Tehran: Farhang-e Gofteman.

Ghobadzadeh, N. (2004). Value changes in Iran (Second decade of the Islamic revolution). *Discourse: An Iranian Quarterly, 6*(2), 77–108.

Ghobadzadeh, N., & Rahim, L. Z. (2012). Islamic reformation discourses: Popular
sovereignty and religious secularisation in Iran. *Democratization, 19*(2), 334–351.

Ghoochani, M. (2007). *Montaghed-e Rohaniyat ya Jaygozin-e On?* [Critic of clergy or
clergy's successor?]. Retrieved October 20, 2011, from http://www.drsoroush.
com/Persian/On_DrSoroush/P-CMO-SoroushDarTarazoo.html.

Gieling, S. (1997). The "Marja'iya" in Iran and the nomination of Khamanei in
December 1994. *Middle Eastern Studies, 33*(4), 777–787.

Glasner, P. E. (1977). *The sociology of secularisation: A critique of a concept.*
London: Routledge & K. Paul.

Gleave, R. (2002). Political aspects of modern Shi'a legal discussions: Khumayni
and Khu'i on *ijtihad and qada'. Mediterranean Politics, 7*, 96–116.

Godazgar, H. (2001). Islamic ideology and its formative influence on education in
contemporary Iran. *Economía, Sociedad y Territorio, 3*(10), 321–336.

Godazgar, H. (2002). Islamism and education in modern Iran, with special reference to gendered social interactions and relationships. *Economía, Sociedad y
Territorio, 3*(11), 489–503.

Godazgar, H. (2007). Islam versus consumerism and postmodernism in the context of Iran. *Social Compass, 54*(3), 389–418. doi: 10.1177/0037768607080835.

Golkar, S. (2012). Cultural engineering under authoritarian regimes: Islamization of universities in postrevolutionary Iran. *Digest of Middle East Studies, 21*(1), 1–23.

Goudarzi, M. R., Jawan, J. A., & Ahmad, Z. B. (2009). The roots of formation of Ayatollah Khomeini's political thought. *Canadian Social Science, 5*(6), 65–80.

Goudarzi, M., Jawan, J., & Ahmad, Z. (2010). Ayatollah Khomeini and the foundation of legitimacy of power and government. *Canadian Social Science, 5*(6), P103–114.

Greeley, A. M. (1989). *Religious change in America.* Cambridge, MA: Harvard University Press.

Gulen, F. (2006). A comparative approach to Islam and democracy. In M. Kamrava (Ed.), *The new voices of Islam: Rethinking politics and modernity—a reader* (pp. 99–104). Berkeley: University of California Press.

Hadad-Adel, F. (2004). Naghd o barrasi ketab-e rahnamaye haghayegh be onvan-e manifest-e Fadaeian-e Islam [Reviewing the book of guidline for truth as the charter for Fadaeian-e Islam]. *Zamane, 3*(24), 27–38.

Hadavi-Tehrani, M. (1998a). Hokumat-e Islami [Islamic government]. *Ketab-e Naghd, 2*(7), 167–221.

Hadavi-Tehrani, M. (1998b). *Valey-e Faqih: Mabani, adeleh va ekhtiarat* [Valey-e Faqih: Essences, reasons, and authorities]. Tehran: Kanon-e Andish-e Javan.

Hadden, J. K. (1987). Toward desacralizing secularization theory. *Social Forces, 65*(3), 587–611.

Haeri, A. (1977). *Shi'ism and constitutionalism in Iran: A study of the role played by the Persian residents of Iraq in Iranian politics.* Leiden: E.J. Brill.

Haeri, A. (1985). *Tashayo va mashrotiyat dar Iran* [Shi'a and constitutionalism in Iran]. Tehran: Amir Kabir.

Haeri, S. K. (1996). Sabet va motaghayer dar din [Fixed and variable in religion]. *Hoze va Daneshgah, 3*(6), 95–100.

Haeri-Yazdi, M. (1994). *Hekmat va hokumat* [Wisdom and government]. London: Shadi.

Haghighat, S. S. (2010). *Mabani-e andish-e siyasi dar Islam* [The foundations of political thought in Islam]. Tehran: Samt.

Haidari, M. (2008). Dastane- jedal motaghabel-e Shariati va ruhanion [The story of confrontation between Shariati and clergy]. *Shahrvand-e emrooz, 3*(50), 1–4.

Haeri, A.-H. (1976). Why did the ʿUlamā participate in the Persian Constitutional Revolution of 1905–1909? *Die Welt des Islams, 17*(1/4), 127–154. doi: 10.2307/1570343.

Hajjarian, S. (2001). *Az shahede qodsi ta shahede bazari: Urfi shodan-e din dar sepehr-e siyasat* [From the sacred witness to the profane witness: The secularization of religion in the sphere of politics]. Tehran: Tarh-e No.

Hajjarian, S. (2007). *Jomhoriat: Afsoonzodaeeazghodrat* [Republicanism: Demystification of power]. Tehran: Tarh-e No.

Halperin, S. W. (1947). Italian anticlericalism, 1871–1914. *Journal of Modern History*, 19(1), 18–34.

Hamid, S. (2014). *Temptations of power: Islamists and illiberal democracy in a new Middle East*. New York: Oxford University Press.

Hammond, P. E. (1985). *The sacred in a secular age: Toward revision in the scientific study of religion*. Berkeley: University of California Press.

Hanafi, H. (2010). Islamism: Whose debate is it? In R. C. Martin & A. Barzegar (Eds.), *Islamism: Contested perspectives on political Islam* (pp. 63–66). Stanford, CA: Stanford University Press.

Hanafi, H., & Wahyudi, Y. (2006). Hassan Hanafi on Salafism and secularism. In I. M. Abu-Rabi (Ed.), *The Blackwell companion to contemporary Islamic thought* (pp. 257–270). Malden, MA: Blackwell.

Harmon, D. E. (2005). *Ayatollah Ruhollah Khomeini*. Philadelphia: Chelsea House.

Harris, I. (1994). *The mind of John Locke: A study of political theory in its intellectual setting*. Cambridge: Cambridge University Press.

Harub, K. (2010). *Political Islam: Context versus ideology*. London: Saqi.

Hashemi, N. (2009). *Islam, secularism, and liberal democracy: Toward a democratic theory for Muslim societies*. New York: Oxford University Press.

Hashemi, N. (2010). The multiple histories of secularism: Muslim societies in comparison. *Philosophy Social Criticism*, 36(3–4), 325–338. doi: 10.1177/0191453709358842.

Hashemi, N. (2014). Rethinking religion and political legitimacy across the Islam–West divide. *Philosophy and Social Criticism*, 40(4–5), 439–447.

Hashemi-Najafabadi, A. (2010). Imamate and leadership: The case of the Shi'a fundamentalists in modern Iran. *Canadian Social Science* 6(6), 192–205.

Hashemi-Shahroudi, M. (1998). Shoura, aalamiyat, Marjaiat va Velayat-e Faqih [Consultant, superiority in learning and Velayat-e Faqih]. *Eram* (3), 27–35.

Hashmi, N. (2013). Why Islam (properly understood) is the solution: Reflections on the role of religion in Tunisia's democratic transition. *The American Journal of Islamic Social Sciences*, 30(4), 137–145.

Heng, M. S. H., & Ten, C. L. (2010). *State and secularism perspectives from Asia*. New Jersey: World Scientific.

Hiro, D. (1985). *Iran under the Ayatollahs*. London: Routledge & K. Paul.

Hirschl, R. (2010). *Constitutional theocracy*. Cambridge, MA: Harvard University Press.

Hooker, R. (1996). Divine right of kings. *European enlightenment glossary*. Retrived December 12, 2010, from http://richard-hooker.com/sites/worldcultures/glossary/divright.htm.

Hosen, N. (2013). Religious pluralism, inclusive secularism, and democratic constitutionalism: The Indonesian experience. In L. Z. Rahim (Ed.), *Muslim secular democracy: Voices from within* (pp. 211–232). New York: Palgrave Macmillan.

Hunter, S. (2009). *Reformist voices of Islam: Mediating Islam and modernity*. Armonk, NY: M.E. Sharpe.

Hunter, S. (2009). *Reformist voices of Islam: Mediating Islam and modernity*. Armonk, NY: M.E. Sharpe.

Hunter, S. T. (2009). Islamic reformist discourse in Iran: Proponents and prospects. In S. T. Hunter (Ed.), *Reformist voices of Islam: Mediating Islam and modernity* (pp. 33–97). Armonk, NY: M.E. Sharpe.

Hussain, A. (2010). Terminological problems for Muslim lives. In R. C. Martin & A. Barzegar (Eds.), *Islamism: Contested perspectives on political Islam* (pp. 57–62). Stanford, CA: Stanford University Press.

Hussain, J. M. (1982). *The occultation of the Twelfth Imam: A historical background*. London: Muhammadi Trust.

Husseinzadeh, A. (2003). Moorori bar hayat va andisheh siasi-e Shaykh Muhammad Isma'il Gharavi Mahallati [A review of the life and political thought of Shaykh Muhammad Isma'il Gharavi Mahallati]. *Amoozeh, 2*(3), 321–340.

Hutson, J. H., & Jefferson, T. (1999). Thomas Jefferson's letter to the Danbury Baptists: A controversy rejoined. *William and Mary Quarterly, 56*(4), 775–790.

Ibn Khaldūn. (2005). *The Muqaddimah: An introduction to history*. F. Rosenthal (Ed.) & N. J. Dawood (Trans.). Princeton, NJ: Princeton University Press.

Jadallah, D. (2013). State sovereignty and citizen agency: The nationalist-Islamic discourse of Shaykh Muhammad Mahdi Shams al-Din. *Mathal/Mashal, 3*(1), 4.

Jafaryan, R. (2008). *Naghsh-e khandan-e Karaki dar taasis va tadavom-e doulat-e Safavi* [The role of Karaki clan in establishment and permanence of Safavids]. Tehran: Nashr-e Elm.

Jahanbakhsh, F. (2001a). Abdolkarim Soroush: New revival of religious sciences. *ISIM Newsletter, 1*(8), 21.

Jahanbakhsh, F. (2001b). *Islam, democracy and religious modernism in Iran, 1953–2000: From Bazargan to Soroush*. Leiden: Brill.

Jahanbakhsh, F. (2003). Religious and political discourse in Iran: Moving toward post-fundamentalism. *Brown Journal of World Affairs, 9*, 243–254.

Jahanbakhsh, F. (2004). The emergence and development of religious intellectualism in Iran. *Historical Reflections, 30*(3), 469–480.

Jahanbegloo, R. (2000). The role of the intellectuals. *Journal of Democracy, 11*(4), 135–138.

Jahanbegloo, R. (2007). Iranian intellectuals: From revolution to dissent. *World Affairs, 11*(1), 80–90.

Jakelic, S. (2010). Secularism: A bibliographic essay. *Hedgehog Review, 12*(3), 49–56.

Jakobsen, J. R., & Pellegrini, A. (2008). *Secularisms*. Durham, NC: Duke University Press.

Javadi-e Amoli, A. (1989). *Piramoon-e vahy va rahbari* [On revelation and leadership]. Qom: Al Zahra.

Javadi-e Amoli, A. (2002). *Velayat-e Faqih; velayat-e feqahat va edalat* [Velayat-e Faqih; guardian of jurisprudence and justice]. Qom: Asra.

Javaherian, A. (2010). Iran: State, civil society, and social emancipation. *Critique, 38*(2), 267–282.

JMHEQ. (2010). What is the opinion of JMHEQ about Sheikh Sanei's Marjaiat? *JMHEQ*. Retrieved November 11, 2011, from http://alef.ir/vdciqvaq.t1au32bcct.html?6wml.

Johnston, D. L. (2010). *Evolving Muslim theologies of justice: Jamal al-Banna, Mohammad Hashim Kamali and Khaled Abou El Fadl.* Pulau Pinang: Penerbit Universiti Sains Malaysia.

Jørgensen, M., & Phillips, L. (2002). *Discourse analysis as theory and method.* London: Sage Publications.

Kadivar, M. (1992). Mabaniy-e eslah-e sakhtar-e amoozeshi-e hawzahay-e elmiyeh [Principles for reforming the educational structure of seminaries]. *Kaihan-e Andisheh, 7*(42), 5–15.

Kadivar, M. (1994). Nazariyeh hay-e doulat dar figh'h-e Shi'ia [The theories of state in the Shiite jurisprudence]. *Rahbord* (4), 1–42.

Kadivar, M. (1997). *Nazariyehay-e doulat dar fiqh Shi'a* [The theories of state in Shiite *fiqh*]. Tehran: Nashr-e Nay.

Kadivar, M. (1998). Hawza va hokumat [Hawza and state]. *Rah-e No, 1*(2), 16–20.

Kadivar, M. (1999a). *Hokumat e vela'i* [Theocratic state]. Tehran: Nashr-e Ney.

Kadivar, M. (1999b). Taamoli dar masaaly-e velayat-e faqih [A thought on the issue of rule of the Islamic jurist]. Retrieved May 20, 2014, from http://kadivar.com/?p=889.

Kadivar, M. (2000a). *Daghdaghehayeh hokumat dini* [The concerns of a religious state]. Tehran: Nashr-e Nay.

Kadivar, M. (2000b). Hokumat-e entesabi [Appointive government]. *Aftab, 1*(2), 8–13.

Kadivar, M. (2000c). Ruhaniyat va ghodrat [Clergy and authority]. *Jameh-e Madani, 1*(2), 1–7.

Kadivar, M. (2000d). Yek bar-e digar hokumat-e velaei [Government by mandate again]. *Doran-e Emrooz, 1*(80), 9.

Kadivar, M. (2001a). *Dindari-e digaran* [Others' religiosity]. Retrieved February 4, 2010, from http://kadivar.com/wp-content/uploads/2001/12/800912-011.pdf.

Kadivar, M. (2001b). *Hawza va donyai-e Jadid* [Hawza and the new world]. Retrieved October 4, 2010, from http://kadivar.com/?attachment_id=6585.

Kadivar, M. (2001c). Khobregan-e mansoub [Appointed experts]. *Aftab, 2*(6), 58–65.

Kadivar, M. (2001d). *Payambari: Tbaligh-e din bbedoon-e mozd* [Prophecy: Free propagation of religion]. Retrieved October 07, 2011, from http://kadivar.com/?p=5905.

Kadivar, M. (2002a). Az Islam-e tarikhi be Islam maanavi [From historical Islam to virtual Islam]. In M. M.-S. A. Soroush, M. Malekian, & M. Kadivar (Eds.), *Sunnat va secularism* [Tradition and secularism] (pp. 431). Tehran: Serat.

Kadivar, M. (2002b). Velayat-e Faqih and democracy. Paper presented at the Middle East Studies Association of North America conference, Washington, DC.

Kadivar, M. (2003). An introduction to the public and private debate in Islam. *Social Research, 70*(3), 659.

Kadivar, M. (2003a). *Fiqhahat va siyasat* [Jurisprudence and politics]. Retrieved February 10, 2010, from http://kadivar.com/?p=5743.

Kadivar, M. (2003b). Hughogh-e basher va roshanfekri-e dini [Human rights and religious intellectualism]. *Aftab, 4*(27 & 28).

Kadivar, M. (2003c). *Mohemtar az fiqh* [More important than *fiqh*]. Retrieved August 7, 2010, from http://kadivar.org/?p=2365.

Kadivar, M. (2004). God and his guardians. *Index on Censorship, 33*(4), 64–71.

Kadivar, M. (2005a). *Naghsh-e ruhaniat dar gozar be democracy* [Clergy's role in the transition to democracy]. Retrieved October 19, 2010, from http://kadivar.com/?p=5647.

Kadivar, M. (2005b). *Sazegary-e Islam ba hogough-e basher va democracy* [The compatibility of Islam with human rights and democracy]. Retrieved February 10, 2010, from http://www.ettelaat.net/extra_05_09/m_kadivar_s_islam_b_h_b_va_d.asp.

Kadivar, M. (2006a). Ghera'ate faramoosh shodeh; bazkhani nazariyeh "ulemaye abrar", talaghy-e avally-e Islam-e Shiie az asl-e imamat [Forgotten reading: A review of the notion of "pious clerics", the first Shi'ite understanding of pontificate]. *Madraseh, 2*(3), 92–102.

Kadivar, M. (2006b). Islam va democracy: Sazegari ya nasazegari? [Islam and democracy: Compatibility or incompatibility?]. *Aeen*(3), 43–49.

Kadivar, M. (2006c). *Siasat-nameh Khurasani: Qgata'ate siasi dar athare Akhund Mulla Mohammad Kazem Khurasani, sahebe Kefayeh* [Khurasani's political philosophy: Political statements in the works of Akhund Mulla Mohammad Kazim]. Tehran: Kavir.

Kadivar, M. (2006d). Tabghebandi-e e'teghadat-e dini [Categorization of religions beliefs]. *Madraseh, 2*(5), 21–26.

Kadivar, M. (2007a). *Baz shenasi-e aghl: Pish-Shart-e sazegari-e din va hughooghe basher* [Re-acknowledging the right of wisdom: Pre-condition of compatibility between religion and human rights]. Retrieved September 15, 2010, from http://kadivar.com/?p=179.

Kadivar, M. (2007b). *Huzoor-e democratic-e din dar arse omomi* [Democratic presence of religion in the public sphere] Retrieved May 5, 2010, from http://kadivar.com/?p=2108.

Kadivar, M. (2008). *Daftar-e aghl: Madjmou'eh maghalat-e falsafi kalaami* [The Book of reason: Articles on Islamic philosophy and theology]. Tehran: Etelaat.

Kadivar, M. (2009). Human rights and intellectual Islam. In K. Vogt, L. Larsen, & C. Moe (Eds.), *New directions in Islamic thought: Exploring reform and Muslim tradition* (pp. 47–73). London: I.B. Tauris.

Kadivar, M. (2010a). *Estizahe rahbari* [Impeachment of the leader]. Retrieved September 16, 2011, from http://kadivar.com/?p=45.

Kadivar, M. (2010b). *Islam-e rahmani* [Compassionate Islam]. Retrieved September 20, 2010, from http://kadivar.com/?p=12.

Kadivar, M. (2010c). *Islam-e taksahati* [One-dimensional Islam]. Retrieved November 05, 2010, from http://kadivar.com/?p=8.

Kadivar, M. (2010d). *Montazeri va fiqh-e rahaee bakhsh* [Montazeri and redeemer *fiqh*]. Retrieved December 27, 2010, from http://www.rahesabz.net/story/29907/

Kadivar, M. (2010e). *Montazeri va fiqh-e rahaee bakhsh* [Montazeri and redeemer *fiqh*]. Retrieved December 27, 2010, from http://www.rahesabz.net/story/29907/

Kadivar, M. (2011a). *Jodaei hoghoghi-e nahad-e din az doulat* [Legal separation of the institution of the state from religion]. Retrieved September 02, 2011, from http://kadivar.com/?p=98.

Kadivar, M. (2011b). *Sair-e tahavol-e andish-e siasi-e Ayatollah Montazeri* [Changing trend of Montazeri 's political thought]. Retrieved June 24, 2011, from http://kadivar.com/?p=5568.

Kadivar, M. (2013a). *Mokhalefan-e Marjaiat dar Jame-e Modaressin* [Dissidents of Marjaiat in the Society of the Lecturers of the Qom seminary (JMHEQ)]. Retrieved February 10, 2014, from http://www.rahesabz.net/story/75456/

Kadivar, M. (2013b).*Asnadi az shekaste shodan-e namous-e enqelab: Neghahi be sal-haye payani-e zendeghani-e Ayatollah Seyyed Kazim Shari'atmadari* [Evidence of dishonoring the revolution: Examining the last years of Ayatollah S. Kazim Shari'atmadari's life]. Retrieved January 13, 2014 from http://kadivar.com/wp-content/uploads/2013/12/Ayatollah-Shariatmadari-.pdf.

Kadivar, M. (2014a). Routinizing the Iranian revolution. In J. T. Kenney and Ebrahim Moosa (Eds.), *Islam in the modern world* (pp. 351–368). New York: Routledge.

Kadivar, M. A. (2014b). *The battle over higher education in Iran.* Retrieved February 27, 2014, from the Middle East Research and Information Project, http://www.merip.org/mero/mero022014.

Kadivar, M. (2014c). *Faraz wa forud-e Azari-Qomi: Seiri dar tahawwol-e mabaniy-e afkar-e Ayatollah Ahmad Azari-Qomi* [The rise and fall of Azari Qomi: The evolution of Ayatollah Ahmad Azari-Qomi's thought]. Retrieved from http://kadivar.com/wp-chttp://kadivar.com/?p=13166.

Kadivar, M., & Kamali-Ardakani, A. A. (2004). Mardomsalari dar araye Shaikh Mohammad Mehdi Shams al-Din va Doctor Mehdi Haeri-Yazdi [Democracy in the thought of Mohammad Mehdi Shams al-Din and Mehdi Haeri-Yazdi] *Nameh Mofid* 10(44), 61–82.

Kamali, H. (1995). *The theory of expansion and contraction of religion: A research program for Islamic revivalism* (February 1995). Retrieved April 25, 2101, from http://www.drsoroush.com/English/On_DrSoroush/E-CMO-19950200-1.html.

Kamali, M. (2007). Multiple modernities and Islamism in Iran. *Social Compass, 54*(3), 373–387. doi: 10.1177/0037768607080833.

Kamrava, M. (2003). Iranian Shiism under debate. *Middle East Policy, 10*(2), 102–112.

Kamrava, M. (2008). *Iran's intellectual revolution.* New York: Cambridge University Press.

Kamrava, M. (2011). Iranian Shi'ism at the gates of historic change. In M. Kamrava (Ed.), *Innovation in Islam: Traditions and contributions* (pp. 58–84). Berkeley: University of California Press.

Kamrava, M., & Dorraj, M. (2008). *Iran today: An encyclopedia of life in the Islamic Republic.* Westport, CN: Greenwood Press.

Karbalaie, A. (2001). Pishineh Velayat-e Faqih [The History of Velayat-e Faqih]. *Fiqh* (29–30), 259–336.

Katouzian, H. (2010). The Iranian revolution at 30: The dialectic of state and society. *Middle East Critique, 19*(1), 35–53.

Katouzian, N. (2002). Gozari bar tadvin-e pishnevis-e Ghanoon-e Asasi [A review of the writing of the primary version of the Constitution]. *Hughogh-e Asasi, 1*(1), 115–137.

Kazemeini-Boroujerdi, S. H. (2008). *Biography: The extract of challenging biography of Iranian apolitical and independent religious leader Ayatollah Sayyed Hossein Kazemeini Boroujerdi.* Retrieved September 10, 2011, from http://www.bam azadi.org/p/biography.html.

Kazemi, A. (2008). *Jamee shenasi roshanfekri-e dini dar Iran* [Sociology of religious intellectualism in Iran]. Tehran: Tarh-e No.

Kazemi, A. V., & Faraji, M. (2003). Orfi shodan va zendegi roozmareh [Secularization and daily life]. *Nameh Ulom-e Ejtemaie, 21,* 243–269.

Kazemipur, A., & Goodarzi, M. (2009). Iranian youth and religion: An empirical study. *Middle East Critique, 18*(2), 161–176.

Kazemipur, A., & Rezaei, A. (2003). Religious life under theocracy: The case of Iran. *Journal for the Scientific Study of Religion, 42*(3), 347–361.

Keane, J. (2000). The limits of secularism. In J. L. Esposito & A. Tamimi (Eds.), *Islam and secularism in the Middle East* (pp. 29–37). New York: New York University Press.

Kechichian, J. A. (1986). The role of the Ulama in the politics of an Islamic state: The case of Saudi Arabia. *International Journal of Middle East Studies, 18*(1), 53–71.

Keddie, N. (2003). Secularism and its discontents. *Daedalus, 132*(3), 14–30.

Keddie, N. R. (1980). Iran: Change in Islam; Islam and change. *International Journal of Middle East Studies, 11*(4), 527–542.

Keddie, N. R. (1997). Secularism and the state: Towards clarity and global comparison. *New Left Review* (226), 21.

Keddie, N. R., & Richard, Y. (2003). *Modern Iran: Roots and results of revolution.* New Haven, CN: Yale University Press.

Kennedy, E. (2006). *Secularism and its opponents from Augustine to Solzhenitsyn.* New York: Palgrave Macmillan.

Kenny, A., & Smyth, G. (1997). Secularism and secularisation. *Studies: An Irish Quarterly Review, 86*(344), 315–330.

Keyman, E. F. (2010). Assertive secularism in crisis: Modernity, democracy, and Islam in Turkey. In L. E. Cady & E. S. Hurd (Eds.), *Comparative secularisms in a global age* (pp. 143–158). New York: Palgrave Macmillan.

Khalaji, M. (2006). The last Marja: Sistani and the end of traditional religious authority in Shiism. Retrieved July 3, 2011, from http://www.washingtoninsti tute.org/uploads/Documents/pubs/PolicyFocus59final.pdf.

Khalaji, M. (2008). Jomhori-e Islami va nazm-e novin rohniyat [Islamic Republic of Iran and the new order of clerical establishment]. *Iran Nameh* [Journal of Iranian studies], 24(2&3), 1–36.

Khamanei, A. (1995). *Supreme Leader's Speech* [Bayanat-e magham-e moazzam-e rahbari]. Retrieved October 20, 2011, from http://www.ghadeer.org/imam_rah/ byanat/byanat.html.

Khamanei, A. (2009). *Velayat-e Faqih va hokm-e hakem* [Velayat-e Faqih and the order of ruler]. Retrieved January 25, 2010, from http://farsi.khamenei.ir/ treatise-content?uid=1&tid=8.

Khatam, A. (2009). The Islamic republic's failed quest for the spotless city. *Middle East Report* (250), 44–49. doi: 10.2307/27735285.

Khoei, A. (1998). Velayat-e motalagh-e Faqih [Absolute rule of Islamic jurist]. *Rah-e No, 1*(21), 16–17.

Kholdi, S. (2010). The hedging mullah: A historical review of the clergy's struggle for hegemony and independence in modern Iran. *Constellations, 17*(1), 31–49.

Khomeini, R. (1944). *Kashf al-asrar* [Secrets unveiled]. Qom: Azadi Publication.

Khomeini, R. (1976). *Namei az Emam Khashef al-Ghata* [A letter by Imam Khashef al-Ghata]. Qom: Unknown.

Khomeini, R. (1983). Interview with Rueters. In R. Khomeini (Ed.), *Taliay-e enghelab-e Islamic* [Herald of Islamic revolution: Collection of interviews in Najaf, Paris, and Qum]. Tehran: Markaz-e Nashr-e Daneshgahi.

Khomeini, R. (2000). *Sahifeh nour* [Book of light] (Vol. 10). Tehran: Moasseh Tanzim va Nashre Asare Imam.

Khomeini, R. (2005). *Islamic government.* London: Alhoda.

Khomeini, R. (2006a). *Kitab al-Bay* [The Book of Business Transactions] (Vol. 2). Tehran: Moasseh Tanzim va Nashre Asare Imam.

Khomeini, R. (2006b). *Sahifeh nour* [Book of light] (Vol. 21). Tehran: Moasseh Tanzim va Nashre Asare Imam.

Khomeini, R. (2006c). *Sahifeh nour* [Book of light] (Vol. 5). Tehran: Moasseh Tanzim va Nashre Asare Imam.

Khomeini, R. (2006d). *Sahifeh nour* [Book of light] (Vol. 6). Tehran: Moasseh Tanzim va Nashre Asare Imam.

Khomeini, R. (2006e). *Sahifeh nour* [Book of light] (Vol. 20). Tehran: Moasseh Tanzim va Nashre Asare Imam.

Khomeini, R. (2006f). *Sahifeh nour* [Book of light] (Vol. 21). Tehran: Moasseh Tanzim va Nashre Asare Imam.

Khomeini, R. (2008). *Tahrir al-wasilah* [A clarification of questions]. S. M. B. Mousavi Hademani (Trans.). Tehran: Dar al-elm.

Khomeini, R., & Algar, H. (1981). *Islam and revolution: Writings and declarations of Imam Khomeini*. Berkeley, CA: Mizan Press.

Khosrokhavar, F. (2001). Neo-conservative intellectuals in Iran. *Critique: Critical Middle Eastern Studies, 10*(19), 5–30.

Khosrokhavar, F. (2004). The new intellectuals in Iran. *Social Compass, 51*(2), 191–202. doi: 10.1177/0037768604043006.

Khosrokhavar, F. (2007). The new religiosity in Iran. *Social Compass, 54*(3), 453–463. doi: 10.1177/0037768607080842.

Khosroshahi, S. H. (1992). Shahid Beheshti va masale-e hokumat-e Eslami [Shahid Beheshti and the issue of Islamic state]. *Tarikh va Farhang-e Moaaser, 2*(3–4), 444–465.

Khosroshahi, S. H. (2000). *Fadaeian-e Islam: Tarikh, amalkard, anidsheh* [Devotees of Islam: History, activities, and thought]. Tehran: Etelaat.

Kian-Thiebaut, A. (1999). Political and social transformations in post-Islamist Iran. *Middle East Report, 29*(212), 12–16.

Kosmin, B. A., Keysar, A., & Tabatabaei, S. J. (2007). *Secularism and secularity: Contemporary international perspectives*. Hartford, CT: Institute for the Study of Secularism in Society and Culture.

Künkler, M. (2013). How pluralist democracy became the consensual discourse among secular and nonsecular Muslims in Indonesia. In M. Künkler & A. C. Stepan (Eds.), *Democracy and Islam in Indonesia* (pp. 53–72). New York: Columbia University Press.

Künkler, M., & Stepan, A. C. (2013). *Democracy and Islam in Indonesia*. New York: Columbia University Press.

Kurtz, P. (2010). *Multi-secularism: A new agenda*. New Brunswick, NJ: Transaction Publishers.

Kuru, A. (2013). Muslim politics without "Islamic" state. *Policy Briefings* (2), 1–10.

Kuru, A. T. (2007). Passive and assertive secularism: Historical conditions, ideological struggles, and state policies toward religion. *World Politics, 59*(4), 568–594.

Kuru, A. T. (2009). *Secularism and state policies toward religion: The United States, France, and Turkey*. New York: Cambridge University Press.

Kuru, A. T., & Stepan, A. C. (2012). *Democracy, Islam, and secularism in Turkey*. New York: Columbia University Press.

Kurzman, C. (2001). Critics within: Islamic scholars' protests against the Islamic state in Iran. *International Journal of Politics, Culture, and Society, 15*(2), 341–359.

Ladier-Fouladi, M. (2012). Sociodemographic changes in the family and their impact on the sociopolitical behavior of the youth in postrevolutionary Iran.

In N. Nabavi (Ed.), *Iran: From theocracy to the Green Movement* (pp. 137–165). New York: Palgrave Macmillan.

Lakzaee, N. (1997). Dar amadi bar andisheh siasi Mohaghegh Sabzevari [An introduction to the political thought of Mohaghegh Sabzeravi]. *Hokumat-e Islami, 2*(3), 141–160.

Lawrence, B. B. (1989). *Defenders of God: The fundamentalist revolt against the modern age.* San Francisco: Harper & Row.

Levey, G. B., & Modood, T. (2009). *Secularism, religion and multicultural citizenship.* Cambridge: Cambridge University Press.

Locke, J., & Vernon, R. (2010). *Locke on toleration.* New York: Cambridge University Press.

Logan, F. D. (2002). *A history of the church in the Middle Ages.* London: Routledge.

Lotfi, A. (1996). *Taabod va taaghol dar ahkam-e sharie* [Devotion and reasoning in religious commandments]. *Fiqh, 3*(7 & 8), 325–352.

Maclure, J., & Taylor, C. (2011). *Secularism and freedom of conscience.* Cambridge, MA: Harvard University Press.

Madaninejad, B. (2011). *New theology in the Islamic Republic of Iran: A comparative study between Abdolkarim Soroush and Mohsen Kadivar.* Retrieved March 20, 2012, from https://repositories.lib.utexas.edu/bitstream/handle/2152/etd-ut-2011-08-4238/madaninejad-dissertation.pdf.

Madeley, J. (2003). A framework for the comparative analysis of church–state relations in Europe. *West European Politics, 26*(1), 23–50.

Mahallati, M. I. (2010). Dar partov-e mashrouteh khahi [In light of constitutionalism]. *Etelaat Siasi va Eghtesadi, 24*(11), 80–89.

Mahallati, M. I., & Rouhani, I. (2007). *Dar partov-e mashrouteh khahi* [In light of constitutionalism]. Tehran: Samadiyeh.

Mahdavi, M. (2014). One bed and two dreams? Contentious public religion in the discourses of Ayatollah Khomeini and Ali Shariati. *Studies in Religion/Sciences Religieuses, 43*(1), 25–52. doi: 10.1177/0008429813496102.

Main, B. (1994). Khomeini's search for perfection: Theory and reality. In A. Rahnama (Ed.), *Pioneers of Islamic revival* (pp. 64–124). London: Zed Books.

Mandaville, P. G. (2007). *Global political Islam.* New York: Routledge.

Marshall, J. (1994). *John Locke: Resistance, religion, and responsibility.* New York: Cambridge University Press.

Martin, D. (1978). *A general theory of secularization.* New York: Harper & Row.

Martin, D. A. (1969). *The religious and the secular: Studies in secularization.* New York: Schocken Books.

Martin, R. C., & Barzegar, A. (2010). *Islamism: Contested perspectives on political Islam.* Stanford, CA: Stanford University Press.

Martin, V. (1993). Religion and state in Khumaini's *"Kashf al-asrar"*. *Bulletin of the School of Oriental and African Studies, University of London, 56*(1), 34–45.

Martin, V. (2000). *Creating an Islamic state: Khomeini and the making of a new Iran.* New York: I.B. Tauris.

Matin-asgari, A. (1997). Abdolkarim Sorush and the secularization of Islamic thought in Iran. *Iranian Studies, 30*(1–2), 95–115. doi: 10.1080/00210869708701861.

Matsunaga, Y. (2000). Examining the views of 'Allamah Majlisi on legitimate political authority *(saltanat-i mashru 'ah)* and the guardianship of the jurist *(wilayat-i faqih). Orient, 35,* 12–22.

Matsunaga, Y. (2007). Mohsen Kadivar, an advocate of postrevivalist Islam in Iran. *British Journal of Middle Eastern Studies, 34*(3), 317–329.

Mazinani, M. S. (1996). Ghalamrove Velayat-e Faqih az didghah-e Moghadas Ardebili [Jurisdiction of Velayat-e Faqih in Moghadas Ardebili's thought]. *Figh, 3*(9), 115–146.

McGinness, F. J. (2004). Anticlericalism. In J. Dewald (Ed.), *Europe, 1450 to 1789: Encyclopedia of the Early Modern World* (Vol. 1, pp. 73–75). New York: Charles Scribner's Sons.

Menashri, D. (1980). Shi'ite leadership: In the shadow of conflicting ideologies. *Iranian Studies, 13*(4), 119–145.

Menashri, D. (2001). *Post-revolutionary politics in Iran: Religion, society, and power.* London: Frank Cass.

Mesbah-e Yazdi, M. T. (1997). *Rah va rahnemashenasi* [The study of the path and guidance]. Qom: Imam Khomeini Institution.

Mesbah-e Yazdi, M. T. (1999). *Hokumat-e Islami va Velayat-e Faqih* [Islamic state and Velayate-e Faqih]. Tehran: Chap o Nashre Beinolmelal.

Mesbah-Yazdi, M. T. (1999). *Porseshha va pasokhha* [Questions and answers] (Vol. 2). Qom: Imam Khomeini Institution.

Mesbah-Yazdi, M. T. (2005). Jumhoriyat hich esalati nadard [Republicanism does not have any essentiality]. *Didgahha.* Retrieved October 23, 2011, from http://www.didgah.net/maghalehMatnKamel.php?id=9462.

Mesbah-Yazdi, M. T. (2011). *Ahmadinejad's mentor sides with Khamenei.* Retrieved February 20, 2012, from www.insideiran.org/media-analysis/ahmadinejad's-mentor-sides-with-khamene.

Michael, M. (2011). Poll: Less than 1% of Egyptians favour Iran-style Islamic theocracy. In *Washington Times.* Retrieved June 7, 2011, from http://www.washingtontimes.com/news/2011/jun/5/poll-less-than-1-of-egyptians-favor-iran-style-isl.

Milani, A. (2010). The good Ayatollah. *Foreign Policy Foreign Policy* (178), 25–26.

Milani, M. M. (1993). Power shifts in revolutionary Iran. *Iranian Studies, 26*(4), 359–374.

Mirsepassi, A. (2000). *Intellectual discourse and the politics of modernization: Negotiating modernity in Iran.* New York: Cambridge University Press.

Mirsepassi, A. (2010). *Democracy in modern Iran: Islam, culture, and political change.* New York: New York University Press.

Mitchell, J. (1990). John Locke and the theological foundation of liberal tolera-tion: A Christian dialectic of history. *Review of Politics, 52*(1), 64–83.

Mneimneh, H. (2009). The Arab reception of Vilayat-e-Faqih: The counter-model of Muhammad Mahdi Shams al-Din. *Current Trends in Islamist Ideology, 8,* 39–51.

Moatamedi, A. (2012). *Pol-e naft sar-e sofreh Chiniha* [Oil money on the Chinese table]. Retrieved March 12, 2012, from http://www.roozonline.com/persian/news/newsitem/archive/2012/march/12/article/-a0926f2fbe.html.

Modood, T. (2009). Moderate secularism and multiculturalism. *Politics, 29*(1), 71–76.

Modood, T. (2010). Moderate secularism, religion as identity and respect for reli-gion. *Political Quarterly, 81*(1), 4–14.

Mohammad Hadi, M. (1998). Velayat-e Faqih [The rule of the Islamic jurist]. *Ketab-e Naghd* (7), 167–221.

Mohammadi, M. (2000). *Liberalism-e Irani* [Iranian liberalism]. Tehran: Jama-e Iranian.

Mohammadi, M. (2008). *Sar bar astan-e ghodsi, del dar gerov-e orfi* [Thinking in sacred area, enthusiasm for secularism]. Tehran: Nogreh.

Mohammadi-Golpayegani, M. (2011). Establishment of a centre to survey jurispru-dential issues [Taasis-e markazi baraye barrasi masael-e feghhi]. In *BBC Persian* (November 19, 2011). Retrieved November 25, 2011, from http://www.bbc.co.uk/persian/iran/2011/11/111119_l44_gholpaighani_fetwas_in_iran.shtml.

Mohammadi-Rayshahri, M. (2004). *Khatereha: Mohammad Mohammadi Rayshahri* [Memories: Mohammad Mohammadi Rayshari] (Vol. 2). Tehran: Markaz-e Asnad-e Enghilab-e Islami.

Mohaqhegh Damad, S. M. (2009). *Qavaed-e fiqh: Bakhsh-e madani* [The rules of jurisprudence: Civil section]. Tehran: Samt.

Mohmmadi-Gilani, M. (1993). Nazarkhahi az fughaha piramoon-e Marjaiat [Jurists' perspective on Marjaiat]. *Rahnmoon, 2*(7), 115–144.

Moin, B. (1999). *Khomeini: Life of the Ayatollah.* New York: I.B. Tauris.

Mojtahed Shabestari, M. (2000). Iman, siyasat va hokumat [Faith, politics, and gov-ernance]. In M. Mojtahed Shabestari (Ed.), *Iman va azadi* [Faith and freedom] (pp. 34–45). Tehran: Tarh-e No.

Mojtahed Shabestari, M. (2004). *Taamolati bar gheraat-e ensani az din* [Some thoughts on the humanly reading of religion]. Tehran: Tarhe No.

Mojtahed-Shabestari, M. (1995). Se gone danesh dar se ghalamrov [Three kinds of knowledge in three areas]. *Naghd o Nazar, 2*(5), 296–300.

Mojtahed-Shabestari, M. (1996). *Hermeneutics, ketab, sunnat* [Hermeneutics, the book, and tradition]. Tehran: Tarh-e No.

Mojtahed-Shabestari, M. (1997). *Iman va azadi* [Faith and freedom]. Tehran: Tarh-e No.

Mojtahed-Shabestari, M. (1998). Din va azadi [Religion and freedom]. *Faslnam-e Uloom-e Siyasi* [Political science quarterly], *1*(3), 23–45.

Mojtahed-Shabestari, M. (1999). Bastar-e maanavi va ughalaei-e fiqh [Abstract and rational context of jurisprudence]. *Kiyan* (46), 5–13.

Mojtahed-Shabestari, M. (2000). Haq, taklif, hokumat [Right, duty, state]. *Aban* (121), 4.

Mojtahed-Shabestari, M. (2001). Zolmat-e siasy va ameriyyat mottlaq [Political tyranny and absolute authority]. *Baztab-e Andishe* (15), 7–13.

Mojtahed-Shabestari, M. (2003). Rah-e doshvar-e mardomsalari [Difficult path to democracy]. *Aftab*, 4(22), 30.

Mojtahed-Shabestari, M. (2004). *Taamolati dar gheraat-e ensani az din* [Some thoughts on the humanly reading of religion]. Tehran: Tarhe No.

Mojtahed-Shabestari, M. (2005). *Naghdi bar gheraat-e rasmi az din: Bohranha, chaleshha va rah-e hallha* [A critique of the official reading of religion: Crises, challenges and solutions]. Tehran: Tarhe No.

Mojtahed-Shabestari, M. (2006). Zarorat-e marzbandi mafahim-e khoda, ghodrat va zoor [The necessity of setting a border between God, political power, and coercion]. In *Anjoman-e Ehyagaran-e Falsafhe* (1312). Retrieved October 5, 2009, from http://aboutphilosophy.blogfa.com/post-421.aspx.

Mojtahed-Shabestari, M. (2007a). Geraat-e nabavi az jahan [Prophetic reading of the world]. *Madraseh, 3*(6), 92–100.

Mojtahed-Shabestari, M. (2007b). *Ya hoqhogh-e basher ya hoqhoghe Khoda? moghalet-e ast* [Human rights or God's rights? A sophistry]. Retrieved June 15, 2010, from http://www.islahweb.org/html/modules.php?op=modload&name=News&file=article&sid=665&mode=thread&order=0&thold=0.

Mojtahed-Shabestari, M. (2008a). Amal be ayaei dar Quran hamishegi Nist [Practicing a verse of Quran is not perpetual]. *Radio Zamaneh*. Retrieved May 18, 2010, from http://www.zamaaneh.com/seraj/2008/12/post_11.html.

Mojtahed-Shabestari, M. (2008b). Islam is a religion, not a political agenda. In *Qantara* (July 7, 2008). Retrieved June 16, 2010, from http://www.qantara.de/webcom/show_article.php/_c-478/_nr-783/i.html.

Mojtahed-Shabestari, M. (2014). *Tanghih mahal-e nezae ba faghihan: Hazrat-e Mohammad ghanoongozar nabood and Quran ketab-e ghanoon nist* [Revising dispute with jurists: Prophet Mohammad was not a lawmaker and Quran is not a book of law]. Retrieved February 24, 2014, from http://mohammadmojtahed shabestari.com/printable.php?id=271.

Mojtahed-Shabestari, M., & Kiderlen, E. (2007). Kare tafsir-e Quran payan napazir ast [Interpretation of the Quran is an unceasing project]. In *Süddeutsche Zeitung* (November 24, 2007). Retrieved June 18, 2010, from http://neeloofar.ir/thinker-/59-1388-10-19-19-52-43/442-1388-12-11-21-06-37.html.

Momayesi, N. (2000). Iran's struggle for democracy. *International Journal on World Peace*, 17(4), 41.

Momen, M. (1985). *An introduction to Shi`i Islam: the history and doctrines of Twelver Shi`ism*. New Haven: Yale University Press.

Monsma, S. V., & Soper, J. C. (2009). *The challenge of pluralism: Church and state in five democracies* (2nd ed.). Lanham, MD: Rowman & Littlefield.

Montazeri, H. (1991). Mabani va sabk-e Estenbat-e Ayatollah Broujerdi [Ayatollah Broujerdi's Essenes and methods of reasoning]. *Howza*, 9(43), 254.

Montazeri, H. (2000a). *Democracy and constitution*. Retrieved November 28, 2010, from http://www.amontazeri.com/farsi/f1.asp.

Montazeri, H. (2000b). *Khaterate Ayatollah Montazeri I* [Ayatollah Montazeri's memoirs I]. Qom: The Office of the Grand Ayatollah Montazeri.

Montazeri, H. (2000c). *Khaterate Ayatollah Montazeri II* [Ayatollah Montazeri's memoirs II]. Qom: The Office of the Grand Ayatollah Montazeri.

Montazeri, H. (2000d). *Mabani-e feqhi-e hokumat-e Islami* [The jurisprudential foundations of the Islamic state] (Vol. 2). Tehran: Saraei.

Montazeri, H. (2003). *Didgahha I*: Payamha va Nazarat-e Montasher Shodeh [Perspectives I: Messages, opinions, and interviews]. Qom: The Office of the Grand Ayatollah Montazeri.

Montazeri, H. (2006a). *Didgahha II*: Payamha va Nazarat-e Montasher Shodeh [Perspectives II: Messages, opinions, and interviews]. Qom: The Office of the Grand Ayatollah Montazeri.

Montazeri, H. (2006b). *Mosahebeh Doctor Diner Herman khabarnegar-e nashriy-e frankfurter allgemeine zeitung with Ayatollah Montazeri* [Ayatollah Montazeri's interview with Dr. Diner Herman, reporter from the *Frankfurter Allgemeine Zeitung*] (interview). Retrieved October 28, 2010, from http://www.amontazeri. com/farsi/payamha/117.HTM.

Montazeri, H. (2008). *Hokumat-e dini va hughogh-e ensanha* [Religious state and human rights]. Tehran: Saraei.

Montazeri, H. (2010). *Didgahha III* [Perspectives III: Messages, opinions, and interviews of Grand Ayatollah Montazeri]. Qom: The Office of the Grand Ayatollah Montazeri.

Montazeri, H. A. (2008). *The rights of Baha'is*. Retrieved June 20, 2010, from http:// www.amontazeri.com.

Montazeri, H., & Salavati, M. (2007). *Mabani-e feqhi-e hokumat-e Islami* [The jurisprudential foundations of the Islamic state] (Vol. 8). Tehran: Saraei.

Morgan, E. S. (1978). *Inventing the people: The rise of popular sovereignty in England and America*. New York: Norton.

Morrison, K. F. (2003). Dictatus Papae. *New Catholic Encyclopedia* (2nd ed., Vol. 4, pp. 735–736). Detroit: Gale.

Mortazavi, S. K., & Manouchehri, A. (2004). Gera'at-e dini-e Mojtahede-Shabestari va rabbet-e on ba araye siyasi-e vay [Religious ideas of Mojtahed Shabestari and its relations with his political thoughts]. *Ulom-e Ijtimaei*, 11(4), 69–82.

Motahhari, M. (1992). *Vahy va nobowat* [Revelation and prophecy]. Tehran: Sadra.

Motahhari, M. (1993). *Piramoon-e enghilab-e Islami* [On the Islamic revolution]. Tehran: Sadra.

Motahhari, M. (2010). *Dah goftar* [Ten lectures]. Qom: Entesarat-e-Sadra.

Motahhari, M., Arshad, F., & Dabashi, H. (2000). The fundamental problem in the clerical establishment. In L. S. Walbridge (Ed.), *The most learned of the Shi'a: The institution of the Marja'i Taqlid* (pp. 161–182). New York: Oxford University Press.

Mottahedeh, R. (2000). *The mantle of the prophet*. Oxford: Oneworld.

Mottaqi, M. (2002). Karname karyabe Soroush [Soroush's flourishing workbook]. *Aftab, 3*(19), 44–51.

Mousavi, M. H. (2010). The Green Movement charter [June 16, 2010]. Retrieved June 25, 2011, from http://www.pbs.org/wgbh/pages/frontline/tehranbu reau/2010/06/the-green-movement-charter.html.

Moussalli, A. S. (2003). Islamic democracy and pluralism. In O. Safi (Ed.), *Progressive Muslims: On justice, gender and pluralism* (pp. 286–305). Oxford: Oneworld.

Moussavi, A. K. (1985). The establishment of the position of Marja'iyyt-i Taqlid in the Twelver-Shi'i Community. *Iranian Studies, 18*(1), 35–51.

Moussavi, A. K. (1992). A new interpretation of the theory of Vilayat-i Faqih. *Middle Eastern Studies, 28*(1), 101–107.

Moussavi, A. K. (1994). The institutionalization of Marja'-i Taqlid in the nineteenth-century Shi'ite community. *Muslim World, 84*(3–4), 279–299. doi: 10.1111/j.1478-1913.1994.tb03602.x.

Moustafa, T. (2014). Judging in God's name: State power, secularism, and the politics of Islamic law in Malaysia. *Oxford Journal of Law and Religion, 3*(1), 152–167.

Movahedi-Savoji, M. H. (2011). *Ayatollah Montazeri va ghanoon-e asasi* [Ayatollah Montazeri and the constitution] (July 11, 2011). Retrieved January 2, 2012, from http://www.rahesabz.net/story/39774/

Mulcahy, M. R. (2007). *Islam is the solution: Demystifying Islamization in Morocco and Egypt*. Retrieved July 4, 2011, from http://digitalcommons.macalester.edu/ intlstudies_honors/2.

Nabavi, N. (2003). *Intellectual trends in twentieth-century Iran: A critical survey*. Gainesville: University Press of Florida.

Nadon, C. (2014). The secular basis of the separation of church and state: Hobbes, Locke, Montesquieu, and Tocqueville. *Perspectives on Political Science, 43*(1), 21–30.

Naeini, M. M. H. (2003). *Tanbih al-Umma wa tanzih al-milla* [Admonishment of the Umma and the purification of the nation/religious community]. Qom: Boostan-e Kitab.

Nasr, S. V. R. (1996). *Mawdudi and the making of Islamic revivalism*. New York: Oxford University Press.

Nasr, S. V. R. (1998). Religion and global affairs: Secular states and religious oppositions. *SAIS Review, 18*(2), 32.

Nasr, V. (2003). Lessons from the Muslim world. *Daedalus, 132*(3), 67–72.

Nasr, V. (2006). When the Shiites rise. *Foreign Affairs, 85*(4), 58–74.

Neuhaus, R. J. (2009). Secularizations. *First Things: A Monthly Journal of Religion and Public Life*, (190), 23–28.

Newman, A. J. (1992). The nature of the Akhbārī/Uṣūlī dispute in late Ṣafawid Iran. Part 1: 'Abdallāh al-Samāhijī's "Munyat al-Mumārisīn". *Bulletin of the School of Oriental and African Studies, 55*(1), 22–51. doi: 10.2307/620475.

Nikfar, M. (2003). Zaat-e yek Pendar [Essence of a thought]. *Negah-e No, 13*(57), 16–27.

Niknam, A. (1999). The Islamization of law in Iran: A time of disenchantment. *Middle East Report* (212), 17–21. doi: 10.2307/3012908.

Norris, P., & Inglehart, R. (2004). *Sacred and secular: Religion and politics worldwide*. New York: Cambridge University Press.

Norton, A. R. (2007). *Hezbollah: A short history*. Princeton, NJ: Princeton University Press.

Nouraie, F. M. (1975). The constitutional ideas of a Shi'ite Mujtahid: Muhammad Husayn Na'ini. *Iranian Studies, 8*(4), 234–247.

Panikkar, R. (1985). Religion or politics: The Western dilemma. In P. H. Merkl & N. Smart (Eds.), *Religion and politics in the modern world*. New York: New York University Press.

Parker, K. I. (2004). *The biblical politics of John Locke*. Waterloo, ON: Wilfrid Laurier University Press.

Parliament. (1989). *Mashroh-e mozakerat-e majles-e khobregan-e ghanoon-e asasi* [Elaboration of the debates in the Constituent Assembly] (Vol. 2). Tehran: Sazman-e Entesharat-e Enghilabe Islami.

Pedram, M. (2003). *Roshanfekran-e dini va moderniteh dar Iran pas az enqelab* [Religious intellectuals and modernity in Iran after the revolution] Tehran: Gam-e No.

Princeton. (2009). *Society of the lecturers of Qom seminary (JMHEQ)*. Retrieved November 11, 2011, from http://www.princeton.edu/irandataportal/parties/modaressineqom.

Princeton. (2011). *Ordinance for the Special Prosecutor's Offices and Courts of the Clergy*. Retrieved November 11, 2011, from http://www.princeton.edu/irandata-portal/legislation/scc.

Rabiee, A. (2001). *Sociology of changes in values: A review of voters behaviour in the second of Khordad 1997*. Tehran: Farhang & Andisheh.

Rafat, A. (2007). *We have lost international trust*. Retrieved December 07, 2011, from http://www.adnkronos.com/AKI/English/Politics/?id=1.0.1961831205.

Rafipoor, F. (1997). *Tazad o toseh: kosheshi dar jahat-e tahlil-e enghelab-e eslami va masael-e ejtemaei-e Iran* [Modernization and conflict: An attempt toward the analysis of the Islamic revolution and social problems of Iran]. Tehran: Shahid Beheshti University Publication.

Rafi-pour, F. (2003). Din va rohaniyat dar naghsh-e jadid [Religion and clergy in new position]. *Negah-e hawza* (139), 112–124.

Rahim, L. Z. (2013). The Spirit of Wasatiyyah democracy. In L. Z. Rahim (Ed.), *Muslim secular democracy: Voices from within* (pp. 1–27). New York: Palgrave Macmillan.

Rahimi, B. (2005). Ayatollah Ali al-Sistani and the democratization of post-Saddam Iraq. *Peace Research Abstracts, 42*(3), 1–24.

Rahimi, B. (2008). *The discourse of democracy in Shi'i Islamic jurisprudence. The two cases of Montazeri and Sistani.* Florence: European University Institute.

Rahimi, B. (2012). The sacred in fragments: Shi'i Iran since the 1979 revolution. In N. Nabavi (Ed.), *Iran: From theocracy to the Green Movement* (pp. 55–76). New York: Palgrave Macmillan.

Rahnama, A. (1994). Ali Shariati: Teacher, preacher, rebel. In A. Rahnama (Ed.), *Pioneers of Islamic revival* (pp. 208–250). London: Zed Books.

Rahnama, A. (2000). An Islamic utopian: A political biography of Ali Shariati. London; New York: I.B. Tauris.

Rajaee, F. (2007). *Islamism and modernism: The changing discourse in Iran.* Austin: University of Texas Press.

Ramazan-Narjesi, R. (2002). Taasis va roshd-e marakez-e tahghigati-e hawza elmi-yeh Qom [Establishment and development of research centers in the Qom seminary]. *Pajhohesh va hawza, 3*(11), 127–130.

Ranjbar, M. (2003). Fazay-e tanafosi Shi'a: Goftman eslah dar hawza elmiy-e Qom [Shiite breathing space: Reformation discourse in Qom seminary]. *Zamane, 2*(16), 22–30.

Rauf, F. A. (2010). Why Islamism should be renamed. In R. C. Martin & A. Barzegar (Eds.), *Islamism: Contested perspectives on political Islam* (pp. 116–124). Stanford, CA: Stanford University Press.

Rawls, J. (1993). *Political liberalism.* New York: Columbia University Press.

Razmjoo, H. (1994). *Postin-e Varooneh* [Reversed fur]. Tehran: Avay-e Noor.

Richard, Y. (1981). Contemporary Shi'i thought. In N. R. Keddie & Y. Richard (Eds.), *Roots of revolution: An interpretive history of modern Iran* (pp. 202–228). New Haven, CN: Yale University Press.

Ridgeon, L. V. J. (2005). *Religion and politics in modern Iran: A reader.* London: I.B. Tauris.

Robbins, T., & Anthony, D. (1981). *In gods we trust: New patterns of religious pluralism in America.* New Brunswick, NJ: Transaction Books.

Robertson, R. (1987). Church–state relations in a comparative perspective. In T. Robbins & R. Robertson (Eds.), *Church–state relations: Tensions and transitions.* New Brunswick, NJ: Transaction Books.

Rohbakhsh, R. (2001). Miras-e Ayatollah Broujerdi [The heritages of Ayatollah Broujerdi]. *Goftogu, 9*(32), 7–36.

Roy, O. (1999). The crisis of religious legitimacy in Iran. *The Middle East Journal, 53*(2), 201–216.

Roy, O. (2001). *The failure of political Islam.* Cambridge, MA: Harvard University Press.

Roy, O. (2002). The crisis of religious legitimacy in Iran. *Peace Research Abstracts, 39*(2), 155–306.

Roy, O. (2004). *Globalised Islam: The search for a new Ummah*. London: Hurst.

Roy, O. (2007). *Secularism confronts Islam*. New York: Columbia University Press.

Roy, O. (2013a). Secularism and Islam: The theological predicament. *The International Spectator, 48*(1), 5–19.

Roy, O. (2013b). There will be no Islamist revolution. *JOD: Journal of Democracy, 24*(1), 14–19.

Saad-Ghorayeb, A. (2002). *Hizbullah: Politics and religion*. London: Pluto Press.

Sachedina, A. (2001). *The Islamic roots of democratic pluralism*. New York: Oxford University Press.

Sachedina, A. A. (2009). *Islam and the challenge of human rights*. Oxford: Oxford University Press.

Sadeghi-Fadaki, S. A. (2009). *Naghsh-e Ayatollah Haeri da ehyay-e hawza Qom* [The Role of Ayatollah Haeri in the revival of the Qom seminary]. Retrieved May 20, 2010, from http://www.tebyan.net/index.aspx?pid=11152.

Sadjadpour, K. (2009). *Reading Khamenei: The world view of Iran's most powerful leader*. Washington DC: Carnegie Endowment for International Peace.

Sadri, M. (2001). Sacral defense of secularism: The political theologies of Soroush, Shabestari, and Kadivar. *International Journal of Politics, Culture, and Society, 15*(2), 257–270.

Saffari, S. (1993). The legitimation of the clergy's right to rule in the Iranian Constitution of 1979. *British Journal of Middle Eastern Studies, 20*(1), 64–82.

Safi, O. (2003). *Progressive Muslims: On justice, gender and pluralism*. Oxford: Oneworld.

Sahabi, E. (2010). *Nim gharn khatereh va tajrobe* [Half a century of memories and experiences]. Tehran: Farhang-e Saba.

Sajo, A. (2008). Preliminaries to a concept of constitutional secularism. *International Journal of Constitutional Law, 6*(3–4), 605–629. doi: 10.1093/icon/mon018.

Salehi-Najafabadi, N. (1984). *Velayat-e Faqih: Hokumat-e salihan* [Velayat-e Faqih: Rule of righteousness]. Tehran: Rasa.

Salehpour, J. (1995). Farayand-e urfi shodan-e fiqh-e Shi'a [The process of secularizing Shiite fiqh]. *Kiyan, 5*(24), 17–23.

Salehpour, J. (1999). Imam Khomeini: Faqih-e dorane gozar [Imam Khomeini: A jurist for transition period]. *Kiyan, 9*(46), 26–37.

Salim, A. (2008). *Challenging the secular state: The Islamization of law in modern Indonesia*. Honolulu: University of Hawaii Press.

Sánchez, J. M. (1972). *Anticlericalism: A brief history*. Notre Dame, IN: University of Notre Dame Press.

Savyon, A. (2002). *The call for Islamic Protestantism: Dr. Hashem Aghajari's speech and subsequent death sentence*. Retrieved August 08, 2011, from the Middle East Media Research Institute (MEMRI), http://www.memri.org/report/en/0/0/0/0/0/0/770.htm#complete.

Scharffs, B. G. (2011). Four views of the citadel: The consequential distinction between secularity and secularism. *Religion and Human Rights, 6*(2), 109–126.

Schemm, P., & Bouazza, B. B. (2014). Tunisia basks in praise over its new constitution. Retrieved February 20, 2014, from http://bigstory.ap.org/article/tunisia-basks-praise-over-its-new-constitution.

Schirazi, A. (1997). *The constitution of Iran: Politics and the state in the Islamic Republic.* London: I.B. Tauris.

Schmid, P. D. (2003). Expect the unexpected: A religious democracy in Iran. *Brown Journal of World Affairs* (9), 181–196.

Sciolino, E. (2000). *Persian mirrors: The elusive face of Iran.* New York: Free Press.

Sealy, A. V. (2011). "In Their Place": Marking and unmarking Shi'ism in Pahlavi Iran. Ph.D. diss., University of Michigan, Detroit.

Seo, M. (2012). Defining "religious" in Indonesia: Toward neither an Islamic nor a secular state. *Citizenship Studies, 16*(8), 1045–1058.

Shams al-Din, M. M. (1999). Din, siyasat, Marjaiat [Religion, politics, Marjaiat]. *Tarjoman-e Siyasi* (199), 24–30.

Shanahan, R. (2004). Shi'a political development in Iraq: The case of the Islamic Da'wa Party. *Third World Quarterly, 25*(5), 943–954.

Shanahan, R. (2005). Hizballah rising: The political battle for the loyalty of the Shi'a of Lebanon. *Peace Research Abstracts Journal, 42*(4).

Shariati, A. (2000). *Ba mokhatabhay-e ashena* [With the familiar addressees]. Tehran: Chapakhsh.

Shariati, A. (2009). *Islam shenasi* [Knowing Islam]. Tehran: Ghalam.

Shariati, A. (2011). *Hossein varese adam* [Hossein heir of Adam]. Tehran: Ghalam.

Sharif al-Radi, M. i. a.-H., & Jafery, M. A. (1984). *Nahjul Balagha—Peak of eloquence: sermons, letters, and sayings of Imam Ali ibn Abu Talib.* Elmhurst, NY: Tahrike Tarsile Qur'an. Retrieved from http://www.worldcat.org/title/nahjul-balagha-peak-of-eloquence-sermons-letters-and-sayings-of-imam-ali-ibn-abu-talib/oclc/12557165&referer=brief_results.

Shimamoto, T. (2006). Leadership in Twelver Imami Shi'ism: Mortaza Motahhari's ideas on the Imamate and the role of religious scholars. *Journal of the Interdisciplinary Study of Monotheistic Religions (JISMOR), 2*(2), 37–57.

Shiner, L. (1967). The concept of secularization in empirical research. *Journal for the Scientific Study of Religion, 6*(2), 207–220.

Shorish, M. M. (1988). The Islamic revolution and education in Iran. *Comparative Education Review, 32*(1), 58–75. doi: 10.2307/1188473.

Siegel, E. (2001). The politics of shahide jawid. In R. Brunner & W. Ende (Eds.), *The Twelver Shia in modern times: Religious culture and political culture* (pp. 150–177). Leiden Brill.

Sindawi, K. (2007). Hawza instruction and its role in shaping modern Shiite identity: The hawzas of al-Najaf and Qumm as a case study. *Middle Eastern Studies, 43*(6), 831–856.

Sistani, A. A. (2005). Nazar-e Ayatollah Sistani dar barei Velayat- Faqih [Ayatollah Sistani's statement about Velayat-e Faqih]. Retrived July 20, 2010, from http://www.tabnak.ir/fa/pages/?cid=111473.

Smith, D. E. (1970). *Religion and political development, an analytic study.* Boston: Little, Brown.

Sobhe, K. (1982). Education in revolution: Is Iran duplicating the Chinese Cultural Revolution? *Comparative Education, 18*(3), 271–280.

Soroush, A. (1993). *Farbeh tar az ideology* [Sturdier than ideology] *Kiyan, 3*(14), 2–20.

Soroush, A. (1994a). *Danesh va dadgari* [Wisdom and religious conviction]. *Kiyan, 4*(22), 10–15.

Soroush, A. (1994b). Ideology-e dini va din-e ideologic [Religious ideology and ideological religion]. *Kiyan, 4*(16), 24–28.

Soroush, A. (1994c). Khadamat va hasanat-e din [The functions and benefits of religion]. *Kiyan, 4*(27), 2–16.

Soroush, A. (1994d). *Qabz va bast-e teorik-e shari'at: nazariy-e takamul-e ma'refat-e dini* [Theoretical constriction and expansion of Shari'a: The theory of evolution of religious knowledge] (4th ed.). Tehran: Serat.

Soroush, A. (1995a). Hurriayt va ruhaniyat [Liberty and clergy]. *Kiyan, 4*(24), 2–11.

Soroush, A. (1995b). Mabani-e teorik-e liberalism [Theoretical foundations of liberalism]. In A. Soroush (Ed.), *Razdani va roshanfekri va dindari* [Wisdom, intellectualism, and religious conviction] (pp. 117–152). Tehran: Serat.

Soroush, A. (1995c). Saqf-e maishat bar sutoun-e shariat [The ceiling of livelihood upon the pillar of religion]. *Kiyan, 5*(26), 25–31.

Soroush, A. (1996a). *Farbeh tar az ideology* [Sturdier than ideology]. Tehran: Serat.

Soroush, A. (1996b). Ideology va din-e donyavi [Ideology and worldly religion]. *Kiyan, 6*(31), 2–11.

Soroush, A. (1996c). Tahlil-e Mafhoom-e Hokumat-e Dini [Analyzing the concept of religious government]. *Kiyan, 6*(32), 2–13.

Soroush, A. (1998a). Dianat, modara va madaniyat [Religiosity, tolerance, and civilization]. *Kiyan, 8*(45), 20–37.

Soroush, A. (1998b). Din-e agalli va aksari [Minimalist and maximalist conceptions of religion]. *Kiyan, 8*(41), 2–9.

Soroush, A. (1998c). Velayat-e bateni va velayat-e siasi [Spiritual guardianship and political guardianship]. *Kiyan, 8*(44), 10–20.

Soroush, A. (1998d). Zati va arazi-e dar din [Substantial and accidental in religion]. *Kiyan, 9*(42), 4–19.

Soroush, A. (1999). *Serathay-e Mostagheem* [Straight paths]. Tehran: Serat.

Soroush, A. (2000). *Reason, freedom, and democracy in Islam: Essential writings of Abdolkarim Soroush.* M. Sadri & A. Sadri (Eds.). New York: Oxford University Press.

Soroush, A. (2003). *Hekmat-e yonanian, Hekmat-e Iranian* [Greek wisdom, Iranian wisdom] Retrieved November 09, 2010, from http://www.drsoroush.com/Persian/News_Archive/F-NWS-13821010-Gooya.html.

Soroush, A. (2004a). *Akhlagh-e hhodayān* [Moral of gods]. Tehran: Serat.

Soroush, A. (2004b). *Islam dini secular ast* [Islam is a secular religion]. Retrieved November 20, 2009, from http://www.drsoroush.com/Persian/News_Archive/F-NWS-13830601-ILNA.html.

Soroush, A. (2004c). Islam niyazi be senf-e rohani nadarad [Islam does not need clergy]. *Baztab-e Andishe, 5*(57 & 58), 70–78.

Soroush, A. (2004d). *Tazabzob-e amali-e Khatami risheh dar tazabzob-e fekri-e ishan darad* [Khatami's practical hesitation is rooted in uncertainty in his thoughts]. Retrieved June 2, 2010, from http://www.drsoroush.com/Persian/News_Archive/F-NWS-13830903-Gooyanews.htm.

Soroush, A. (2005a). Secularim-e siasi va secularism-e falsafi [Political secularism and philosophical secularism]. *Baztab-e Andishe, 6*(64), 21–31.

Soroush, A. (2005b). *Tashayyo va Chalesh-e Mardomsalari [Shi'a and the challenges of democracy].* Retrieved May 20, 2010, from http://www.drsoroush.com/Persian/News_Archive/P-NWS-1384-05-10-LectureInParis.html.

Soroush, A. (2006a). *Bast-e tajrubih-e nabavi* [The expansion of prophetic experience]. Tehran: Serat.

Soroush, A. (2006b). *Rohaniayt menhay-e Islam* [Clergy without Islam]. Retrieved June 10, 2010, from http://drshariati.org/show.asp?ID=70&q=

Soroush, A. (2007). *Khatami's election victory was detrimental to Kiyan.* Retrieved August 4, 2009, from http://www.drsoroush.com/English/Interviews/E-INT-Kian.htm.

Soroush, A. (2008a). *Aeen-e shariari va dindari* [Urban ritual and religious convictions]. Tehran: Serat.

Soroush, A. (2008b). Din-e secular [Secular religion]. In A. Soroush (Ed.), *Modara va modiriyyat* [Administration and tolerance] (pp. 157–173). Tehran: Serat.

Soroush, A. (2008c). *Islam, Catholicism, and the secular: A conversation with José Casanova and Abdolkarim Soroush.* Retrieved January 29, 2010, from http://berkleycenter.georgetown.edu/events/islam-catholicism-and-the-secular-a-conversation-with-jose-casanova-and-abdolkarim-soroush.

Soroush, A. (2008d). *Modara va modiriyyat* [Administration and tolerance]. Tehran: Serat.

Soroush, A. (2009a). An open letter to President Hashemi-Rafsanjani. In *Siyasat-nameh* [Political letter] (pp. 47–51). Tehran: Serat.

Soroush, A. (2009b). Dr. Soroush speech in Georgetown University, December 27, 2009 (video). Retrieved June 24, 2010, 2010, from http://www.youtube.com/watch?v=6HEEkNqd6eo&feature=related.

Soroush, A. (2009c). Ghiam alaihe hokumat-e dini [Revolt against the religious state]. Retrived July 13, 2010, from http://www.balatarin.com/permlink/2012/3/12/2962971.

Soroush, A. (2009d). *Jashn-e zaval-e estebdad-e dini* [Celebration at the downfall of religious dictatorship]. Retrieved December 16, 2010, from http://www.drsoroush.com/Persian/By_DrSoroush/P-NWS-13880619-JashneZevaleEstebdadeDini.html.

Soroush, A. (2009e). *Siyasat-nameh* [Political letter]. Tehran: Serat.

Soroush, A. (2010a). *Deghul bab: Falah-e khlagh va salah-e ulama* [Knocking on the door: Prosperity of people and interest of clergy]. Retrieved November 20, 2011, from http://www.drsoroush.com/Persian/By_DrSorous h/P-NWS-13890302-DagholBab.html.

Soroush, A. (2010b). *Democracy is not extractable from Islam.* Retrieved Aprli 27, 2010, from http://www.roozonline.com/persian/news/newsitem/article/democracy-is-not-extractable-from-islam.html.

Soroush, A. (2010c). *Din dar sepehr-e omomi* [Religion in the public sphere]. Retrieved August 1, 2011, from http://www.drsoroush.com/Lectures-89.htm.

Soroush, A. (2010d). Islam va secularism [Islam and secularism]. Retrived March 8, 2011, from http://lectures.drsoroush.com/Persian/Lectures/2010/Islam_and_Secularism_Session2_2010_11_03_DrSoroush.mp3.

Soroush, A. (2010e). *Razdani, roshanfekri va dindari* [Wisdom, intellectualism, and religious conviction]. Tehran: Serat.

Soroush, A. (2010f). *The rise of intellectual reform in Islam* (April 20, 2010). Retrieved August 10, 2010, from http://fora.tv/2010/04/20/The_Rise_of_Intellectual_Reform_in_Islam.

Soroush, A. (2011). *Siyasat, Marjayiat va nobovvat* [Politics, the institution of the source of emulation, and prophecy]. Retrieved January 04, 2011, from http://www.drsoroush.com/Persian/Interviews/P-INT-20110105-SiasatMarjayatVaNobovat.html.

Soroush, A., & Kadivar, M. (2000). *Pluralizm-e dini* [Religious pluralism]. Tehran: Salam.

Soroush, A., Mobasser, N., & Jahanbakhsh, F. (2009). *The expansion of prophetic experience: Essays on historicity, contingency and plurality in religion.* Boston: Brill.

Soroush, A., Sadri, M., & Sadri, A. (2000). *Reason, freedom, and democracy in Islam: Essential writings of Abdolkarim Soroush.* New York: Oxford University Press.

Stark, R. (1999). Secularization, R.I.P. *Sociology of Religion, 60*(3), 249–273.

Stark, R., & Iannaccone, L. R. (1994). A supply-side reinterpretation of the "secularization" of Europe. *Journal for the Scientific Study of Religion, 33*(3), 230–252.

Stepan, A. (2012). Tunisia's transition and the twin tolerations. *Journal of Democracy, 23*(2), 89–103.

Stepan, A. C. (2000). Religion, democracy, and the "twin tolerations". *Journal of Democracy, 11*(4), 37–57.

Stepan, A. C. (2001). The world's religious systems and democracy: Crafting the "twin tolerations". In A. C. Stepan (Ed.), *Arguing comparative politics* (pp. 213–253). New York: Oxford University Press.

Stepan, A. C. (2011). The multiple secularisms of modern democracies and autocracies. In C. J. Calhoun, M. Juergensmeyer & J. VanAntwerpen (Eds.), *Rethinking secularism.* Oxford: Oxford University Press.

Sukidi. (2005). The traveling idea of Islamic Protestantism: A study of Iranian Luthers. *Islam and Christian-Muslim Relations, 16*(4), 401–412.

Sultan-Mohammadi, A. (2001). Velayat-e Faqih az didghah-e Allameh Majlisi [Velayat-e Faqih in Allameh Majlisi's thought]. *Uloom-e Siasi*, 4(4), 105–120.

Tabatabaee, M. (2005). *Barrasi ara-e Akhbari va Usuli* [Review of Akhbari and Usuli thought]. Tehran: Mostafa Tabatabaee.

Tabatabaei, S. J. (2007). Roshanfekri-e dini: Tarkibi motazad va bimaani [Religious intellectualism: A paradoxical and nonsense syntax]. *Talash*, 5(25). Retrieved July 14, 2011, from http://talashonline.net/1384/12/ roshanfekri-dini-tarkibi-motezad-va-bimaena.

Taghavi, F. (2007). *Secular apparition: The resurgence of liberal-democratic intellectual discourse in post-revolutionary Iran*. Ph.D. diss., University of California, ProQuest dissertations & theses full text dataset. Retrieved July 2, 2010, from http://ezproxy.library.usyd.edu.au/login?url=http://search.proquest.com/docvi ew/304875412?accountid=14757 (304875412).

Taji-Farouki, S. (2004). *Modern Muslim intellectuals and the Quran*. Oxford: Oxford University Press.

Tamadonfar, M. (2001). Islam, law, and political control in contemporary Iran. *Journal for the Scientific Study of Religion*, 40(2), 205–219.

Tamimi, A. (2001). *Rachid Ghannouchi: A democrat within Islamism*. Oxford: Oxford University Press.

Taqavi, M. A. (2004). *The flourishing of Islamic reformism in Iran political Islamic groups in Iran (1941–61)*. New York: Routledge.

Taylor, C. (1998). Modes of secularism. In R. Bhargava (Ed.), *Secularism and its critics* (pp. 31–53). Delhi: Oxford University Press.

Taylor, C. (2007). *A secular age*. Cambridge, MA: Belknap Press of Harvard University Press.

Taylor, C. (2008). Secularism and critique. In *The immanent frame*. Retrieved March 21, 2011, from http://blogs.ssrc.org/tif/2008/04/24/secularism-and-critique.

Taylor, C. (2009). *The future of the secular*. Retrieved January 19, 2010, from http://fora. tv/2009/03/05/Charles_Taylor_The_Future_of_the_Secular#fullprogram.

Tazmini, G. (2009). *Khatami's Iran: The Islamic Republic and the turbulent path to reform*. New York: Tauris Academic Studies.

Terhalle, M. (2007). Are the Shia rising? *Middle East Policy*, 14(2), 69–83.

Tibi, B. (2001). *Islam between culture and politics*. New York: Palgrave.

Ullmann, W. (1972). *A short history of the papacy in the Middle Ages*. London: Methuen.

UNDP. (2014). *New constitution a historic landmark on journey to democracy for Tunisia*. Retrieved February 20, 2014, from http://www.undp. org/content/undp/en/home/presscenter/articles/2014/01/27/new-constitution-a-historic-landmark-on-journey-to-democracy-for-tunisia/

United States Department of State. (2014). *In special visit, Kerry recognizes Tunisia's "model" constitution*. Retrieved February 20, 2014, from http://iipdigital.usem bassy.gov/st/english/inbrief/2014/02/20140218293256.html#axzz2tpd3jATS.

Updegraff, J. J. (2006). *Westernization or modernization: The political, economic and social attitudes and desires of the post-Khomeini generation in Iran.* Retrieved November 25, 2011, from http://cgsc.cdmhost.com/u?/p4013coll3,777.

Uysal, A. (2013). Insights for Egypt's and Tunisia's Islamists from Turkish experience of democratic transition. *Insight Turky, 15*(4), 69–76.

Vahdat, F. (2000a). Post-revolutionary discourses of Mohammad Mojtahed Shabestari and Mohsen Kadivar: Reconciling the terms of mediated subjectivity—Part II: Mohsen Kadivar. *Critique: Critical Middle Eastern Studies, 9*(17), 135–157.

Vahdat, F. (2000b). Post-revolutionary discourses of Mohammad Mojtahed Shabestari and Mohsen Kadivar: Reconciling the terms of mediated subjectivity—Part I: Mojtahed Shabestari. *Critique: Critical Middle Eastern Studies, 9*(16), 31–54.

Vahdat, F. (2004). Post-revolutionary Islamic modernity in Iran: The intersubjective hermeneutics of Mohamad Mojtahed Shabestari. In S. Taji-Farouki & Institute of Ismaili Studies. (Eds.), *Modern Muslim intellectuals and the Quran* (pp. 193–224). New York: Oxford University Press.

Vahdat, F. (2011). *The process of societal secularization in Iran.* Paper presented at the "Concept of Secularism and Its Iranian Permutations" conference, March 27, 2010, Illinois, USA.

Vakili, V. (2001). Abdolkarim Soroush and critical discourse in Iran. In J. L. Esposito & J. O. Voll (Eds.), *Makers of contemporary Islam* (pp. 150–176). New York: Oxford University Press.

Varei, S. J. (2003). *Pajhoheshi dar andish-e siasi-e Naeini* [A study on the political thought of Naeini]. Tehran: Dabir Khaneh Majles-e Khobregan-e Rahbari.

Varei, S. J. (2010). Faghihan-e asre mashrouteh va masael-e mostahedeseh siasi [Jurists in the constitutionalism era and relevant political issues]. *Ulom-e Siasi, 13*(49), 95–127.

Varisco, D. M. (2010). Inventing Islamism: The violence of rhetoric. In R. C. Martin & A. Barzegar (Eds.), *Islamism: Contested perspectives on political Islam* (pp. 33–50). Stanford, CA: Stanford University Press.

Varzi, R. (2006). *Warring souls: Youth, media, and martyrdom in post-revolution Iran.* Durham, NC: Duke University Press.

Vasigh, S. (2005). *Laïcité chist* [What is Laïcité]. Tehran: Akhtaran.

Vogt, K., Larsen, L., & Moe, C. (2009). *New directions in Islamic thought: Exploring reform and Muslim tradition.* London: I.B. Tauris.

Voll, J., Mandaville, P., Kull, S., & Arieff, A. (2012). Political Islam in the Arab Awakening: Who are the major players? *Middle East Policy, 19*(2), 10–35.

Volpi, F. (2011). *Political Islam: A critical reader.* London: Routledge.

Waldron, J. (2002). *God, Locke, and equality: Christian foundations of John Locke's political thought.* New York: Cambridge University Press.

Witte Jr., J. (2006). Facts and fictions about the history of separation of church and state. *A Journal of Church and State, 48*(1), 15.

Wood, J. E. (1967). Christianity and the state. *Journal of the American Academy of Religion, 35*(3), 257–270.

Wootton, D. (1986). *Divine right and democracy: An anthology of political writing in Stuart England.* New York: Penguin Books.

Wu, B. (2007). Secularism and secularization in the Arab world. *Journal of Middle Eastern and Islamic Studies, 1*(1), 55–65.

Yamane, D. (1997). Secularization on trial: In defense of a neosecularization paradigm. *Journal for the Scientific Study of Religion, 36*(1), 109–122.

Yasuyuki, M. (2009). The secularization of a faqih-headed revolutionary Islamic State of Iran: Its mechanisms, processes, and prospects. *Comparative Studies of South Asia, Africa and the Middle East, 29*(3), 468–482.

Yavuz, M. H. (2009). *Secularism and Muslim democracy in Turkey.* Cambridge: Cambridge University Press.

Yavuz, M. H., & Esposito, J. L. (2003). *Turkish Islam and the secular state: The Gülen movement.* Syracuse, NY: Syracuse University Press.

Yazdi, M. (1987). Vojoohat va maliat [Religious remuneration and taxes]. *Noor-e Elm, 3*(9), 76–90.

Yazdi, M., Hashemi-Shahroudi, M., & Mohmmadi-Gilani, M. (1995). Vojooh-e sharie dar nezam-e Islami [Religious payments in the Islamic state]. *Fiqh-e Ahl-e Bait, 1*(2), 13–51.

Yousefi Eshkevari, H. (2014). *Roshanfekran-e musalman va secularism dar Iran* [Religious intellectuals and secularism in Iran]. Retrieved February 22, 2014, from http://yousefieshkevari.com/?p=4235.

Yusefi-Eshkevari, H. (2011). Faithful life in an Urfi state. *Comparative Studies of South Asia, Africa and the Middle East, 31*(1), 23–26.

Zagorin, P. (2003). *How the idea of religious toleration came to the West.* Princeton, NJ: Princeton University Press.

Zakariyya, F. (2005). *Myth and reality in the contemporary Islamic movement.* London: Pluto Press Ltd.

Zooalam, A. (2000). *Changes in social values after the Islamic revolution.* Tehran: Islam Culture and Thought Research Centre.

Index